From
Class to Caste
in American Drama

Recent Titles in
Contributions in Drama and Theatre Studies

America's Musical Stage: Two Hundred Years of Musical Theatre
Julian Mates

From Farce to Metadrama: A Stage History of *The Taming of the Shrew*, 1594–1983
Tori Haring-Smith

Prophet of the New Drama: William Archer and the Ibsen Campaign
Thomas Postlewait

The Theatre of Meyerhold and Brecht
Katherine Bliss Eaton

Ten Seasons: New York Theatre in the Seventies
Samuel L. Leiter

Sam Shepard's Metaphorical Stages
Lynda Hart

The Letters and Notebooks of Mary Devlin Booth
L. Terry Oggel, editor

Carlo Gozzi: Translations of *The Love of Three Oranges*, *Turandot*, and *The Snake Lady* with a Bio-Critical Introduction
John Louis DiGaetani

The Critics' Canon: Standards of Theatrical Reviewing in America
Richard H. Palmer

Eugene O'Neill in Ireland: The Critical Reception
Edward L. Shaughnessy

Spotlight on the Child: Studies in the History of American Children's Theatre
Roger L. Bedard and C. John Tolch, editors

Orson Welles on Shakespeare: The W.P.A. and Mercury Theatre Playscripts
Richard France

Divine Madness and the Absurd Paradox: Ibsen's *Peer Gynt* and the Philosophy of Kierkegaard
Bruce G. Shapiro

Broadway Talks: What Professionals Think About Commercial Theater in America
Arvid F. Sponberg

From
CLASS to CASTE
in American Drama

Political and Social Themes
Since the 1930s

RICHARD G. SCHARINE

Contributions in
Drama and Theatre Studies, Number 32

GREENWOOD PRESS

New York • Westport, Connecticut • London

Library of Congress Cataloging-in-Publication Data

Scharine, Richard G.
     From class to caste in American drama : political and social
themes since the 1930s / Richard G. Scharine.
          p.   cm.—(Contributions in drama and theatre studies, ISSN
0163-3821 ; no. 32)
     Includes bibliographical references and index.
     ISBN 0-313-26737-5 (alk. paper)
     1. American drama—20th century—History and criticism.
2. Political plays, American—History and criticism.   3. Social
problems in literature.   I. Title.   II. Series.
     PS338.P6S33   1991
     812'.509358—dc20   90-43386

British Library Cataloguing in Publication Data is available.

Library of Congress Catalog Card Number: 90-43386
ISBN: 0-313-26737-5
ISSN: 0163-3821

First published in 1991

Greenwood Press, 88 Post Road West, Westport, CT   06881
An imprint of Greenwood Publishing Group, Inc.

Printed in the United States of America

The paper used in this book complies with the
Permanent Paper Standard issued by the National
Information Standards Organization (Z39.48-1984).

10 9 8 7 6 5 4 3 2 1

Copyright Acknowledgments

The author and publisher gratefully acknowledge permission to use the following:

Excerpts from *The Trial of the Catonsville Nine* by Daniel Berrigan. Copyright ©
1970 by Daniel Berrigan. Reprinted by permission of Beacon Press.

Excerpts from *Black Elk Speaks* by Christopher Sergel. Based on the work *Black Elk
Speaks* by John G. Neihardt. Copyright © 1976 by The Dramatic Publishing Company. Reprinted by permission of The Dramatic Publishing Company. Permission to
produce the play *Black Elk Speaks* must be obtained from The Dramatic Publishing
Company.

Excerpts from *In the Matter of J. Robert Oppenheimer* by Heinar Kipphardt. Copyright © 1968. Reprinted by permission of Methuen Drama.

Excerpts from *Johnny Johnson* by Paul Green. Copyright © 1936, 1937 by Paul
Green. Copyright © (In Renewal) 1963, 1964 by Paul Green. Copyright © 1971,
revised and rewritten by Paul Green. Reprinted by permission of Samuel French, Inc.

"1936" by Stephen Vincent Benét in *Selected Works of Stephen Vincent Benét, I:
Poetry.* Copyright © 1936 by Stephen Vincent Benét. Copyright renewed © 1963 by
Thomas C. Benét, Stephanie B. Mahin, and Rachel Benét Lewis. Reprinted by
permission of Brandt & Brandt Literary Agents, Inc.

Excerpts from *Getting Out* by Marsha Norman. Copyright © 1980. Reprinted by
permission of the William Morris Agency.

Excerpts from *Waiting for Lefty* in *Six Plays of Clifford Odets* by Clifford Odets.
Copyright © 1979. Reprinted by permission of Grove Press, Inc.

Excerpts from *The Mighty Gents* by Richard Wesley. Copyright © 1979. Reprinted
by permission of Dramatists Play Service, Inc.

Excerpts from *The Autobiography of Malcolm X* by Malcolm X. Copyright © 1977.
Reprinted by permission of Random House, Inc.

Excerpts from *Sticks and Bones* by David Rabe. Copyright © 1972. Reprinted by
permission of Blueman, Ball, and Len.

Contents

Introduction

Trent: Why a play . . .
Stone: Because the theater, sir, alone among the arts, engages in equal measure, the emotion and the intellect. And both must be touched here, if we are to survive.[1]

—*The End of the World*, by Arthur Kopit

I am convinced that fine art is the subtlest, the most seductive, the most effective means of propaganda in the world . . . because it works by exhibiting examples of personal conduct made intelligible and moving to crowds of unobservant, unreflecting people to whom real life means nothing.[2]

—George Bernard Shaw

As its title implies, this book examines selected issues which shaped the development of the United States from the Depression to the AIDS crisis, as they were portrayed in selected American plays first produced between 1933 and 1985. It chronicles a dramatic concern with the mythos of American capital labor conflicts—conflicts which also affected and were affected by American problems of caste (social rank based on unalterable biological conditions, such as race, cultural ancestry, sex, and sexual orientation). In our contemporary United States, class and caste remain inextricably entwined.

From Class to Caste in American Drama, therefore, draws upon fifty years of American social and political history, as well as the history of the American theatre and American political theatre. Although the book begins by examining a number of American definitions of political theatre and proposes a theory of how a political play is constructed, no attempt is made to chronicle the histories of political theatre or any politically oriented theatre companies, except as is required for the understanding of the dramas.

Political Theatre: Definition and Usage

All definitions of political theatre note its rhetorical nature, that is, its purpose is to persuade. As Eric Bentley put it in his keynote address to the Columbia/City University of New York "Political Theatre Today" conference in May 1985, "Clearly the bone of contention is propaganda."[3] In *The Drama of Attack*, his analysis of American social drama of the 1930s, Sam Smiley describes didactic drama as emphasizing thought over plot and character.[4] Discussing the same period in *Drama and Commitment*, Gerald Rabkin differentiates between ideological and aesthetic theatre.[5]

Yet, the purpose of all literature is rhetorical, in the attempt to convince us of the author's viewpoint. In *Feminist Drama: Definition and Critical Analysis*, Janet Brown cites Kenneth Burke as her authority for refusing to separate author message for artistry.[6] Certainly, no author was more message-oriented than Mao Tse-tung, who said, "Works of art which lack artistic quality have no force, no matter how progressive they are politically."[7] Similarly, works of art created without political intent can have political consequences. One of Jacques Ellul's three forms of propaganda is "integration propaganda . . . a self-producing propaganda that seeks to obtain stable behavior, to adapt the individual to his everyday life, reshape his thoughts and behavior in terms of the permanent social setting."[8] Indeed, to be apolitical is a political act under certain circumstances. In the heyday of Soviet socialist realism, it was for "formalism" that Vsevelod Meyerhold spent his last days in Siberia.

To follow such reasoning to its logical end is to conclude that all art is political—a statement that is both true and a discussion closure. It might be more accurate to say any drama may be produced for a political purpose, but this requires an analysis of individual productions that is beyond the scope of this book. We will limit our analysis of political drama to written scripts whose political implications were inherent at the time of their composition.

This is by no means as narrow a limit as might be implied. Ellul's two other forms are agitation propaganda and dialectical propaganda. Agitation propaganda "is most often subversive . . . and has the stamp of opposition. It is led by a party seeking to destroy the government or the established order. "9 Its intention is to point out previously unrecognized or uncontested social problems. Dialectical propaganda is more subtle. "It is a theatre which attempts to demystify, by depicting separately, interactively, and always clearly, the basic elements which comprise a confused social or historical situation."10

It is agitation propaganda which is usually defined as political theatre. Caspar Nammes, whose 1948 *Politics in the American Drama* was a pioneer in American political theatre analysis, restricted his discussion to "plays directly dealing with such political subjects as candidates running for office, corruption in government, politics and specific political issues; plays based upon a political philosophy, such as Fascism, Nazism or Communism; [and] plays whose plots stem obviously from political situations."11 Michael Kirby, in *A Formalist Theatre* (1987), is even more circumspect. His thesis is not in sympathy with political theatre which can only be described subjectively, that is, it has no unchangeable "formal" elements and depends entirely upon the intent of the playwright and/or the production and its effect upon the audience. "Theatre is political if it is *concerned with* the state or *takes sides* in politics. This allows us to define 'political theatre' in a way that distinguishes it from other kinds of theatre: it is a performance that is intentionally engaged in or consciously takes sides in politics."12

However, agitation propaganda theatre, as Professor Kirby admits, can also motivate and inspire. "It can give [believers] the feeling that they are not alone in their beliefs, that others are actually involved and pursuing the same goals."13 This is without doubt most true of the political theatre which involves caste. Indeed, it is at the point where "consciousness-raising" becomes cultural rather than issue-oriented that agitprop evolves into the demystification associated with dialectical propaganda.

The drama of all emergent social groups begins with group members describing their own experiences. Their discovery that the experiences are similar gives them validity both as individuals and as a social group. For example, playwright Megan Terry describes the empowering potential of women's consciousness-raising sessions: "One of the things feminist theatre can do is to explore the possibilities of what a woman could be like because we've had so many outlines and definitions forced on us." She defines feminist drama as any drama that gives women confidence by showing themselves to themselves free of imposed masculine standards.14 Substitute the words *black* and *Chicano* for *feminist*, and *white* for *masculine*, and the definition applies equally well to Ed Bullins's "black rituals" at Harlem's New Lafayette Theater and El Teatro

Campesino's *actos* performed on the picket lines during the Delano, California, grape strikes. Such actions lack political significance only if you regard the potential alteration of the nation's social, economic, and aesthetic life as apolitical.

In a caste theory of culture, one culture is the norm. All others deviate from it. The advantage of political theatre as a consciousness-raiser is its insistence that each group has its own norm—different from, but in no way inferior to, that of the dominant culture. In that way, the move of El Teatro Campesino from the agitprop *actos* of the Delano fields to its *corridas* and *mitos* of the seventies was a necessary political step if it was to provide an alternative rather than a reaction to gringo society. Similarly, the "Black Arts Movement" could see the necessity for "a radical reordering of the western cultural aesthetic . . . a separate symbolism, mythology, critique, and iconology."15

Finally, from the viewpoint of a personal cultural base, the unquestioned classics of dominant art may be examined as cultural artifacts whose close study may reveal the assumptions and tactics by which the dominant culture remains dominant. The feminist deconstruction of *The Oresteia* and of Shakespeare in Sue-Ellen Case's *Feminism and Theatre*16 is the critical counterpart to the dramatic demystification provided in the dialectical propaganda defined by Elull. Such a criticism is capable of taking up the questions asked by the French critic Hippolyte Taine in the nineteenth century: "Given a literature, a philosophy, a society, an art, a group of arts, what is the moral condition which produced it? What are the conditions of race, milieu, moment most fitted to produce this moral condition?"17

At its best, the purpose of political theatre is to answer Taine's questions, and with those answers to alter the moral condition described. The chance of achieving that alteration in a specific case is slim. As Carlos Fuentes says:

I do not believe that literature has an immediate, partisan role to play, but I do believe that literature is revolutionary and thus political in a deeper sense. Literature not only sustains a historical experience and continues a tradition. It also—through moral risk and formal experimentation and verbal humor—transforms the conservative horizon of the readers and helps liberate us all from the determinisms of prejudice, doctrinal rigidity, and barren repetition.18

Further, one could cite Tom Stoppard's comparison of the relative influences of South African playwright Athol Fugard and *Guardian* correspondent Adam Raphael, whose 1970s newspaper series prompted South African mine owners to raise wages:

The plain truth is that if you are angered or disgusted by a particular injustice of immorality, and you want to do something about it, *now, at once*, then you can hardly do worse than write a play about it. That's what art is bad at. But the less plain truth is that *without* that play and plays like it, without artists, the injustice will *never* be eradicated. In other words, because of Athol Fugard . . . *The Guardian* understood that the Raphael piece was worth leading the paper with, worth printing.[19]

Comparing Political Theatre with Traditional Theatre

For our purposes we will define political theatre as those plays showing public policy, laws, or unquestioned social codes unfairly and systematically threatening the existence or quality of human life. Classical tragedy, as Aristotle defined it, imitated the events of the real world in such a way as to show their inevitability. Its aim was to reconcile the spectator with his world by purging him of the tensions the world aroused in him. Worrying about what could not be changed was wasted effort. This philosophy, the German playwright/theorist Bertolt Brecht insisted 2,300 years later, served entirely to support the status quo. Augusto Boal, the Brazilian director and Brecht admirer, called the Aristotelian system "coercive."[20] Greek tragedy, for instance, shows the gods punishing those who violate the structure-supporting codes of religion (blasphemy toward the gods), society (betrayal of a host), and family (the harming of a blood relative). Such plays are integrationist propaganda.

Brecht, who spent the last thirty years of his life trying to perfect political drama, first called his theatre "epic," and later "dialectic." He suggested that the modern world could only be described to an audience in terms of its alterability. The actor's performance and the elements of staging do not aim to imitate real life, but attempt rather to show how real life works—an intellectual rather than an emotional experience. Fate (inevitably) is the product of social and economic realties, and thus is a historical (changeable) condition. Human behavior is created by historical conditions, and is a part of historical conditions. Dialectical theatre should so distance the audience that it may understand why something is happening, rather than share the feelings of those to whom it happens.[21]

In a political tragedy, the system is the antagonist. The trials faced by a good man because of the machinations of a bad man are melodramatic. The trials faced by any man (or Everyman) because of an unjust system, no matter how honestly administered, are political. In political tragedy, the social norm is basically antihuman (destructive to human beings instead of geared to their survival). In such plays, characters who are "good" are destroyed because the corruption in the system is too strong for them to combat, or so accepted as to be invisible. At the same time, those who accept the values of the system are destroyed because the system shows no favorites and consumes its own.

Traditional comedy falls into two categories, romantic and judicious. Romantic comedy—from Shakespeare to Neil Simon to sitcom—is the more familiar form because it is less bound to a particular culture or time. It presumes the efficacy of the social norm, that is, society is basically good and the comic character (the one whom we laugh at or ridicule) is funny because he deviates from the norm of a society. The comic character pretends to be something other than what he is, or else fails to understand what the norm of society is, or why the norm is correct. Comedy reinforces the social norm by making the audience fear the laughter that accompanies deviation from it.

The basic premise of political theatre, on the other hand, is that the social norm or some part of it is in error. Therefore, in a political comedy, that erroneous norm will be laughed at in an attempt to convince the audience to bring it into line with real social needs. Called judicious comedy, this drama was evident in Aristophanes' attacks on the Peloponnesian War, corrupt Athenian officials, and the blasphemy he perceived in the rise of sophism. Its ancestors were the fertility rites that directed ridicule against those forces of nature and society which stood in the way of the human drive for pleasure and procreation.

If there is an inherent shortcoming in political comedy, it may lie in the nature of laughter itself, which traditionally has been a means of release in tense situations. The classic line with which Owen Wister's "Virginian" averted a gunfight, "Smile when you say that, pardner," is understood by any guerrilla theatre performer. Freud knew that every joke is a disguised attack, but the street performer knows that a joke may get his message across without risk of a broken head. The problem is that when tension is released, the need for taking action is often released with it. Playwright Peter Barnes notes that jokes are a way of accepting existing conditions: "If a man is doubled up with laughter, he can't very well change the injustices that are afflicting him. It seems to me that those received opinions about humour must be examined very cooly and intensely."[22]

Structuring Political Theatre

Dramatic action in political theatre is naturally organized around an idea—the exposure of a societal flaw and the formulation of a plan of action to change it. Political theatre is not limited to a single type of plot.

Plays whose subjects are as diverse as the congressional pork-barreling in Maxwell Anderson's *Both Your Houses* and the AIDS crisis of William Hoffman's *As Is* still use the "well-made play" structure, itself older than Aristotle. In the opening scenes, the playwright sets up the situations and the desires and motivations of certain characters (who are in support of, in opposition to, or indifferent toward some aspect of the existing social system). Out of the conflicts between the characters' goals and their interrelationship with the existing situation, all later events develop. Attempts to surmount the obstacles make up the substance of the play, with each scene growing out of the last until a crisis is reached where either the supporter(s) of the system or the rebel(s) against it must triumph. That triumph is often measured by the movement of the indifferent, previously neutral, group of characters to a position of systemic opposition or support.

The "well-made play" is often politically effective because of its determinist structure—specific causes lead to specific results—and because of the audience's familiarity with the form. This familiarity, however, has inherent difficulties. The "well-made play" is synonymous with realism, which in television, film, and the theatre has concentrated on individual motivations rather than social causes. Playwright David Edgar sees this as the predicament in writing political plays for TV's large audience: "The countless other drama serials, series, and plays that are part of a television audience's experiential baggage will lead them to take an individual-psychological view of events if they are given any opportunity."[23]

Still, the political message cannot become part of the "audience's experiential baggage" by refusing the openings available. Trevor Griffiths calls this procedure "strategic penetration," and Hal Foster has asserted that it is only sensible to practice "counterhegemonic and resistant" art wherever "the cultural is an arena in which active contestation is possible."[24]

Nevertheless, a political message is often more likely to be perceived if the audience's expectations are altered. The most common method is to separate events into dramatically complete episodes. In the classic agitprop play, a symbolically representative character encounters the symbolic manifestation of a system in a single episode. Longer episodic dramas follow one of two forms. In the first, a central character undertakes a sort of picaresque pilgrimage in which he encounters various examples of a central flaw in society. Eventually, the character identifies the problem and acts against it—often unsuccessfully, leaving the audience disturbed and angry. Plays as different as Paul Green's *Johnny*

Johnson and Marsha Norman's *Getting Out* use this structure. Alternately, the protagonist does not recognize this problem, but thanks to his or her struggles, the audience does, and therefore is made responsible for doing something about it.

In the second type of episodic political theatre, different characters face different aspects of the same societal problem in a number of separate episodes. When they come to realize that their separate problems are part of the same problem, they unite together to fight, inviting the audience to join them. Examples in this book include the chronicle plays *In White America* by Martin Duberman and *Black Elk Speaks* by Christopher Sergel, and the granddaddy of them all, Clifford Odet's *Waiting for Lefty*.

The best of traditional theatre demands personal involvement in the form of emotional commitment. However, political theatre makes the assumption that if the audience knows what is really happening and what to do about it, they will extend their commitment to action. Erwin Piscator, certainly one of the most overtly political of theatre directors from the end of World War I to his death in 1966, attempted to physicalize this commitment by including his working-class audience in the historical scenes of mass revolution in plays like *Red Rumble* and *In Spite of Everything* in the mid-1920s. The Communist Party, to which he was devoted, was quick to point out his error to him:

In this formulation, the danger of "direct literature" and especially the theater comes clear: the stage and the experience communicated by it as a substitute for the collectivism lacking in reality, as a substitute for an experience of the masses which in the real world, in political life, does not happen to the revolutionary party. The stage becomes, as in the bourgeois theater, a place where the inadequacy felt in reality disappears, where the negative complexes can be swept out of sight. . . . It is the substitution for the real class struggle by the demonstration of a copy on the stage.[25]

The purpose of a political play is not to reassure the audience, but to arouse it to complete *outside* of the theatre an action suggested in the play. In order to assure that fact, political theatre plays must tread the fine line of not ending happily (resulting in audience complacency), while seeing its goals as reachable (retarding audience despair).

The Political Theatre Character

The problem of the political dramatist has been to make systems and values theatrically moving. A drama's effectiveness depends upon the audience's identification with a character whose subsequent triumph or defeat becomes the audience's own. Unfortunately, as we have already noted, the personalization of the viewer's reaction causes the character's circumstances to be perceived as individual and unique, fated in the view of Aristotle, neurotic in the view of Freud. It is difficult to see the character (and, by extension, ourselves) as the product of history, that is, politically changeable systems and values.

The political playwright frequently attempts to counter this difficulty by creating characters who are representative of large social groups. The dramatic ancestors of these "generic" characters are to be found in the symbolist plays of August Strindberg, in the expressionists, and, going back to the Middle Ages, in the "Mankind" and "Everyman" of the morality plays. Paul Green's Johnny Johnson carries the name most found among American World War I soldiers. Angus Buttonkooper, the Little Man in search of a home in *One-Third of a Nation*, was already familiar to Federal Theatre audiences from a previous "Living Newspaper," *Power*. The Vietnam-shattered family of David Rabe's *Sticks and Bones* bore the inferences of having the names associated with one of television's most beloved sitcom's: Ozzie, Harriet, David, and Ricky. The antagonists (those associated with the system's error) are no less generic than the protagonists. Harry Fatt is the aptly named "capitalist pig" in *Waiting for Lefty*, while those charged with brainwashing the minds and souls of blacks in *The Death of Malcolm X* are identifiable by Uncle Sam suits and other symbols of Western white culture.

Progress in political dramas can often be measured by the movement of neutral characters to a point of commitment. Fanny and David in Lillian Hellman's *Watch on the Rhine* learn that fascism cannot be appeased and join with Kurt Muller to oppose it. Bella, Honey, and Cousin Roy find that racism cannot be quietly ignored in *Deep Are the Roots*, and find themselves taking a reluctant stand. The white man who comforts a Little Rock black girl at the conclusion of *In White America* has discovered the link between her and his own fifteen-year-old daughter.

In the earlier plays, the result of this movement from neutrality to commitment is the creation of the collective hero, who has the power to oppose a system which would crush individuals, for example, the strike committee (and the audience) in *Waiting for Lefty*, the tenement dwellers in *One-Third of a Nation* who plan "to keep on hollering until they admit in Washington it's just as important to keep a man alive as it is to kill him," and so on.

In drama where caste is a factor, however, unity becomes the goal. Marianne Van Kerhoven of Brussels University has noted three distinct stages in political theatre since the 1960s: (a) the attempt to change society, (b) the attempt to discover group identity, and (c) the attempt to maintain that identity.[26] It is an evolutionary pattern which tells much about the magnitude of the problem ahead. In *As Is*, the sense of self-acceptance that Rich achieves because of the support of his family and loved ones is as important as the victory he will probably never win over AIDS; and in *Getting Out* Arlene must come to accept all facets of her personality before she can even begin the task of self-determination. Sometimes the realization of the need for unity comes too late, and the process is never without its difficulties. In *Black Elk Speaks*, the Native American tribes are finally forced to give up their individual identities and accept the white man's designation of them as "Indians" so that they can effectively fight back. For Yellow Woman, the recognition that she must side with her people against all white men is made particularly bitter by the fact that she is married to one.

Political Theatre Imagery

As in all good theatre, the visual aspects of political drama carry a message. Most often the setting serves as a metaphor for the system under which the characters live, while at times scenic elements themselves comment directly on the play's action or theme.

By definition, political theatre puts aspects of public life on trial. All of Heinar Kipphardt's *In the Matter of J. Robert Oppenheimer* and Daniel Berrigan's *The Trial of the Catonsville Nine*, and parts of Arthur Miller's *The Crucible*, take place in courtrooms where the protagonists are being tried as much as anything for the judgments they have drawn about their own societies. All are convicted, but the evidence presented in the process reverses the verdict in the minds of the audience who are to be stirred to action by the law's unfairness. *The Crucible* is a larger metaphor, substituting the hysteria of the Salem witchcraft trials for the McCarthyist Red-baiting of the early 1950s. Sidney Kingsley's adaption of Arthur Koestler's *Darkness at Noon* is similar. However, the latter, set in the Russia of Stalin's Purge Trials, can also be seen as a straightforward condemnation of a revolution congealed into a reign of terror. It is only in retrospect that its ambivalence surfaces. *Darkness at Noon* is set in a prison of the protagonist's own making. *Getting Out* is more subtle. Its central setting—a motel room which is to be the first outside home for a paroled ex-prostitute—is a literal inset in a larger grouping of prisons and other institutions whose judgments keep her at the mercy of a male hierarchy.

Even more clearly, domestic settings are metaphors for America in sum. The spacious, tastefully simple living room of *Watch on the Rhine*, with its inviting classlessness, unlocked front door, and liberal patriarch's portrait on the wall, is America, even as Fanny Farrelly's acceptance of her German grandchildren marks America's recognition of itself as part of the World Family. In contrast, the similarly tastefully living room of *Sticks and Bones* is America as a television advertisement, its consumerist falsity as vulnerable to the realities of a racist war as a picture tube is to a combat boot. The living room of Ed Bullins's *The Gentleman Caller* is less realistic, but the message of its trophy wall decorated with black, Chinese, Vietnamese, and Native American heads is no less clear.

The Gentleman Caller shares with *The Death of Malcom X* a use of visual stereotypes to comment on the plays' actions, among them the Uncle Sam suits worn by the officials of the Institute for Advanced Black (brainwashing) Studies in the latter and the white (and dead) Mr. Mann in the former. *The Death of Malcolm X* also provides a properly symbolic award for an integrationist Uncle Tom: a jewel-encrusted watermelon. *Johnny Johnson*, as befits a musical by Kurt Weill, has scenic elements which sing their message (including a Statue of Liberty trenody about the futility of symbols and cannons which mourn not being plowshares), as well as others which bear witness in eloquent silence (including a statue of Christ which conceals a sniper and a tombstone dedicated to peace). In *One-Third of a Nation*, the set *is* the protagonist, an "old-law" (pre-1901) tenement which comments on the society which allows it to continue to exist. The original setting of Luis Valdez's *Las Dos Caras del Patroncito* was a comment, but not a metaphor. The only agitprop play included for discussion, it was performed in the fields in order to explain the Delano grape strike to those who were participating in it.

The Conjunction of Historic and Dramatic Themes

The bulk of *From Class to Caste in American Drama* is divided into seven chapters. Each chapter has three aspects: (a) a history of the period of cultural phenomena studied in relation to an evolving principle, (b) a detailed analysis of particular American dramas which illustrate that evolution, and (c) a suggestion of other plays in which the evolution may be further studied.

The twenty-one dramas which receive detailed analysis include nineteen American plays, one German docudrama whose dialogue is totally drawn from American published sources, and one film. All were selected for the insight they provide into the cultural attitudes of the United States and the political ramifications of those attitudes. The priority given to those insights is the criterion which justifies the inclusion of the German play and the film.

The seven historically labelled chapters of *From Class to Caste in American Drama* are as follows: (1) The Great Depression; (2) World War II; (3) The Cold War (4) Vietnam; (5) Civil Rights; (6) Civil Rights Theatre—Race; and (7) Civil Rights Theatre—Gender. The conditions and problems of each period should be seen as deriving to some extent from the solutions imposed in the era preceding it. For example, our involvement in Vietnam is clearly the result of our assumptions about ourselves and the world which were the product of the Cold War, while the rise of the women's movement in Chapter 6 was inspired by both the accomplishments and the shortcomings of the civil rights movement. The relationship of the major plays analyzed to the evolving cultural attitude is described below.

The Great Depression (1933–1938)

The dominating idea of this period is class analysis: the bankruptcy of the rugged individualism ideal, and the subsequent rise of the collective hero and the sense of government responsibility to its citizens. *Both Your Houses*, Maxwell Anderson's 1933 Pulitzer Prize winner, believes in as little government as possible. Government policy is the tool of a big business which built America in order to steal it. But Manifest Destiny has passed, and the people who once prospered riding on the coattails of these thieves are now starving. *Waiting for Lefty*, by Clifford Odets (1935), shows all "producing members of society" to be equally oppressed by capitalism, and unites them all together to "strike" for a Marxist society in which they will control the means of production. Based on FDR's second inaugural address, Arthur Arent's *One-Third of a Nation* (1938) became the best known of the Federal Theatre's "Living Newspapers." It could alter the specifics of its slum descriptions to fit the city in which it was being played, and argued (not for the last time) that federal money spent on armaments could be better used to relieve social inequities at home.

World War II (1936–1945)

The dominant idea of this period is the growth of America's responsibility toward the world's oppressed people. The trend toward a "family of man" viewpoint in which an ideal, classless, democratic world will be a reflection of a classless democratic America reflects the rise of the United States as a world power and will lead to a belief in our ability to "Americanize" the world. Set to a Kurt Weill score, Paul Green's *Johnny Johnson* (1936) fights the "War to End All Wars" and is put in an asylum as a "peace monomaniac." A reflection of Oxford Pledge pacifism, the play accepts the "merchants of death" explanation of our entry into World War I and suggests (without much hope) the League of Nations as an alternative to nationalist inhumanity. Lillian Hellman's pro-interventionist *Watch on the Rhine* (1941) opened seven months before Pearl Harbor. By the simple expedient of making a family half-German and half-American, the play depicts a responsibility to the World Family of freedom fighters. Arnaud D'Usseau and James Gow's *Deep Are the Roots* (1945) showed America the irony of its self-image of world freedom fighter by showing us the racial caste system which institutionalized a second-class citizenry. What happens to a black college graduate, designated by act of Congress an officer and a gentleman, when he returns to a home in which front doors are forbidden to him and he must have a note from a white person to use the public library?

The Cold War (1950–1964)

In our attempt to "never again" allow tyranny to work its will in the world, we found ourselves confusing a national struggle with the Apocalypse, endangering the very liberties we were sworn to protect. *Darkness at Noon*, Sidney Kingsley's 1950 adaptation of Arthur Koestler's novel, describes an idealistic revolution gone wrong because of an unquestioning acceptance of historical determinism and "the end justifying the means." Although the setting is the Stalin Purge Trials of the late 1930s, it is equally applicable to America's "anti-Red" purges following World War II. In Arthur Miller's *The Crucible* (1953), the Salem witch trials of 1692 provide a parallel to the McCarthy Communist hunts of the early 1950s. A comparison between the Puritan theocracy and America's sense of itself as God's chosen people shows the danger of equating dissenting viewpoints with heresy, turning accusations into convictions, and presuming all human differences to be the product of demonic conspiracy. Heinar Kipphardt's *In the Matter of J. Robert Oppenheimer* (1964) is culled from the transcripts of the physicist's Atomic Energy Commission (AEC) hearing in 1954. Oppenheimer is seen to have lost his AEC clearance because of his association with Communists in the 1930s and his reluctance to develop the hydrogen bomb, and as a warning to other scientists to do their work without questioning its consequences.

Vietnam (1957–1971)

The concentration in this period is on our growing awareness of the gap between ideals and means—the principles which drew us into the war and the realities of our national institutions—and our reluctance to face this gap. *China Gate*, Samuel Fuller's 1957 pro-interventionist film about American soldiers of fortune fighting for the French in Indochina, sees racism as the barrier to Western success in Asia. The issues are made clear by having the native Communists be the puppets of an unscrupulous Russian major, and the prize be the hearts of a Eurasian girl and her Vietnamese son—last seen happily clutching a baseball glove and other assorted American paraphernalia. Derived from the trial transcripts by one of the defendants who burned Maryland draft records with napalm, Daniel Berrigan's *The Trial of the Catonsville Nine* (1969) is a litany of the breakdown of the ideals of the Catholic church, the American legal system, domestic racial practices, and imperialist business policies. David Rabe's *Sticks and Bones* (1971) shows the extent to which America will go to avoid seeing that the terrors of Vietnam are merely the reflection of racial/sexual/materialist attitudes at home. David, blinded perhaps by the war or perhaps by congenital disease, insists on bringing the realities of the war home to Ozzie, Harriet, and Ricky. When they can no longer bear the guilt of these realities, his family "assists" David's "suicide."

Civil Rights (1963–1976)

What appeared to be a problem of black and white in America dissolved on close examination into endless shades of gray as black American drama evolved from protest to Black Power to the postrevolutionary blues. *In White America*, Martin Duberman's 1963 docudrama, proceeds chronologically from the slave ships to Little Rock. The first act ends with Emancipation, but the more important second act concludes with an example of acceptance on a personal level. In Ed Bullins's *The Gentleman Caller* (1969), a seemingly stupid "Mammy-type" maid cuts the throat of her master (whose false beard symbolizes his potency) before shooting her mistress *and* the "sophisticated Negro" who appears ready to assume his place in white society. She then reveals herself as an apostle of black aesthetics and Black Power nationalism. In

The Death of Malcolm X (1969), LeRoi Jones sees Malcolm's assassination as part of an anti–Third World conspiracy by American government/business/military, the Ku Klux Klan (KKK), and "Uncle Tom" Negroes. The members of Richard Wesley's *The Mighty Gents* (1976), a once powerful street gang now grown older, see only three ways out of their dead-end ghetto life: (1) early death as drunken panhandlers, (2) material success as pimps and thieves preying on their own kind, or (3) the creation of children to whom they can pass on their unfulfilled hopes. They make the wrong choice.

Civil Rights Theatre Sequel I—Race

The principle theme is the extension of the challenge to white male hegemony from black Americans to other "minority" groups (Chicanos, Native Americans, women, gays, etc.) whose rights and virtues have been denied. Until each has established its fundamental worth as a separate group, a truly unified society is seen as impossible. Luis Valdez's *Las Dos Caras del Patroncito*, "The Two Faces of the Boss," (1965) is one of a series of one-act plays produced by El Teatro Campesino for Cesar Chavez's striking United Farm Workers in California. Like most protest drama, it provides an alternative view of history which explains the worker's position in it and denigrates that of the boss. Christopher Sergel's *Black Elk Speaks* (1976), adapted from John Neihardt's 1930–1931 interviews with the Oglala Sioux medicine man, centers around the Plains Indian Wars, beginning with the Minnesota Santee Sioux in 1862 and ending with Wounded Knee in 1890. Christianity and gold justified the white man's slaughter of the red man, but these actions are seen in the light of Black Elk's vision, which calls for the unity of all living things and the earth which produced them.

Civil Rights Theatre Sequel II—Gender

Women, gay men, and lesbians are alike in that their political difficulties are associated with gender and gender roles. In specifics, however, they may be distinctly different. A lesbian, for example, knows that most of the demands of gay men could be met without dismantling the patriarchy that oppresses her as a woman. She also knows that many women's liberationists are capable of dismissing lesbian issues as "lavender herrings," as Betty Friedan did.

Sent to reform school by a sexually abusive father, and to prison by a sexually exploitive pimp, the heroine of Marsha Norman's *Getting Out*

(1978) is divided against herself, robbed of the spirit which might have permitted her to survive, and sent back into the environment which originally sent her to prison. Finally, the discovery by a young man that he has AIDS in William M. Hoffmann's *As Is* (1985) throws into sharp relief the homophobia which distorts the American psyche and the American legal system. Before these can be changed, his family and friends, and even the victim himself, must learn to accept him "As Is."

Notes

1. Arthur Kopit, *The End of the World* (New York: Hill and Wang, 1984), I, 32.
2. George Bernard Shaw, "The Author's Apology" from *Mrs. Warren's Profession*, in *European Theories of the Drama*, ed. Barrett H. Clark (New York: Crown Publishers, 1947), 472–73.
3. Eric Bentley, "Writing for Political Theatre," in *Political Theatre Today*, ed. Jane House (New York: Institute on Western Europe, Columbia University, and Center for Advanced Study in Theatre Arts, City University of New York, 1988), 1.
4. Sam Smiley, *The Drama of Attack* (Columbia: University of Missouri Press, 1972), 6.
5. Gerald Rabkin, *Drama and Commitment* (Bloomington: Indiana University Press, 1964), 295.
6. Janet Brown, *Feminist Drama: Definition and Critical Analysis* (Metuchen, N.J.: Scarecrow Press, 1979), 1.
7. Quoted by Catherine Itzin, in *Stages in the Revolution* (London: Eyre Methuen, 1980), 1.
8. Quoted by George H. Szanto, in *Theater and Propaganda* (Austin: University of Texas Press, 1978), 74.
9. Szanto, *Theater and Propaganda*, 73.
10. Szanto, *Theater and Propaganda*, 75.
11. Caspar H. Nammes, *Politics in the American Drama* (Philadelphia: University of Pennsylvania Press, 1950), vii.
12. Michael Kirby, *A Formalist Theatre* (Philadelphia: University of Pennsylvania Press, 1987), 85.
13. Kirby, *A Formalist Theatre*, 94.
14. Quoted by Dinah Leavitt, in *Feminist Theatre Groups* (Jefferson, N.C.: McFarland, 1980), 12.
15. Larry Neal, "The Black Arts Movement," *Tulane Drama Review,* 12, no.4 (Summer 1968): 29.
16. Sue-Ellen Case, *Feminism and Theatre* (New York: Methuen, 1988), 6–27.
17. Quoted by Leo Weinstein, in *Hippolyte Taine* (New York: Twayne Publishers, 1972), 85.
18. Quoted by Eric Bentley, in "Writing for Political Theatre," in *Political Theatre Today*, ed. Jane House (New York: Institute on Western Europe, Columbia University, and Center for Advanced Study in Theatre Arts, City University of New York, 1988), 4.

19. Quoted by Catherine Itzin and Simon Trussler, in "Ambushes for the Audience: Towards a High Comedy of Ideas," *Theatre Quarterly* 4, no. 4 (May–July 1974): 14.

20. Augusto Boal, *Theater of the Oppressed* (New York: Urizen Books, 1979), 33–50.

21. Bertolt Brecht, *Brecht on Theatre*, ed. and trans. John Willet (New York: Hill and Wang, 1964), 69–99.

22. Quoted by Susan Carlson, "Comic Collisions: Convention, Rage, and Order," *New Theatre Quarterly* 3, no. 12 (November 1987): 308.

23. David Edgar, "Ten Years of Political Theatre, 1968–78," *Theatre Quarterly* 8, no. 32 (Winter 1978): 30.

24. Hal Foster, *Recoding* (Port Townsend, Wash.: Bay Press, 1985), 149.

25. Ernst Shumacher, "Piscator's Political Theater," in *Brecht: A Collection of Critical Essays*, ed. Peter Demetz (Englewood Cliffs, N.J.: Prentice-Hall, 1962), 89.

26. Marianne Van Kerkhoven, in "Round Table with Stanley Kauffmann," in *Political Theatre Today*, ed. Jane House (New York: Institute on Western Europe, Columbia University, and Center for Advanced Study in Theatre Arts, City University of New York, 1988), 98.

From
Class to Caste
in American Drama

The Great Depression—Social Themes in the Theatrical Mainstream

As a national disaster, only the Civil War ranks with the Great Depression. Between 1929 and 1933, the gross national product shrank from $87 billion to $41 billion. Inversely, estimated unemployment went from 3.2 percent to between one-quarter and one-third of the working population.[1] Farmers, who had been encouraged to expand their acreage and their debt during World War I, were even worse off. In 1929, farmers' earnings were only 30 percent of the American average.[2] Two years later, they had dropped by three-quarters. By the winter of 1932–1933, a third of the value of all farms was pledged to banks and insurance companies.[3]

Try to visualize those statistics in human terms. In 1931, four New York hospitals reported ninety-five starvation deaths. In Washington, a congressman argued that eleven cents a day could feed an Indian child. A single parish in San Antonio buried thirty-nine persons in one month, "mostly children." In Carlisle, Pennsylvania, a starving man suffocated his three small daughters rather than see them starve to death. In 1933, the Children's Bureau reported that one child out of five was inadequately fed.[4]

Even the surviving unemployed lost their self-esteem and found their community status in danger. They felt a sense of personal guilt at having failed in what they had been told was the richest country in the world, wondering if the Depression, like the monster in *Frankenstein* (the most popular movie of 1930), was not God's retribution for their hubris. In some locales, families on relief lost the right to vote.[5] College students, those perennial "hopes of the future," found that one-third of the class

of 1933 had been unable to find employment, and another one-third had
gotten jobs for which they had no interest, talent, or training. As "An
Ode to Higher Education," a popular ditty of the time, put it:

> I sing in praise of college,
> of M.A.'s and Ph.D.'s.
>
> But in pursuit of knowledge
> We are starving by degrees.[6]

What had caused this disaster? In theory, laissez-faire economics—the
free market system—prevented economic crises because demand controlled supply, and competition (Adam Smith's "great regulator of
industry") undercut potential abuse by the supplier.[7] However, Adam
Smith had built his theory on a relatively equal distribution of wealth.
By 1929, 200 corporations held 22 percent of America's total wealth and
49 percent of its corporate wealth. In 1931, 65 percent of American
industry was in the hands of 600 corporations.[8] This imbalance was to
prove a major factor in the economy's downward spiral.

From 1920 to 1929, disposable income rose 9 percent for all Americans, but 75 percent for the richest 1 percent. One-tenth of 1 percent of
the population had annual incomes of $100,000 or more, while 71 percent
had incomes of under $2,500. This unequal distribution was a problem
for the rich as well as the poor. For how could the poor (demand) buy
from the rich (supply) without money? The answer was credit. Aided by
the developing new industry of advertising, outstanding installment
credit increased from $1.38 billion in 1925 to $3 billion in 1929. Three
out of every five cars and four out of every five radios during this period
were purchased on "time."[9]

The rich were buying on credit too. After 1926, the Federal Reserve
Board permitted 90 percent margins, selling stock at ten cents on the dollar.
This encouraged speculation, or the buying of stock based not on the real
value of the company, but on the hope that the price of the stock would go
up. For example, the Radio Corporation of America (RCA), without ever
paying a dividend, went from 94.5 in March 1929 to 505 in September.
An investor with $945 in March could have bought one hundred shares on
margin, selling them in September at a profit of nearly $42,000.[10] The
market reached its peak on September 3, 1929, and when it crashed on
Black Thursday, October 24, the loss of values in the day's trading
amounted to almost as much as America had spent to fight World War I.[11]

The collapse of the market meant a collapse of credit. Business cut
back on production to reduce inventory and on credit to increase real

assets. This meant laying off workers, who, lacking either cash or credit, reduced purchases. As unpurchased items clogged inventories, industry cut back again, further reducing worker purchasing power.

Internationally, America cut back on its loans to Germany, but continued to demand war debts owed by France and Great Britain. These debts, in turn, had been financed by German reparations. As Germany teetered toward bankruptcy, Hitler found the unemployed to be his strongest supporters. An early victim of the 1930 Smoot-Hawley Tariff (intended to protect American industry against foreign competition) was Japan. Its foreign trade fell by nearly 50 percent between 1929 and 1931, leading to a military takeover and the resumption of an aggressive expansionist policy that had been dormant for a decade.[12] By March 1932, revolutions had toppled governments in seven Latin American countries.[13] When a 10 percent reduction was made in the salaries of federal employees that summer, President Hoover sent a secret message to Congress asking that the armed forces be exempted, as their services might be needed soon to assist in the suppression of civil dissent. [14] War and revolution appeared to be in a deadly race.

Few doubted that the United States was on the brink of radical change. The obvious options were communism and fascism. According to John A. Simpson of the National Farmers Union: "The capitalistic system is doomed. It has as its foundation the principles of brutality, dishonesty, and avarice." When AFL (American Federation of Labor) president William Green threatened a Senate subcommittee with a "universal strike" if relief was not forthcoming, Senator Hugo Black of Alabama asked, "That would be class war, practically?" "It would be that," said Green. "That is the only language that a lot of employers ever understand—the language of force."[15]

On the other hand, when the Bonus Army (World War I veterans seeking immediate payment of $1,000 due in 1945) marched on Washington in the summer of 1932, Army Deputy Chief of Staff General George Van Horne Moseley worked on a plan to send dissidents "to one of the sparsely inhabited islands of the Hawaiian group . . . to stew in their own filth until their cases were finally disposed of with the return of normal conditions."[16] Governor Eugene Talmadge of Georgia had unwanted nonresidents put on chain gangs, and when textile workers went on strike, had pickets put into barbed-wire concentration camps. Frank Hague, the political boss of Jersey City, called for similar camps in Alaska for "Native Reds." Even so moderate a man as Kansas governor Alfred M. Landon, who was to be the 1936 Republican candidate for president, stated a preference for "the iron hand of a national dictator" over social chaos.[17]

The most touching and most out-of-touch option was suggested by President Herbert Hoover: "national character." In 1922, exhausted by his herculean efforts in feeding the refugees of the World War I and saddened by the xenophobia displayed at the Versailles Peace Conference, the then-secretary of commerce wrote a book entitled *Rugged Individualism*, in which he described the greatest American resource as the moral character of its people—their ability to find answers to their problems individually or by mutual cooperation without government interference or coercion. Nine years later, as the Depression deepened, Hoover still believed in "character and idealism and high intelligence over the councils of despair or prudence and material comfort."[18]

It is a myth of enormous appeal—that strength of character and hard work is a national virtue which can overcome any social, physical, and economic adversity. It has inspired Americans—including Hoover, a deeply religious, self-made millionaire—to achieve much. It inspires them still. Like all myths, however, it has its dark side: the implication that those who cannot overcome lack virtue, are not good Americans. Thus, Treasury Secretary Andrew Mellon could speak of the benefits of the Crash: "People will work harder, live a more moral life."[19] And Senator Albert Gore could speak of unemployment relief as "the paresis of the soul and it defies all cure, defies all remedy."[20] This myth presumes Americans are universally, not just geographically, blessed, and has sometimes led us to confuse our national interests with Divine interests.

In retrospect, it is plain that rugged individualism was not to be the myth of the 1930s. The lesson of the thirties, played out on stage as well as in politics, had also been heard before in America: "United we stand, divided we fall." The collective hero will have his moment in the spotlight, eventually lose focus and decline into the team player or the corporation man. But before his star fades, he will (as Proteus rather than as Zeus) make his government over into his own image. As Franklin D. Roosevelt asserted at the 1932 Democratic National Convention: "Modern society, acting through its government, owes the definite obligation to prevent the starvation or the dire want of any of its fellow men and women who try to maintain themselves and cannot."[21]

Both Your Houses

When Maxwell Anderson's *Both Your Houses* opened on March 6, 1933, it was already outdated. It is true that few would have said so at the time. After all, it was the year's Pulitzer Prize winner. It raised issues which have yet to be resolved in the present. It expressed a philosophy which enjoyed a remarkable national resurgence in the late seventies and early eighties. As a political drama, it was well constructed. The through line of action (the spine of the action) is built around the progress of a money bill in the House of Representatives, and the audience can always get its bearings by examining the condition of the bill and its distance from passage. The characters are generic—interesting but easily recognizable—and again are identifiable by their relationship to the bill. Although the audience is clearly invited to sympathize with some characters more than others, the play is essentially a judicious comedy in which the real villain is the System. Furthermore, in the best tradition of political theatre, the System defeats the hero, leaving the audience the task of achieving in life what was not achieved in the theatre.

Perhaps *Both Your Houses* was only three days late. On March 4, 1933, Franklin Delano Roosevelt was inaugurated as president of the United States. Late that night he established a nationwide bank holiday, to last until the federal government determined which institutions were financially sound. At that moment, Maxwell Anderson's "Get the Government Off the People's Back" thesis went into a half-century of political dormancy from which (rhetoric and changes of focus aside) it has yet to emerge.

The son of a roving Baptist minister, who migrated westerly from Pennsylvania to Ohio, Iowa, and North Dakota, Maxwell Anderson earned a B.A. from the University of North Dakota and an M.A. from Stanford University (Herbert Hoover's alma mater). Like Alan McClean, the protagonist of *Both Your Houses*, Anderson was a teacher—twice fired for pacifism—and, like McClean's father, was later a journalist in North Dakota, San Francisco, and New York.[22] Of his first eight plays, only *What Price Glory* (coauthored by Lawrence Stallings) was a great success. Then in 1930 *Elizabeth the Queen* catapulted Anderson into a hitherto undreamed-of tax bracket and provided the stimulus for a new play.

The purpose of the appropriations bill which is the unifying thread of *Both Your Houses* is to supply the $40 million supposedly needed to finish a Nevada dam originally budgeted at $400 million and which has already cost $790 million. The present struggle is to keep the deficiency bill's pork-barrel additions small enough so that the total package will not exceed $200 million.

As the play's *Romeo and Juliet*-inspired title suggests, Congress will not get high marks here for frugality and sensible action. The motives behind the deficiency bill additions vary, but few are defensible. Eddie Wister—a "pocket" congressman whose vote is owned by Appalachian Steel, his district's major employer—wants $15 million for the rehabilitation of two battleships, despite the fact that their military capabilities are limited to the sinking of disarmament conferences. Solomon Fitzmaurice schemes to have the Atlantic fleet winter off the coast of a resort area where he has holdings (a feat actually achieved by Representative Fred Britton of Long Island) at the cost of an additional $200,000 to the public. Sol needs the money to cover four years of disallowed tax exemptions: "What have you got to be in this carrion government to get your income tax fixed? A Secretary of the Treasury?" "It helped before," a friend reminds him.[23]

Ironically, the only literally illegal provision scheduled for cutting is $15,000 requested by a congresswoman for the dissemination of birth control information to the poor. It is unfortunate that even today the congresswoman's complaint remains relevant: "Doesn't the President consider uncared for babies an item in the national defense?" (*Both Your Houses*, II, ii, 127)

Enter freshman Nevada congressman Alan McClean. Like those of the other key characters in the play, McClean's name is refreshingly indicative. Solomon Fitzmaurice is a font of wisdom as to the operations of the House; Simeon Gray is an honest politician stained by a dishonest atmosphere; and McClean is the epitome of integrity elected on an economy platform. Alan was fired for exposing the misappropriation of funds at an agricultural college where he taught, a firing he turned into a campaign issue. Added to the appropriations committee because he is from the dam's district, Alan suspects that his financial backers—contractors on the project—had a conflict of interest in supporting him, that if construction bidding were open, completion of the dam would cost less than $40 million. Beyond that, he thinks it would be better for the country if the bill, and its expensive riders, were abandoned: "I was elected and sent here because I told my people I'd do what I could to reduce taxes and cut down even necessary expenditures. And there's nothing in the bill that can't be done without." (*Both Your Houses*, I, ii, 49)

Levering, the party whip, accuses Alan (without receiving a denial) of being one of the "Sons of the Wild Jackass," that is, a Western Progressive—proagriculture, prolabor, antibanking and anti–Gold Standard, often isolationist, and only nominally a major party member. The appellation is only partly accurate. McClean wants a reduction in taxes, but the most famous of the Progressives, William Jennings Bryan, won the Democratic presidential nomination three times by appropriating the

Populist Party's "Free Silver" demand. In Anderson's native North Dakota, the Nonpartisan League (formed in 1915) was both nominally Republican and well to the economic left of either major political party. Fueled by resentment of out-of-state marketing practices, the League gained control of the legislature in 1918 and established a state grain elevator, state hail insurance, a state bank, bank deposit insurance, workmen's compensation, women's suffrage, and increased funding for rural schools. In fact, the three loudest voices in their demands for massive state economic support—the late Huey Long's "Every Man a King" movement, Robert Townsend of the Old Age Pension Plan, and Father Coughlin (the radio priest)—united behind Nonpartisan North Dakota congressman Bill Lemke as a 1936 third-party presidential candidate.[24]

The governing of the country in *Both Your Houses* is merely a by-product of Congress's real purpose: levying $4 billion in taxes for congressmen to invest for themselves, or, more accurately, for the financial powers which engineer their elections. This difficulty in finding a balance between individual interest and collective interest is the oldest of charges against capitalism. As the wise Solomon Fitzmaurice explains it, pork-barreling is the only way to get the opportunity to work for other people: "Everybody wants something, everybody's trying to put something over for his voters, or his friends, or the folks he's working for. So they all get together, and they put those things in bills, and everybody votes for 'em. All except the opposition. They don't vote for 'em because they don't get anything. That's all there is to it. That's the whole government. If you want to be in Congress, you have to do it." (*Both Your Houses*, I, ii, 54–55)

Alan's natural ally against wasteful pork-barreling ought to be the hard-working, cost-cutting chairman of the Appropriations Committee, Simeon Gray. However, as his name suggests (and as he is aware), he has been tainted by the process he has struggled to work within: "I'd say that honesty was so rare as to be almost unknown in any government, and impossible under our system." (*Both Your Houses*, I, ii, 175–76) Because a bank of which he is a director has falsely listed assets, Gray has scheduled a penitentiary to be built in that district—thus pumping badly needed federal money into the area, saving the bank and preventing his own exposure. Although he agrees with Alan philosophically, Gray must support the bill.

Alan's Congress-wise secretary, Bus, teaches him how to form the small voting block of farmer-laborites and nonpartisans who have been excluded from the bill that he will need to tip the scales against it.

Although this ploy eventually fails (Alan has not sufficient talent in making promises to gain the necessary votes), he has by this time learned the system well enough to formulate his own plan.

Gray has included within the dam bill just enough items to insure a majority vote on the floor. Wister and Sol have used their knowledge of Gray's banking difficulties to blackmail the rehabilitation of the battleships and the redeployment of the Atlantic fleet onto the list. Nevertheless, Gray has excluded the pet projects of three of the seven committee members. With McClean added, they make up a majority of the committee. Alan merely points out whose items are included within the bill, and moves that all those previously struck be reinserted—at a total cost of $475 million. His logic is that Congress will not dare pass so bloated a bill in a Depression, and even if they did, the president is pledged to veto it.

"You give everybody what he wants, including the opposition, and lo! there ain't no opposition." (*Both Your Houses*, III, ii, 170) McClean underestimates the greed of his fellow representatives, of course. The bill gets a veto-proof two-thirds majority. As in so many political theatre plays, the main action ends in failure—hopefully spurring audience offstage reaction.

But what should the reaction be? In 1938 Dorothy Thompson wrote: "Two souls dwell within the bosom of the American people. The one loves the Abundant Life, as expressed by the cheap and plentiful products of large-scale production and distribution. The other soul yearns for former simplicities, for decentralization, for the interests of the 'little man,' revolts against high pressure salesmanship, denounces 'monopoly' and 'economic empires,' and seeks ways of breaking them up."[25] Alan McClean doesn't believe in "communism or fascism or any other political patent medicine!" (*Both Your Houses*, III, ii, 175) A more radical congressman, Joe Ebner, thinks that Congress's economic excesses will cause the common man to overthrow the System. The one "common man" in the play—Mark, the black janitor—is not initially certain that the revolution isn't a good idea: "If it went over—maybe I'd be on the upside." (*Both Your Houses*, I, i, 12) Significantly, his view changes at the suggestion that nonpassage of the bill may affect his job. Sol's answer to the Depression is to return the country to the thieves who made it great: "Brigands built up this nation from the beginning. They stole billions and gutted whole states and empires, but they dug our oil wells, built our railroads, built up everything we've got, and invented prosperity as they went along. . . . We can't have an honest government, so let 'em steal plenty and get us started again." (*Both Your Houses*, III, ii, 176)

Sol is frightening, persuasive, and perhaps a little bit of a prophet. The 1933 National Recovery Act is often remembered for extending collective bargaining to workers, but it also suspended certain antitrust laws for industry. The development of the material wealth of this country has depended not a little upon the possibility of getting rich doing it. The freedom to get rich has depended not a little upon capital's sharing some of those riches with labor. Certainly Sol's speech is given more substance than Alan's frustrating last statement, which sees a coming revolution without telling the audience which direction to look: "You think you're good and secure in this charlatan's sanctuary you've built for yourselves. You think the sacred and senseless legend poured into the people of this country will protect you. It won't. It takes about a hundred years to tire this country of trickery—and we're fifty years overdue right now." (*Both Your Houses*, III, ii, 178)

The question this play never answers is overdue for what? The United States has probably never been closer to revolution that it was in the last days of the Hoover administration while *Both Your Houses* was being rehearsed. No one knew if reform would be enough.

Labor and the Left

Both organized labor and the Communist Party promised to be major players in the United States that emerged from the Great War. The link between the two was obvious in theory, if largely unconsummated in practice. Nevertheless, during the 1920s both were to decline in significance.

Under the supervision of a National War Labor Board, industrial workers had achieved (a) an eight-hour work day, (b) the banning of lock-outs, (c) the right to organize and bargain collectively through worker-selected representatives, (d) equal pay for women doing equal work, and (e) the principle of "a living wage to insure the subsistence of the worker and his family in health and reasonable comfort."[26] Yet, a decade later, union membership had fallen by a third, and, although manufacturing workers' hourly pay increased 8 percent between 1923 and 1929, corporation profit was up 62 percent.[27]

Hard times (the twenties began with a recession and ended with a depression) are traditionally difficult for labor organizing. However, the main problems unions faced in the postwar era were philosophical. The American Revolution and subsequent populist and progressive movements had been oriented toward individual property owners. In 1921, "open shop" adherents (employers who preferred to hire outside of union affiliation) united under the rubric "The American Plan," which purported to allow "every man to work out his own salvation, and not to be bound by the shackles of organization to his own detriment."[28]

What this meant, in fact, was one-man/one-company labor contracts in which the worker sold his "property" (labor) to an employer at what the market would bear. While it was the right of every worker to receive a living wage, the Supreme Court ruled—while invalidating a minimum-wage law as violation of liberty of contract—that it is unconstitutional for the state to force the employer to provide such a wage. An earlier postwar Supreme Court decision ruled the secondary boycott illegal and declared that taking away an employer's strike-blocking injunction "deprived him of property without due process."[29]

Philosophically, bolshevism challenged American populist egalitarianism at its weakest point—the urban industrial worker. Karl Marx contended that a classless society would occur in an industrialized world when the value system of the worker achieved hegemony and the workers assumed control of the means of production. Communism, by defining property as the product of labor, placed the worker at the top of the social hierarchy and categorized all others as nonproductive parasites.[30] Since both communism and organized labor denied hegemony to property, both found themselves in opposition to the existing American legal system. That the two would form an alliance is less surprising than the ineffectiveness of the alliance formed.

When the first Comintern (Communist International) was formed in March 1919, the name did not appear to be an exaggeration. During the "Two Red Years" of 1919–1921, Bolshevik revolutions achieved temporary successes in Bavaria, Hungary, and Finland, and reaction to a near-victory drove Italy into the arms of Mussolini in 1922. In 1919 there were thirty to forty thousand Communists in the United States. After a decade of factionalism and foreignism, the Party boasted one-quarter that number. During the twenties, the Communist Party and the Communist Labor Party were more interested in internecine warfare than class warfare. Even in the 1930s, however, the Communist Party of the United States of America (CPUSA) was literally an "alien entity." In the fall of 1934, the circulation of the English-language *Daily Worker* was 50,000, compared to 131,000 for the Party's non-English newspapers. Not until mid-1936 would the American-born Party members equal in number the foreign-born.[31] In addition, the Party demanded strict adherence to a constantly changing, mentally exhausting ideological labyrinth of a political policy, designed and controlled by a country halfway around the world to meet its own needs. Not surprisingly, few employed industrial workers had the energy or the proclivity for mental gymnastics to remain a member for long.

The inroads made among the American intelligentsia were more productive, if no more permanent. The John Reed Literary Clubs, named for the journalist and American Communist buried in the Kremlin, were formed in 1929. However, the big breakthrough among "fellow travelers" (radicalized non-Communist intellectuals) was made two years later, when critic and *New Republic* editor Edmund Wilson called for a movement to "take Communism away from the Communists" and make it a major force in American recovery. The first important "front" group, the National Committee for the Defense of Political Prisoners, supported striking miners in Harlan County, Kentucky, protested Japanese aggression in China, and denounced a bill by Martin Dies (who was to become the first chair of the House Un-American Activities Committee in 1938) to deport alien Communists. This group, including Theodore Dreiser, Michael Gold, Sherwood Anderson, Lincoln Steffens, Elmer Rice, Malcolm Cowley, and Edna St. Vincent Millay, provided the nucleus (with Langston Hughes, Countee Cullen, and John Dos Passos) of the League of Professional Groups for William Z. Foster and James Ford, the 1932 Communist presidential ticket.

As was to happen in the future, the League foundered on the unwillingness of fellow travelers to structure either their literary outputs or their political viewpoints to the Party line. After Hitler seized power in Germany, members Sidney Hook and James Rorty called for a united front against fascism. However, during the Comintern's "Third Period" (1928–1934), the Party saw the Fascists as merely another weapon in the battle against bourgeois capitalism. Consequently, Hook, Rorty, and those of a similar mind soon found themselves blistered in the Communist press as "objective enemies of the working class."[32]

After 1933, Communists came to recognize that Hitler was a military threat to Russia herself. On September 18, 1934, Moscow joined the League of Nations and set about arranging security pacts.[33] Between 1935 and the nonaggression treaty signed with Germany on August 23, 1939, the Party encouraged a worldwide anti-Fascist "Popular Front" movement and gave local support to any liberal government it felt might be enlisted. The League of American Writers was formed in 1935, and one of its members was Clifford Odets.

Waiting for Lefty

"The point is that so deep was the crisis at this time, that virtually every conscious person was attempting to find a basic answer to society's jitters, and for the moment they were willing to consider any idea promising a solution, no matter how extreme or unpopular."[34]

As recalled by Harold Clurman, a cofounder and director of the Group Theatre, such was the mood at a 1932 literary reception for a new book by Communist presidential candidate William Z. Foster. Within two years, several members of the Group Theatre were Communist Party members, including its subsequently best-known alumni, director Elia Kazan and playwright Clifford Odets.

Waiting for Lefty was produced by the Marxist New Theatre League on January 5, 1935, in New York's Civic Repertory Theatre as part of a benefit for New Theatre Magazine. The inspiration for the play was the 1934 New York taxi drivers' strike, and its setting is a taxi driver union hall. The audience in the auditorium (plus an occasional "plant") takes the role of rank and file union members. There is no fourth wall between them and the stage. The play's action is episodic, taken from the lives of the strike committee members and played in a semicircle formed by their chairs. At the end of these episodes, each of which depicts the moment which brought the committee member to his present political position, they (and, hopefully, the audience) will find they have the same enemy: capitalism.

Indeed, the physical manifestation of capitalism is the sole link to all the play's episodes: Harry Fatt, the union boss, whose porcine characteristics are used to link capitalism, organized crime, and anticommunism. Fatt declares: "Red and yellow makes a dirty color, boys. . . . Give those birds a chance and they'll have your sisters and wives in the whorehouses, like they done in Russia. They'll tear Christ off his bleeding cross. They'll wreck your homes and throw your babies in the river."[35] It is the intention of Fatt (and the gunman leaning against the proscenium arch) that the drivers not reduce company profits by going out on strike. As a stand-in for capitalism, Fatt will always be present during these scenes (played to stall the vote while the strike committee "waits for Lefty" Costello, their chairman), sometimes taking part, sometimes merely blowing cigar smoke (confusion) from the edge of the circle.

Despite the care he takes to make the audience dislike Fatt, Odets only gradually introduces communism as an alternative to capitalism. The first strike committee member establishes his Americanism fast. Joe Mitchell "ain't a red boy one bit!" He is a wounded war veteran and his concerns are concrete, not ideological. His furniture has been repossessed, his two blond children are threatened by rickets and lack school shoes, and, in order to save the children, his wife is contemplating leaving him for another man. As Edna points out, capitalism's refusal to pay him a living wage is killing his kids and his marriage:

Joe: I'm not so dumb as you think. But you are talking like a Red.

Edna: I don't know what that means. But when a man knocks you down you get up and kiss his fist! You gutless piece of baloney. . . . Get those hack boys together! Sweep out those racketeers like a pile of dirt! Stand up like men and fight for the crying wives and kids. (*Waiting for Lefty*, ii, 258–59)

In subsequent episodes, the evidence against capitalism accumulates. Miller, a lab technician, is offered a raise and job security if he will make poison gas and spy on his immediate superior for some unseen decision maker named Siegfried (Odets was Jewish). Fayette, the capitalist industrialist, is shown as racist, anti-ethnic, and antihuman.

Fayette: I like sobriety in my workers . . . the trained ones, I mean. The Pollacks and niggers, they're better drunk—keeps them out of mischief . . . You're doing something for your country. Assuring the United States that when those goddam Japs start a ruckus we'll have offensive weapons to back us up! . . .

Miller: They say twelve million men were killed in the last one and twenty million more wounded or missing.

Fayette: That's not our worry. If big business went sentimental over human life there wouldn't be big business of any sort! (*Waiting for Lefty*, iii, 260–62)

An important secondary theme is introduced in episode three when Sid, a young cabbie unable to marry because of poverty, talks of his brother, who, like many other college graduates of the thirties, joined the navy just to eat. The myth of the rugged individualist is used to shame men who failed during the Depression, and to encourage them to regain their manhood by fighting wars which benefit only capitalists. Sam's naval destination is Cuba, where the American military is overthrowing yet another government in the name of American sugar companies, but Sid hints of a different revolution to come: "They'll teach Sam to point the guns the wrong way, that dumb basketball player." (*Waiting for Lefty*, iv, 268)

Other faces of the capitalist evil appear. An actor discovers that capitalists turn artists into prostitutes. Fittingly, the producer—played by the Harry Fatt actor—has just had his Russian wolfhound emasculated. Back at the union hall, a labor spy is exposed by a brother who knows true fraternity is not a question of blood but of worker loyalty. Later, a doctor finds that his skill is not so important as his being Jewish ("The USSR is the only country where anti-Semitism is a crime against the State," one of the strike committee Greek chorus yells from the edge of the playing circle), and that a woman's illness is not so important as her being a charity patient. By now it is an aristocratic, patriarchal doctor who is urging a class war in which the workers take charge: "Doctors don't run medicine in this country. The men who know their jobs don't run anything here. The honest workers were sold out . . . in '76. The Constitution's for rich men then and now." (*Waiting for Lefty*, vii, 279)

The workers are learning with the audience. A stenographer gives the actor a copy of *The Communist Manifesto*: "Come out in the light, Comrade." Doc Benjamin (played by Odets) elects to fight class distinction here rather than practice socialized medicine in Russia, and as Agate Keller bursts onstage, word comes that Lefty has been found murdered, shot in the back of the head behind the carbarns. Throughout his speech, Keller (played by Elia Kazan) is backed up by the other six workers, so it is plain that the whole group is speaking: "What's the answer, boys? The answer is, if we're reds because we wanna strike, then we take over their salute too! . . . [makes Communist salute] What is it? An uppercut! The good old uppercut to the chin! . . . Working class, unite and fight! Tear down the slaughter house of our old lives! Let freedom really ring. . . . What are we waiting for?" (*Waiting for Lefty*, viii, 282)

What is clear is that we cannot "wait for Lefty." A classless society cannot be the work of one man, who, like a Hitler or a Mussolini, could lead us to disaster. The thirties hero was collective, refusing to be bound by outdated American myths. "It was the birth cry of the thirties. Our youth had found its voice. It was a call to join the good fight for a greater measure of life in a world free of economic fear, falsehood, and craven servitude to stupidity and greed. "Strike! . . . not alone for a few extra pennies of wages or for shorter hours of work, strike for greater dignity, strike for a bolder humanity, strike for the full stature of man."[36]

The WPA and the FTP

Franklin Delano Roosevelt, the man who heard "the birth cry of the thirties" most clearly, was struggling to save capitalism, not to replace it. He understood Thomas Macaulay's dictum, "To preserve, it is necessary to reform," even if some capitalists did not. "One of my principal tasks," he said in 1934, " is to prevent bankers and businessmen from committing suicide."[37] In the famous "hundred days" following his first inauguration, Congress passed sixteen bills intended to alleviate the ills of the Depression. The Federal Deposit Insurance Act reassured a public which had seen 1,456 banks fail in 1932. The three million young men of the Civilian Conservation Corps (CCC) advanced national forestry programs from five to fifteen years prior to World War II.[38] The Public Works Administration (PWA) built the Grand Coulee Dam, New York's Triborough Bridge, fifty-one public housing projects and two-thirds of the nation's new schools.[39]

Even labor was making progress of which Karl Marx might have approved: first, through a government more representative of its values, and, second, through its own efforts. The National Industrial Recovery Act (NIRA) of 1933 restated organizing and collective bargaining rights, set minimum-wage and maximum-hour codes, and created the National Labor Board to mediate management/labor disputes. Although the NIRA was invalidated by the Supreme Court, its labor guarantees were included in New York senator Robert Wagner's 1935 National Labor Relations Act, which also banned a number of unfair labor practices (including company unions) and established the National Labor Relations Board to oversee union elections.[40]

That same year, the Congress of Industrial Organizations (CIO) was formed. Unlike the older, craft-organized American Federation of Labor, CIO unions were industry-wide, giving them the capability of shutting down an industry with a single strike. The AFL doubled its membership between 1932 and 1937, despite ejecting the "classless" industrial unions in 1936. However, the CIO, under the leadership of the United Mine Workers' John L. Lewis, staged some spectacularly successful strikes in the auto and steel industries and by the end of 1937 was the larger organization.[41]

It was obvious early that the most effective New Deal programs were those that provided labor and training, and in 1935 Roosevelt decided to end federal relief. The "alphabet soup" of agencies which provided work—the CCC, the PWA, and the National Youth Administration (which provided part-time employment to over 4.6 million young people of school age)—were kept. The rest of the unemployed were to be engaged by the new Works Progress Administration (WPA), whose $1.39 billion allotment was in the hands of Harry Hopkins. Many of the eight million workers employed by the WPA during its tenure built the 20,000 playgrounds, schools, hospitals, and airfields which are its most visible legacy.[42] But it was Harry Hopkins's peculiarly un-American contention that artists were workers like everybody else and deserved to be employed in the field of their expertise. The result was the Federal Arts Project:

including (a) the Federal Writers Project, which produced almost a thousand publications and employed such then-unknown writers as Tennessee Williams, John Cheever, and Richard Wright; (b) the Federal Art Project, which supported Jackson Pollock and Willem de Kooning and whose public murals were alternately praised for their vigor and condemned for their politics; (c) the Federal Music Project, which underwrote William Schumann and fully six Los Angeles symphony orchestras; (d) the Federal Dance Project; and (e) the Federal Theatre Project (FTP), under the direction of Hopkins's former Grinnell College classmate, Hallie Flanagan (Davis).[43]

Like that of the other WPA components, the function of the FTP was not artistic or educational, but was rather to put professionals back to work. Secondarily, the intention was to present native dramatic entertainment nationwide at little or no cost, hopefully of such quality that the U.S. government could be proud to sponsor it. In all cases, 90 percent of the WPA funds were to pay for labor, and 90 percent of this labor was to come from the relief rolls.[44] Every employee was supposed to have made a living in the theatre in the past and be capable of making one in the future, but there was no provision for the development of new talent. Fortunately, many neophytes were employed by the Federal Theatre, which launched careers of the caliber of actors Arthur Kennedy, E. G. Marshall, and John Randolph, directors John Huston, Nicholas Ray, and Sidney Lumet, composer Lehman Engel, designer Howard Bay, and writers Arthur Miller and Dale Wasserman.[45]

Before funding for the Federal Theatre Project was cancelled on June 1, 1939, twelve hundred productions in thirty-five states had been presented (not counting the three thousand radio programs produced each year through the Federal Theatre of the Air). It also published the *Federal Theatre Magazine*, established community theatres and actor-training classes, held playwriting contests in colleges and CCC camps, did psychodrama experimentation in hospitals, and created the National Service Bureau, which did drama research, read, wrote, and translated plays, and distributed its work nationwide.[46] At its peak, 15,500 theatre and circus people were employed to entertain a weekly audience over 350,000 in six different languages and mime. Although 65 percent of all FTP productions were free, and admissions when charged ranged from a nickel to an all-time high of $1.65 for an Orson Welles/John Houseman Broadway presentation,[47] the Federal Theatre still earned over $2 million. Finally, including dependents, the FTP supported an average of 50,000 people a year for nearly four years at a cost of just over $46 million, roughly the price of a battleship.[48]

Given the Federal Theatre's scope, origin, and historical epoch, it would have been impossible for it to ignore political subjects entirely. The presence of sixteen Negro dramatic units in a country where even the CCC camps were segregated and many southern administrators barred blacks from the WPA was a political act in itself. The Living Newspaper—a documentary committed to investigating the extent, nature, and origin of a social problem—was by its very nature political.

On her Guggenheim Fellowship, Hallie Flanagan had travelled to Russia and eleven other European countries, where she became familiar with the idea of the theatre as a didactic instrument. She was particularly impressed with the Epic Theatre methods of Erwin Piscator, who made use of loudspeakers, projections, newsreel techniques, segmented stages, and comic-strip dioramas to make political comments in the socialist-affiliated Volksbuhne of Berlin. Hallie Flanagan adapted these methods to plays she directed for Vassar's Experimental Theatre, including such leftist, agitprop street plays as *Miners are Striking* and *We Demand*, as well as the original *Can You Hear Their Voices?*, based on a *New Masses* story about the 1931 Arkansas hunger riots.[49] Even the term "Living Newspaper" came from the Russian "Blue Blouse" theatres which used Epic Theatre techniques to educate areas of low reading or political literacy. By the early 1930s there were several American Blue Blouse groups. The origin of the form and the fact Hallie Flanagan was once a contributing editor to the magazine of the League of Workers Theatre would later be cited to prove the FTP to be the vanguard of a Communist takeover.[50]

The first Living Newspaper was *Ethiopia*—the story of its invasion by Italy. White House censorship prevented its opening in 1936 on the grounds that it depicted living people, but actually because it compromised American neutrality. The FTP New York administrator, playwright Elmer Rice, resigned, and many predicted the demise of the Living Newspaper form. But *Triple-A Plowed Under*, having as its subject the disastrous Agriculture Adjustment Act, ran a surprising eighty-five performances in New York and was later produced in Chicago, Los Angeles, Cleveland, and Milwaukee. Later Living Newspapers included *Injunction Granted* (a history of the labor union movement), *Power* (a call for public ownership of utilities), *One-Third of a Nation*, and—in Chicago—*Spirochete* (a history of syphilis). Equally challenging locally created Living Newspapers included *Dirt* (about agribusiness in Iowa), *Timber* (lumber in Washington state), *Tapestry in Linen* (Oregon's flax industry), and *King Cotton* (textile mills in the South).[51] *Liberty Deferred* (chronicling America's continuing civil rights deficiencies) was never produced.

One-Third of a Nation

I see millions of families trying to live on incomes so meager that the pall
of family disaster hangs over them day by day. . . . I see one-third of a
nation ill-housed, ill-clad, ill-nourished.
                          —FDR's second inaugural address (January 30, 1937)

The term "one-third of a nation" and its relationship to substandard
housing originated not with Roosevelt, but with Dr. Edith Elmer Wood's
1919 book, *The Housing of the Unskilled Wage Earner*. Dr. Wood's most
important discovery flew in the face of the common perception of why
slums exist. It was generally believed that slums were a collecting ground
for moral refuse. Therefore, housing regulations were seen as a means
of enforcing morality upon the degenerate. To the contrary, as early as
1913 Wood determined that people lived in slums because they had no
other housing available, and condemned: "Any remedial measure which
simply forces them out of the alleys and makes no provision for their
future is a very great hardship upon . . . people who in the majority of
cases are deserving of every consideration."[52]

The idea for basing a Living Newspaper on the Roosevelt inaugural
occurred when the Wagner-Steagall Housing Bill was introduced in
Congress. Twenty reporters began researching (the Living Newspaper
was sponsored by the Newspaper Guild) and a "morgue staff" scoured
daily papers for relevant material. In May 1937, City Editor Richard
McManus delivered the research results to author Arthur Arent: "What
stood out in my mind was the repetitive quality of the whole
thing. . . . Lousy, stinking holes, called homes, in 1850—and in 1938,
the same holes, still occupied by human beings."[53]

One-Third of a Nation begins with a 1924 tenement fire and ends with
one in 1938, a metaphor for the cyclical nature of housing problems.
Through a maze of historic and legal entanglements, the audience
accompanies the pilgrimage of a home-seeking little Everyman named
Angus K. Buttonkooper (already familiar to Living Newspaper viewers
from *Power*). His mentor is the disembodied voice of a loudspeaker, but
the play's central character is real estate, and its villain is the profit
motive.

Fourteen people died in the 1924 fire in an "old-law tenement" (a
pre-1901 building not under the jurisdiction of current safety codes).
There were 67,000 such tenements in New York, and it would have taken
the city's entire staff of inspectors three years to visit each building just
once. The landlord could be questioned only if it could be proved there

were violations of pre-1901 laws—of which the wooden wainscoting which turned the stairwells into a five-story torch was not one.

At an investigative hearing, the landlord justifies himself to a tenant who lost his wife and sons in the fire: "You'll have to go back in history and blame whatever it was that made New York City real estate the soundest and most profitable speculation on the face of the earth!"[54]

New York City speculation began with grants of free land to Trinity Church in 1705, the tax-free leases of which were divided among its most influential vestrymen. Trinity was also the first subject of a commission studying such speculation, an investigation which was called off when the commission's chairman, Aaron Burr, received one of the leases himself.

The relationship of land leasing to the growth of the city is the key to the growth of the slums. "A man's got to have a place to live" is the play's refrain. So long as working people do not own the space on which they live, and so long as the city itself remains a growing and profitable venture, the wealth of the landowner will automatically increase as the competition for living space increases. In the play's most marvelous image, a landowner unrolls on stage a small grass mat representing five acres of land at Broadway and Canal Street in 1775 and sits on it. The Voice of the Town Crier notes the passing of time to 1781, 1800, and 1845, and during each period an increasing number of tenants pay increasing sums of money to rent smaller and smaller parcels of the landowner's land in order to have places to live—a concept visualized by their occupation of places on the grass mat. By the end of the scene not a blade of grass is showing and the tenants can barely move.

An unfortunate side effect of the competition for living space is the space's deterioration. Since there is a waiting list for any available apartment, the landlord has no economic incentive to maintain those in existence. Their value increases at the same rate they become less suitable to live in. The same competition for living space makes new housing too expensive for tenants. In 1936 there were thirty-six hundred people living in old-law tenements for every individual space opened in new housing units. This competition lifted rents so that on the average only 1 percent of those tenants living in housing demolished to make way for new apartments could afford to live in them. Ninety-nine percent has to move into the remaining old-law tenements, increasing their crowding.

"Speculation in misery," the play's Loudspeaker/Conscience calls it, and the misery is more than mere inconvenience. Following a guide into the 1850s, Angus Buttonkooper discovers the third New York cholera epidemic in twenty-two years.

The resulting investigation by the Health Inspector of New York merely called for the fox to clean up the henhouse: "The remedy lies with the humane and philanthropic capitalists by whom houses might be erected with all the comforts and conveniences of separate rooms, running water and so forth, which could yield a fair interest on their value and make thousands of people happy!" (*One-Third of a Nation*, I, v, 59–60)

The cholera-infected rooms are soon occupied again: "In case you're forgetting . . . you've got to have a place to live!" (*One-Third of a Nation*, I, vi, 65). And while cholera has been subdued in the twentieth century, death rates for tuberculosis, diphtheria, and spinal meningitis in old-law tenements from 1919 to 1934 were more than double those of the New York average.

The slums are also a nationwide breeding ground for crime. Twenty-five percent of Seattle's juvenile delinquency is found in the 6.5 percent area which constitutes its slums. Fifty percent of all Richmond, Virginia's, juvenile delinquency occurs in the 18 percent area of its city slums. In Cleveland, the figures are 47 percent in 17 percent, and in Philadelphia, they are 46 percent in 9 percent. (*One-Third of a Nation*, II, i, 82–83)

Even when laws are passed, the cycle continues. Between 1867 and 1887, new laws required fire escapes, water on every floor, a toilet for every twenty occupants, and no windowless rooms. Unfortunately, such laws were seldom enforced, and when enforced were challenged in court. In 1895 Judge Roger A. Pryor upheld Trinity Church's contention that being forced to supply water for its tenants was not "a proper exercise of police power": "A conclusion contrary to the present decision would involve that species of socialism under the regime of which the individual disappears and is absorbed by a collective being called 'the State' . . . a principle utterly repugnant to the spirit of our political system and necessarily fatal to our form of liberty." (*One-Third of a Nation*, II, 1, 70–71)

It is, of course, precisely collective action and the state that the play presents as a solution to urban housing problems. Even the 1901 reforms could do nothing about tenements built before that date, or inadequate maintenance, or racial discrimination and the "hot bed" (one room rented to three different tenants for the eight hours they are presumed to be sleeping in it). Inspired by the example of unions and the discovery that the police assessed each landlord $25 per room for the carrying out of evictions, some tenants forced rent controls and apartment repairs with building-wide "rent strikes." But holding the line on rents did nothing to improve housing, and there was no incentive to build low-cost housing because there was no money in it.

One-Third of a Nation suggests that the answer lies in government-financed housing, bracing itself for the inevitable charges of socialism, invasion of private rights, contravening of economic laws, and unconstitutionality. The Wagner-Steagall Housing Bill, introduced in 1937 and budgeted at $1 billion, also faced the familiar insinuations that slums were the creation of the people who live in them, that those who occupy slums are aliens, not Americans, and that (according to Darwinian logic) we have no right saving those who are unable to save themselves. The original appropriation is cut in half, and New York City, the replacement of whose slums would cost $2 billion alone, can expect to get no more than $30 million. But the question is not one of government funding, but of government priorities.

Mrs. Buttonkooper: Say, Mister, how much was the appropriation for the Army and Navy?

Loudspeaker: The appropriation for the Army and Navy for the last four years was three billion, one hundred and twenty-five million dollars. . . .

Little Man: Why that's more than enough money to clean out every slum in New York! (*One-Third of a Nation*, II, iv, 120)

The preamble to the U.S. Constitution gives the insurance of domestic tranquility and the promotion of the general welfare the same emphasis as providing for the common defense. And, as the play ends with the same kind of fire that took fourteen lives at its opening curtain, we are reminded of the continuing cost of not living up to its promise.

One-Third of a Nation ran most of 1938 in New York and was seen by two hundred thousand people. Subsequently, it was produced in ten other cities, appropriately changed to mirror local conditions. Nevertheless, the Federal Theatre Project was abolished on June 30, 1939—a sacrifice to the political realities of the times. Congressman Everett Dirkson labeled the FTP productions "salacious tripe." Eighty-one of the 830 play titles in the FTP records were attacked by the House Un-American Activities Committee (HUAC), including 5 plays not produced, 46 not originating with the project, 3 Living Newspapers, *Candide*, *The Trojan Women*, and *Sing for Your Supper* (whose finale, "Ballad for Americans," was chosen as the theme for the 1940 Republican National Convention).[55] The ostensible reason given for the FTP's cancellation was economy, although the entire Arts Program cost less than three-quarters of 1 percent of the WPA appropriation.[56] The FTP was also called a hotbed of Communist-inspired radical activity. HUAC member (later chairman) J.

Parnell Thomas of New Jersey offered his opinion of the FTP's *Prologue to Glory*, a play showing a youthful Lincoln battling politicians: "That is Communist talk. . . . This is simply a propaganda play to show all politicians are crooked." Thomas later went to federal prison for defrauding the government.[57] When Hallie Flanagan was called for a single morning's testimony on December 6, 1938, the level of HUAC's understanding was probably best illustrated by the attempt of Congressman Joe Starnes of Alabama to determine if Christopher Marlowe was a Communist.[58]

The congressional elections of 1938 had crippled Roosevelt's majority, and the new Congress had a mandate to make relief cuts. The FTP was a highly visible and relatively inexpensive scapegoat, and WPA officials decided not to fight for it. Still, the very existence of the Federal Theatre is a reminder of how much the government's influence in our daily lives increased in the five years these three plays covered. In 1931, President Hoover's belief that government intervention was the siren song for the death of American character was still generally accepted, and the position of Alan McClean as the protagonist of *Both Your Houses* shows it. But by 1938 the majority of Americans believed the government had a responsibility to answer Mrs. Buttonkooper's call. They agreed with President Roosevelt's acceptance speech at the 1936 Democratic National Convention: "Governments can err; Presidents do make mistakes, . . . but better the occasional faults of a Government that lives in a spirit of charity than the consistent omissions of a Government frozen in the ice of its own indifference."[59]

American Myth, Dramatic Manifestation

More than any other decade in American history, the 1930s conjures up the image of politically committed theatre. Perhaps this is because we experienced that theatre twice—once when it was first written and performed, and once when it was refuted and (less often) defended by many of its participants before congressional committees during the Cold War. In fact, considering the social desperation of the period, relatively few dramatic challenges were mounted against the political, economic, legal, and social systems of the nation. According to Sam Smiley, "Of the 1,540 plays professionally produced in New York during the thirties, only 177 (11 percent) were directly *engage*, and less than a third of those could be called didactic [plays which *compel* an audience to learn]."[60]

Nevertheless, organizations like the League of Workers Theatres, the Workers' Laboratory Theatre, the Theatre Union, the Theatre of Action, and even the Group Theatre are purely 1930s phenomena. That these theatrical collectives give way to the equally unique Federal Theatre in the last third of the decade reinforces this chapter's dominant theme: the evolution of our national self-perception from rugged individualism to collective action to government responsibility. As Elmer Rice declared in 1935: "The rugged individualism so beloved by Mr. Hoover is now a museum piece. It is no longer a part of the social scene. The old system in the theatre is finished."[61]

It is not surprising that so few social dramas of the 1930s emulate *Both Your Houses'* call for less government. Until 1933, "I am the master of my fate, I am the captain of my soul" was not just an American ideal; it was a national imperative. Grover Cleveland stated it best when he vetoed the 1887 Texas Seed Bill: "Though the people support the Government, the Government should not support the people."[62] Less government was the norm, and until it ceases to be effective, the norm is invisible.

In the twenties, American drama was less concerned with the social individual than with the individual psychology. Whatever Eugene O'Neill may have had to say about the social position of Afro-Americans (*The Emperor Jones, All God's Chillun Got Wings*), workers (*The Hairy Ape*), or women (*Strange Interlude*), the drama lay in the workings of their minds. Even in a social drama like *Gods of the Lightning*, Maxwell Anderson and Harold Hickerson's 1928 treatment of the Sacco-Vanzetti case, the protest is not against a particular governmental system, but against the unfair relationship of any individual to the will of government.

As the 1930s progressed, the ability of the individual to stand clear of his or her government became less a matter of ruggedness than escapism. Gerald Weales has demonstrated how the power imbalance between authority and the individual became a theme for traditional comedy (plays in which the social status quo is upheld or restored) after 1935. He cites a number of popular farces—*Sailor Beware, She Loves Me Not* (1933), *Boy Meets Girl, Three Men on a Horse* (1935), *Brother Rat* (1936), *Room Service* (1937), and *What a Life* (1938)—in which the efforts of self-described rugged individualists lead from one fiasco to another, only to have the difficulties resolved by an authority figure. In the Kaufman and Hart/Rodgers and Hart musical, *I'd Rather Be Right* (1937) that authority figure is no less than Franklin D. Roosevelt himself. Even when the government is in the opposition, as when the IRS and the FBI intrude upon the eccentric family of Kaufman and Hart's *You Can't Take It with You* (1936), the problem is solved by a pure fluke and never reaches the confrontation stage. "The farces were obviously popular partly because people wanted to laugh in and in spite of a Depression decade, but the implicit appeal, I suspect, came from the fact that their pose of irreverence, their bouncing sense of the individual in action was hedged by the comforting assurance that someone out there was taking care of things."[63]

As for the anti-authoritarian rugged individualist, his true 1930s manifestation was in the gangster, a last gasp of the nineteenth century in other ways as well. He was a Darwinian product of his environment, for example, "Baby-Face" Martin in Sidney Kingsley's *Dead End* (1935), as well as a Romantic hero in conflict with it: "But I knew him when we were kids. He had a lot of fine stuff. He was strong. He had courage. He was a born leader. He even had a sense of fair play. But living in the streets kept making him bad."[64] In Robert Sherwood's *The Petrified Forest* (1935), Duke Mantee "represents the bankruptcy of the free-enterprise system—free enterprise exhausting itself in the compulsive acquisition of money that can never be used."[65] He must be destroyed, but, metaphorically more important, so must the environment that produced him.

The class-conscious collective hero of *Waiting for Lefty* is far more overtly present in the 1930s. The discussion of his awakening to action makes up a large part of many excellent books to which the reader is referred—among them Gerald Rabkin's *Drama and Commitment: Politics in the American Theatre of the Thirties*, Sam Smiley's *The Drama of Attack: Didactic Plays of the American Depression*, Malcolm Goldstein's *The Political Stage: American Drama and Theater of the Great Depression*, Jay Williams's *Stage Left*, and R. C. Reynolds's *Stage Left: The Development of the American Social Drama in the Thirties*.[66] This book is indebted to them for their historical and dramatic perspectives. It remains only to note some of the earliest of the capitalist/labor conflict plays to go beyond the agitprop form, and to cite one play as especially relevant in terms of both class and caste.

In May 1931, Hallie Flanagan and Margaret Ellen Clifford of Barnard College presented *Can You Hear Their Voices?* at Vassar's Experimental Theater. Based on a Whittaker Chambers's story published in the *New Masses* that March, the Flanagan/Clifford play drew upon the 1930 Arkansas food riots. Close enough to the typical capitalist/agitator conflicts of the time to be accepted by workers' theatre audiences (if not by Third Period doctrinaire theorists), *Can You Hear Their Voices?* featured individual characterization and, although episodic, its scenes built to a conventional dramatic point which trusts the audience's ability to draw conclusions. One of the authors' conclusions that so annoyed contemporary Marxist critics was that the play demanded the relief for which the Communists called, without stating that only through a Communist revolution could it come about.[67]

That December, Claire and Paul Sifton's *1931—* was both more explicit, more ambitious, and less successful. The second production of the fledgling Group Theatre and the first play of its kind to be presented on Broadway, it closed after nine performances. The structure and protagonists (Adam Coaldigger and The Girl) of *1931—* have obvious agitprop ancestry. Ten interludes in which nameless unemployed workers gather at the gates of factories are interspersed among fourteen scenes in which Adam loses his job, his home, and his self-respect, and The Girl becomes pregnant, a prostitute, and a victim of venereal disease. Scene by scene, the crowd of unemployed workers increases in size and anger, until at last, singing the "Internationale," they are joined by Adam in a march through the streets. As Harold Clurman noted, *1931—* did good balcony business throughout its run, but an audience for its more expensive seats was still years away from the theatre.[68]

Until the birth of the Federal Theatre, blacks were only slowly losing their invisibility. The works of Langston Hughes, the best (as he was in so many other fields) Afro-American dramatist, will be discussed in Chapter 5. For the most part, black viewers—if able to enter a usually segregated theatre—had to be content with an occasional telling moment in an otherwise white play, such as "Supper Time" in *As Thousands Cheer* (1933), in which Ethel Waters sings about the problem of telling children that their father has been lynched, or the bitter supposition by the black "death row" prisoner in John Wexley's *The Last Mile* (1930) that heaven and hell will be as segregated as the America he has known. Exceptions were the many plays on the subject of the "Scotsboro Boys"—the nine young blacks who were unjustly accused of raping a white prostitute in a boxcar of an Alabama freight train. Wexley's *They Shall Not Die* (1934) was the best of these.

One play to effectively combine class struggle and caste struggle was *Stevedore* by Paul Peters and George Sklar. The Theatre Union production, which ran for 175 performances in 1934 New York, also fostered a road tour and a London production with Paul Robeson.[69] Because he is trying simultaneously to organize a stevedore's union and combat white dominance, a black dockworker is jailed on the charge of raping a white woman. Following his escape, he rallies his neighbors to fight off a white mob intent on burning down the ghetto. He is shot, but his white fellow dockworkers arrive in time to save the neighborhood and demonstrate class solidarity across caste lines. Stated bluntly, the plot sounds crude, but viewers as diverse as Groucho Marx and Bill ("Bojangles") Robinson were enthralled by it. *Herald-Tribune* critic Percy Hammond summed up what was probably the general reaction: "Being a white man and a capitalist, I ought to resent *Stevedore*. But [the authors] write so theatrically and with such fascinating violence about wrongs and rectifications that I am lost in admiration of their showmanship."[70]

Finally, both the birth and the death of the Federal Theatre are a tribute to the decade's growing perception of the power theatre can have as a social force. The title of the first book on the FTP, *Bread and Circuses*, accurately implies that it was intended to be a form of creative relief for out-of-work artists. However, the linking of *One-Third of a Nation* with FDR's second inaugural address and the Wagner/Steagall Housing Bill showed how far administration thinking had travelled in three years. On a different road, the FTP's opposition had travelled just as far, and whether it feared communism or just losing an election, it knew that theatre, with its ability to show the action being done, had far more political potential than pamphlet or speech.

Notes

1. Gerald Nash, *The Great Depression and World War II: Organizing America 1933–45* (New York: St. Martin's Press, 1979), 6.

2. Robert McElvaine, *The Great Depression: America 1929–1941* (New York: Times Books, 1984), 21.

3. Goronwy Rees, *The Great Slump: Capitalism in Crisis 1929–1933* (New York: Harper & Row, 1970), 223, 275.

4. Edward Ellis, *A Nation in Torment: The Great American Depression 1929–1939* (New York: Coward-McCann, 1970), 236–45.

5. Ellis, *Nation in Torment*, 253.

6. Hal Draper, "The Student Movement of the Thirties: A Political History," in *As We Saw the Thirties*, ed. Rita James Simon (Urbana: University of Illinois Press, 1967), 156.

7. Gene Smith, *The Shattered Dream: Herbert Hoover and the Great Depression* (New York: William Morrow, 1970), 94.

8. Martin Fausold, *The Presidency of Herbert C. Hoover* (Lawrence: University Press of Kansas, 1985), 37.

9. McElvaine, *Great Depression*, 38–41.

10. Ellis, *Nation in Torment*, 37.

11. Smith, *Shattered Dream*, 14.

12. Rees, *Great Slump*, 200–201, 214–15.

13. Smith, *Shattered Dream*, 95.

14. Rees, *Great Slump*, 212.

15. McElvaine, *Great Depression*, 91.

16. Smith, *Shattered Dream*, 135.

17. Ellis, *Nation in Torment*, 254–56.

18. Smith, *Shattered Dream*, 64.

19. Smith, *Shattered Dream*, 57.

20. Rees, *Great Slump*, 211–12.

21. Quoted by Bernard Hirschhorn in "What's a Government For?" *Showcasing American Drama: "One Third of a Nation,"* ed. Vera Jiji (New York: Research Foundation of CUNY, 1984), 21.

22. Alfred S. Shivers, *Maxwell Anderson* (Boston: Twayne Publishers, 1976), 24–25.

23. Maxwell Anderson, *Both Your Houses* (New York: Random House, 1933), II, i, 78. All subsequent references to this play will be noted in the text. For every person with a million-dollar income, Secretary of the Treasury Andrew Mellon's 1926 Revenue Act meant a $600,000 tax break.

24. Ellis, *Nation in Torment*, 443.

25. McElvaine, *Great Depression*, 157.

26. Foster Rhea Dulles and Melvyn Dubofsky, *Labor in America* (Arlington Heights, Ill.: Harlan Davidson, 1984), 218.

27. Fausold, *Presidency of Herbert C. Hoover*, 67.

28. Dulles and Dubofsky, *Labor in America*, 238.

29. Dulles and Dubofsky, *Labor in America*, 240.

30. Paul Seabury, *The Rise and Decline of the Cold War* (New York: Basic Books, 1967), 89–90.

31. Harvey Klehr, *The Heyday of American Communism* (New York: Basic Books, 1984), 91, 166, 381.

32. Klehr, *Heyday of American Communism*, 74–84.

33. Klehr, *Heyday of American Communism*, 168–69.

34. Harold Clurman, *The Fervent Years* (New York: Hill and Wang, 1945), 113.

35. Clifford Odets, *Waiting for Lefty*, in *Twenty One-Act Plays*, ed. Stanley Richards (Garden City, N.Y.: Doubleday, 1978), i, 251–52. All subsequent references to the play will be included within the text.

36. Clurman, *Fervent Years*, 138–39.

37. McElvaine, *Great Depression*, 252.

38. Ellis, *Nation in Torment*, 305–7.

39. Hirschhorn, "What's a Government For?" 21–22.

40. Nash, *Great Depression and World War II*, 21, 56.

41. Dulles and Dubofsky, *Labor in America*, 284–94.

42. McElvaine, *Great Depression*, 265–66.

43. Nash, *Great Depression and World War II*, 87–89.

44. Hallie Flanagan, *Arena* (New York: Duell, Sloan and Pierce, 1940), 29–30.

45. John O'Connor and Lorraine Brown, *Free, Adult, Uncensored* (Washington, D.C.: New Republic Books, 1978), 4–5.

46. Willson Whitman, *Bread and Circuses* (New York: Oxford University Press, 1937), 30–31.

47. Glen Loney, "Hallie Flanagan's Vision," in *Showcasing American Drama: "One-Third of a Nation,"* ed. Vera Jiji (New York: Research Foundation of CUNY, 1984), 11.

48. Flanagan, *Arena*, 435–37.

49. Gerald Warshaver, "An American Cultural Studies Approach to *One-Third of a Nation*," in *Showcasing American Drama: "One-Third of a Nation,"* ed. Vera Jiji (New York: Research Foundation of CUNY), 6.

50. Vera Mowry Roberts, "One-Third of a Nation": A Living Newspaper Production in *Showcasing American Drama: "One-Third of a Nation,"* ed. Vera Jiji (New York: Research Foundation of CUNY, 1984), 25.

51. O'Connor and Brown, *Free, Adult, Uncensored*, 11–14.

52. Eugenie Ladner Birch, "Woman-Made America: The Case of Early Public Housing Policy," in *Showcasing American Drama: "One-Third of a Nation,"* ed. Vera Jiji (New York: Research Foundation of CUNY, 1984), 25.

53. Paul Sann, "Repetitious History of Our Slums Presented as an Absorbing Dramatic Piece by the WPA Federal Theatre Project," in *Showcasing American Drama: "One-Third of a Nation,"* ed. Vera Jiji (New York: Research Foundation for CUNY, 1984), 31–32.

54. Arthur Arent, *One-Third of a Nation*, in *Federal Theatre Plays*, ed. Pierre de Rohan (New York: Random House, 1938), I, ii, 23. All subsequent references to this play will be included within the text.

55. Flanagan, *Arena*, 432–34.

56. Flanagan, *Arena*, 334.

57. O'Connor and Brown, *Free, Adult, Uncensored*, 31–33.

58. Eric Bentley, *Thirty Years of Treason* (New York: Viking Press, 1971), 25.

59. McElvaine, *Great Depression*, 349.

60. Sam Smiley, *The Drama of Attack: Didactic Plays of the American Depression* (Columbia: University of Missouri Press, 1972), 26.

61. Quoted by Gerald Rabkin, in *Drama and Commitment: Politics in the American Theatre of the Thirties* (Bloomington: Indiana University Press, 1964), 248.

62. McElvaine, *Great Depression*, 7.

63. Gerald Weales, "Popular Theatre of the Thirties," *Tulane Drama Review* 11, no. 4 (Summer 1967): 67.

64. Sidney Kingsley, *Dead End: A Play in Three Acts* (New York: Random House, 1936), III, 112.

65. Malcolm Goldstein, *The Political Stage: American Drama and Theater of the Great Depression* (New York: Oxford University Press, 1974), 148.

66. R. C. Reynolds, *Stage Left: The Development of the American Social Drama in the Thirties* (Troy, N.Y.: Whitston Publishing Co., 1986).

67. Goldstein, *Political Stage*, 43–46.

68. Clurman, *Fervent Years*, 71–72.

69. Goldstein, *Political Stage*, 69.

70. Jay Williams, *Stage Left* (New York: Charles Scribner's Sons, 1974), 116.

2

World War II—Theatrical Themes from Antiwar to Prowar to Postwar

Fifteen years ago came the Armistice and we all thought it was to be a new world. It is! But a lot worse than it was before. Ten million men were killed and many more maimed, fifty billion dollars worth of property destroyed, and the world saddled with debts. And what for? Would it have been any worse if Germany had won? Ask yourself honestly. No one knows.[1]
—William Allen White (November 11, 1933)

In America, periods of self-sacrifice and disillusionment follow one another with cyclic regularity. The 1920s probably would have reacted cynically to the "War to Make the World Safe for Democracy"—a claim which must have puzzled allies like the Czar of Russia and the Mikado of Japan—even if it had attained its aims. But clearly it had not.

Woodrow Wilson's "Fourteen Points" encouraged the Central Powers to sue for a "peace without victory." However, at the 1919 Peace Conference, Wilson was unable to forbid secret treaties and war reparations, or initiate freedom of the seas, universal disarmament, and self-determination by nationalities. He did achieve Point 14—the formation of a League of Nations.[2]

The rejection of the League by the isolationist Right (as embodied in the Republican-controlled Senate) was predictable. Article 10 of the League's charter made it necessary for every member to take part in the common defense of the victim of an aggressive act. Article 11 made a war or the threat of war "a matter of concern" to all League members, whether directly involved or not. Finally, Article 16 defined any war begun in violation of the League's covenant as a war against all members of the League.[3] A people torn equally between the desire to return to nineteenth-century "normalcy" and the pleasure of flexing their newly acquired economic muscle were not about to yield international autonomy to any non-American deliberative body. That included the League's most important creation, the Permanent Court of International Justice (the World Court). When the United States did apply for membership in 1926, it attached such reservations as to force a rejection. A compromise was worked out in 1929, but Senate opponents of the Court blocked its consideration until 1935. That January the application finally seemed destined for victory, but a flood of letters, telegrams, and petitions inspired by the Hearst newspapers and Father Coughlin, the radio priest, prevented the required two-thirds majority.[4]

Nevertheless, as Depression desperation drove country after country to find military solutions to their economic problems, it was obvious that America had to adopt some legal policy toward acts of international belligerency. Japan invaded Manchuria in 1931, and in 1933 Hitler withdrew Germany from the Geneva Arms Limitation Conference and the League of Nations, reinstated the draft, and began to build up the air force. But it was Italy that inspired the First Neutrality Act by threatening to invade Ethiopia over an incident at Walwel, a fort on the Ethiopia–Italian Somaliland border, in December 1934.

The policy was suggested by Charles Warren, Wilson's World War I assistant attorney general, in the April 1934 *Foreign Affairs* magazine, and the president signed it into law on August 31, 1935. It forbade arms sales and private loans to all belligerents and forbade American citizens to travel on ships of warring countries.[5]

The shortcomings of the First Neutrality Act were many. Most notably, it made no distinction according to blame. No matter who started the war or for what purpose, the sale of arms was forbidden to both sides. Nevertheless, it offered Roosevelt the perfect political compromise: (1) Italy, the obvious aggressor, was denied arms which landlocked Ethiopia couldn't purchase anyway; (2) Italian-American voter support was spared; (3) in this year of the WPA, the legislative deck was cleared for social programs; and (4) the bill was only for six months.

The Isolationist Reaction to the Great War

Hidden in the language of the Neutrality Act is a common assumption of the 1930s which was shared by the isolationist Right and the internationalist Left alike: that our military involvement in the Great War was a direct result of our economic involvement.

As the prestige of the capitalist dissolved with the stock market, he was retroactively tried and convicted of war crimes in the public consciousness. In 1934 and 1935, a series of books and articles about the international arms trade popularized the phrases "merchants of death" and "blood brotherhood." An anonymous article in the March 1934 *Fortune* presented the industry's axiom: "When there are wars, prolong them; when there is peace, disturb it."[6] *Merchants of Death*, by H. C. Engelbrecht and F. C. Hanighen, described arms-makers as "one of the most dangerous factors in world affairs—a hindrance to peace, a promoter of war."[7] George Seldes's *Iron, Blood, and Profits* depicted them as "organized into the greatest and most profitable secret international of our time—the international of bloodshed for profits."[8] Walter Millis's *Road to War: America 1914–1917* showed Allied war purchases as both ending America's 1914 business slump and aligning us so completely with the Allies as to provoke the German submarine attacks which brought us into the war.[9]

In 1935, South Dakota senator Gerald Nye began investigating the World War I munitions industry, eventually documenting the huge war profits by such firms as Remington Arms, Bethlehem Steel, and DuPont (whose earnings increased sixteenfold between 1914 and 1916), close ties between arms makers and the Army and Navy Departments, and questionable techniques by which sales were made to Latin America and China.[10]

Many Depression-era analysts saw World War I and the interim period which followed it as a struggle between rival imperialisms for colonies, trade, raw materials, and world markets of all descriptions. The rise of Hitler was, therefore, a product of the reparations imposed on Germany by the treaty of Versailles. The annexation of Manchuria by Japan and the Italian Ethiopian invasion could be similarly explained.[11]

The Antiwar Movement of the 1930s

Viewing the events of 1936, the Council on Foreign Relations's annual survey concluded that the American people now feared "that another general war was in the making, more destructive than the last, and its Day was not far off."[12] Nevertheless, from Congress to classroom to church, Americans were far from resigned to the war's inevitability.

The 1933 Commission on the Coordination of Efforts for Peace listed 12 international, 28 national, and 17 local peace societies in the United

States.[13] A November 1935 poll showed that 75 percent of Americans favored a national referendum before war could be declared. That year Congressman Ludlum of Indiana introduced a constitutional amendment requiring such a referendum. When the Japanese bombed an American gunboat on a Chinese river late in 1937, the amendment suddenly had 218 cosigners.[14]

On April 13, 1934, 25,000 college students left their classrooms in a "Student Strike Against the War." In 1935, when 130 colleges and universities participated nationwide, the number increased to 150,000.[15] In 1935, about 81 percent of 65,000 college students polled by the *Literary Digest* said that they would not bear arms for the United States if it invaded another country. One-sixth refused to fight even if the United States were invaded.[16]

The most imaginative student antiwar group, the "Veterans of Future Wars," was created at Princeton University and spread rapidly to three-hundred college campuses. This "VFW" demanded a $1,000 bonus paid on June 1, 1935 (plus 3 percent interest compounded semi-annually for thirty years) on the grounds that there would be no "postwar" for the soldiers of the next apocalypse. They also asked that their mothers, the Future Gray Ladies of America, be sent to Europe to visit the potential gravesites of their sons. An aptly named Texas representative, Maury Maverick, got this group a congressional hearing, but to no avail.[17]

In replay to a 1931 poll by *The World Tomorrow* magazine, 54 percent of the Protestant ministers responding said they planned "not to sanction any future war or participate as an armed combatant." Sixty-two percent wanted their church to state formally its opposition to war. When the poll (now including Jewish rabbis) was retaken in 1934, 62 percent refused to support wars as individuals and 67 percent wanted their church to take the same stand. Even Catholics argued that no modern war could fulfill St. Augustine and Thomas Aquinas's concept of a "just war."[18]

American Antiwar Drama in the 1930s

> All night they marched, the infantrymen under pack
> But the hands gripping the rifles were naked bone
> And the hollow pits of the eyes stared, vacant and black,
> When the moonlight shone.
> "It is eighteen years," I cried. "You must come no more.
> We know your names. We know you are the dead.
> Must you march forever from France and the last, blind war?"
> "Fool! From the next!" they said.[19]
>
> —"1936," by Stephen Vincent Binét

Nowhere was the concern over the "War to Come" more vividly expressed than on the New York stage, where, from 1932 to 1937, no fewer than seven plays depicted the beginning of World War II, illustrated its causes, and, in doing so, suggested ways by which it might be avoided. They were *Men Must Fight* by Reginald Lawrence and S. K. Lauren (1932), *Peace on Earth* by George Sklar and Albert Maltz (1933), *If This Be Treason* by John Haynes Holmes and Reginald Lawrence (1935), *Idiot's Delight* by Robert Sherwood (the Pulitzer Prize winner for 1936), *Bury the Dead* (1936), *Johnny Johnson* by Paul Green and Kurt Weill (1936), and *The Ghost of Yankee Doodle* by Sidney Howard (1937). Read today, they are monuments to futility, their bad reviews etched on millions of tombstones. Yet they often show remarkable prescience, and, although their targets are America's most cherished institutions, their attacks reveal a belief in the ideals of those institutions that revisionist historians may well envy.

The first of these targets is national honor, with its attendant surrender of individual conscience, often to an economically self-serving, jingoistic propaganda machine which promotes concepts of heroism and masculinity that justify the expense of human life in the name of abstractions. Only second comes capitalism, whose warfare is seen as class-based, with its dividends earned by those who work and fight, and paid to those for whom war is good business. The plays see nationalism as a carrier for capitalism, made palatable by appeals to a religion inextricably linked to messianic xenophobia.

In most of the plays, the experiences of characters in the Great War are cited as documentation. In *Men Must Fight*, the father of Laura Seward's son allows himself to be sacrificed in an air mission he knows is suicidal in order to fulfill what he sees as his duty as a man. The philosophy professor hero of *Peace on Earth* is aware from his service in a World War I propaganda unit of how the beliefs of a country are conditioned. The pacifistic U.S. president of *If This Be Treason* speaks of one of World War I's most moving symbols: "They are all unknown soldiers tonight, waiting for the tombs that I am asked to build."[20] The heroine of *The Ghost of Yankee Doodle* lost her husband in the war, and her wealthy, liberal brothers-in-law have devoted their fortunes to antiwar movements. Robert Sherwood, himself a veteran of the Canadian Black Watch, chose to use his only identified ex-soldier in *Idiot's Delight* to comment on the folly of nationalism. A border resident, he lost not only the war but his country when the Versailles Treaty ceded his Austrian hometown to Italy. At the end of the play, he is in uniform again for his "new country." Only *Bury the Dead*, set in the second year of "the War that is to begin tomorrow night,"21 avoids direct reference to World War I.

Bury the Dead is also the only play to give no hint of America's new adversaries, whose diversity in the other plays is startling. *Peace on Earth* presumes a lineup much like World War I. *If This Be Treason* is closer to the mark, predicting a Japanese air attack on Manilla more than six years before Pearl Harbor. *Idiot's Delight* also begins with an air attack, this time by Italy on France, with Germany and England drawn into the war by treaty commitments. Most imaginative are *Men Must Fight*, which depicts a 1940 U.S. war with a united South America, fighting with Japanese support, and *The Ghost of Yankee Doodle*, in which the sinking of a cargo ship in the act of carrying war materials to Italy plunges us into war with France.

In the end, however, it does not matter who our opponents are. All the plays find that the seeds of war are self-planted. Once the killing starts, it is national honor that demands it continue. In *Men Must Fight*, an ambassador to Uruguay, politically appointed for his billions, insults the government and is shot by a revolutionary, triggering the Atlantic fleet. It is the Pacific fleet in *If This Be Treason* whose aggressive posture (unreported to the American people) forces Japan to seize Manilla as a defensive buffer zone.

Honor-inspired war is a crime in which the victims create themselves. Even the most articulate of internationalists, a Leninist who has been attending a United Front workers conference in *Idiot's Delight*, protests the bombing of his native France in tones so strident that they lead him to a firing squad. As a jailed worker ruefully notes while enlistments mount in *Peace on Earth*: "They're products of a system. The system goes to war and they go along with it."22

Nor is it sufficient that soldiers die for their country. They must be stripped of their individual humanity in order to serve as a mass abstraction in whose name others must die. In *Bury the Dead*, a panicked general realizes the consequences of the living's contact with the discontented dead: "Wars can be fought and won only when the dead are buried and forgotten. How can we forget the dead who refuse to be buried?" (*Bury the Dead*, 149) Perhaps the ultimate example occurs at the end of *The Ghost of Yankee Doodle* when a corrupt newspaper tycoon loses his about-to-enlist son in a plane crash: "My son and the first hero of the new war. . . . I've found a way to tie Steve's death in with national honor."23

If the war dead are to be exploited as a mass symbol, the living are to be drummed into lockstep by the mass media. The popular wisdom is expressed by Edwin Seward, the secretary of state, who sees his peace treaty destroyed in *Men Must Fight*: "After war is declared, it is the duty of every American to surrender his life, his goods, and even his conscience to the command of his country, so that we may face the common enemy with an unbroken and united front."24 However, his adopted son is closer to the truth when he responds to a similar statement by his fiancée: "Cut it, Peg! Don't talk like the newspapers." (*Men Must Fight*, II, 65) In *Peace on Earth,* a blues singer sways her hips to a throaty "I wanna man with a uniform on" *(Peace on Earth*, III, 116), and when a ship running contraband arms to Italy is sunk by France in *The Ghost of Yankee Doodle*, the subsequent war is sold through the cinema: "They're making a movie called 'The Farragut's Daughter.' It seems the captain of the *Farragut* did have a daughter. She's been through two divorces and runs a pet shop in Atlantic City, but she's going to be Shirley Temple on the screen!" (*The Ghost of Yankee Doodle*, v, 108)

It is in the name of religion that the women of *Bury the Dead* are urged to convince their men to lie down. In *Peace on Earth* (to a chorus of "Onward, Christian Soldiers") a minister calls upon his parishioners to "smite down the Heathen, smite down the barbarian hordes. I say to you that if Jesus walked the earth today he would be the first to join the fight." (*Peace on Earth*, III, 117)

But no matter the means of manipulation, the motivation is money. If "the first casualty of war is truth," the 1930s believed that business collected the life insurance. In *If This Be Treason*, the presidential press secretary cheerily congratulates a steel magnate turned hawkish congress-man: "That was a nice jump Jennings Steel took this morning—90 to 110. Broke the amateur record, the boys tell me." (*If This Be Treason*, II, 81) When war news is desired in *Idiot's Delight*, a finger is pointed at a vacationing arms-dealer: "Because he *made it.* . . . Because he is a master of the one *real* League of Nations . . . the League of Schneider-Creusot, and Krupp, and Skoda, and Vickers and Dupont. The League of Death! And the workers of the world are expected to pay him for it, with their sweat, and their life's blood."25 As a reporter puts it in *Peace on Earth*, "Why do you think they converted your mills, because the world stopped wearing underwear?" (*Peace on Earth*, I, 27)

As the scenes above suggest, the plays see internationalism and class consciousness as the logical alternative to economically mandated mur-der. *If This Be Treason* invokes international law in the form of the Kellogg-Briand antiwar pact of 1928, and its final scene was inspired by the Russian army's refusal to fire on Petrograd revolutionaries in 1917. *Peace on Earth's* German sailors, upon discovering that they are loading guncotton instead of soap, join with striking longshoremen to throw it in the sea. In *Bury the Dead*, a woman from the slums realizes that her husband's mistake is not in refusing to be buried at the Front, but rather is not standing up to his boss at home. Among the young, Robert Seward of *Men Must Fight* struck a responsive chord: "Wars may be started by old men, but they have to be fought by fellows our own age. If enough of us refuse to take any part in it—and continue to refuse—there won't be any war." (*Men Must Fight*, II, 62)

Nevertheless, of the seven plays, only *If This Be Treason* can truly be said to end happily. On the stage, as in life, the war could not be avoided. Robert Seward was given an "international" education for the purpose of training him as an antiwar diplomat. Yet, at the play's end, he flies off to meet a death as certain as his father's in the last war. In *Peace on Earth*, a character leads his country in joining the League of Nations. But the proposal is only the dream of a man about to be executed, not for the murder with which he is charged, but for his opposition to the war. The four countries one can see from the high window above the staircase in the ski resort of *Idiot's Delight* are interchangeable in their snowy mountain beauty. But that does not prevent the guests who share the resort so amicably from heeding their countries' call to war. Nationalistic paranoia, propaganda, and profits have their way. Nowhere is that unholy trio more prominent than in the group's one antiwar musical.

Johnny Johnson

About this time there had arrived from abroad the composer whose *Three-Penny Opera* (on records) might have been described as a Group [Theatre] pastime. We befriended Kurt Weill, and Stella Adler insisted that he must do a musical play for us along lines he had made known in Germany. Weill suggested one day he would like to do an American equivalent of the comic Czech war novel *The Good Soldier Schweik*, which had been dramatized and produced with success in Berlin. . . .

On a visit to Chapel Hill to discuss a play about college life that Paul Green had submitted to us, I learned something about Paul's past that he had never before mentioned. He had fought overseas in the last war and had an intimate acquaintance with the American soldier of that day. I mentioned Kurt Weill's suggestion, particularly since Paul was fascinated with the element of music in the theatre.[26]

Johnny Johnson owes a great deal to *Schweik*, as it does to the picaresque novel and the medieval morality play. Its central character is an Everyman ("John Johnson" was the most common name among American soldiers in World War I) whose pilgrimage through the world changes his perception of it. The play is international and class-conscious (without ever using those terms), suggesting both the necessity for world government based on mediation and the guilt of political/economic leaderships who manipulate nationalist aims for their own benefit without ever facing the consequences personally. *Johnny Johnson* may be unique among American musical comedies in that it denigrates patriotism, questions that any country may have a special relationship with God, and undercuts any comfortable assumptions we may have about love.

The play begins on April 6, 1917, the day the United States entered World War I, and ends on the eve of a new war. Johnny's pilgrimage can be divided into four movements or levels of political awareness. In the first, he searches for a justification of the newly declared conflict and finds it in the idea of a "war to end all wars." In the second, he enlists, planning to stop the fighting by winning the German people away from the warlords who are misusing their loyalty. In the third section, Johnny discovers that his own leaders are as inhuman as those of the Germans and is arrested for trying to end the war. Finally, Johnny realizes that belief in peace is considered as insanity, but continues the increasingly hopeless struggle.

Johnny Johnson opens in a small American town's cemetery at one of those appropriately ambiguous ceremonies of mourning and rededication called a memorial service. The two hundredth anniversary of a treaty with the local Indians provides an occasion for dignitaries to pontificate upon the importance of peace and the horrors of the current European war. The speeches are to be followed by a poem, "Democracy Advancing," recited by Minny Belle Tompkins, the town's prettiest girl, and the unveiling of a statue carved by Johnny Johnson, the town's artisan/artist and tombstone maker. Where this democracy will "advance" is hinted at early when a stirring reminiscence by Civil War veteran Grandpa Joe Tompkins of the charge up Chikamauga Hill turns the crowd into a bloodthirsty, chauvinist mob. Indeed, when word arrives of the declaration of war, the town's citizens, with Minny Belle in the lead, immediately march off to the courthouse to volunteer.

Only Johnny hesitates, unable to comprehend how he and his idol, Woodrow Wilson, came to such radically different conclusions. In frustration he yanks the drawstring hanging down from the monument: "The drape rolls up and reveals the deep-cut bas-relief of a plump-breasted dove with a leaf in its mouth, its wings outspread in flight. Engraved above this in large and wide-spaced letters is the single word, 'Peace'"[27] As the scene ends with the courthouse bell tolling in the distance, the play is provided with the first of its many striking images, and the American peace movement with a fitting symbol: a tombstone.

Minny Belle, Johnny's beloved, is also being wooed by Anguish Howington, a rising young capitalist and manufacturer of rotten mineral water. Eventually, he will become mayor, governor, and a leading supporter of national defense, but at the moment, he is running an understandably distant second in Minny Belle's affections. For her part, Minny Belle calls on both men to enlist, assuming the role of "The Girl He Left Behind," smiling through her tears as she sends her man off to do or die for God and country. A large part of her subsequent communication with Johnny is an oft-repeated "How many Germans did you kill?"—a reminder of how often in wartime a lovely image is used to sell death.

However, Anguish Howington will never see action. Aggie Tompkins, Minny Belle's mother, afraid that Johnny will never "amount to a row of pins (too good—wishy-washy—no backbone)," introduces Anguish to a time-honored Tompkins tradition: self-mutilation in place of service.

Despite *his* lack of physical disabilities, Johnny resists Minny Bell's proddings to enlist: "Like if by going I could help—well . . . put an end to—sort of like the idea of—say, a war to put down war. . . . Then I'd feel the cause was worth it, and I'd go as quick as scat. When it was over the democratic nations maybe could league up and unite for peace." (*Johnny Johnson*, I, ii, 24–25) With the printing of the full text of Wilson's War Address in the evening newspaper, Johnny is naturally off to the recruiting office.

On the troop ship to France, another startling visual image reinforces one of the play's themes—the futility of dying for an abstraction. Before he lies down, Johnny swears an oath to the Statue of Liberty that he will find a way to halt the war. As he sleeps, the statue comes to life and sings the trenody of the dead, in wondering contempt of creatures who will use inanimate idols to justify their actions. (*Johnny Johnson*, I, iv, 44–45)

> A million years I dreamless lay,
> Insensate in the quiet earth,
> Unformed and will-less till the day
> Men rived me forth and gave me birth
> And set me up with queer intent
> To swear their pride and folly by,
> And I who never nothing meant
> Am used to send men forth to die.
>   (*Johnny Johnson*, I, iv, 44–45)

Time passes slowly in the French trenches, and the soldiers hope for peace. "With genial cruelty," the English sergeant propounds the "merchants of death" theory to explain why it won't come: "This war will last ten years. The big blighters back home don't want it to end. Who'd they

sell their munitions to if we have peace? Ten years? It might last twenty."
(*Johnny Johnson*, I, vi, 49) Johnny spends his spare time writing letters
addressed to the common German soldiers. When others laugh at his
belief that the war can be ended with words, he snaps back: "Well, we
don't seem to be able to end it with guns." (*Johnny Johnson*, I, vi, 54)
A veteran English soldier describes the Christmas of 1914, when the two
armies sang carols to one another, played a soccer game between the
trenches, and exchanged gifts. An American private—a Chicago gangster
in civilian life—reads John 3:16 from his Bible, prompting a chuckle
from Johnny: "I was just thinking the Germans are praying to the same
God on their side too. Human begins are a funny race, ain't they?"
(*Johnny Johnson*, I, vi, 57)

The Bible of Private Fairfax is not the only religious artifact used to
prop up questionable actions. Amidst the shattered tombstones of a
shell-torn churchyard, Johnny encounters the enemy in the form of a
cleverly hidden sniper: "a huge black wooden statue of Christ, leaning
a bit awry and showing in its posture something of the beaten and
agonized torture of an El Greco figure. . . . And now, through a great
wounded hole in the breast of Christ where the heart should be, is pushed
the ugly muzzle of a telescopic rifle with a silencer attached. The muzzle
comes to rest on the outstretched hand of the Redeemer." (*Johnny
Johnson*, I, vii, 62)

When Johnny captures the sniper, he finds under the false mustache
and Kaiser Wilhelm helmet only a sixteen-year-old, terrified by stories
about the monsters he must fight. The boy's name is Johann (Johnny in
German) and his sergeant, who was formerly his teacher, also believes
that the ordinary soldiers are being sacrificed for "Faterland und Kaiser."

Johnny releases Johann, sending him back to his own troops with the
speeches of Woodrow Wilson and some of his own, "which come to the
point quicker," and accidentally picks up a posterior wound in the
process. While in the hospital, Johnny learns that his efforts are bearing
fruit and general discontent is developing in the German lines. He also
learns that the Allied High Command plans to capitalize on this discontent
with a new offensive rather than a peace plan.

Seated in the luxury far from the front on the eve of battle, "these
mighty keepers of men's destiny speak forth their arguments and plans
with puppet pomp and solemn precision," playing out a high-stakes poker
game with the lives of their men. The goal is not peace, or even victory,
but national honor—with tiny Belgium struggling to earn respect by
raising its pledge of dead from 30,000 to 50,000 and exhausted France
risking revolution by striving to meet the English bid of 100,000 dead.

As he listens, Johnny realizes that he has even more in common with the ordinary German soldier than he had supposed.

During the great battle that Johnny fails to prevent, an organ plays "the stately chant music of a church prayer" while on opposite sides of a stage-rear backdrop the projections of a German and an American priest pray the same prayer for deliverance from the enemy in their respective languages. Johnny finds the body of Johann beside the shattered and mutilated statue of Christ. Kneeling in the mud, Johnny holds the dead Johann, "naked save for a piece of torn cloth tied around his middle, his body marked with sweat and powder burns"—a pietà of waste, rather than redemption: "I had this war stopped once. Maybe there's no sense in that. They said so. But you wouldn't say so—no, you wouldn't. . . . Would you!" (*Johnny Johnson*, II, iii, 96)

Johnny returns to America and the confines of an insane asylum, where he is incarcerated as a "peace monomaniac." Late in the play, we are shown an assembly of elderly men, many of whom have the appearance of well-known U.S. senators and other dignitaries. A man resembling Thomas R. Marshall, Woodrow Wilson's vice president, presides over them, and for a moment it seems that we are listening again to the debate over the establishment of the League of Nations: "The disorganized countries of the earth, frightened, suspicious, jealous of one another—loaded with the ever-increasing weight of vast armaments—sufficient already to destroy every human being under the sun—are praying to someone to show them the way out of their dilemma. . . . And in this covenant of a united world we show them." (*Johnny Johnson*, II, vi, 110)

The timelessness of this argument—more relevant today than it was in 1936—cannot be denied, and after heated discussion, the League is this time approved. The assembly is then quieted for an appearance by the new chairman of the hospital board, Anguish Howington (now married to Minny Belle), and we realize that we are still in the asylum, where to make peace the first order of business is the mark of insanity.

At the play's end, Johnny, now freed from the asylum, stands on a street corner selling wooden toys he has carved in the shape of living things. A Boy Scout—accompanied at a distance by his mother (Minny Belle)—tries to buy a toy soldier from Johnny, an item he does not make:

"I'm named after my father. He's mayor of the town, you know. And he's going to be governor. . . . Daddy says that we're in for another big war and all the people have got to be ready to keep the enemy from destroying us." [*From the distant stadium where the people are gathering, cheering is heard and then the soaring, somewhat hysterical voice of a political rabble rouser in a splurge of raspy, indistinguishable words—even as Gog Magog from the Bible or a Tower of Bable madness.] (Johnny Johnson*, II, vii, 119–20)

We have come full circle to a new memorial service. Alone, Johnny continues to sing his song of hope, refusing to be drowned out by a brass band blaring the "Democracy March."

From Isolationism to Internationalism

In the presidential-election year of 1936, the foreign policy plank of the Republican Party platform pledged "to promote and maintain peace by all honorable means not leading to foreign alliances in foreign affairs." The Democrats (whose candidate won a landslide 46 out of 48 states) went even further in their platform, promising to "work for peace and to take the profits out of war; to guard against being drawn, by political commitments, international banking or private trading, into any war which may develop anywhere."[28]

Given the realities of American political parties, it can be safely assumed that antiwar isolationism was what the American voter wanted. Yet five years later, on December 10, 1941 (thirteen months after electing the same presidential candidate to an unprecedented third term, and three days after the Japanese bombing of Pearl Harbor), a poll found that the nation had approved Congress's declaration of war by 96 percent in favor to 2 percent opposed.[29] What happened to change our minds?

A plausible answer might be "Nothing." Our war with Japan began when Japan attacked us. At the time when the poll was taken, we were not yet at war with Germany and Italy. That would come the next day, when they declared war on us. In this scenario, our participation was an act of pure self-defense of our lives and our national honor.

Such an analysis, however accurate, falls somewhat short of the whole truth. Until well into the twentieth century, the United States had maintained a traditional neutrality, partly derived from geography and partly from our view of ourselves. In the 1930s, the neutrality was reinforced by our economic circumstances, revisionist views of our involvement in World War I, our always ambivalent relationship with communism, and a very real concern with the military might of Germany.

Neutrality and the 1930s

George Washington's farewell address may have warned his countrymen "to steer clear of permanent alliances," but he was neither the first nor the last of the Founding Fathers to give that advice. Between the world wars, it was common to imagine that our two-ocean cushion could effectively quarantine us from any undesirable foreign contract. Perhaps we were close enough in time to remember that the United States had devoted the whole first half of the nineteenth century to extending its geographic borders against the British, French, and Spanish influences that surrounded it. The Louisiana Purchase, the War of 1812, the annexations of Florida and Texas, the War with Mexico, the Gadsen Purchase, the division of Oregon, and even the Civil War were in part attempts to define a continent free of European pressures. By the end of the nineteenth century, Americans were calling this process Manifest Destiny. Still later, revisionists called it the beginning of imperialism. It was really self-preservation.

This is not to suggest that American expansion had no connection to an idealistic philosophy. The American Revolution marks the beginning of the Age of Revolution (roughly 1775–1850), the political parallel to the Age of Romanticism. The United States is largely a Romantic country. Its early leaders were the intellectual children of Jean-Jacques Rousseau and John Locke. The likelinesses of their fathers are stamped on its institutions and documents, of which Thomas Jefferson's *The Declaration of Independence* is only the most obvious example. America saw itself as the haven of individual accomplishment, in harmony with nature, and in opposition to older, man-structured societies which Romantic philosophy saw as a corruption of God's original creation. As historian Paul Seabury put it:

In conventional American folklore, populistic nationalism has rested upon certain assessments of America's novel relationship to world politics. The New World, which the nation represented, was pervaded by an individualistic and egalitarian ethos. It was juxtaposed to an Old World; its newness arose from the fact of America's recent birth and settlement (which rendered it in a certain sense "historyless"); its newness depended upon the newness of applied principles. The *novus ordo seculorum* was not simply the antithesis of the Old World. It was a qualitatively new and better system of politics.[30]

Our traditional neutrality, then, has been a fortunate blend of realpolitik and religion. The Depression probably reinforced both. The classic horror films of the times are thinly disguised metaphors depicting the dangers of departing from God's (and the American) Way. *Dracula* (1931) with its suave European aristocrat sucking the lifeblood out of innocent American beauty, clearly warned against involvement with Continental decadence. Only the Cross and the shining light of the sun can protect us against the undead children of the European night. On the level of practical politics, any officeholder publicly more concerned with international affairs than the day-to-day survival of his constituents would have had a short political life. The quotes from the 1936 foreign policy planks are easy to excerpt because the originals were so short.

Earlier in the chapter, we took note of the "merchants of death" theory—the supposition that our entry into World War I was engineered by industrialists who traded American blood for inflated profits. Another widely advanced revisionist theory was that we had become, during the war, a pawn of British foreign policy. Under this hypothesis, Great Britain always follows a strategy of "divide and rule," supporting the second military power on the Continent as a means of checking the ambitions of the most powerful. Prior to World War I, it was not German militarism that threatened democratic freedoms, but rather German mercantilism that threatened British imperialism. After the war, however, Germany was bereft of all armaments and curbed by huge war reparations, while France maintained a large standing army and (after 1932) a military alliance with Russia. To counter France, Great Britain supported Germany's rebuilding of its navy. Even as late as 1934, Montagu Norman arranged for the Bank of England to loan Hitler 750,000 pounds.[31]

In World War I, the path America had followed to "save democracy" had been greased by British indoctrination—a mechanism amply documented in such books as Harold Lasswell's *Propaganda Technique in the World War* (1927), James Squires's *British Propaganda at Home and in the United States from 1914 to 1917* (1935), and Horace Peterson's *Propaganda for War: The Campaign Against American Neutrality, 1914 to 1917* (1939).[32] As a second world war began, Hitler was just another British-created Frankenstein monster to many Americans, and the idea that we should defend Great Britain again seemed cruelly absurd.

Furthermore, many Americans and Britains believed that a strong Germany would be a stabilizing factor in Europe. In 1937, Lord Lothian, later Great Britain's ambassador to the United States and its most effective propagandist in the period between their respective entries into World War II, expressed the idea that German control could end the Depression in Central Europe: "Germany and the smaller countries to the east and south are largely economically correlative, and the present economic sub-division of Eastern Europe cannot be permanent."[33] When, on March 12, 1938, Austria yielded to German military pressure and allowed itself to be incorporated into greater Germany, Senator William E. Borah of Idaho, the author of the 1936 Republican foreign policy platform, wrote a constituent: "Austria was really a German state and the Versailles peacemakers had ruined, crippled and dismembered it, and [it] could not stand alone."[34]

As it happened, neither could Czechoslovakia. In September, Germany demanded that that country (itself a polyglot product of the Versailles Treaty) surrender the Sudetenland, Czechoslovakia's German-speaking western border. Great Britain and France, nominal allies to the Czechs, vacillated and appealed to the United States. On September 26, President Roosevelt sent telegrams urging peace to the heads of all the states involved. At the same time, he refused a French request that he offer to mediate the dispute and Chamberlain's request for radio time to explain British policy. The following day, Roosevelt sent two more telegrams: one to Hitler, assuring him that the United States took no responsibility for ensuing negotiations, and one to Mussolini, asking him to influence Germany toward peace. At the Munich conference on September 29–30, Hitler offered a choice: appeasement or war. Without American support and without consulting the Czechoslovakian government, Great Britain and France yielded. Hitler declared himself satisfied. Germany would require no further acquisitions of land in Europe. In a radio address, American under secretary of state Sumner Welles was delighted, seeing the post-Munich era as presenting the best opportunity since Versailles to establish "a new world order based upon justice . . . and law."[35] Late the following March, Germany occupied the remainder of Czechoslovakia, and two weeks later Italy annexed Albania without opposition.

Thirty days after Munich, Orson Welles and the Mercury Theatre of the Air broadcast their version of H. G. Wells's *War of the Worlds* over CBS radio. It was told in the form of radio news bulletins interrupting regularly scheduled programming—such as those with which the public had become very familiar during the year's European crises. Of the six million people listening, approximately 20 percent believed America was actually being invaded. Follow-up questionnaires, however, showed that many believed the attackers were not actually Martians, but rather German airships in disguise.[36]

The Spanish Civil War

At Munich, England and America embarked on similar courses for different reasons. In Spain, often cited as the classic case of appeasement, their motives were very similar: a sense that they had more to fear from Communist Russia than from Fascist Germany. As George Orwell asserted: "In essence it was a class war. If it had been won, the cause of the common people everywhere would have been strengthened. It was lost, and the dividend-drawers all over the world rubbed their hands. That was the real issue; all else was froth on its surface."[37]

That there was an uprising in Spain surprised no one. By the twentieth century, Spain's two most venerable institutions, the Crown and the Church, had declined greatly in popular support. A military dictatorship was in force for much of the twenties, and King Alfonso XIII fled the country in 1931. Coalitions of first the Left and next the Right ruled the following five years, until the elections of February 1936, when a Left-Center alliance was victorious. Months of unrest followed, and on July 17 a faction of the military, primarily led by General Francisco Franco in Spanish Morocco, went into open revolt. The immediate availability of German transports to ferry Franco's troops from Morocco clearly established the ideology of his rebellion.

On August 15, 1936, Great Britain and France pledged to "rigorously abstain from all interference, direct or indirect, in the internal affairs of Spain." Within two weeks, nearly two dozen other nations, including Italy, Germany, and the Soviet Union, pledged nonintervention and agreed to establish an international committee to enforce an embargo on all arms sales. Nevertheless, within six weeks, Germany and Italy had supplied Franco with dozens of tanks, nearly 200 warplanes, and 10,000 rifles and machine guns. By January, 20,000 Italian "volunteers" (one-fifth of the eventual total) would be in the rebel zone.[38]

For the Western democracies, however, it was "eyes left." As early as January 1925, the State Department was checking rumors of an impending Comintern-guided revolution against Spain's military dictatorship. In December 1930, when a Republican overthrow of the monarchy misfired, American charge d'affaires Sheldon L. Crosby attributed the insurrection to "very decided left and Comuno-Bolshevist influences in this country doubtlessly directly inspired from Moscow."[39]

Equipment from Soviet Russia did bolster the defenses of the Republican government. However, Italian troops and armor, fresh from their conquest of Ethiopia, and German air power and the Condor Legion, which had recently occupied the Rhineland, made up much of the Fascist military force in Spain.[40] Modern air warfare began with terror bombings of civilians in Madrid, and then in April 1937, in Guernica—the inspiration for Pablo Picasso's impression of his birthplace's destruction.

The Spanish Civil War was replete with ugly ironies. On August 2, 1936, Admiral Jean Darlan—later to become infamous as a Fascist collaborator in German-occupied France—warned an international group about "the establishment of a Francist regime in Spain allied with Italy and Germany." Sir Samuel Hoare, the first lord of the British Admiralty, scoffed at Darlan: "On no account must we do anything to bolster up Communism in Spain, particularly when it is remembered that Communism in Portugal, to which it would probably spread, . . . would be a grave danger to the British Empire."[41] As late as 1938, Lord Londonderry, former British air minister, wrote: "The robust attitude of Germany, Italy and Japan, which whole-heartedly condemn communism and bolshevism . . . is an attitude of mind which is not properly appreciated in this country."[42]

As was already suggested in Chapter 1, America's relationship with communism was slightly more complex. Its promise of hegemony to industrial workers was less of a physical threat than a threat to our ideological identity. Abroad, however, it was a menace to our multinational corporations, and we sensed its shadow on every trade agreement with a country with marginal standards of living.

Furthermore, if American politicians had no reason to worry about Spanish communism, they did have to be concerned with Catholic voters in the United States. In the early weeks of the war, hundreds of priests and nuns were indiscriminately slaughtered as "Fascist fifth communists," and although anticlerical feelings were not limited to the Communists, their professed ideology did provide fuel for yet one more stand against "godless atheism." Even Pope Pius XI openly supported the Fascists.

Unfortunately for the Republican government (which tried seriously to limit its excesses), the working-class Left also provided the most effective military defense against Franco's rebels. The International Brigade, which provided 40,000 anti-Fascist volunteers (including 3,000 Americans in the Abrahm Lincoln Brigade) was also recruited largely from Communists. In addition, whatever Russia cost in goodwill, she was not always able to make up in support. Initially generous in goods and equipment, Russia was within the year bogged down in a major civil disturbance of its own—the Great Purge Trials. Between 1937 and 1939, the Communist Party was expunged of one-third of its membership, including 214 of its top army commanders. The decimation was even higher in the navy.[43] Other than a few advisors, Russian participation in the Spanish Civil War was limited by necessity.

Stalin ceased support of the Republican government in the summer of 1938, but by then many non-Russian participants, including Orwell and Arthur Koestler, had become disillusioned by the men of the NKVD (People's Commissariat of Internal Affairs) among the Soviet advisors, who were more concerned with enforcing Party conformity than preserving Spanish democracy.

America's Neutrality Act, which had been extended on February 29 until May 1, 1937, did not cover civil wars. Therefore, on August 7, the State Department declared a moral embargo, requesting that American companies treat the Spanish situation like a war between two national belligerents. When a New Jersey scrap dealer insisted that business superseded morality and tried to sell airplane parts to the Republican Loyalists, Congress passed special legislation blocking the sale of war materials to Spain. The legislation went into effect on January 8, 1937, and was lifted immediately after the fall of Madrid on March 28, 1939, signalled Franco's victory.[44] When the skies over Madrid became quiet, the blitzkrieg of Poland was only five months away.

In February 1937, Joseph E. Davies, the American ambassador to Moscow, was surprised to find that European diplomats in the U.S.S.R. believed that an understanding between Hitler and Stalin was not beyond possibility. In the following two years, Russia sought in vain for Western help in Spain. On May 3, 1939, Foreign Commissar Maxim Litvinov, the architect of the Popular Front Movement, was dismissed from office and replaced by V. I. Molotov.[45] On August 18, 1939, Germany and Russia concluded a trade treaty, and five days later, Hitler announced a Nazi-Soviet non-aggression pact. Freed of the fear of a two-front war, on September 1 Germany invaded Poland. Unable to vacillate any longer, Great Britain and France declared war on September 3. "Fascism," said Molotov, "is a question of point of view."[46]

In the end, it is impossible to disagree with the assessment of Julio Alvarez del Vayo, Republican Spain's last foreign minister: "Today, no one should be able to deny that the collapse of the Spanish Republic was due to Non-Intervention. . . . [Events] have confirmed our contention that appeasement, which reached the limits of folly in Spain, would lead inevitably to war."[47]

The Curtain Rises on Interventionism

> For twenty years, I've devoted myself to decrying war and the war makers, agitating for disarmament, for a world commonwealth. But more and more, I began discovering to my horror that my facts and my arguments were being used in ways that I never intended, by rabid isolationists, by critics of democracy, even by Nazi propagandists. And . . . it's knocked the props from under me.[48]
>
> —*Flight to the West* by Elmer Rice (1940)

Anti-Fascist drama was neither frequent nor unheard of between Hitler's ascendancy to the German chancellorship in 1933 and Pearl

Harbor. S. N. Behrman's Comedy of Manners suffered under the strain of his protest against anti-Semitism in *Rain from Heaven* as early as 1934. The story that a German-Jewish music critic tells about the annihilation of the Last Jew was a parable then, but the Third Reich was already planning how to turn it into a reality. Georgi Dimitroff, the Bulgarian Communist falsely tried for setting fire to the Reichstag, provided a hero for two plays of 1934: *Dimitroff*, a (Marxist) New Theatre League agitprop piece written by Group Theatre moonlighters Art Smith and Elia Kazan; and *Judgment Day*, a thinly disguised full-length treatment by Elmer Rice. The same story inspired *Till the Day I Die*, a more imaginative one-act play which Clifford Odets wrote as a companion piece for the Broadway production of *Waiting for Lefty* in 1935. Sinclair Lewis's novel *It Can't Happen Here*, as dramatized by the author and John Moffit in 1936, provided an occasion for the Federal Theatre's most heroic production effort—the opening of twenty-one separate performances in seventeen different cities on the same day[49]—but not its finest play. The subject was a Fascist overthrow in the United States, a possibility also warned against by Elmer Rice in *American Landscape* (1938). That same year, *Kiss the Boys Goodbye* by Claire Boothe (Luce) hid an allegory of a Fascist takeover so well that those who did not read the preface to the published version could be excused for missing the point. More interesting from our thematic standpoint, and, ultimately, from the standpoint of drama as well, were the agonizing reappraisals of authors who had earlier opposed wars of any kind. The farce of "neutrality" in Spain and the 1938 Nazi annexations of Austria and the Sudetenland resolved their conflict. At the beginning of 1937, Maxwell Anderson's *A Masque of Kings* suggested that any overthrow of tyranny could only bring about a counter-tyranny, and the hero of his *High Tor* decided that nothing was worth fighting for and headed west. However, by *Knickerbocker Holiday* (1938), Anderson's protagonist decides in favor of a democracy which is less efficient in removing freedom than the corporate state, and in *Key Largo* (1939), King McCloud finally concludes that it is more important for values to survive than individuals. During the Spanish Civil War, McCloud abandoned his men when they refused to retreat from a military position which was untenable in a war that was already lost. Given a second chance, he sacrifices himself to destroy a more personalized fascism in the form of the gangster, Murillo: "A man must die for what he believes—if he's unfortunate enough to have to face it in his time—and if he won't, then he'll end up believing in nothing at all—and that's death too."[50]

Irwin Shaw, the author of *Bury the Dead*, also wrote about ordinary men fighting back against gangsters in *The Gentle People* (1939), a Group Theatre–produced allegory about the necessity for peace lovers to resist fascism. The same year the Group produced *Thunder Rock* by Robert Ardrey (of whom we shall hear later). In conversations with ghosts from the past, the play's lighthouse-bound hero decides that the progress of mankind is inevitable, and he cannot withdraw from the world simply because the evil that opposes it is just as inevitable.

In the postscript to the published version of his 1936 Pulitzer Prize winner, *Idiot's Delight*, Robert Sherwood, who had fought with the Canadian Black Watch in World War I, predicted the effect of a second world war: "The world will soon resolve itself into the semblance of an ant hill, governed by commissars who owe their power to the profundity of their contempt for the individual members of their own species."[51] In 1938, however, he won his second Pulitzer for *Abe Lincoln in Illinois*, about "a man of peace who had to face the issue of appeasement or war."[52] His Lincoln decides to oppose slavery even if it divides the Union. Following the Russian invasion of Finland, Sherwood won his third Pulitzer in 1940 for *There Shall Be No Night*, in which a scientist who has spent his life investigating the causes of insanity suddenly finds his country and family trapped by the madness of war. Ironically, by 1943, when Alfred Lunt and Lynn Fontanne took the play to London, Russia was again an ally of the Western democracies, and Sherwood was forced to reset the action during the Italian invasion of Greece.[53] In *Watch On The Rhine* (premiering April 1941), Lillian Hellman could have faced a similar problem with a hero who was both German and Communist.

Watch on the Rhine

Lillian Hellman's *Watch on the Rhine* is the perfect American political drama. It has a very specific political purpose, but very little political theory. What theory exists in the play is spoken by a child. The values of the adult world are embodied in action, and, as in any good political drama, there is one action to which the audience can contribute after the curtain is down. Although we are presented with logical arguments in support of that action, it is the emotional appeal of the situation and the characters with whom we identify that motivates us. Even the setting has made its peace with the realities of American commercial theatre production, and every incident in this advocate of interventionism takes place in the living room of a well-to-do American family, not far from Washington, D.C.

In its early nineteenth-century origins, its space, its simplicity, and above all, its eclecticism, the Farrelly living room is a metaphor for America. It has its own traditions and has encompassed many visions that have coexisted without losing their individuality. The front door is unlocked, and always has been. On the wall is a portrait of Joshua Farrelly, who, without every appearing, will be in some ways the most important character in the play. It is he who gives this family/nation its particular flavor, and it is his values that must be perpetuated. It is Hellman's particular genius that without ever leaving this living room or introducing a single bona fide Nazi into it, she brings home to America the realities of the war and makes the best possible case for our participation in it.

The house is owned by Fanny Farrelly. An old-line Washington aristocrat, she is consciously imperious, demanding, unreasonable, manipulative, and charming. One of the chief targets of all these qualities is her son, David, a Washington bachelor and lawyer whose actions, ideas, and taste in women Fanny compares unfavorably with those of his father. Joshua Farrelly was a diplomat, Renaissance man, and the sole architect of Fanny's standard of values. Extended guests in the household are Teck de Brancovis, a Romanian count whose current American exile is the result of a wrong guess taken when the Nazis came to power, and his wife, Marthe, an American heiress whose fortune and affections the count long ago dissipated. Marthe is now in love with David, and in-house relationships are becoming strained.

Watch on the Rhine is set late in the spring of 1940, at a time when German forces are knifing their way through Belgium on their way to Paris. But this action is never referred to. The uproar in the house is because Sara, Fanny and Joshua's other child, is returning home for the first time in twenty years. Shortly after World War I, Sara married Kurt Muller, a German engineer, and they settled (much against her mother's wishes) in his homeland where they raised three children. In recent years, however, Sara's letters have carried frequently changing postmarks, both from within Germany and from the countries on its borders, and have been increasingly less specific about the family's daily life. When they arrive, it is on an earlier-than-expected, cheaper, train. They have had no breakfast and Sara's dress is obviously outdated. The children show extraordinary discipline, but are amazed at the house's luxury and, especially, its unlocked front door. The real enigma, however, is Sara's husband, Kurt, who is outside of the family's frame of reference, but who strikes a chord of recognition in the more worldly, opportunistic Teck de Brancovis.

Kurt's task in America is to pick up money donated to the anti-Fascist cause. Hellman's task is to take this German national, World War I American opponent, and likely Communist, and create a hero with whom American audiences can identify. To do this, she invests him with typical American heroic virtues.

To begin with, Kurt is a man of action, not talk. Because opportunities to demonstrate anti-Fascist heroism in an upper-class living room are necessarily limited, Hellman assigns the task of explaining Kurt's attitudes to others.

When we want to know what Kurt's beliefs are, we need only listen to his children. What would seem priggish in the speech of a grown man is precocious and endearing when baldly stated or even slightly garbled by nine-year-old Bodo. And yet we are fully aware that the children, who have been constantly on the move under ideologically hostile circumstances, could only have learned their ideals from their father and mother. As ever, well-disciplined, intelligent children with good sets of values reflect with favor on their parents.

In addition, who could be a more convincing witness to a man's quality than an enemy. Desperate to obtain the reentry into the Nazi political sphere that the exposure of a major underground anti-Fascist would get him, Teck borrows a "most-wanted" list from the German embassy. Reviewing Kurt's record as a courier, a soldier in Spain, a spy, and a pirate radio operator, even the count expresses admiration for Kurt's skill and bravery.

When Kurt finally is moved to action, it is to return to Germany to save fellow agents captured by the Gestapo. With him he intends to take the money raised in America to fight fascism—money that Teck demands for not identifying Kurt to German intelligence.

Teck is presented as the antithesis to Kurt. The image of a Central European count who achieved his sustenance through blood money is too tempting to resist. Teck is a Dracula challenging Kurt's Parsifal, acknowledging no commitment beyond himself. He is not even a true Nazi, as power is his only ideology. Both Teck and Kurt made judgments about National Socialism in 1931. Kurt correctly evaluated its evil and enlisted in the fight against it. Teck underestimated Nazi strength, and found himself dealt out of a game more important to him than the principles of those who control the deal. The ability to deliver Kurt might earn Teck another hand, but for political gamblers—like actors—timing is everything: "[Some Fascists] came late: some because they did not jump in time, some because they were stupid, some because they were shocked at the crudity of the German evil, and preferred their own evil, and some because they were fastidious men. For those last, we may well some day have pity. They are lost men, their spoils are small, their day is past."[54] But Teck is clever, patient, and ruthless. He wants only to be on the winning side, and he will not play his hand recklessly. To see the Tecks of the world on the other side is to see that the odds are not in your favor.

If Teck and Kurt represent the extremes of Europe, Fanny, David and Marthe stand in for uncommitted America. Marthe married Teck at seventeen to fulfill her mother's fantasies. Now only Teck's threats hold this marriage together. The count and countess are the beneficiaries of the Farrellys' "unlocked front door" and unsuspicious natures. The family now must pass through the classic pattern of American involvement with European fascism: first, failure to recognize its existence; second, failure to see it as a personal threat; and third, appeasement.

When Fanny and David realize that Kurt will not give up the underground's money and that Teck is equally determined to betray Kurt to German intelligence, they agree to protect Kurt by meeting Teck's price. However, Teck's true aim is power, not wealth, and Kurt is aware that such ambitions cannot be bought off: "If they are willing to try you on this fantasy, I am not. What ever made you think I would take such a chance? Or *any* chance? You are a gambler. But you should not gamble with your life." (*Watch on the Rhine*, III, 387–88)

Once again, Teck has underestimated commitment, and Kurt kills him (overpowering him, by the way, not with a perfectly convenient Luger, but in true American fashion with his bare hands). It is now time for the Farrellys to make their commitment. They can either call the police and retain their isolationism, or they can give Kurt the car and the two days he needs to hide the body and get a head start, and become accomplices to a murder. Two factors will influence their decision.

The first is Fanny's late husband, Joshua Farrelly, by whose standards she measures everything. In a key early exchange, the connection is made between Joshua and Kurt when Fanny reminds her eldest grandchild (and her husband's namesake) that he bears a great name. "My name is Muller," the boy replies. (*Watch on the Rhine*, I, 341) After Teck's murder, Fanny reflects on one of Joshua's last statements: "A Renaissance man . . . is a man who wants to know. He wants to know how fast a bird will fly, how thick is the crust of the earth, what makes Iago evil, how to plow a field. He knows there is no dignity to a mountain, if there is no dignity to man. You can't put that in a man, but when it's *really* there, and he will fight for it, put your trust in him." (*Watch on the Rhine*, III, 392)

Nine-year-old Bodo provides an early description of Kurt: "He likes to know how each thing of everything is put together." (*Watch on the Rhine*, I, 349) By the time Fanny remembers the discussion above, we have already seen Kurt as a loving husband and father and as a musician, are aware of his past as an engineer and a farmer, and have been shown documentation of the exceptional range of his anti-Fascist activities. We know that he is willing to give his own life and to kill in the service of his beliefs. We are also able to anticipate Fanny's decision.

But then how could she decide otherwise? For if Kurt is anti-Fascist Europe and the Farrellys are America, it must be concluded that Joshua, Babette, and Bodo belong to both. In 1941, Hellman has revived the concept of the Popular Front by embodying it in the international family. In *Watch on the Rhine*, we are urged to fight, not for abstractions or foreigners, but for children whom we have come to love and look upon as our own. In a moving farewell to his children, Kurt recalls a family reading and discussion of *Les Misérables:*

The world is out of shape, we said, when there are hungry men. And until it gets in shape, men will steal and lie and . . . kill. But for whatever reason it is done, and whoever does it—you understand me—it is all bad. . . . But you will live to see the day when it will not have to be. All over the world, in every place and every town, there are men who are going to make sure it will not have to be. They want what I want: a childhood for every child. For my children, and I for theirs. (*Watch on the Rhine*, III, 394–95)

With this evocation of the World Family, Kurt returns to Germany, leaving Sara and his children in the Farrelly house, taking with him Fanny and David's commitment and the money they had raised to bribe Teck, soon to be followed by other Americans who believe they might turn Kurt's dream into a reality.

War and the Revelations of Caste

The Negro is a born anti-fascist. Long before Hitler walked across the face of the earth we knew him. For three centuries, we tasted the bitterness of Nazism under the name of lynchocracy. . . . . Yet we love America.[55]
—Adam Clayton Powell, Jr. (1945)

It was W. E. B. Du Bois who predicted in 1903 that, for America, "the problem of the Twentieth Century is the problem of the color line."[56] At no time has that problem been more obvious than during wartime. George Washington was but the first of many American commanders to reverse himself on the policy of using black troops, but only because he had been outflanked by Lord Dunamore, the royal governor of Virginia, who promised freedom to any slave who would join the British army. By April 1776, the British tactic was so successful that South Carolina instituted the death penalty for blacks who fled to the enemy side or persuaded others to do so.[57]

Nine months after the declaration of the War of 1812, blacks were permitted to enlist in the navy, and eventually formed nearly 20 percent of what were integrated crews. At least 600 black troops at the Battle of New Orleans contributed to the worst British defeat since Yorktown.[58]

The North was widely perceived as losing the Civil War before Lincoln's Emancipation Proclamation, followed by War Department Order G0143 on May 22, 1863, allowing Negro enlistment. In the war against the Gray, 180,000 of those who fought for the Blue were black. They received fourteen Congressional Medals of Honor; the casualty rate of their units was 40 percent higher than white units; and their pay was 40 percent lower.[59] The fact that black troops were segregated for the first time did not seem to dampen their enthusiasm for battle.

When the peacetime army was reorganized in 1866, four black regiments were established as a permanent part of the nation's armed forces. The Ninth and Tenth Cavalry regiments—called "Buffalo soldiers" by the Indians—fought the Plains Wars, and "Smoked Yankees" (as the Spanish called them) preceded Teddy Roosevelt's Rough Riders up San Juan Hill during the Spanish-American War. But even before "Black-Jack" Pershing (given his nickname because he commanded black troops) led the Tenth Cavalry across the Mexican border in pursuit of Pancho Villa, Woodrow Wilson's administration was preparing for World War I by reducing the black role in the military.[60]

In January 1913, a House of Representatives bill called for repeal of the statutes authorizing the four black regiments. In July 1914, Representative Frank Park of Georgia introduced a bill to prevent blacks from serving as commissioned or noncommissioned officers. Two years later, southern congressmen sponsored a bill against the enlistment or reenlistment of "any person of the Negro or colored race," in the U.S. military service.[61] In July 1917, Colonel Charles Young, one of only three black line officers at the onset of the war, was "invalided" out of service, lest his next promotion give the United States its first black general.

Only one out of every nine black draftees was assigned to a (segregated) combat unit.[62] The Ninety-second Infantry Division was commanded by white American officers, who characterized their men as cowardly, stupid, and sexually brutal. The Ninety-third served under the French, spending 191 consecutive days in a frontline position without ever losing a foot of ground. The French awarded the Ninety-third the Croix de Guerre and requested that the United States send to France all black units which could be spared. A French liaison officer serving in General Pershing's headquarters sent to the French Military Mission a memo entitled "Secret Information Concerning Black Troops": "We cannot deal with them on the same plane as with white American officers without deeply wounding the latter. We must not eat with them, must not shake hands or seek to meet with them outside the requirements of military service. We must not commend too highly the black American troops."[63]

In 1917, the first year of American participation in World War I, the number of lynchings at home doubled to thirty-eight. In 1918 there were sixty-two lynchings of blacks, and in 1919—the first full year of "peace"—seventy-seven Negroes were lynched, including ten veterans, several still in uniform.[64] This was the year that the American Legion segregated black members, and that on France's Bastille Day march, the British and the French included black troops, and the Americans did not. In 1924, when a federal bureau dedicated a plaque inscribed with the names of servicemen killed during the war, the black dead were immortalized on a separate tablet. In 1930, when Gold Star mothers and widows were invited to visit the European graves of their loved ones dead in the war, black women were sent on a separate ship.[65] In 1935, when the Lincoln Memorial was dedicated in Washington, D.C., no blacks were included in the ceremonies honoring the Great Emancipator, and those attending were not allowed to sit in front.

With the approach of World War II, the past was prelude for the Negro serviceman. The first Navy Cross winner of World War II was Dorie Miller, a mess steward aboard the USS *West Virginia* at Pearl Harbor, who pulled his wounded captain to safety and, taking over a machine gun, brought down four Japanese planes. In 1944, Dorie Miller died on a ship sunk by Japanese torpedoes. He was still a messman, the only position in which the Navy accepted blacks when he enlisted.[66]

Everything in the beginning was aimed at making World War II a race war. It was proclaimed as "a white man's war"—against "those yellow rats," the Japs. We were formally at war with Germany and Italy but we set up concentration camps for Japanese only, even when they were American born. . . . While we, the colossus of the West, slumbered, the Japanese slaughtered millions of Chinese with our scrap iron and our gasoline. Yet, we included Chinese from our shores. Even after we had been at war for some time, the yellow men, good enough to fight our enemy, were not considered good enough to emigrate to America.[67]

It is a record of racism that Hiroshima and Nagasaki did little to alleviate.

On the Western Front we faced an opponent whose goal of world domination was stated in terms of racial superiority so marked that it justified genocide. Hitler, the architect of this policy, was clearly a monster and a madman. The comparison with our own racial policies should have embarrassed us, but it was an embarrassment we concealed remarkably well. As Alabama's senator William B. Bankhead (the father of Tallulah) put it when he was asked if a Nazi was superior to a Negro: "He's white, isn't he?"[68]

Nevertheless, the value systems of all combatants are early casualties in wartime, and war's most fortunate side effect is that the less sustenance a value has, the sooner a survival-minded society will jettison it. During World War II, blacks made inroads, not only in the military, but in the economy as well. In the autumn of 1940, the disappointment of blacks in the position they had been given in the country's burgeoning wartime economy and expanding military began to be heard from the NAACP (National Association for the Advancement of Colored People), the National Urban League, and newer organizations like the Allied Committees on National Defense. The proposal which most caught the public's imagination was that of A. Philip Randolph of the Brotherhood of Sleeping Car Porters, calling for 50,000 blacks to march on Washington, D.C., on July 1, 1941. On June 24, the president issued Executive Order 8802, prohibiting discrimination in defense production industries and establishing the President's Committee on Fair Employment Practice (FEPC) to enforce this policy. The percentage of black workers in skilled, semiskilled, and single-skilled jobs increased by two-thirds between 1940 and 1944. The percentage of black-filled federal jobs in Washington, D.C., doubled, with most of the gains made in positions from which blacks had previously been barred.[69]

In the spring of 1946, with the war safely over, Congress cancelled the FEPC, not to reactivate it until new civil rights pressures were felt in 1957. About the March on Washington's second demand, desegregation of the armed forces, EO-8802 said nothing.[70] The implications of that segregation were found in other than duty situations. In defiance of all science, the Red Cross "Jim-Crowed" blood donations—at a time when the blood blank of England was under the direction of a black American doctor, Charles Drew of Howard University.[71] The white officers of a black artillery company in Pennsylvania determined that "any association between the colored soldiers and white women, whether voluntary or not, [will] be considered rape," and authorized the death penalty.[72] Particularly galling to the average black soldier were privileges and hospitalities accorded to German prisoners of war—as recorded by poet Wittner Bynner.

On a train in Texas German prisoners eat
With white American soldiers, seat by seat,
While black American soldiers sit apart—
The white men eating meat, the black men heart.[73]

In *The Fire Next Time*, James Baldwin expressed the feelings of many black Americans: "The treatment accorded the Negro during the Second World War marks, for me, a turning point in the Negro's relation to America. To put it briefly, and somewhat too simply, a certain hope died."[74]

Nevertheless, blacks in the armed forces became a presence to be reckoned with by friend and foe alike during the war. The air corps began to accept black applications in March 1942. The navy opened up branches other than messman in April. The Coast Guard began accepting blacks in May, followed by the marines in June. By the end of 1944, there were 40 percent more black officers in the military than there were enlisted men in 1939. Except in the air corps, the training of officers was integrated from the beginning of the war. In August 1944, the navy began to experiment with integrated ships. The need for infantry replacements during the Battle of the Bulge forced the first army modification of segregation. Negro enlisted men who were willing to sacrifice all rank were allowed to volunteer for all-black platoons within white companies. A survey taken in seven of the eleven divisions where this policy was tried found that 84 percent of the white officers and 81 percent of the white enlisted men found that black soldiers performed "very well" in combat, while the 16 percent of the officers and 17 percent of the enlisted men thought blacks did "fairly well." Performance ratings were highest where combat was the most severe.[75]

Given a taste of equality and success, how would the black soldier react to a South determined to maintain its traditions? According to the National Opinion Research Center of the University of Denver in August 1944, four out of five white Southerners expected race relations to grow worse after the war.[76] "You know what my main job in the Army was? It was to make my men believe they were fighting for a better world for themselves, as well as for you. . . . All through this war we've been living on promises—we've had to fight on faith. Now the promises have to be made good, even if we have to begin at the beginning."[77]

Shortly before the end of World War II, Gunnar Myrdal, the Swedish sociologist, published the classic treatise on white racism, *An American*

Dilemma, One of its features that was to have great significance in the postwar mutual readjustment between blacks and the South was the "White Southerner's Rank Order of Discrimination"—a listing of privileges whites were least likely to yield to blacks: (1) interracial sex, (2) social equality, (3) desegregated public facilities, (4) the right to vote, (5) equality before the law, and (6) economic opportunity.[78]

Deep Are the Roots

The major thematic points of *Deep Are the Roots* (opening September 26, 1945, and set the preceding spring) are probes of the "Rank Order of Discrimination," tests of its flexibility and response risk. The plot, however, creaks along on such readily recognizable elements as a linen-suited, silver-haired southern senator, a missing family heirloom, a conveniently remembered lynching, and a porcine southern sheriff. Arnaud d'Usseau and James Gow take no chances with their protagonist—a college graduate, academic enough to be offered a Ph.D. scholarship in biochemistry from the University of Chicago, and altruistic enough to reject it for the principalship at the local "colored" school; sensitive enough to play Othello at fourteen, and sensible enough to reject the grown-up Desdemona when she offers herself; and, in addition, an officer and gentleman with six Battle Stars, seventeen pieces of shrapnel in one leg, and a Distinguished Service Cross. Aligned with First Lieutenant Brett Charles and the winds of change are Genevra ("Nevvy") Langdon, his childhood friend, and Howard Merrick, a liberal northern novelist, unnecessary *raisonneur*, and fiancé of Nevvy's sister, Alice. Preservers of tradition are Alice Langdon, Senator Ellsworth Langdon (the girls' father), and Bella Charles (Brett's mother and a longtime family servant). Two other characters, Honey (a maid scorned by Brett) and Roy Maxwell (a cousin of the family and a congressional candidate) are important because they have no fixed ideological position and, thus, are indicators of the flow of public opinion. It is Honey who yields to the senator's pressure to help frame Brett for the theft of a watch, and who later recants when she comes to understand the temper of the black community. And it is Cousin Roy who, like any good politician, senses that a change is coming in the power structure and wants desperately to gauge its direction so that he can get out in front and lead it.

As the son of Senator Langdon's trusted housekeeper, Brett Charles grew up with the senator's two daughters. Alice was his teacher and mentor, guiding him through Fisk University, and obtaining for him the University of Chicago scholarship. Nevvy was his playmate until Alice caught then rehearsing the murder scene from *Othello* when Brett was fourteen and Nevvy twelve. Brett's independence in choosing the local principalship over the northern scholarship distresses Alice. Reluctantly, she supports him to the extent of insuring that a new (segregated) schoolhouse will be built, but presumes that other past niceties will continue to be observed: for example, that this ex-officer and decorated war hero will continue to enter from the side door, and that this school principal will get a note from her permitting his withdrawal of a book from the public library. He will not attempt to travel on a "whites only" Pullman car to an Atlanta conference which she considers Communist-infiltrated, and he will not—literally on pain of death—lay hands on her younger sister.

For his part, Senator Langdon dislikes Alice's championship of Brett, not realizing that her patronizing is merely the flipside of his contempt. He glowers when his daughter's fiancé dares to shake hands with Brett, and disputes Merrick's eyewitness account of Brett's conduct in the public library. The senator senses that Brett is the vanguard of change, and his suspicions are especially aroused when Brett chooses to take the school-master job: "Sounds innocent enough; but I can see through you. Get hold of the colored folk around here and make them dissatisfied—put ideas in their heads—stir up trouble. . . . If he told you the truth, you'd probably find that over there he slept with white women!" (*Deep Are the Roots*, I, 61)

For all his stereotypical ravings, the senator is closer to the truth than any other white in the household. Brett's collisions with tradition are not those of a native son with a bad memory. They reflect a specific political agenda. The black community did not just offer him the principalship. He actively campaigned for it by letter before even arriving home. His speech of acceptance is designed to confront rather than conciliate: "telling our good-hearted darkies that segregation *is morally wrong* and that it won't always exist." (*Deep Are the Roots*, II, 102) Before going into the library, Brett makes sure there is "no written law or regulation prohibiting colored folk entering that front door." (*Deep Are the Roots*, II, 109) The Atlanta conference on racial problems gives him a double opportunity for challenge: The subjects to be discussed—education, job opportunities for returning servicemen, the poll tax, and so on—are important, but so is the method of getting there. Brett has Nevvy buy him a Pullman car ticket to see if they will turn him away while he is wearing his country's uniform. Inasmuch as interstate transportation was the issue upon which the Supreme court made its "separate but equal" decision in *Plessy vs. Ferguson* (1896), Brett is disputing constitutional law as well as local tradition. Whatever his actions, Brett's motivations are clear: "In Italy I was an American officer. Here I'm a nigger. I had forgotten some of the things that means."[79] (*Deep Are the Roots*, II, 84)

It could be said that Brett's relationship with Nevvy is his only nondeliberate flouting of the "Rank Order of Discrimination." While Howard Merrick (Alice's fiancé) sees Brett as the New South, someone with whom he can "connect" without having to endure the embarrassing obsequiousness with which many southern blacks "get over" on whites, Nevvy's emotions are more complex.

On one level, Brett is her first love, now grown tall and heroic. On the other, she is moved to expiate white southern guilt. When Brett is arrested falsely for the theft of a family watch, inscribed, ironically, "Honor Above All," Nevvy sees in the face of her father the sick ecstasy she witnessed as a child on the faces of a lynch mob: "There will be men sitting on the porch of the Country Club, and they'll talk about what a problem the 'niggers' are getting to be, and there'll be a little bit of that look on their faces. . . . When [my father] searches Brett's room it's a tiny little lynching. It's an act of cruelty and he's enjoying it." (*Deep Are the Roots*, II, 118–19)

In her way, Bella is as much of a traditionalist as Langdon and Alice. However, her motivations are far different. Bella is fully aware that the sincerity of Nevvy and Brett's feelings will not keep Brett alive if the rest of the white community realizes that there is a relationship between them. The South of 1945 has upper and lower classes, but it lives and dies according to caste. Bella's standing as the senator's housekeeper and Brett's education and military record place them high in the class system of the black community, but it cannot give them the rights and privileges which are reserved for whites, many of whom are their inferiors in all other measurable factors. The penalty for attempting to cross the caste line would be death for Brett and ostracism for Nevvy—a bitter irony for Bella, who knows that racial sexual barriers are quite permeable from the top: "No, we ain't good enough to claim a place among the chosen people. But we're good enough to share the white man's bed. And when we do, God punishes us as he sees fit—but nobody calls the sheriff." (*Deep Are the Roots*, III, 184–85)

It is Alice who calls the sheriff when a letter from an anonymous redneck accuses her of walking late at night with Brett. Realizing that Nevvy has been mistaken for her, Alice reveals how "deep are the roots" of her prejudice: "I have to do what I know is right." (*Deep Are the Roots*, II, 144)

Alice's betrayal challenges the widespread myth that it is the aristocracy, the "quality folk," who will bring abut equality for blacks. Booker T. Washington inaugurated the policy of "courting the best people," believing that as Negroes increased in thrift, education, and efficiency, whites would gradually admit them to full citizenship. This doctrine of conciliation, expediency, and gradualism was adopted without substantial change by a whole generation of southern black leaders. The flaw of the doctrine lay not in the sensibility of its actions, but in that it encouraged an "inferior caste" mind-set. Since Negroes were discriminated against for their "blackness," visible evidence of white ancestry—first courted for its social and economic value—came to be seen as a good in itself, creating a caste within a caste.[80] The cry of the sixties, "Black is beautiful," is a political affirmation as well as an aesthetic one. Aligning the black cause with white values and white upper-class interests was a "double whammy," ignoring the possibilities of both racial solidarity and class solidarity across the caste line.

The racial solidarity does come. Like many another political hero, Brett achieves more as a martyr than as a crusader. Not only does Bella denounce the senator and Alice in blistering terms, the rest of the help quits in protest of the family's breach of faith. Honey returns the "Judas money" the senator gave her to lie about the watch because of "colored town" pressure. Even in the white community, there are those who understand that such blatant discrimination has repercussions. Cousin Roy Maxwell is terrified by the fact that returning veterans will actually make blacks the majority in the country, but his sense of injustice is touched as well: "I'm told he was beaten up while wearing his uniform. There are a lot of people who don't like that. And you know something? I'm one of them." (*Deep Are the Roots*, III, 164)

Brett is released and put on a train to the North. He leaves it, however, and returns to the Langdon house for a final confrontation: "My men were right. . . . They knew when it comes right down to it, it's white against black—the black underneath. They had the satisfaction of hating—hating all white people." (*Deep Are the Roots*, III, 195)

As Merrick points out, this is an unworkable conclusion for Brett. To hate all white people, he would have to hate Nevvy too. For her part, Alice admits the nature of her prejudice and asks for forgiveness. Nevertheless, it is not until she allows Nevvy and Brett to make their own decision concerning marriage that we discern any real progress in her attitude.

Actually, the progress asked for has been moderate, even by 1945 standards. The code that the play finally affirms could be described as the "White *Northerner's* Rank Order of Discrimination," in that economic, political, and legal equality are upheld, but except for the abandonment of certain social forms, separateness is never seriously challenged. Housing is never discussed, and as a school principal, Brett is concerned with a new building, not integration. Even miscegenation is a tantalizing red herring, as Brett twice turns down offers of marriage which Nevvy makes without so much as onstage hand-holding. At the final curtain, race relations have extended only to the point of Brett dropping the obligatory "Miss" in speaking to Alice, who is moved to spontaneously shake his hand.[81]

Caste Lists in the Postwar Theatre

Deep Are the Roots was the earliest and most successful of four plays by white authors dealing with the problems of the returning minority veteran during the 1945–1946 New York theatre season. Robert Ardrey's *Jeb* had a similar story: a disabled Silver Star winner gets a job running an adding machine in the mill of his Louisiana hometown, only to lose it because running an adding machine is a white man's job. Later, he is driven out of the South on a fabricated charge of dating a white woman. As his would-be employer explains it, "When we say a nigra wants a white man's girl, what we mean it's a nigra wants a white man's job."[82] Despite the presence of Ozzie Davis and Ruby Dee in the cast, *Jeb* failed. Maxine Wood's *On Whitman Avenue* (produced by and starring Canada Lee) centered on a white liberal college girl's attempt to rent an apartment in a restricted suburb to a Negro veteran and his wife, and was slightly more successful.

In the long run, a play in which no blacks appear probably had a greater affect on race relations in the United States than any of the preceding three. Arthur Laurents's *Home of the Brave* explored the guilt of a Jewish soldier who survives the ambush in which his gentile best friend dies. The play ran only sixty-seven performances in 1945–1946, but as a film with the Jewish character replaced by a black, *Home of the Brave* was one of the top motion pictures of 1949.[83]

We should also note a play that focused on another aspect of black/white relationships that war seemed to exacerbate in the United States: lynching. In 1944, Lillian Smith published a novel entitled *Strange Fruit*, taking her title from the Lewis Allan song which Billie Holiday made so unforgettably her own, and in 1945, Ms. Smith and her sister, Esther, dramatized the story. Late the following year, even before *Deep Are the Roots* had finished its Broadway run, President Truman was listening to national black anger over postwar lynchings. His Civil Rights Commission, appointed that December, took only ten months to produce a report entitled *To Secure These Rights*, a blueprint for many of the court decisions of the fifties and for the congressional civil rights acts of the mid-sixties.

As the forties waned, America was becoming increasingly aware that her internal affairs could not be separated from the impression she had upon the rest of the world.

A lynching in Georgia is not ignored by textile workers in Bombay. A race riot in Detroit does not escape the notice of the dock worker in Shanghai. The existence of our Negro ghettos is known to the Chinese peasant and the South African mine worker even though many Americans continue to ignore it. . . . During World War II we appealed to such people for support against a regime that posed a theory of racial superiority as part and parcel of a program of world domination. We are appealing to them now in our world wide opposition to what many regard as an equally repugnant ideology; we seek their support against a dire threat to our national interest and to the democratic potentials of other countries. . . . The colored races over the world are likely, however, to judge us by what we do and not by what we say. . . . As the world becomes smaller, our neighbors not only can look over our back fence; but they also can examine the contents of our closet. Many of them—black or yellow or of some other hue—will not like what they see.[84]

For good or for ill, civil rights was now a battlefield in the Cold War, and the two would never be separated again.

Notes

1. Quoted by Lawrence S. Wittner, in *Rebels Against War: The American Peace Movement, 1941–1960* (New York: Columbia University Press, 1969), 3.

2. The idea of a League of Nations (referred to in the 1917 War Address as a "League of Honor") evolved from a suggestion made to Wilson by Charles William Eliot, the former president of Harvard, on August 6, 1914. Edwin Borchard and William Lage, *Neutrality for the United States* (New Haven: Yale University Press, 1937), 236–37.

3. Charles G. Fenwick, *American Neutrality: Trial and Failure* (New York: New York University Press, 1940), 17.

4. Robert A. Divine, *The Illusion of Neutrality* (Chicago: University of Chicago Press, 1962), 83.

5. Divine, *The Illusion of Neutrality*, 68–72.

6. Divine, *The Illusion of Neutrality*, 65–66.

7. H. C. Engelbrecht and F. C. Hanighen, *Merchants of Death: A Study of the International Armament Industry* (New York: Dodd, Mead, 1934), 9.

8. George Seldes, *Iron, Blood, and Profits* (New York: Harper & Brothers, 1934), 13.

9. Walter Millis, *Road to War: America 1914–1917* (Boston: Houghton Mifflin, 1935), 82–102.

10. Robert A. Divine, *The Reluctant Belligerent* (Chicago: University of Chicago Press, 1965), 9.

11. John K. Nelson, "The Peace Prophets: American Pacifist Thought, 1919–1941," in *The James Sprunt Studies in History and Political Science*, Vol. 49 (Chapel Hill: University of North Carolina Press, 1967), 60–61.

12. Divine, *The Reluctant Belligerent*, 9.

13. Charles Chatfield, *For Peace and Justice: Pacifism in America 1914–1941* (Knoxville: University of Tennessee Press, 1971), 94–97.

14. Wittner, *Rebels Against War*, 29.

15. Hal Draper, "The Student Movement of the Thirties: A Political History," in *As We Saw the Thirties*, ed. Rita James Simon (Urbana: University of Illinois Press, 1967), 168–72.

16. Chatfield, *For Peace and Justice*, 259–60.

17. Nelson, "Peace Prophets," 32–33.

18. Nelson, "Peace Prophets," 24–26.

19. Stephen Vincent Benét, "1936," in *Selected Works of Stephen Vincent Benét, Vol. 1: Poetry* (New York: Farrar & Rhinehart, 1942), 454–55.

20. John Haynes Holmes and Reginal Lawrence, *If This Be Treason* (New York: Macmillan, 1935), I, 53. Subsequent references to this play will be included within the text.

21. Irwin Shaw, *Bury the Dead*, in *New Theatre and Film, 1934 to 1937*, ed. Herbert Kline (San Diego: Harcourt, Brace, and Jovanovitch, 1985), 130. Subsequent references to this play will be included within the text.

22. George Sklar and Albert Maltz, *Peace on Earth* (New York: Samuel French, 1936), III, 92. Subsequent references to this play will be included within the text.

23. Sidney Howard, *The Ghost of Yankee Doodle* (New York: Charles Scribner's Sons, 1938), vii, 152. Subsequent references to this play will be included within the text.

24. Reginald Lawrence and S. K. Lauren, *Men Must Fight* (New York: Samuel French, 1933), II, 58. Subsequent references to this play will be included within the text.

25. Robert E. Sherwood, *Idiot's Delight* (New York: Charles Scribner's Sons, 1936), II, i, 79–80. Subsequent references to this play will be included within the text.

26. Harold Clurman, *The Fervent Years* (New York: Hill and Wang, 1945), 172.

27. Paul Green, *Johnny Johnson* (New York: Samuel French, 1936), I, i, 14. Copies of this play, in individual paper covered acting editions, are available from Samuel French, Inc., 25 W. 45th St., New York, N.Y. 10036 or 7623 Sunset Blvd., Hollywood, Calif. 90046, or from Samuel French, (Canada) Ltd., 80 Richmond Street East, Toronto M5C, 1P1, Canada. Other references to the play are in the text.

28. Wayne S. Cole, *Roosevelt and the Isolationists* (Lincoln: University of Nebraska Press, 1983), 199.

29. Wittner, *Rebels Against War*, 34.

30. Paul Seabury, *The Rise and Decline of the Cold War* (New York: Basic Books, 1967), 88–89.

31. Porter Sargent, *Getting US into War* (Boston: Porter Sargent, 1941), 20–21.

32. Donald Drummond, *The Passing of American Neutrality, 1937–1941* (New York: Greenwood Press, 1968), 40–41.

33. Sargent, *Getting US into War*, 29.

34. Cole, *Roosevelt and the Isolationists*, 278.

35. Drummond, *Passing of American Neutrality*, 77–78.

36. Howard Koch, *The Panic Broadcast* (Boston: Little, Brown, 1970), 103.

37. George Orwell, "Looking Back on the Spanish War," in *A Collection of Essays by George Orwell* (San Diego: Harcourt Brace Jovanovich, 1946), 203.

38. Douglas Little, *Malevolent Neutrality: The United States, Great Britain, and the Origins of the Spanish Civil War* (Ithaca, N.Y.: Cornell University Press, 1985), 246–48.

39. Little, *Malevolent Neutrality*, 50–53.

40. During World War II, Hitler was to present a neutral Spain with a 374-million-reichsmark bill for services rendered.

41. Little, *Malevolent Neutrality*, 240–41.

42. Sargent, *Getting US into War*, 26, 28.

43. M. K. Dzienwanowski, *A History of Soviet Russia* (Englewood Cliffs, N.J.: Prentice-Hall, 1979), 130–31.

44. Divine, *The Illusion of Neutrality*, 170–71.

45. Drummond, *Passing of American Neutrality*, 49, 87.

46. Quoted by Alan Landsburg, in *Between the Wars: The Spanish Civil War* (Wilmette, Ill.: Films Incorporated, 1978).

47. Little, *Malevolent Neutrality*, 17.

48. Elmer Rice, *Flight to the West* (New York: Coward-McCann, 1941), I, 22–23.

49. John O'Connor and Lorraine Brown, *Free, Adult, Uncensored* (Washington, D.C.: New Republic Books, 1978), 59.

50. Maxwell Anderson, *Key Largo* (Washington, D.C.: Anderson House, 1939), II, 118.

51. Robert E. Sherwood, "Postscript," *Idiot's Delight* (New York: Charles Scribner's Sons, 1936), 189–90.

52. Quoted by Gerald Rabkin, in *Drama and Commitment: Politics in the American Theatre of the Thirties* (Bloomington: Indiana University Press, 1964), 110.

53. Malcolm Goldstein, *The Political Stage: American Drama and Theater of the Great Depression* (New York: Oxford University Press, 1974), 352.

54. Lillian Hellman, *Watch on the Rhine*, in *Modern American Plays*, ed. Frederic G. Cassidy (Freeport, N.Y.: Books for Libraries Press, 1970), III, 383. Subsequent references to this play will be included within the text.

55. Adam Clayton Powell, Jr., *Marching Blacks* (New York: Dial Press, 1945), 4–5.

56. W.E.B. DuBois, *The Souls of Black Folk* (New York: New American Library, 1969), ix.

57. Jack D. Foner, *Blacks and the Military in American History* (New York: Praeger Publishers, 1974), 6–15.

58. Foner, *Blacks and the Military*, 22–25.

59. John S. Butler, *Inequality in the Military: The Black Experience* (Saratoga, Calif.: Century Twenty-One Publishing, 1980), 23.

60. Foner, *Blacks and the Military*, 106–7.

61. Butler, *Inequality in the Military*, 24–25.

62. Richard M. Dalfiume, *Desegregation of the Armed Forces* (Columbia: University of Missouri Press, 1969), 13–14.

63. Butler, *Inequality in the Military*, 25–26.

64. Arthur Waskow, *From Race Riots to Sit-in, 1919 and the 1960's* (Garden City, N.Y.: Doubleday, 1966), 9–12.

65. Foner, *Blacks and the Military*, 124–27.

66. Foner, *Blacks and the Military*, 173–74.

67. Powell, *Marching Blacks*, 126.

68. Powell, *Marching Blacks*, 32.

69. Arnold Rose, *The Negro in America* (New York: Harper & Brothers, 1948), 134–35.

70. Dalfiume, *Desegregation of the Armed Forces*, 115–22.

71. Powell, *Marching Blacks*, 127.

72. Dalfiume, *Desegregation of the Armed Forces*, 69.

73. Foner, *Blacks and the Military*, 153.

74. James Baldwin, *The Fire Next Time* (New York: Dell Publishing Co., 1964), 76.

75. David G. Mandelbaum, *Soldier Groups/and Negro Soldiers* (Berkeley: University of California Press, 1952), 103–4.

76. Powell, *Marching Blacks*, 6–7.

77. Arnaud d'Usseau and James Gow, *Deep Are the Roots* (New York: Random House, 1945), I, 63–64. All subsequent references to this play will be noted in the text.

78. Rose, *The Negro in America*, 24.

79. Brett's experience in the post office was typical. After World War II many black veterans in the South were unable to take advantage of the GI Bill of Rights, because post offices would not give them the necessary applications. Rose, *The Negro in America*, 178.

80. Adam Clayton Powell, Jr., called self-hatred, which resulted from blacks valuing a white skin "one of the most disastrous forces retarding the progress of the race." Powell, *Marching Blacks*, 12–13.

81. The fates, which subsequently befell some of those people involved with the original production of *Deep Are the Roots*, were scarcely encouraging. On the tour of the play through the South, the original Brett Charles (Gordon Heath) became so depressed from the discrimination he faced that he quit the show and moved to Paris, from where he never returned. Arnaud d'Usseau and the play's director, Elia Kazan, found themselves accused of being Communists before the House Un-American Activities Committee in the 1950s. The original Nevvy (Barbara Bel Geddes) wound up on *Dallas*.

82. Robert Ardrey, *Jeb*, in *Plays of Three Decades* (New York: Atheneum, 1968), II, 149.

83. Rob Edelman, "*Home of the Brave*," in *Magill's Survey of Cinema, Second Series* 3, ed. Frank M. Magill. (Englewood Cliffs, N.J.: Salem Press, 1981), 1047.

84. Wilson Record, *The Negro and the Communist Party* (Chapel Hill: University of North Carolina Press, 1951), 2–3.

3

The Cold War—Onstage
Sublimated Protest and the Marx of
Satan

There is in this global war literally no question, military or political, in which the United States is not interested.[1]
—Franklin Delano Roosevelt (October 1944)

This war is not as in the past. Whoever occupies a territory also imposes on it his own social system as far as his army can reach. It cannot be otherwise.[2]
—Joseph Stalin (April 1945)

It shouldn't have taken genius to predict antagonism between the United States and the Soviet Union in 1945. Their friendship was based on their mutual enmity toward Hitler, and even that bond was relatively recent. In 1939, the Soviet Union, despairing of gaining any meaningful military alliance with the Western democracies, signed a nonaggression pact with Germany, selling its principles for Eastern Poland and triggering World War II. Twenty-one months later, Hitler, stalled at the English Channel and unaware that another Axis partner, Japan, was about to drag the United States into the war, turned his legions eastward into the expanses which had swallowed up Napoleon. The Communist Party of the United States, which had shifted from Popular Front to pro-isolationism in 1939, did another 180-degree flip while balancing precariously on the Party line and called for a "second front" in Western Europe. "D-Day" came on June 6, 1944, and when Russian and American troops met at the Elbe River in Germany on April 15, 1945, the end of the war in Europe was only thirteen days away. However, the first Cold War battle had already been fought in early February in a southern Russia resort town named Yalta.

The myth of Yalta is an extremely flexible one. One version tells of a naive and already fatally ill Roosevelt who "sold out" Poland and the rest of Eastern Europe to a Stalin, who, sensing American weakness of will, set into motion the vast acquisitory machinery of the Communist monolith. The Russian interpretation of the story pictures a Polish corridor, through which Germany had twice in three decades struck at Mother Russia, being groomed for a government controlled by those who failed to come to her aid in the past. A third reading is at least as believable. Still engaged in a bloody Pacific war and unaware of the role the atomic bomb would play in it, Roosevelt wanted the cooperation of the Red Army in the invasion of Japan, and agreed to a document capable of multiple interpretations, the particulars of which both he and Stalin expected to negotiate to national advantage.

Whether the Cold War was avoidable from that point is conjecture. American revisionist historians of the 1960s accused the United States of using economic pressures, atomic blackmail, and the rebuilding of the totalitarian prewar powers of Germany, Japan, and Italy as anti-Bolshevik bulwarks.[3] In contrast, no less an expert than Earl Browder, at that time secretary of the Communist Party of the United States of America, has stated that "Stalin needed the Cold War to keep the sharp international tensions by which he alone could maintain such a regime in Russia."[4] In the long run, both Russia and the United States were affected by their belief in another myth, the myth of Hitler.

Ernest May's *"Lessons" of History* explains the Cold War as an exercise in "preventing World War II." President Truman (who came to office following Roosevelt's death in April 1945) and his closest advisors all had their first exposure to national power during the period when Hitler's expansionism was the greatest threat to world peace. Once these men drew parallels between Russian action and German imperialism of the 1930s, direct opposition was their only option. Ambassador to Poland Arthur Bliss Lane saw "appeasement or apparent appeasement . . . as dangerous to United States interests as it . . . was in 1940 or 1941."[5] Gaddis Smith, the biographer of Dean Acheson, describes Truman's secretary of state from 1949 to 1953 and "his colleagues in the State and Defense Departments, his contemporaries in Congress, the press, the universities, his superior in the White House [as] driven by the ghost of Hitler and secondarily by hatred for Communist ideology or a desire to achieve a world-wide 'open door' for American trade."[6]

Understandably incensed at being equated with an enemy which had killed twenty million of their people, the Russians formulated Hitler analogies of their own. In March 1946, when Winston Churchill made his famous "Iron Curtain" speech in Fulton, Missouri, Stalin replied: "He also begins the work of unleashing a new war with a race theory, asserting that only English-speaking nations are full-fledged nations, who are called upon to decide the fortunes of the entire world."[7]

Nevertheless, Russia and communism—it would be a long time before we would consider separating the two—were making disturbing gains in the years following World War II. In Eastern Europe between 1945 and 1948, Communist regimes were imposed on Poland, Hungary, Romania, Bulgaria, and Czechoslovakia. Perhaps we might have been more skeptical about the Communist monolith had we noted that it was the two Eastern European countries with indigenous Communist parties, Yugoslavia and Albania, that maintained the greatest independence from Russia—Yugoslavia breaking relations with Moscow in 1948 and Albania supporting Communist China in the late 1950s.[8] At the time, however, with Russian troops in Iran and threatening Turkey, insurgent Communists waging civil war in Greece, large Communist parties in Italy and France, and a legitimate Russian occupation presence in Germany and Austria, America was not in a mood for subtle distinctions.

But even as the United States prepared to meet it, Russian influence in Europe and the Middle East peaked and began to recede. Under U.S. pressure, the Soviets withdrew from Iran in 1946, willingly abandoned the Greek rebels (who were supplied by Yugoslavia) in 1947, and never gained control of the Italian and French Communist parties (which, in turn, never gained control of their governments). On March 12, 1947, in a speech to Congress requesting aid for Greece and Turkey, President Truman promised "to support free peoples who are resisting attempted subjugation by armed minorities or by outside pressures."[9] The "Truman Doctrine" meant, according to George Kennan in the July 1947 issue of *Foreign Affairs*, a "policy of containment, designed to confront the Russians with unalterable counterforce at every point where they show signs of encroaching upon the interests of a peaceful world."[10]

Moscow's last overt European gambit was against West Berlin, the "bone in the Russian throat" (as Nikita Khrushchev was to call it). In late June 1948, the Soviets imposed a complete blockade of all surface routes through East Germany to West Berlin for the purpose of forcing American, British, and French occupying forces out. Truman responded with a plan to supply the city's two million inhabitants entirely by air. Russia yielded after eleven months, having inspired a formal Western military alliance—the North Atlantic Treaty Organization—and the uniting of the Western occupation zones into the German Federal Republic.[11] The battleground was rapidly shifting to the Far East.

If post–World War II Russia evoked the ghost of Hitler, our revulsion to Far Eastern communism owed much to Pearl Harbor-era racism. In September 1945, Secretary of the Navy James Forrestal argued against sharing atomic energy secrets because "the Russians, like the Japanese, are essentially Oriental in their thinking" and could not, therefore, be trusted.[12] I recall a 1950s army training lecture preparing us to combat the "only white Orientals." This level of thought explains not only our inability to separate Russian and Chinese communism, but our subsequent miscalculations in Korea and Vietnam.

In 1927 Mao Tse-tung's faction became the first Communist party to rebel against Moscow. It was not until twenty years later, when even Secretary of State George Marshall had determined that Mao's opposition, the Nationalists of Chiang Kai-shek, had no chance of winning the Chinese civil war, that Russia again undertook to support the indigenous Communist party.[13] Nevertheless, when the inevitable evacuation of Chiang's army to Formosa occurred early in November 1949, America's Cold War began to turn in on itself.

The Cold War as Holy War

In *The Arrogance of Power* (1968), Senator William Fulbright noted that Americans "are not God's chosen savior of mankind but only one of mankind's most successful and fortunate branches, endowed by our Creator with about the same capacity for good and evil, no more or less, than the rest of humanity."[14] What Fulbright was denying was, in fact, what most Americans believed (and possibly still believe). The "New World" was seen as precisely that: A new Eden of individual opportunity superseding the corruption and inflexibility of the Old World and redeeming the promise of its Creator.

In the twentieth century, however, spokesmen such as Eugene V. Debs, Lincoln Steffens, and Upton Sinclair prodded a generation of Americans to reconsider the moral and physical implications of capitalism, industrialism, and urbanization. Under such circumstances, the 1917 Bolshevik revolution, with its pretension to being the perfect system for the industrial worker, threatened America's always fragile national ego. If America (and its developed institutions) was the new Eden, then communism must be the serpent tempting the faithful, and our reaction to it could only be apocalyptic. "Communism was a synonym for the forces of Satan that opposed God's kingdom, and to a large proportion of the American people the term came to signify anything that was socially unorthodox, radical, left-wing, or merely liberal. Communism, thus conceived, was to be contained, and it was to be fought wherever it might manifest itself, whether in Russia, in South-East Asia, in Washington, or in American intellectual communities."[15]

World War II was proof enough for most Americans that representative democracy and private enterprise was justified by both history and God. Alone in the civilized world, America's living standards were higher than they had been before the war. At home, Truman's "Fair Deal" proposed to more equitably distribute the gains of Roosevelt's New Deal. Abroad, the United Nations (her charter framed in San Francisco and her body housed in New York) promised to "save succeeding generations from the scourge of war; to reaffirm faith in fundamental human rights; to establish conditions under which justice and respect for . . . international law can be maintained; and to promote social progress and better standards of life."[16]

Time's Henry R. Luce called it "the American Century," and our nuclear monopoly guaranteed that it would remain so. Like Thomas Moore's *Utopia*, we excluded from public office (at least de facto) all those who did not publicly profess a belief in God. Our World War II military leader, Dwight David Eisenhower, was even, as president, to insert the words "under God" between "one nation" and "indivisible" in our Pledge of Allegiance.

Nevertheless, five years later the war's end, we had seen all of Eastern Europe and the planet's most populous nation fall under the sway of an alien ideology preached by a former ally which we believed owed its very survival to us. We were embroiled in an Asian land war we apparently had no intention of winning, and Russia, whose atomic bomb had followed ours by over four years, was working on a hydrogen bomb which would be ready only nine months after ours. Luce's American Century had given way to Auden's "Age of Anxiety."

How could God's chosen people be seriously threatened by the Devil unless some of the best and the brightest of the Host (like Lucifer an hour before he fell) be the Devil's own? Furthermore, although the serpents in our new Eden might be recognizable, the Eves who did the Devil's will did not even recognize themselves. In July 1949, playwright/congresswoman/ambassador Claire Boothe Luce suggested that our not aiding Nationalist China derived from original sin in the State Department, a pride preventing diplomats from seeing they were being used as Communist dupes.[17]

Thus, the enemies of God ("our way of life") fit into three categories: (a) Communists, who betrayed intentionally, (b) dupes, who betrayed inadvertently, and (c) the injudicious, who betrayed with poor judgment. The imperiling of the chosen people was a punishment for sin. The evil, however, could be separated from the merely weak. If the latter would honestly recognize their sins, confess them publicly, and denounce the evil ones who had lured them into sin, they might still be saved. If, on the other hand, they insisted on maintaining their innocence (or in shielding others), they must be cast forth from America's protection as doctrinal or judgmental dangers to its citizens.

Ironically, in its need to prove the existence of a demonically conspiratorial opposition, America's postwar Communist witch-hunts most resembled in structure (if not in magnitude) the great Stalinist purges of 1936–1938. Both sets of trials shared the assumption that the current system and policy were perfect. Therefore, any systemic failure—present or past—derived from ideological betrayal. That such betrayals were improbable only showed the vastness of the conspiracy, a conspiracy that the defendants' confessions were obliged to confirm. For example, in his 1936 trial, Lev Borisovich Kamenev, one of the creators of the revolution, questioned rhetorically the nature of his own guilt: "Is it an accident that alongside of [me] . . . are sitting emissaries of foreign secret police departments, people with fake passports, with dubious biographies and undoubted connections with the Gestapo? No, it is not an accident."[18] In 1954, Canadian sociologist Dennis Wrong noted the similarity between McCarthy's questioning technique and the GPU (Soviet secret police) during the Purge Trials: "McCarthy too displays less interest in the witnesses appearing before his committee than in finding out who recommended them, and who gave them security clearance, thereby expanding his proscribed minority to include . . . not only Communist Party members but anyone opposing him who ever had any commerce with the Party, real or imaginable."[19]

The purpose of both sets of trials was to insure unquestioning unity in the coming conflict with the enemy. War was clearly on the horizon in 1936. Russia's lag in technology virtually assured that an Eastern Front war would be fought on Soviet soil in an area where the government had recently subjected millions of peasants to unimaginable suffering, while forcing on them a bitterly resented social and economic system. Since initial defeats were probable, it was equally likely that many citizens might turn to any available alternative to Stalin. The trials were intended to show that opposition to Stalin was the equivalent of opposition to communism itself. Therefore, any past or potential future opponents of the dictator were treasonous by definition. Between 1937 and 1939, approximately 850,000 Party members were purged (see Chapter 2), and when massive military defeats did accompany the German invasion of 1941, potential dissidents had no leadership to turn to.[20]

The (Iron) Curtain Rises

Even as it is possible to describe the tactics of the Cold War as an attempt to prevent World War II, it is only natural that dramatists who were writing about the war after its outcome could be anticipated would be concerned with causes rather than descriptions. Given the time required for a play to travel from the writing desk to the proscenium arch (not to mention the motion picture screen), it is equally natural that the play's audiences should be tempted to apply the lessons of war's causes to the postwar world in which they lived.

The conclusion such plays drew was pretty much what national leaders had concluded: never again appeasement. A typical example is Lillian Hellman's *The Searching Wind* (1944) which reached most of us as a film a year after the war ended. Hellman's central character is an ex–World War I soldier turned American diplomat. Present at Mussolini's 1922 takeover in Italy, the beginning of the Weimar Republic's death throes, and pre-Munich Paris, Alexander Hazen suffers the double paralysis of the thirties: a belief that no war is worth the cost, and a fear that opposition to tyranny may hurt family foreign investments. In the final scene, Hazen must face a war amputee son (Montgomery Clift on the stage, Douglas Dick in the movies) who leaves no doubt as to his opinion of his parents' vacillation: "I am ashamed of both of you and that's the truth. I don't want to be ashamed that way again. I don't like losing my leg. . . . I'm scared—but everybody's welcome to it as long as it means a little something and helps to bring us out someplace."[21]

That sense that we should be able to recognize the "right" and stand up for it, even if we must sacrifice personally, permeates much of the later, war-inspired, drama. (Arthur Miller's *All My Sons* is an excellent example.) Certainly, communism as a threat is not a frequent theme in postwar American drama. It provides a joke in the opening scene of *Born Yesterday* and an excuse for Nancy Walker to organize college radicals in Max Shulman's *Barefoot Boy with Cheek* (1947). Campus Communists will never be funny again. Vulnerability of atomic secrets provides melodrama in Herman Wouk's *The Traitor* (1949), while scientific anguish over the potential of those secrets in Donald Ogden Stewart's *How I Wonder* (1947) looks forward to *J. Robert Oppenheimer*.

Even the most philosophical treatment of the perils of communism—Maxwell Anderson's *Barefoot in Athens* (1951)—chose to treat the subject obliquely. It was Anderson's contention that in the later dialogues Plato used Socrates as a front man for his growing disaffection with democracy, until in *The Republic* he created the prototype of a Communist dictatorship. Faced with a choice between the absolutist benevolence of Pausanias, the Spartan king, and a restored democracy that will probably kill him, Socrates—as did Brom Broeck in *Knickerbocker Holiday* (1938)—chooses democracy. Anderson's premise is in his preface:

> The democratic—or republican—method is the best we know; though it's not too admirable, with its local and national bosses, its inevitable spoils system, its routine corruption. The communist system, with its gang of assassins in office, is the worst we know. Plato was sufficiently astute to see that the right structure of a communist society could be maintained only by a ruthless use of assassination, yet he chucked democracy and came out for [Spartan] communism. At least his philosopher-kings, once chosen, would that way be safe from the mob.[22]

Thus, the search for truth is superior to any imposed truth (whatever its results). It is instructive that another serious anticommunist play, Henry Denker and Ralph Berkey's *Time Limit* (1956), deals with Communist brainwashing techniques used in the Korean War, in which men are broken by a combination of torture and being forced to decide between two equally valid "rights."

Darkness at Noon

"Anyone who understands the history of the political activity in Hollywood will appreciate the fact that innocent, sincere persons were used by the Communists to whom honesty and sincerity are as foreign as the Soviet Union is to America. I was duped and used. I was lied to. But, I repeat. I acted from good motives, and I never knowingly aided Communists and any Communist cause."[23]

Edward G. Robinson's contrite appearance before the House Un-American Activities Committee on April 30, 1952, made an ironic contrast to his performance as a revolutionary commissar imprisoned by the logic of a police state apparatus he had helped to create. Sidney Kingsley's dramatization of Arthur Koestler's 1940 novel opened in New York on January 13, 1951. Koestler's original novel, although derived from the Purge Trials and his own imprisonment during the Spanish Civil War, does not specifically identify the tyranny that is his protagonist's creation and downfall. This slight distancing helps us to concentrate on the mode of thinking which produces a police state, rather than to associate all evil with a particular police state. As a play, *Darkness at Noon* is very specific in its Russian references.

The play begins with the middle-of-the-night imprisonment of N. S. Rubashov, "ex-Commissar of the People, ex-member of the Central Committee, ex-General of the Red Army, [and] bearer of the Order of the Red Banner."[24] All his life, Rubashov has lived by a set of beliefs. The first is that he was fighting to relieve the oppression of the people. The second is that the socio-economic-political system he represents is the only methodology under which the oppression can be permanently relieved: "We have already arrived at the truth. Objective truth and with us—Art is its weapon." (*Darkness at Noon*, I, 22)

"Objective truth" is Marx's predictions concerning the development and outcome of the class war. Rubashov's third major belief is the logical extension of the first two. If the price of saving the masses is the sacrifice of some individuals, then the sacrifice must be made. If the law of historic inevitability is in force, then current due process is irrelevant.

All trials are studies of past events with the aim of determining if a law has been broken, and, if so, by whom. In *Darkness at Noon*, the evidence of the crime is in the living conditions of the people. Yet the "objective truth" is that applied Marxism is the perfect system for meeting human needs. In the Russian classification of education, history is listed as science. Given a perfect system and imperfect results, success and failure can be explained by adherence to or deviation from Party policy. Objectively, all deviants are equally guilty, for he who does not further Party aims impedes them, whatever may be his intentions. But if subjective loyalty does not automatically qualify as patriotism, neither does material achievement. In his only contribution to Marxist theory, Stalin defined the most dangerous traitor as the potentially greatest contributor: "A real wrecker will from time to time do good work because it is the only way for him to gain confidence and continue working."[25] Like Lucifer, the traitor at this level has looked upon the face of God and chosen damnation.

This is the view of Rubashov held by Gletkin, his first interrogator. Too young to remember the ideals for which the revolution was fought, he accepts the premise that the state it created is ideal. Gletkin's answer to his country's impossible roads and questionable engineering is to arrest the driver of a car that breaks down. Rubashov's contact with political systems other than his own proves his guilt to Gletkin, as do his protestations of innocence. Perfect systems make no false accusations.

Rubashov's second interrogator—his former friend and subordinate, Ivanoff—is more subtle, appealing to his reason rather than his fear. Since Rubashov has given his life to the advancement of the Party, it is only logical that if the Party at the moment needs his confession of treason against the Party, he will give it.[26] To do otherwise, to protect one's innocence when Party unity demands a scapegoat, would be to think mechanistically and reinforce the "petty bourgeois concept [of] the I—the me." Ivanoff tells Rubashov that a war is coming—a war that could bring down the government, or bring it the world: "There's a breach in the Party. In the whole country. The people are restless—dissatisfied. Our economy is in pieces. The breach must be mended first. And you—and those who think like you—must mend it." (*Darkness at Noon*, II, 67)

Ivanoff is sure that Rubashov will make the objectively correct decision, that he will be convicted, and later rehabilitated because his intellect will be needed in the subsequent war effort. Ivanoff fails to recognize that because of his own connections to the past, he is as vulnerable as Rubashov. Before Rubashov ever comes to trial, Ivanoff is executed.

On the final level of interrogation, Rubashov questions himself and discovers that he is the creator of a logic so perfect it cannot admit humanity. In a series of flashbacks, he reexamines his past decisions and finds them to be the building blocks of his cell. He recalls recommending Party membership for a friend who is now being tortured solely to provide Rubashov an object lesson; threatening with exposure a German Party member who was moved at the plight of the liberals being slaughtered by the Gestapo; and turning in to the government an Italian Communist who refused to support a Russian shipbuilding deal with Mussolini: "Dialectically, . . . whatever does not serve the long distance aims of the Party is an enemy of the Party and therefore even though he may think himself subjectively an anti-Fascist, he is in fact, objectively, a Fascist." (*Darkness at Noon*, II, 54)

Most of all, however, Rubashov recalls Luba Loshenko, the secretary who honestly loved him.[27] Luba is the antithesis of Rubashov's hardness. A believer in the soul and the worth of her own feelings, she sees no reason to deny the joy of today for a worker's paradise tomorrow. But she is also capable of seeing truths that escape ideologies—that production at the plants is down because the workers are overworked, and afraid because those who fear are arrested; that the machines are overworked too and, not understanding dialectic, break down.

With Luba, Rubashov is softened in spite of himself. Listening to Beethoven's *Appassionata*, he expresses a sentiment historically ascribed to Lenin:[28] "This music is dangerous. When you listen to this—and you realize human beings can create such beauty—you want to pat them on the head. That's bad, you see. They'll only bite your hand off." (*Darkness at Noon*, I, 27) Rubashov eventually allows Luba to be arrested without protest, knowing that the accusation is tantamount to conviction, and that she is being used as a mere pawn to destroy him.

In his final session with Gletkin, Rubashov breaks, his three beliefs shattered. Already aware of his people's misery, he comes to realize that the philosophy under which he has labored can never alleviate that misery. In the transcripts of Luba's interrogation, he discovers that no purely materialistic ideology can ever encompass human needs.

Confronted at every turn in his interrogation by teachings from his own books, Rubashov begins to understand that he is the spiritual father of Gletkin. By always placing ideological truth ahead of human truth, he has created a race of men whose only truth is ideological. The terror has been turned against the people; the means have become the end; and the perfect society has become the airtight prison: "My hundred eighty million fellow prisoners. What have I done to you? What have I created? If history is all calculations . . . where in your mathematics, Rubashov, is the human soul? At the very beginning you forget what you were searching for." (*Darkness at Noon*, III, 94)

Casualties on the Home Front

Timing is everything to a conspiracy theory. The Communist capture of mainland China followed the first Russian atomic explosion by about six weeks. Six weeks later (January 21, 1950), Alger Hiss, a former State Department official accused by Whitaker Chambers of being a Communist in the 1930s, was convicted of perjury. On February 2, Klaus Fuchs, a German-born British nuclear physicist who had worked at Los Alamos, was arrested on the charge of giving atomic secrets to the Russians, an event leading to Julius and Ethel Rosenberg's arrest and conviction. On February 9, 1950—five days before the Soviet Union and Communist China signed a thirty-year mutual-aid pact—Senator Joseph McCarthy of Wisconsin found a ready audience for his accusation that the State Department housed 205 known Communists.[29]

If God and America were one, and the struggle against America's enemies a holy war, then any action taken to defeat those enemies was morally justified. As a government panel headed by former President Hoover reported in 1954, the United States "must learn to subvert, sabotage, and destroy our enemies by more clever, more sophisticated and more effective methods than those used against us."[30]

In 1950 the U.S. Navy blanketed San Francisco for six days with a pneumonia-causing serratia to test the possibilities of bacteriological warfare. In 1953 the army tested cloud-seeding as a means of chemical warfare over St. Louis and Winnipeg, Canada. At least one suicide resulted from a CIA experiment which tested the effects of LSD on unaware subjects. Between 1945 and 1963, an estimated 250,000 servicemen were stationed as close as 3,500 yards from Hiroshima-plus–sized atomic blasts to test the ability of soldiers to survive on a nuclear battlefield. Dr. Joseph Lyon, a Utah state epidemiologist, testified in April 1979 that children growing up in state's fallout areas in the 1950s suffered 250 percent more leukemia than children living there before and after the tests.[31]

American institutions and individuals were also victimized on non-physical levels. Before he became chairman of the House Un-American Activities Committee, Congressman Harold Velde of Illinois was known for introducing a bill to require the Librarian of Congress to mark the subversive passages in all nine million books under his care. Such thinking did not bode well for the nation's colleges and universities when HUAC, the Internal Security Committee of Senator Albert Jenner of Indiana, and McCarthy's Senate Government Operations Committee all decided to investigate them in 1953.[32]

J. B. Matthews, the ex-Methodist missionary and ex-Communist who was an important source of information for the very first HUAC Committee in 1938, was staff director of McCarthy's committee by 1953. That year, Matthews followed his May *American Mercury* article, "Communism and the Colleges," with a July entry entitled "Reds and Our Churches." Its opening sentence was bound to catch the eye: "The largest single group supporting the Communist apparatus in the United States today is composed of Protestant clergymen."[33] According to Matthews, the Communist conspiracy contained seven thousand such ministers, ninety-five of which he actually named. A number of these were already dead, while a good many others had signed petitions favoring social reforms which Communists had supported as well.

The State Department was an obvious target. Respected China experts, like John Stewart Service and John Paton Davies lost their jobs—not for having been on McCarthy's list, but for having accurately predicted Chiang Kai-shek's downfall. (A couple dining in a Houston restaurant was jailed overnight for the same prediction.) George C. Marshall, WW II chief of staff and the architect of a rebuilt Western Europe, had tried unsuccessfully to convince the Nationalists and Communists in China to form a coalition government in 1946. For this, McCarthy launched a 60,000-word attack on Marshall and his successor, Dean Acheson, on Flag Day in 1951.[34] Acheson had not only defended America's nonintervention in China, but had also "encouraged" the invasion of South Korea by judging it to be outside of our natural defense perimeter.[35]

In *Inquisition in Eden*, Alvah Bessie listed seventeen prominent Americans who died of suicide or stress-related "natural causes" following appearances before HUAC or McCarthy.[36] The American Legion picketed movie theaters showing *Limelight*, a 1952 film by Charlie Chaplin, with whose political statements they disagreed, and attacked the University of Nebraska for using a textbook with a chapter by Owen Lattimore, who had been smeared by McCarthy. A Chicago congressman blocked the playing of Aaron Copeland's *Lincoln Portrait* at President Eisenhower's inauguration because of Copeland's alleged associations. Pressure from the Veterans of Foreign Wars forced the Voice of America to ban the music of Roy Harris, who had dedicated a symphony to the Soviet Union during World War II. Columnist and radio commentator Elmer Davis sympathized: "Why Harris did not withdraw his dedication (on demand) as Beethoven, without demand, had withdrawn his dedication of the *Eroica* to Napoleon, I do not know. . . . Maybe he still likes the Soviet Union, or maybe he just didn't like the demand. Maybe he doesn't like to be pushed around, and if this country ever runs out of people who don't like to be pushed around, we are done for."[37]

Insofar as such hearings were essentially "show trials," it is only fitting that some of the most dramatically interesting witnesses were in show business, ranging in the 1950s from Arthur Miller to Zero Mostel. The scenarios faced by some of the "Hollywood Ten" accused writers and directors (including Albert Maltz, coauthor of *Peace on Earth*) rivaled anything they had concocted for the screen. More insidious were the entertainment industry blacklists, which denied those named not only the right to face their accusers, but even notification that they were on the list. "The [motion picture] industry blacklist policy was extended to cover every person subpoenaed by [HUAC] who failed to answer all the questions put to him, or who having been named by a witness, did not appear voluntarily to clear himself."[38]

In radio and television, the blacklist was even more arbitrary and producers even more cautious. To be named in the magazine *Red Channels* as having even a "pinkish tinge" was fatal professionally. Vincent Hartnett of AWARE, Inc., had a thriving business throughout the 1950s passing on the political reliability of on-air and on-camera talent for networks, producers, and advertisers for a fixed fee (generously reducing the cost for a name that appeared a second time). Everett Sloane, a veteran character actor, found himself on the list for having the same last name as an actor in *Red Channels*. Unable to find work, he arranged to appear on United Nations radio because such appearances required an FBI clearance. He then approached AWARE board member Paul Milton, who was unimpressed: "We at AWARE have different standards of clearance than the United States government's agencies. We are a little more stringent. We feel that they are a little lenient."39

Millard Lampell, a writer who was on the blacklist throughout the 1950s, tells of one television writer who had *himself* investigated rather than risk a careless charge: "[While] probing him, the investigator questioned a number of network executives. He assured them that it was only a routine check and L. was not under suspicion. Their reaction was skeptical. 'Where there's smoke, there's fire.' L. haunts the waiting room of the networks, a gaunt ghost desperately brandishing his certificate. He has not worked in eight months."40

The secrecy of the blacklist had side effects. Lampell records the ebbing of his confidence in his talent as producers who previously had used his work seemingly lost interest. John Henry Faulk, a performer who wrote his own material, felt both skills atrophy as he remained isolated from the public: "I began to understand why some artists had capitulated to the other side—traded their integrity to Satan, as it were—in order to get back into their profession."41

How did one prove one's loyalty and get off the blacklist? When John Henry Faulk sued AWARE, Inc., for libel, radio producer and director Hiram Brown testified he was allowed to present a radio series starring Joseph Cotton only after the sponsor agreed to yield one of its commercial spots for a patriotic statement. Actress Kim Hunter reappeared on television after sending a pro-AWARE telegram to her union, AFTRA (Associated Federation of Radio and Television Artists).42 Usually, however, the proper procedure involved the confirmation of the existence of a conspiracy and the naming of those who were involved in it: "If one knew no such names, the lawyer would obligingly supply some, in one case arguing away the qualms of a famous choreographer who was anxious to clear himself but reluctant to become an informer with the reassuring thought, 'Hell, they've all been named already, so you're not really doing them any harm. They can't be killed twice.'"43

Hidden Faces of 1952

In an era in which to be suspect is to be condemned, committed drama is infrequent, and when present, cloaked in ambiguity. Anyone studying American theatre which resisted the Red Scare of the fifties owes a debt to Albert Wertheim's *Theatre Journal* article "The McCarthy Era and the American Theatre." Professor Wertheim's particular contribution was to go beyond the openly challenging plays to study revivals and allegories whose significance would have been recognized by the audiences of the time. He even searched out plays by well-known authors whose failure to get them produced may be traced to the hysteria of the period.

Two such plays which date from 1952 are Albert Maltz's *The Morrison Case* and William Saroyan's *The Slaughter of the Innocents*. Maltz, a screenwriter who was one of the Hollywood Ten and went to prison for contempt of Congress, produced in Pete Morrison a hero not unlike the philosophy professor of his *Peace on Earth*. It is not CPUSA membership that costs Morrison his job, but the fact that he was curious enough about the Party to read their literature: "It don't make no difference I'm not a Communist. I think your job is to get rid of anybody who thinks different from you do. . . . I read a newspaper you don't like, I own some books you don't like—that's it! . . . I think my job was done the minute I was charged, before I walked in there."[44] Saroyan's play has a number of targets—among them drama critics whose qualifications consist of "a life-long history of cynicism, indifference, and irresponsibility"[45]—but it is primarily concerned with a legal system which is only an excuse for punishing individuality: "Do you think for a minute that you can live in your *own* world, in the fantasy world you have made out of your panic and fear? A world in which you are terrified even of a child. . . . Where do you think *you* are going to live in this world you have made?" (*The Slaughter of the Innocents*, II, i, 49)

More successful (and better plays) were the 1952 revivals of James Thurber and Elliot Nugent's *The Male Animal* (1940) and Lillian Hellman's *The Children's Hour* (1934). In the former, a mild-mannered English professor loses his peace of mind and, very probably, his teaching position when he proposes to read to one of his classes the last letter of Bartolomeo Vanzetti as an example of instinctual compositional style: "If I can't teach this letter today, tomorrow none of us will be able to teach anything except what Mr. Keller here and the legislature permit us to teach. . . . We're holding the last fortress of free thought, and if we surrender to prejudice and dictation, we're cowards."[46] The revival of Miss Hellman's play about two young teachers whose occupational and personal lives are destroyed by a never-proved lie, coming only six months after the appearance before HUAC she describes so well in *Scoundrel Time*,[47] had an immediate relevance that did not require analysis.

Wertheim also notes several other plays in which the subject is not political subversion, but deviance from an accepted standard of values. A key example is the case of Tom Lee, the presumed homosexual schoolboy in Robert Anderson's *Tea and Symphony* (1953): "I resent this judgment by prejudice. He's not like me, therefore, he is capable of all possible crimes. He's not one of us . . . a member of the tribe!"[48] Given that homosexuals were routinely banned from government service in the 1950s (see Chapter 7) on the basis of their supposed susceptibility to treason-causing blackmail, the political significance of Tom's situation is obvious. Just as obvious was Jerome Lawrence and Robert E. Lee's dramatization of the Scopes Monkey Trial, *Inherit the Wind* (1955). Bertram Cates (the Scopes character) was charged for teaching that a new theory of man's development, evolution, might be more accurate than the accepted biblical view. The real question, however, is the one asked by most of the plays of this chapter: Can a person be prosecuted for his or her ideas?

Another historical figure so prosecuted is Joe Hill, the Industrial Workers of the World (IWW) songwriter and the hero of Barrie Stavis's *The Man Who Never Died* (1958). The real-life Hill was executed for murder in Salt Lake City after a questionable trial in 1915. In Stavis's play, however, a copper tycoon makes it clear that Joe must die because the Labor Movement is a threat to American capitalism: "We are just becoming a great nation. Fifty years ago we were torn apart by the Civil War and now these men are determined to tear us apart in another war. I say it will not be. We stand on the threshold. The golden age of America. The nations of Europe need our steel, lumber, copper. What are they buying it for? It's for guns they're buying it. . . . Two years—three years—and all Europe will be in flames. Their death promotes our life. At the moment they are destroyed, we are ready to step in and take mastery of the world."[49]

Mike Herzog, the mathematician of Robert Ardrey's *Sing Me No Lullaby* (1954) is similarly treated. Plucked out of a Guadalcanal foxhole to work on the Manhattan Project, Mike has since lost his research position, his subsequent teaching job, home after home, and so many other things that the FBI's only present interest in him is whether he can lead them to any other potential subversives. They believe he has done so when he visits an old college friend who ran for Congress as a liberal in 1946: "'What, after all, is patriotism but the force that divides one people from another? . . . Whether we like it or not, we enter now a new world in which old forms of government are obsolete. It is up to the citizen to change that form of government or see it overthrown by forces beyond his control.' . . . There's some more. If you have means of proving that you were misquoted, I'd advise you to do it."[50]

The message is that to think is to be guilty, to have ever thought is to think, and to know someone who has ever thought is to be suspect. Few plays have ever dramatized that message so cogently as Arthur Miller's *The Crucible*.

The Crucible

"The ultimate crime of which McCarthyites and anti-McCarthyites were accusing one another was, make no mistake about it, that of heresy; the passions generated were, make again no mistake about it, passions appropriate not to an intellectual debate but to a heresy hunt, and we shall not understand them, ever, unless we bear that in mind."[51]

"The consequences of our thinking will be felt into the seventh generation. Hence, a wrong thought from us is more criminal than a wrong deed from others." (*Darkness at Noon*, III, 85) In *Darkness at Noon*, Gletkin accuses Rubashov by quoting from one of his own books, reminding us—even as does the Gospel of Matthew—that sin is measured in thoughts as well as deeds. The sinfulness of thought is particularly relevant in *The Crucible*, Arthur Miller's play about the Salem, Massachusetts, witch trials of 1692. Witchcraft is by its very nature a "thought" crime, in that the witch does not attack openly but rather sends a spirit forth to attack the victim. Coming as it did in 1953, when many Americans were confusing political and religious ideologies, it was inevitable that *The Crucible* would be seen as a comment on the Communist "witch-hunts" of the era. Miller himself admitted this inevitability in his June 21, 1956, appearance before the House in Un-American Activities Committee.[52]

The Salem witch-hunt differed from its European counterparts in its brevity, in that no confessed witch was executed, and in the unchallenged acceptance by the judges of "spectral" evidence: that is, the accused did not have to be present at the scene of the crime, except as a "spectral manifestation." This made dreams and hallucinations acceptable legal proof and rendered courtroom defense impossible.

Before common sense led to a recess of the trials, nineteen convicted witches, including some well-respected community citizens, were hung. One man (Giles Corey) was pressed to death for refusing to plead. When the trials resumed in September, spectral evidence was not admitted, and the result was no further convictions. Five years later, one of the judges and one of the "afflicted" girls whose accusations were the main evidence in court asked publicly to be forgiven by the families of the convicted, and in 1711 the Massachusetts legislature posthumously pardoned thirteen defendants and paid reparations to their families. The remainder were not to be officially exonerated until 1957,[53] four years after the premiere of *The Crucible*.

One of the ironies of the Salem tragedy and the Cold War is that both arose in times of relative prosperity following a period when the people's survival was very much in doubt. World War II (and the Depression preceding it) had ended for the United States, while the battle of the Puritan settlers with nature and the Indians was just beginning to yield results. In both cases, consequently, the extraordinary discipline and sense of purpose which had seen them through the crisis was weakening. Freed of the necessity for absolute unity, some people began to question aspects of public policy and demand new freedoms. Salem was a theocracy—a system of government incorporating the principles of a state church and presumably acting as the temporal arm of God. It is a system under which dissidence cannot exist, for to be in opposition to religious leadership is punishable by civil law, and disagreement with the government becomes heresy.

The strength of a messianic state is that it commands unity on all levels. Its weakness is that it assigns all evil to its opposition, and necessarily associates that opposition with the evil one, the Devil. Judge Danforth phrases it best in *The Crucible*: "You must understand, sir, that a person is either with this court or he must be counted against it, there is no road in between."[54]

The problem is that an individual may oppose a church or a government for reasons other than witchcraft or communism. John Proctor stays away from church because he finds the Reverend Mr. Parris to be materialistic, but this does not make him an atheist. Though a person might understandably hide his practice of witchcraft, it does not necessarily follow that *everything* hidden is witchcraft—as the prosecution of Martha Corey on the evidence that she refused to show her husband the books she read indicates. One may also feel guilty for sins of less than apocalyptic import. John Proctor's inability to remember the Seventh Commandment is not diabolically inspired revulsion to Scripture, but rather shame over his adultery with Abigail Williams.

The Reverend John Hale is a sincere scholar of witchcraft, but experts tend to define problems in terms of their expertise, relevant or not. In the service of the court, a bureaucrat like Ezekiel Cheever will find what he is told to find without troubling his conscience over its consequences.

Furthermore, though war against the Devil is holy, not all those who make accusations are. Some are to be pitied, like Ann Putnam, who, driven half mad by the infant deaths of seven of her eight children, alleviates her guilt by accusing Rebecca Nurse, who has had eleven healthy children. Some are to be condemned. Ann's husband, Thomas, sees the trials as a means of gaining the land of his convicted neighbors, and Abigail Williams's longing for John Proctor provides the motive for her condemnation of Elizabeth Proctor.

Two factors complicate the accusation and courtroom procedure: the presence of self-induced and mass hysteria, and the permitting of spectral evidence. In Act II, Scene 2, of *The Crucible*, we are shown an Abigail who has come to believe her own accusations. She is like a consummate actress who has made herself the role she plays, and who can extend her aura to her fellow performers and to the audience. Mary Warren, the Proctors' impressionable servant and one of the accusing girls, describes the sensation which overcomes her in court: "I feel a clamp around my neck and I cannot breathe air; and then—I hear a voice, a screamin' voice, and it were my voice—and all at once I remembered everything she done to me!" (*The Crucible*, II, 57)

Later, when Mary tries to confess to the judges that the accusers were pretending, Abigail and the girls turn the same hypnotic hysteria on her that they used on courtroom observers. In a chilling scene, the girls conjure up a diabolic force which their imaginations make so palpable that Mary is reduced to a screaming acquiescence to their accusations, leading to the arrest of John Proctor.

Spectral evidence was the claim by a witness or a victim—unverifiable even by others who were present—that the witch's spirit had engaged in acts of torture. The discomfort of the victim was the proof of the crime, and the clairvoyance of the witness identified the criminal. That there was no evidence defined the crime as witchcraft, a thought crime. "Witchcraft is *ipso facto*, on its face and by its nature, an invisible crime, is it not? Therefore, who may possibly be witness to it? The witch and the victim. None other. Now we cannot hope that the witch will accuse herself, granted? Therefore, we must rely upon her victims—and they do testify, the children certainly do testify." (*The Crucible*, III, 100) Thus, in cases of suspected witchcraft, punishment could legitimately follow an accusation of the contemplation of (conspiracy to commit) crime—a condition blurring the distinction between civil crime and religious sin.

As was pointed out earlier, Salem was unique among witchcraft trials in that no confessor was executed. Since defense was virtually impossible, after the first hangings only the strongest willed of the defendants maintained their innocence. The Reverend John Hale, initially an official of the court, loses faith in the justice of its decision and finds himself counseling those he believes innocent to confess, solely for the purpose of saving their lives.[55] In *Darkness at Noon*, Ivanoff, who knows Rubashov is not guilty, and Gletkin, his enemy, differ only in the *way* they expect to induce Rubashov to confess. As Lampell noted, confession was the only way off the blacklist. When the New York City Commission voted in 1955 not to allow Arthur Miller to make a film about teenage gangs and the urban problem, one of the commissioners said: "I'm not calling him a Communist. My objection is that he refuses to repent."[56]

John Proctor eventually confesses to a compact with the Devil in order to save his life, only to recant when faced with the confession's second requirement—the naming of others in the compact. Such a naming was necessary not only as an act of contrition, it was necessary also to prove that there was a compact at all. In crimes of thought, there is no evidence except the witnesses' testimony concerning the defendant's spirit, whatever its manifestation. Once we assume a conspiracy exists, then those who testify to bad character are seen as repentant, while those who testify to good character are seen as potential conspirators themselves.[57] For example, in *The Crucible* those Salem citizens who signed a petition affirming the good character of Martha Corey, Rebecca Nurse, and Elizabeth Proctor are "arrested for examination." (*The Crucible*, III, 93–94)

Before HUAC, Miller willingly discussed his own flirtations with the Left, but refused to name anyone he might have met under those circumstances.[58] In this respect, he differed from Elia Kazan, the director of Miller's *Death of a Salesman*. Kazan, who had originated the role of Agate Keller in *Waiting for Lefty* and who had directed *Deep Are the Roots*, volunteered the names of all his associates during his period of Communist Party membership in the 1930s when he appeared before HUAC in 1952. Kazan went on to make *On the Waterfront*, the 1954 Academy Award–winning film, whose hero informs to a congressional committee. Miller wrote *The Crucible*, whose hero dies because he will not inform to his judges. As a result of his hearing, Miller was cited for contempt of Congress, a judgment he successfully appealed two years later.

The final danger of convicting someone for conspiracy, witchcraft, or any other thought crime in which evidence of deed is lacking is that it sets a precedent. In *Darkness at Noon*, those who followed Rubashov were taught the standards and methodology of judgment to use against him. If we convict one on the basis of questionable evidence, we must perforce convict all, a principle evoked by Judge Danforth: "Do you know that near to four hundred are in jail from Marblehead to Lynn, and upon my signature? . . . And seventy-two condemned to hang by that signature? Do you know, Mr. Proctor, that the entire contention of the state in these trials is that the voice of Heaven is speaking through the children?" (*The Crucible*, III, 87–88)

The inability to separate the state from the voice of Heaven and the automatic consignment of those who disagree with it in any form or at any time to the Devil is the real crime of both *The Crucible* and the Cold War. Questioning, as Socrates knew, cannot rot either the moral or political foundation of a state. It can only reveal the rot. Four months before his HUAC hearing, Miller, in a message to a Dostoyevski fete, denounced both "Red and anti-Red curbs on art," sending copies to the Soviet Writers Union, the American Committee for Cultural Freedom, and the American Committee for Liberation from Bolshevism. In his committee testimony, he might still have been speaking to both sides: "Our law is based on acts, not thought. How do we know? Anybody in this room might have thoughts of various kinds that could be prosecuted if they were carried into action."[59]

Theatre of Fact

Officially, the McCarthy era came to an end on December 2, 1954, the day the U.S. Senate censored the junior senator from Wisconsin. Practically, it was to contaminate the longest war in U.S. history, and the faint glow from its fallout's half-life may still be perceived under the right conditions.

"A happy people has no history," the old proverb goes, because until something goes wrong, nobody bothers to investigate it. Since the Cold War, we have had a lot of history, much of it under theatrical conditions. For those cast in invisible roles in the past (anything other than adult, heterosexual WASPs), the history play has been an impetus to "come out" (into the light, out of the closet, etc.). The purpose of such plays is to validate group experience by presenting incidents from American history from the viewpoint of the history-suffering minority instead of the history-writing majority. Such plays include *In White America*, *Black Elk Speaks*, and *Coming Out*.

More demanding and often more effective is the docudrama or Theatre of Fact. Its power derives from the author's contention that all dialogue is taken directly from the spoken or written words of actual, historical characters. It is true that others select and arrange those words, and every lawyer knows the adaptability of statements taken out of context, but such arrangements have an undeniable cumulative power in the theatre.

In its most recent incarnation, Theatre of Fact is an invention of the remarkably efficient Germans. It began with Rolf Hochhuth's *The Deputy* (which in 1963 posed the question of Pope Pius XII's responsibility for the Jewish Holocaust), and was refined by Heinar Kipphardt (*In The Matter of J. Robert Oppenheimer*) and Peter Weiss's *The Investigation* (derived from transcripts of the Nuremberg Trials). The outstanding American examples from the Cold War era are Donald Freed's *Inquest* (1970)—about the arrest, trial, and execution of the accused atom bomb spies, Julius and Ethel Rosenburg—and Eric Bentley's *Are You Now or Have You Ever Been*, compiled from the House Un-American Activities Committee 1947–1958 investigations of show business. Bentley has been so circumspect as to refuse to allow productions of his work to adjust the context of any line for theatrical enhancement.[60] Not all original Theatre of Fact sources showed such integrity.

In the Matter of J. Robert Oppenheimer

Oppenheimer: We scientists have been on the brink of presumptuousness in these years. We have known sin.

Robb: Good, Doctor. We shall speak of those sins.

Oppenheimer: I guess we don't mean the same thing.

Robb: That is something we are going to find out, Doctor.[61]

In the Matter of J. Robert Oppenheimer is a documentary drama composed by Heinar Kipphardt solely from historical data—chiefly the records of the security clearance eligibility hearing initiated against Dr. Oppenheimer by the AEC (Atomic Energy Commission) and published in May, 1954. The play was first performed in Germany in 1964 and selects and condenses the Oppenheimer hearing events for dramatic purposes but does not alter the actual words of the participants.

Like other plays in this chapter, *In the Matter of J. Robert Oppenheimer* focuses on the trial of a previously highly respected member of the society for thought crimes against the structure of a state which views its mission as messianic as well as political. As director of the Los Alamos, New Mexico, laboratories, Oppenheimer was widely known as the Father of the atomic bomb. After the war, he served as chair of the AEC's General Advisory Committee and of the Institute for Advanced Studies at Princeton. Also, as in other plays from this chapter, Oppenheimer conducts a parallel self-examination to determine the true nature of the crime and his guilt in it.

As ever in a thought crime, the first difficulty is proving its existence. Eight years after Hiroshima, the Russians produced a hydrogen bomb whose deliverability was superior to our own. Given the superiority of our political system and our preferred place in the moral configuration of the universe, how could this happen? Senator Joseph McCarthy thought he knew the answer: "And, I ask you, who is to blame? Were they loyal Americans or were they traitors, those who deliberately misled our government, who got themselves celebrated as atomic heroes, and whose crimes must at last be investigated." (*In the Matter of J. Robert Oppenheimer*, I, i, 10)

Having established the existence of a crime and having painted a psychologically satisfying portrait of the criminal, the prosecution must set out to prove that Dr. Oppenheimer fits the frame, that is, that he had the motive, the opportunity, and the ability to commit the crime. There are twenty-four allegations against Dr. Oppenheimer in the hearing's letter of charges. One accuses him of slowing the development of the hydrogen bomb. That is the crime. The other twenty-three deal with his associations with Communists or Communist front organizations, all of which go back at least twelve years. These are the motive.

It is important to remember that Dr. Oppenheimer's hearing has no more real trial legality than the spectral evidence in Salem or Gletkin's interrogations in *Darkness at Noon*. The twenty-three charges of Communist associations were investigated in each of Oppenheimer's previous security clearance checks in 1943, 1947, and 1950 and found irrelevant.[62] Oppenheimer's letters, private records, and public documents were confiscated by the FBI for use by the prosecution, but the defendant was denied access to them, even as he was not allowed to see the rest of the FBI's file on him. Depositions by government witnesses (frequently including hearsay) were used against Oppenheimer, but his lawyers were not allowed to call those witnesses into court for cross-examination. Although the AEC's attorneys were given security clearance, Oppenheimer's lawyers were forced to leave the hearing chambers whenever classified material was being discussed. Most important, there is no evidence connecting Oppenheimer to acts of treason against the United States.

"How clumsy and unscientific is our procedure when, over and above the facts, we do not concern ourselves also with the thoughts, the feelings, the motives which underlie those facts, and make them the subject of our inquiries." (*In the Matter of J. Robert Oppenheimer*, I, i, 21) But if the primary action of the hearing is to examine Dr. Oppenheimer's thoughts, its primary purpose is to control the thoughts of others. Since his Los Alamos days, Oppenheimer's involvement with atomic energy has been largely advisory. His clearance will expire automatically in ninety days, and the Atomic Energy Commission can choose not to renew it without comment.[63] Even if he is denied clearance, the act will be purely symbolic. As Nobel laureate Hans Bethe puts it: "Are the atomic secrets to vanish out of his head if his clearance is withdrawn?" However, as an expendable symbolic sacrifice, Oppenheimer's contribution to unity parallels Rubashov's confession. Counterespionage officer Major Radzi[64] believes that scientists have to learn to become team players, to do their work without question and turn the results over to the politicians and the military who will decide what is to be done with it: "If we want to defend our freedom successfully, we must be prepared to forego some of our personal liberty." (*In the Matter of J. Robert Oppenheimer*, I, vi, 58)

All segments of society must be taught willing submission to the greater needs of the state. In defining the hearing's purpose, Thomas A. Morgan, chairman of the Sperry Gyroscope company and member of the hearing board, sees no contradiction between this submission and the concept of personal liberty: "We should make it clear to the scientists that we don't dictate such and such opinions to them, and that we don't intend to boot them out because they hold this or that opinion. But we must insist on a sharp dividing line between their subjective views and their objective work, because modern nuclear policy is possible only on that basis." (*In the Matter of J. Robert Oppenheimer*, I, v, 43)

If the nation's best-known nuclear physicist can be made to accept this schizophrenia of principle and action, or to pay the consequences of not accepting it, others can certainly be induced into a scientific lockstep.

The crime and the real purpose of the hearing established, the AEC counsels, Roger Robb and C. A. Rolander, set out to prove that Oppenheimer could have produced the hydrogen bomb had he so wished. It is pointed out that he shared with Edward Teller an early patent for a thermonuclear device. He is credited with producing the atomic bomb in an extremely short time, picking its target, and determining the height at which it should be exploded for maximum effect. When Oppenheimer protests that he merely supplied the technical data and did not himself decide to drop the bomb, a decision about which he had definite qualms, Robb reminds him of the Franck Report—a memorandum in which certain physicists advised *demonstrating* the bomb's potential to Japan rather than dropping it on that country.

"The reason I am digging up this old Hiroshima business is this: I want to find out why, at that time, you devoted yourself with such single-mindedness to your tasks, with a hundred percent loyalty, I would say—and why, later, in the matter of the hydrogen bomb, you adopted an entirely different attitude." (*In the Matter of J. Robert Oppenheimer*, I, i, 18) The implication, of course, is that the atomic bomb was originally produced to offset its possible use by a Fascist enemy. The use of the hydrogen bomb, on the other hand, was expected to be against Communist Russia.

Oppenheimer's connections with leftist organizations in the thirties were at the anti-Depression, anti-Fascist variety already previously discussed. They were so common among the intellectuals of the period that Oppenheimer's philosophical interest and monetary support seems moderate.[65] His wife, former fiancée, brother, and sister-in-law, as well as many of his friends and students, were all Communist Party members at one time or another. An earlier husband of his wife died in the Spanish Civil War. Oppenheimer's own "fellow-traveller" tendencies were cooled by the Purge Trials and ended by the 1939 nonaggression pact with Germany—although he was relieved to have Russia as a wartime ally. Nevertheless, Oppenheimer is suspected because he has refused to condemn his former Communist friends. It is not sufficient to hold today's opinions, one must always have held them. "Control of the past depends above all on the training of memory. And if [to do so] it is necessary to rearrange one's memories or to tamper with written records, then it is necessary to forget that one has done so."[66] George Orwell describes the process in *1984*, explaining the "memory hole" and the disappearance of inconvenient past truths down it.

The AEC uses another of these past truths to indicate that even during the anti-Fascist war, Oppenheimer was a security risk. In the Christmas season of 1942, Haakon Chevalier, a friend of Oppenheimer's, told him of an English engineer named Eltenton who claimed the ability to transmit scientific information to the Russians. The incident was forgotten for six months until an intelligence officer's worries about security at the Berkeley (California) laboratory prompted Oppenheimer to bring it up. Instead of telling the whole truth, however, he fictionalized certain parts of the story to protect Chevalier, who was known to have strong left-wing views, and himself. Although no secrets were passed, the surfacing of the truth proved embarrassing for Oppenheimer. In the play the prosecutors use the incident to cast doubt on Oppenheimer's judgment and veracity at best, and, at worst, to infer that he may have sacrificed other Communist agents to save a more important one: himself.

The evidence that Oppenheimer opposed the hydrogen bomb is equally inferential. His objections at specific times to specific aspects of the thermonuclear program are given ideological rather than technical motivations. For example, his objection to a particular thermonuclear model in 1949 as unworkable is presented as his unchanging attitude, while his enthusiasm over new ideas two years later is ignored. He disputes the value of the bomb on military grounds because Russia has only two targets big enough to require such a bomb, while the United States has more than fifty. Politically, he doesn't want the bomb tested before the 1952 elections because it will prevent the new president from making his own decisions concerning test bans. As for his security concerns, many scientists at Los Alamos (including his friend Hans Bethe) complained that Oppenheimer was "too pro-government."[67]

Against Oppenheimer is weighed the opinion of air force scientist David Tressel Griggs, who sees a conspiracy on the part of several nuclear physicists against the Strategic Air Command's defense policy of massive retaliation and in favor of strengthening of air defenses. More impressive because of his reputation as Father of the H-bomb is Edward Teller. It is Teller who argues most convincingly that if Oppenheimer had shown enthusiasm for thermonuclear development, his personality, reputation, and organizational skills would have convinced the cream of the nuclear physicists to apply themselves to the project despite the revulsion inspired in them by Hiroshima. The result would have been the earlier achievement of the ideas which eventually made the H-bomb possible. Inherent in Teller's argument, moreover, is the whole crux of the government's case and the nation's mood of 1954: that despite the fact that both superpowers can now destroy the world many times over, all of America's foreign and domestic problems would not exist if we were to remain militarily ahead of the Communists, and that anyone who disagrees with this truth for whatever reasons is in "the objective sense" a traitor to national security.

When asked if the United States should make some effort toward a nuclear arms agreement with Soviet Russia, Oppenheimer replies: "If the Devil himself were on the other side, one would have to reach an understanding with the Devil." (*In the Matter of J. Robert Oppenheimer*, II, ii, 82) In true messianic fashion, it is the marks of the Devil that Roger Robb traces back to Oppenheimer's alleged sin of unconscious wrong thinking: "This is a form of treason which is not known in our code of law; it is ideological treason which has its origins in the deepest strata of the personality and renders a man's actions dishonest, against his own will." (*In the Matter of J. Robert Oppenheimer*, II, iii, 118)

The hearing finds against Oppenheimer, of course. Like Rubashov and Proctor, he is the victim of an age too frightened to see events in other than black or white reasoning, too self-absorbed to see the means becoming the end, too guilty to see that the Devil's face becomes our own when we "quail to bring men out of ignorance." (*The Crucible*, III, 120) But whatever Oppenheimer's shortcomings may be, he is not unaware of the role he played in placing the world in its vulnerable position. Nor has he lost the quality that made him so useful to physics in the past—his ability to recognize truths before most other men. In his own mind, Oppenheimer owed a debt to mankind for what he had done, not to his country for what he had not done: "We have spent years of our lives in developing ever sweeter means of destruction, we have been doing the work of the military, and I feel it in my very bones that this is wrong. I shall request the Atomic Energy Commission to review the decision of the majority of this Board; but, no matter what the result of that review may be, I will never work on war projects again. We have been doing the work of the Devil, and now we must return to our real tasks." (*In the Matter of J. Robert Oppenheimer*, II, 126–27)

For the last years of his life, Oppenheimer returned to the Princeton Institute of Advanced Studies. Like the executed witches and some of Stalin's Purge victims, he was eventually "rehabilitated," and was awarded the AEC's Encrico Fermi prize at a 1963 ceremony which Edward Teller attended. That was the year of the above-ground nuclear test-ban treaty. The Cold War seemed finally to be over, and our revulsion toward it to parallel that felt at the end of the Salem witch trials.[68]

But no one has yet released the deadly scorpions from their bottle. Nor has America retired from its preoccupation with the battle against the alien ideology, the next round of which was to be devastating, and the last round of which may not have been fought. We have gone for a ride on the tiger, but how long can we stay on its back?

Notes

1. Quoted by Arthur M. Schlesinger, Jr., in *The Cycles of American History* (Boston: Houghton Mifflin, 1986), 181.

2. Quoted by Ralph B. Levering, in *The Cold War, 1945–1972* (Arlington Heights, Ill.: Harlan Davidson, 1982), 15.

3. Paul Y. Hammond, *Cold War and Détente* (New York: Harcourt Brace Jovanovich, 1975), 9.

4. Schlesinger, *Cycles of American History*, 209–10.

5. Ernest R. May, *"Lessons" of History* (New York: Oxford University Press, 1973), 32.

6. Gaddis Smith, *Dean Acheson* (New York: Cooper Square Publishers, 1972), 417.

7. Quoted by Hugh Higgins, in *The Cold War* (New York: Barnes and Noble, 1974), 37.

8. Louis J. Halle, *The Cold War as History* (New York: Harper & Row, 1967), 78–80.

9. Harry S Truman, "The Truman Doctrine," in *America in the Cold War*, ed. Walter LeFeber (New York: John Wiley & Sons, 1969), 53.

10. Marvin F. Herz, *How the Cold War Is Taught* (Washington, D.C.: Georgetown University Press, 1978), 27.

11. Levering, *Cold War, 1945–1972*, 34–35.

12. May, *"Lessons" of History*, 33.

13. Halle, *Cold War as History*, 46–47.

14. Quoted by Michael Parenti, in *The Anti-Communist Impulse* (New York: Random House, 1969), 63.

15. Halle, *Cold War as History*, 285.

16. *Chapter of the United Nations and Statute of the International Court of Justice* (Washington, D.C.: U.S. Department of State, 1945), Publication 2368, p. 1.

17. Claire Boothe Luce, "The Mystery of our China Policy," in *Plain Talk*, ed. Issac Don Levine (New Rochelle, N.Y.: Arlington House, 1976), 151–53.

18. Quoted by Adam B. Ulam, in *A History of Soviet Russia* (New York: Praeger Publishers, 1976), 123.

19. Dennis H. Wrong, "McCarthyism as Totalitarianism", in *The Meaning of McCarthyism*, ed. Earl Latham (Boston: D. C. Heath, 1965), 22.

20. Ulam, *History of Soviet Russia*, 130–31.

21. Lilliam Hellman, *The Searching Wind* (New York: Viking Press, 1944), II, iii, 96.

22. Maxwell Anderson, *Barefoot in Athens* (New York: William Sloane, 1951), xii.

23. Quoted by Eric Bentley, in *Thirty Years of Treason* (New York: Viking Press, 1971), 498.

24. Sidney Kingsley, *Darkness at Noon* (New York: Samuel French, 1951), I, 9. Subsequent references to this play will be made in the text.

25. Ulam, *History of Soviet Russia*, 130.

26. Reading General Krivitsky's *I Was Stalin's Agent* years after writing *Darkness at Noon*, Arthur Koestler was surprised to discover a real-life parallel to the Ivanoff-Rubashov interrogation in the questioning of Mrachkovsky, a legendary hero of the postrevolutionary civil war, by his ex-subordinate, Sloutski. Mrachkovsky was one of only two original Bolsheviks charged who had refused to confess prior to the first Purge Trial in 1935: "Days and nights of argument . . . brought Mrachkovsky to the realization that nobody else but Stalin could guide the Bolshevik Party. . . . One had to remain within the Party even unto death, or dishonour, or death with dishonour, if it became necessary for the sake of consolidating the Soviet power." Arthur Koestler, "Postscript to the Danube Edition," *Darkness at Noon* (London: Hutchinson of London, 1973), 267.

27. Ironically, the originator of the role of Luba was Kim Hunter, who was later coerced into saving her career by supporting a political position with which she disagreed. When CBS-TV dramatized *Fear on Trial* in 1975, Miss Hunter was played by Lois Nettleton, who played the nameless secretary recording Rubashov's confession in the initial production of *Darkness at Noon*.

28. Tom Stoppard uses the quote in *Travesties*, a play featuring Lenin, James Joyce, and Tristan Tzara in 1916 Zurich. Tom Stoppard, *Travesties* (New York: Grove Press, 1975), I, 45.

29. A reporter told McCarthy about a July 1946 letter written by then–Secretary of State James Byrnes, discussing 3,000 persons who had been temporarily transferred to the State Department from various wartime agencies. Of the 3,000, a recommendation had been made against permanently employing 284, for a number of reasons, and 79 of these had already been dismissed. Subtract 79 from 284 and McCarthy had his "205 Communists." Robert Strauss Feuerlicht, *Joseph McCarthy and McCarthyism* (New York: McGraw-Hill, 1972), 54–55.

30. Levering, *Cold War, 1945–1972*, 62–63.

31. Levering, *Cold War, 1945–1972*, 61–62.

32. Elmer Davis, "Through the Perilous Night," in *By Elmer Davis*, ed. Robert Lloyd Davis (Indianapolis: Bobbs, Merrill, 1964), 76–77.

33. Bentley, *Thirty Years of Treason*, 727–28.

34. Feuerlicht, *Joseph McCarthy and McCarthyism*, 81–82.

35. Dean Acheson, "The Triumph of the Communists in China Was Beyond the Control of the United States" (August 1949), in *America in the Cold War*, ed. Walter LeFeber (New York: John Wiley & Sons, 1969), 69–73.

36. Quoted in Bentley, *Thirty Years of Treason*, xix–xx.

37. Davis, *By Elmer Davis*, 74–76.

38. Ring Lardner, quoted in Bentley, *Thirty Years of Treason*, 194.

39. Quoted by John Henry Faulk, in *Fear on Trial* (New York: Grosset & Dunlap, 1976), 189–90.

40. Quoted by Bentley, *Thirty Years of Treason*, 704.

41. Faulk, *Fear on Trial*, 66.

42. Faulk, *Fear on Trial*, 161–74.

43. Quoted in Bentley, *Thirty Years of Treason*, 706.

44. Albert Wertheim, "The McCarthy Era and the American Theatre," in *Theatre Journal*, 34, no. 2 (May 1982): 216.

45. William Saroyan, *The Slaughter of the Innocents*, in *Theatre Arts*, 36, no.2 (November 1952): 47. Subsequent references to this play will be made in the text.

46. James Thurber and Elliot Nugent, *The Male Animal* (New York: Samuel French, 1941), III, 130.

47. Lilliam Hellman, *Scoundrel Time* (Boston: Little, Brown, 1976), 94–111.

48. Robert Anderson, *Tea and Sympathy* (New York: Random House, 1953), III, 164.

49. Barrie Stavis, *The Man Who Never Died* (New York: Dramatists Play Service, 1958), I, ii, 155.

50. Robert Ardrey, *Sing Me No Lullaby* (New York: Dramatists Play Service, 1955), II, 41.

51. Willmoore Kendall, "McCarthyism: The *Pons Asinorum* of American Conservatism", in *The Meaning of McCarthyism*, ed. Earl Latham (Boston: D. C. Heath, 1965), 45.

52. Miller also claimed to have begun thinking about the play in 1938. Bentley, *Thirty Years of Treason*, 818.

53. Chadwick Hansen, *Witchcraft at Salem* (New York: George Braziller, 1969), 207–219.

54. Arthur Miller, *The Crucible* (New York: Penguin Books, 1976), III, 94. Subsequent references to this play will be included in the text.

55. In 1697 the historical Reverend John Hale wrote *A Modest Inquiry into the Nature of Witchcraft*: "Nineteen were executed, and all denied the crime to the death; and some of them were knowing persons, and had before this been accounted blameless livers. . . . It is not to be imagined but that, if all had been guilty, some would have had so much tenderness as to seek mercy for their souls." Quoted by Charles W. Upham, in *Salem Witchcraft*, Vol. 2 (New York: Frederick Ungar Publishing Co., 1959), 476.

56. Quoted in Bentley, *Thirty Years of Treason*, 790.

57. Danforth's speech reminds one of Bernard Baruch's comment during the eighty-four-year-old statesman's 1955 HUAC appearance: "It isn't a case of giving associations. It's a case of giving comfort to the Communists. Anyone who has nothing to fear can speak freely. They'll get a fair hearing." Quoted in Bentley, *Thirty Years of Treason*, 684.

58. Speaking before HUAC in 1956, Miller's attitude paralleled that of Proctor: "I am not protecting the Communists or the Communist Party. I am trying to, and I will, protect my sense of myself. I could not use the name of another person and bring trouble on him. . . . I take the responsibility for everything I have ever done, but I cannot take responsibility for another human being." Quoted in Bentley, *Thirty Years of Treason*, 820.

59. Quoted in Bentley, *Thirty Years of Treason*, 808.

60. Eric Bentley, "Writing for Political Theatre," in *Political Theatre Today*, ed. Jane House (New York: Institute on Western Europe, Columbia University, and Center for Advanced Study in Theatre Arts, City University of New York, 1985), 7–8.

61. Heinar Kipphardt, *In the Matter of J. Robert Oppenheimer* (New York: Hill and Wang, 1968), I, i, 17. Subsequent references to this play will be included in the text. Oppenheimer had discussed the physicists' "sin" in creating the atomic bomb as early as 1948. Peter Goodchild, *J. Robert Oppenheimer: Shatterer of Worlds* (Boston: Houghton Mifflin, 1981), 174.

62. Chairman Lewis Strauss, who knew Oppenheimer's file, was responsible for changing the AEC's security criteria so that Oppenheimer could *not* meet its requirements again. Strauss also requested FBI bugging of Oppenheimer's home beginning January 1, 1954, and passed information from Oppenheimer's discussions with his lawyers on to the AEC attorneys. Barton J. Bernstein, "The Oppenheimer Conspiracy," in *Discover* (March 1985): 22,27.

63. The AEC had to race through its review of Oppenheimer's appeal in order to issue its decision on June 29, 1954, the day before his current clearance's expiration date. Goodchild, *J. Robert Oppenheimer*, 265.

64. The officer testifying was actually Colonel Boris Pash, perhaps too Russian-sounding a name for dramatic purposes.

65. Oppenheimer told *Time* in 1948: "I became a real left-winger, joined the teachers' union, had lots of Communist friends. . . . The Thomas [HUAC] Committee doesn't like this, but I'm not ashamed of it. I'm more ashamed of the lateness. Most of what I believed then, now seems complete nonsense, but it was an essential part of becoming a whole man. If it hadn't been for this late but indispensable education, I couldn't have done the job at Los Alamos at all." Quoted in Goodchild, *J. Robert Oppenheimer*, 174.

66. Quoted by Davis, *By Elmer Davis*, 104.

67. Bethe's testimony was attacked because Klaus Fuchs had served in his division. In fact, Ed Condon, the project associate director, resigned in 1943 because Oppenheimer refused to protest Grove's limiting of contract between the various laboratories in the project. Goodchild, *J. Robert Oppenheimer*, 85.

68. Dr. Bentley (1795), quoted in Upham, *Salem Witchcraft*, 469–70.

4

Vietnam—Theatre as a Mirror to National Institutions

If you people had known even a little bit about my nation, you could have solved the Vietnamese problem in 1945. Just a little history. Just a little culture.[1]

        —Vo Van Kim, University of Hue Vietnamese historian (1968)

Any dispassionate summation of our relationship with Vietnam and the Southeast Asian landmass of which it is a part must conclude that we knew nothing of the history, people, and culture of the area, and, insofar as it did not affect our sense of ourselves as a nation and a people, we did not care.

On April 30, 1970, President Richard M. Nixon announced to the nation that Vietnam-stationed American troops, supported by air power, had invaded Cambodia for the purpose of eradicating North Vietnamese command posts there. In that year, the twenty-seventh of our involvement in Indochina, only one American university (Yale) offered the Cambodian language—to a total of two students. There was no tenured Vietnam specialist on any faculty in the United States. Only six universities offered courses in the Vietnamese language (thirty students).[2] In 1967, when William Lederer visited the American psychological warfare unit in Saigon, he found that there was no American attached to the unit who spoke or read Vietnamese. He concluded that the only function of the Saigon psychological warfare unit was to convince other Americans that the war was going well in Vietnam.[3]

"When the enemy is away from home for a long time and produces no victories and families learn of their dead, then the enemy population at home becomes dissatisfied and considers it a mandate from Heaven that the armies be recalled," declared Marshal Tran Hung Dao, a Vietnamese general in A.D. 1280.[4] Vietnam has been conquered often, but never permanently. The Chinese stayed for over eleven hundred years before they were driven out in A.D. 939. The Mongolians (defeated by Tran Hung Dao), the Ming Chinese (1400), and the Imperial Chinese, late in the eighteenth century, all had their historical moments of domination. The last were defeated by a surprise attack during the Tet New Year celebrations of 1789.

French penetration of Vietnam began with missionaries and traders in the eighteenth century. By 1862 France controlled much of South Vietnam (Cohin China) and Cambodia. Successful wars with China ended with the conquest of Central (Annam) and North (Tonkin) Vietnam (1885) and Laos (1893). Although the country's titular leader was the emperor in Hue, real power in Indochina was in the hands of the French bureaucracy and military.[5]

Or was it? Under the Chinese, the Vietnamese had retained their identity as a people far longer than the fifty unopposed years of French rule. The real power of Vietnam flowed upward from the village culture which had produced 95 percent of its people. In the villages and the land surrounding them are the spirits of the ancestors.[6] Such people felt no kinship with the Cambodians and Laotians, and their sense of nationhood owed nothing to the Annam emperors whose capitulation to the French symbolized the loss of the "mandate of Heaven." Even among the Vietnamese, distinct psychological differences existed between the community-oriented, tightly disciplined Northerners and the more individualistic Southerners which did not bode well for any outside power supporting the latter in a civil war. That almost every civil and military leader the United States supported in Buddhist South Vietnam was northern-born and Catholic did not help either.[7]

From the autumn of 1940 to its defeat in August 1945, Japan occupied Indochina. Except for the confiscation of much of the rice crop, the Japanese did not interfere in the governing of the area until March 1945, when they replaced the French protectorate with a puppet Vietnamese government under Emperor Bao Dai. At the war's end, this government fell to the National Liberation Committee formed by the Vietminh and led by Ho Chi Minh.[8]

Ho was by no means unknown at the end of World War II. Born in Annam in 1890, he left his homeland in his early twenties as a ship's laborer and spent most of the next thirty years abroad. He first became famous under the name Nguyen Ai Quoc when, encouraged by Woodrow Wilson's call for the "self-determination of nations," he tried to discuss freedom for his countrymen at the 1919 Versailles Conference. Rebuffed, Ho became a founding member of the French Communist Party in 1920, while retaining his affection for American anticolonialist principles. In December 1941, he called for cooperation with Washington in its war with Japan. In 1944, in recognition for his saving of a downed American pilot, Ho was made a member of the OSS (Office of Strategic Services), the predecessor of today's CIA.[9] In 1945 the OSS supplied five thousand guns to the Vietnamese rebels, who (until his death on April 12) had a strong supporter in Franklin Roosevelt.

The foreign policy priority of Harry S Truman, on the other hand, was the stabilization of Western Europe: "[The United States has] no interest [in] championing schemes of international trusteeship that would weaken and alienate the European states whose help we need to balance Soviet power in Europe."[10]

At the Potsdam Conference in July 1945, it was decided that Great Britain would accept the Japanese surrender below the sixteenth parallel and China above it. However, Ho Chi Minh was not waiting for the outcome of international conferences. Between August 19 and August 25, the Vietminh gained control of Hanoi, Hue, and Saigon, and secured the abdication of the Emperor Bao Dai. On September 2 in Hanoi, Ho Chi Minh read the Declaration of Independence of the Democratic Republic of Viet-Nam (the DRV).

All men are created equal. . . . They are endowed by their Creator with certain inalienable rights. Among these are life, liberty, and the pursuit of happiness. . . .

A people which has obstinately opposed French domination for more than eighty years, a people who during these last years ranged themselves definitely on the side of the Allies to fight against fascism, this people has the right to be free. This people must be independent.[11]

September 2 was also the day of unconditional Japanese surrender. In the North, the Chinese looted unashamedly, but allowed Ho Chi Minh to administer the government. The British, on the other hand, were primarily concerned with their own impending colonial difficulties in India and Malaya. To evict the Vietminh from Saigon in September, they rearmed not only the French, but also (over bitter protests by General Douglas MacArthur) Japanese prisoners of war.[12]

American actions spoke louder than MacArthur's words. To the returning French we gave $160 million worth of U.S. uniforms, tanks, vehicles, and airplanes. The French used the equipment—American markings still clearly visible—to make war against the Vietminh. Between October 1945 and February 1946, Ho Chi Minh sent eight communications to President Truman and Secretary of State James Byrnes requesting a path to independence similar to that being accorded by the U.S. to the Philippines. They were never answered. In March 1946, with North Vietnam wracked by famine because of Chinese looting, Ho agreed to a French military presence in the North for five years, at the end of which Vietnam (like Algeria) would become a "Free State within the French Union."[13] Nevertheless, by the end of 1946, France and the DRV were at war.

The United States was not insensitive to the injustices of colonialism, but the Truman administration believed that a stable Asia required an economically powerful Japan and that a stable Europe required a militarily powerful France. To achieve the former, Japan would require a non-Communist Southeast Asia as a trading partner.[14] Meanwhile, if France was to play a leading role in the new European Defense Community, it must avoid being stalemated in Indochina.[15] With these goals in mind (and not a little influenced by the sudden involvement of the Chinese in Korea), America made France a military loan of $133 million late in 1950. By the time of the French defeat in 1954, America had given France $2.6 billion and was carrying 80 percent of its Vietnam military budget.[16]

At the time of Dienbienphu, the mountain fortress siege which ultimately decided the war, the United States considered—and rejected—open intervention in the war. Admiral Arthur Radford, chairman of the Joint Chiefs of Staff, discussed with the French the advisability of a mass air attack, possibly using tactical missiles. Air force General Nathan Twining approved, but attached conditions the French were unlikely to agree with. Army General Matthew Ridgeway disapproved, believing bombing in such mountainous terrain would still require ground troops (700,000 of them for ten years).[17] Secretary of State John Foster Dulles wanted a joint intervention involving the British, and Vice President Richard Nixon wanted to go it alone, if necessary. In the end it was President Eisenhower, relying on Ridgeway's estimate and cognizant of a Congress that wanted no more Koreas, who made the decision. Dienbienphu fell on May 7, 1954.[18]

The French government fell with it. The new premier, Pierre Mendes-France, negotiated a settlement with the Vietminh on July 20, and the French military began their evacuation on October 9, 1954 (and were soon to be bogged down in yet another colonial quagmire, Algeria).

Vietnam's non-Communists under the Emperor Bao Dai received extremely generous terms at the 1954 Geneva Conference—due, ironically, to pressure put upon the Vietminh by both Peking and Moscow. The country was temporarily divided at the seventeenth parallel, with the South retrieving much of the territory that Hanoi controlled militarily, until a national plebiscite scheduled for July 1956 determined how the country would be ruled.[19] Realizing that "possibly 80 percent of the population would have voted for the Communist Ho Chi Minh as their leader rather than Chief of State, Bao Dai,"[20] the United States encouraged the denunciation of this election by the South. China took no action in protest, and, in this year of Polish and Hungarian rebellions, Russia's attention was elsewhere.

Vietnam: Early Stages

In *Vietnam War Literature*, John Newman's excellent annotated bibliography, he lists no play written about Vietnam before 1966.[21] While this is an oversight, the relative lack of drama set in Vietnam or even protesting against our involvement there is understandable. As this chapter's opening pages point out, we knew nothing of the language or culture of Southeast Asia. For the Vietnamese, unlike the European or Russian, we lacked even that most basic of dramatic requirements—a recognizable cultural stereotype. When John Wayne's *The Green Berets* (1967) attempted to present our South Vietnamese allies as "a smart-looking, dedicated, efficient force, they [were] made to sound like Tonto."[22] For the rest we had only Fu Manchu, Charlie Chan, Anna May Wong, and a host of inscrutable Orientals whom we could not tell apart.

Politically, we were no better off. During the period when we were forging the chain that bound us to Vietnam, the Communist monolith theory dominated. To suggest that there were Communist parties with purely national aims would have been greeted with the same disbelief accorded the Greek philosophers who first identified seemingly solid matter as composed of atoms. The "other" interpretation of world history is implied in Lyndon Johnson's determination not to "lose" Indochina as Truman "lost" China, and only blood would obscure the way we read it.

When the war did come home, and opposition to it reached dramatic intensity, that drama for the most part was not played out in auditoriums. Even as America's first images of Vietnam appeared on television, our protests against it were frequently a form of public theatre, staged to draw the widest and most instantaneous media coverage possible. "Instant gratification" was less a personality trait of Dr. Spock's permissively raised Baby-Boomers than a technological achievement of network television. The six o'clock news became the staging area of both the theatre of war and the theatre of antiwar.

As Tom Stoppard warned us earlier, if "you want to do something about [injustice] *now, at once*, you can hardly do worse than write a play."[23] However, it is the plays (art) which change the society that produces the injustice. Art is a metaphor for the human condition. By showing human action in a social context from which the viewer can be momentarily detached, a play can reaffirm or inspire values which govern the hegemony of a society.

With that in mind and in the absence of plays, we turn to the films of the period. A "true" anti-Communist film saw the menace as growing from within, as superficially attractive, and as taking advantage of our democratic freedoms in order to subvert us. This type ranged from the obvious, such as *I Was a Communist for the FBI* (soon to have a spin-off radio series and later to resurface as television's *I Led Three Lives*) to the classic *Invasion of the Body Snatchers*. The latter was pure Communist paranoia, with an entire society gradually being absorbed by emotionless, will-less aliens who looked like us, but weren't us. Since these aliens were inhuman as well as un-American, any weapon used against them was moral—be it the pitchforks of the original version or the mass incineration of the 1978 remake which coincided with the reemerging of the "evil empire" concept.

The anti-appeasement "myth of Hitler" maintained its hold on popular culture during the time of our Vietnam involvement, with every serious major war film from *The Longest Day* to *Patton* set in World War II Europe. Pre-Vietnam films that were set in Southeast Asia are primarily notable for the way in which they altered their original sources to serve the anti-Communist impulse.

Any future study of Hollywood's treatment of Vietnam will owe much to Albert Auster and Leonard Quart's *How the War Was Remembered*. Two of the earliest subjects on which they focus are the film versions of Graham Greene's *The Quiet American* (1958) and Eugene Burdick and William Lederer's *The Ugly American* (1963). Greene's novel, published three years earlier, is a cautionary tale about the destructive potential of innocence. In the novel, a solemn, ingenuous CIA agent arrives in French Indochina for the purpose of stimulating a democratic third force which will rule in lieu of the French or the Communists. The chaos he creates prompts an English correspondent, spiritually exhausted by years of failure to penetrate the Vietnamese psyche, to inform on him, bringing about his death.

The film accepts as correct the American ideology. Pyle, the CIA agent, is "a young man with an idea who terrifies the Communists." Now, the correspondent betrays Pyle partly because the Communists convince him that Pyle supports terrorism, but mostly because his Vietnamese mistress is attracted to Pyle. (She, incidentally, is played by a white actress—acceptance of American ideas apparently serving as a racial purifier.) Pyle, as a student, has already met the logical leader of this third force, and the films ends with a dedication to "the people of the Republic of Vietnam . . . and its president, Ngo Dinh Diem."[24]

The Ugly American has lost even more of its plot, probably due to its need to focus more on Marlon Brando as its star, but retains a healthier ambivalence. Brando, the new ambassador to a fictional Southeast Asian country, and the local neutralist leader were friends as OSS agents during World War II. When his friend's faction prefers to stay neutral and ignore the aid the United States can offer, the ambassador supports the building of a modern road to the border of the country's northern enemy—a road for trade purposes, but with military potential. Revolution and war follow. Communists assassinate the neutralist, and the ambassador calls for the intervention of the Seventh Fleet.

The film accurately depicts an America that wants to have it both ways. As a people, we sincerely support the Third World desire for independence, while seeing that desire as futile so long as the threat of communism exists. *The Ugly American* ends with an ambiguous image. As the ambassador makes an impassioned television plea for understanding of the individuality of developing nations, a viewer at home, contentedly mumbling on a pork chop, tunes him out. Has he switched off the message of Third World independence, or that of America's responsibility to protect it from communism? In 1963 no one knew.

China Gate

The essence of the 1950s anti-Communist film was the threat from our own dark side. Samuel Fuller's *China Gate*,[25] despite its "B-picture" production values and a story line that cracks under the weight of its ideology, is both typical and unique as an anti-Communist drama: typical because its conflict is internal, and unique because that conflict is set for the first time in Vietnam. Communism figures in several Fuller films of the fifties. According to Nicholas Garnham, Fuller uses communism "as the Other against which the characters and America define themselves. If Communism wasn't there, it would be necessary for America to invent it."[26] *China Gate*, however, is first of all a journalistic "scoop": "In

1957, before America had committed herself to Vietnam and before most Americans even knew that America was aiding the French . . . before the world knew of Ho Chi Minh, Fuller had huge posters of him in the film and a synopsized newsreel biography of him in the preface. . . . "The year 1954, the day Thursday, the time ten o'clock. . . . Vietnam the barrier between Communism and the Free World."[27]

There are two stories in *China Gate*. One is that of the familiar polyglot squad of soldiers of fortune on a mission to destroy a massive ammunition dump deep behind enemy lines. The other plot concerns the relationship between one of the squad members and the Eurasian wife he deserted years before. For both stories, the mission is only important in that its pressures reveal the characters to themselves.

Ideologically, the war is presented as part of a civilization-wide battle to contain communism. An officer who once fought for his France now speaks of fighting for the "whole free world." The legionnaires, however, are mercenaries, each of whom is fighting to exorcise something within himself. The one Frenchman in the patrol is an ex-policeman who, unable to cope with the restrictions his civilian occupation placed on him, seeks freedom in war. A German veteran of the Hermann Goering Brigade fights now because only during battle does he have something to belong to. In his dreams, a Hungarian reenacts his first killing, that of a young Russian soldier who surprised him in World War II. Goldie, a black American, is the most overtly anti-Communist: "I have come to finish something we didn't finish in Korea. There are still a lot of live Commies." We come closer to the truth, however, when Goldie speaks of his longing for the children he and his wife were unable to have. For each legionnaire, *communism* is the code word for everything that cripples him psychologically.

In no one is this psychological crippling more apparent than in Brock, the white American who leads the patrol. Years earlier, he abandoned his half-Chinese wife (the unmistakably Occidental Angie Dickinson) because their son was born with Oriental features. Yet the war he is fighting is precisely for such children. From the opening documentary footage, Fuller dissolves directly to what he has called "the true image of war," an orphan running through a ruined city. In the five-year-old son of Brock and Lucky Legs is centered the entire free world/communism conflict: under what system is the boy to grow up?

After Brock deserted them, Lucky Legs became a prostitute to keep herself and her son alive. One of her lovers, Chan, a Russian major commanding the area's Vietminh, is willing to marry her and take the boy to grow up in Moscow. Given the rejection of them both by the boy's natural father, logic would dictate that Legs accept Chan.

The central position of the child in *China Gate* raises a number of questions about American attitudes, including those concerning sovereignty, race, and materialism. To begin with, the pivotal Oriental has no say over the culture in which he is to grow up. Nor is the possibility that he could grow up in a Third World culture even suggested. He will either be Russian or American. The very few featured Oriental characters are equally powerless. Only one of the mercenaries (in the pay of the French) is Oriental, and he is Nationalist Chinese. On the Vietminh side, the Russians quite literally call the shots for a revolution in which the natives are only tools. In a display of contempt for both East and West, Major Chan hides his munitions in a Buddhist temple, both desecrating a place of worship and boasting that the Americans and French would never think of bombing it. The idea that the Vietnamese might have the right to revolt, the right to control their own revolution, and the right of respect for their own culture is never raised.

One issue that is met squarely, if not fully resolved, is that of race. Brock's racism is irrational. He married Lucky Legs, who is half-Chinese but does not look Chinese. He rejected his son, who is three-quarters Caucasian but looks Oriental—this from a white man whose best friend is black. How is it possible to have faith in the values and good intentions of an America in which the World Family is a foreign concept, an America which determines the fate of its sons and daughters based solely on racial characteristics?

Lucky Legs is similarly ambivalent. Conscious that it is her mixed blood that Brock has rejected, her subsequent prostitution and her use of herself as a human detonator in blowing up the ammunition dump seems to be an acceptance of that value judgment rather than a triumph over it.

It is Lucky Legs who is determined that her son shall go to America. It is for this reason that she volunteers to lead the mercenaries to the ammunition dump. Typically, ideology has nothing to do with her decision: "I'd prefer to let you and the hammer and sickle boys fight it out alone." On one occasion, she slips the mercenaries past the Vietminh by leading a rendition of "The Marseillaise" in a drunken group which does not understand what it is singing. It is not patriotism that influences her to choose Brock's America over Chan's Russia. It is because their lives are directionless that the members of the Foreign Legion patrol are in Vietnam. Major Chan and communism have answers, but they are negative. In a stark cave beneath the Buddhist temple, Chan shows Lucky

Legs his arsenal, proclaiming his faith to a congregation of gleaming bombs and shells: "I'll show you why it's logical that you should marry me. . . . This is my garden, these are my revelations." Asked to sacrifice her child to the deadly logic of objective truth, Lucky Legs pushes Chan off a cliff and, carrying an activated grenade, throws herself upon the arsenal.

In the end, Brock and his son are seen leaving for America, the latter weighed down by the icons which identify him as an American boy—a puppy and a baseball glove. The film suggests that Brock, having conquered his racism and accepted his son as part of himself, no longer needs to fight a war. This freedom is the gift of Lucky Legs's martyrdom. Goldie, on the other hand, remains behind "to kill Commies" because no one can cure his childlessness. "Around here," as an Alabama farmer once said to John Dos Passos, "Communism's anything we don't like. Isn't it that way everywhere else?"[28]

But what if the war is a scapegoat on a national as well as a personal level? In Vietnam the whole mythology of our country began to break down like an overextended supply line. Our belief in the absolute rightness of our cause had allowed us to make our presence dominant on a huge, exceptionally rich, continent. In doing so we created problems, but the possibilities of the American Dream conspired to push them into the background. Our borders reached, we pressed on to our Manifest Destiny, always confident in our ideal and in the evil of those who opposed us. But after nearly two centuries, our step became less sure. In Vietnam we began to lose the faith. The means that we used to achieve our ideal there seemed to end in corruption and death. This far older culture refused to meet our strengths, and in a kind of spiritual jujitsu, turned them against us. The mandate of Heaven seemed to be changing, and we were forced to turn in on ourselves, to examine not only our present motivations but our past actions. We went home not with Brock but with Goldie, only to find our communism was our sterility.

America and the Vietnam Experience

It is fair to say that most Americans, even most government officials, had nothing material that they wanted in Southeast Asia. We became involved as part of a crusade against the idea of communism, which meant for us the freedom of the individual against the tyranny of the collective. Later, we became more deeply involved, not because the government we were assisting was democratic, but because without our assistance it could never become democratic. Still later, we increased our support because the stability of world peace depended upon our ability to honor our commitments. Finally, we stayed not because we believed in the morality of what we were doing or even in its effectiveness but because having spent so much in lives, money, and honor, to pull out would have been a public act of self-recognition staggering in its implications.

In February 1966, Senator J. W. Fulbright questioned Secretary of State Dean Rusk: "May I ask what is the explanation of why in 1956, contrary to the terms of the Geneva accords, elections were not held? . . . We backed Diem, did we not? Didn't we have much to do with putting him in power?"[29] The first elections held in South Vietnam were on October 24, 1955, when voters were offered the choice between Emperor Bao Dai and a republic with Ngo Dinh Diem, then prime minister, as president. Diem (backed by the CIA) won with 98.2 percent of the vote, polling in Saigon 605,025 votes out of 450,000 registered.[30] Despite his Catholicism and his years of study at Maryknoll seminary in Lakewood, New Jersey, in the early 1950s, Diem attempted to rule South Vietnam like a Confucian monarch, disseminating much of his political patronage to members of his own family, like him northern and Catholic. Best known and most hated were his brother Nhu—the director of the police and secret service and overlord of South Vietnam's extortion, graft, gambling, and opium trade—and his sister-in-law, Madame Nhu, the regime's unofficial publicist.[31] Describing South Vietnam's 16,000 "hamlets of opposition" as "former Vietminh," Nhu systematically executed 75,000 persons and put another 50,000 in prison. General Tran Van Don, Diem's last military chief of staff, later described the excesses: "Had they confined themselves to known Communists or proven Communist sympathizers, we could understand their methods. The repression, however, spread to people who simply opposed their regime, such as heads or spokesmen of other political parties, and against individuals who were resisting extortion by some of the government officials."[32]

Diem's downfall began on May 8, 1963, when troops fired on a crowd in Hue displaying flags in honor of Buddha's birthday. The Buddhists, who made up 70 to 80 percent of the population in comparison to the Catholics' 10 percent, struck back in an unusual way.[33] On June 11, a monk immolated himself in front of newspaper and television cameras at a downtown Saigon intersection. That summer and early autumn, as mass demonstrations packed the streets, six more monks and a Buddhist nun committed similar suicides. Hundreds of protestors were arrested, and on August 21, Nhu's Special Forces raided the pagodas, seizing 1,400 Buddhists.[34] Tired of supporting a leadership disavowed by its own people, the United States imagined the South Vietnamese military would be more effective, and let it be known that a coup would not be opposed. Both Diem and Nhu were assassinated on November 2, 1963, but American public opinion was blunted by the murder of President Kennedy less than three weeks later.

Throughout much of the election year of 1964, Lyndon Johnson deliberately downplayed America's future role in Vietnam, searching for the consensus that would give him the freedom to act. His primary interest was the passing of John F. Kennedy's civil rights program and the creation of its social and economic equivalent in the War on Poverty: "[A Congressional debate on] that bitch of a war [would destroy] the woman I really loved—the Great Society."[35] The public perception of his moderation in contrast to the warlike stance of Republican Senator Barry Goldwater helped Johnson to a landslide victory. Nevertheless, he felt his domestic program could never survive the "loss" of Vietnam or the loss of congressional support. Events in early August were to offer him the opportunity to consolidate both.

While engaging in electronic surveillance in the Gulf of Tonkin on August 1, the destroyer *Maddox* was attacked by North Vietnamese torpedo boats. Three days later, under questionable radar and sonar conditions, the *Maddox* and the *Turner Joy* reported another attack. Johnson ordered a retaliatory bombing attack on North Vietnam and requested Congress to approve a joint resolution pledging full support of U.S. forces "to promote the maintenance of international peace and security in Southeast Asia." On August 7, the Senate approved the Gulf of Tonkin Resolution 88–2, while the House voted its support 416–0.[36] For the rest of his term of office, Johnson was to insist that Congress had given him the necessary authority for whatever action he deemed necessary in Vietnam.

Bui Diem, South Vietnamese ambassador to Washington, was to recall, "I think that most of the time the Americans made decisions and the South Vietnamese government was informed afterwards."[37] Between the fall of Diem and the rise of General Nguyen Cao Ky in February 1965, there were ten South Vietnamese governments.[38]

Nevertheless, all our troops in Vietnam (increased to 16,500 in the summer of 1963 in order to teach the ARVN [Army of the Republic of Vietnam] "counterinsurgency" techniques) were still advisers, and—officially at least—our policy was that the Vietnamese would fight the general war.[39] We would, however, supply heavy air and technical support.

On February 12, 1965, American planes began the systematic bombing of North Vietnam. In 1965, the United States flew 25,000 sorties and dropped 63,000 tons of bombs on North Vietnam; in 1966 there 79,000 sorties and 136,000 tons; and in 1967 108,000 sorties and 226,000 tons at a cost of $30,000 per B-52 sortie. When the $6 billion loss in aircraft between 1965 and 1968 is factored in, the United States spent $9.60 for every $1.00 in damage inflicted on North Vietnam.[40]

Effective air support requires secure air fields. An infiltration attack on the Pleiku U.S. helicopter base which killed 9 Americans, wounded 109, and destroyed five aircraft convinced the administration that marines were needed to protect those bases. By the same reasoning, Vietcong killed in the field *couldn't* threaten landing fields. In May, U.S. military personnel stood at 46,500. By October 23, it was up to 148,300. On June 22, 1967, there were 463,000 American troops in Vietnam, in addition to over 600,000 South Vietnamese and 54,000 third-country troops. Communist strength was estimated at 294,000, including 50,000 North Vietnamese regulars. On March 9, 1968, with U.S. troop strength at 495,000, General William Westmoreland was reported as requesting an additional 206,000 troops.[41] In 1968, 14,592 Americans were to die in Vietnam.

And for what? Other than attrition, we had no plan for winning the war, and attrition in a foreign country is a two-way street. The war would cost the lives of a quarter million of the ARVN (and 1,435,000 civilians).[42] The South Vietnamese soldier's pay was one-sixteenth that of his American counterpart, who often treated him and the people he represented with contempt, and who frequently could not tell the difference between him and the enemy they were supposed to be fighting. His leaders were corrupt—to some extent understandably. A colonel in the provinces made only one-fourth as much as a girl working for the Americans in Saigon. No wonder 124,000 ARVN troops (21 percent of its ground force) deserted in 1966 alone.[43]

Meanwhile, half of the inpatients and 70 percent of the outpatients in the two northernmost corps areas were drug users. During 1969 and 1970 alone, more than 16,000 were discharged for drug abuse.[44] Between 1961 and 1970, 20 percent of South Vietnam's jungles and 36 percent of its mangrove forests were sprayed with herbicides. In 1965, nearly half of the spraying was done on food crops. The major defoliant was Agent Orange, proved in U.S. studies between 1963 and 1967 to cause cancer, birth defects, and other problems.[45] One out of four GIs stationed in Saigon had a venereal disease. Bribes were required in order to receive work permits and driver's licenses. The black market sold everything from whiskey to hand grenades at a 300 percent markup. As Major Pham Van-linh, Vietcong logistics officer, put it: "Without American money, guns, food, and supplies, we of the National Liberation Front would have a hard time surviving."[46]

Some Americans were less concerned with the war's economic and physical corruption than they were with its morality. In a war that had no objective against an enemy seldom seen and hard to identify, frustration, anxiety, and racism sometimes combined to cause incidents which irredeemably shamed their uniform and their country. An example—by no means isolated—which caught the public interest was the "My Lai-4 Massacre."

My Lai-4 was one of several hamlets in the Quang Ngai area where "C Company" of the First Battalion, Twentieth Infantry, had taken heavy casualties from mine fields without ever seeing a Vietcong. As part of a larger "search and destroy" mission on March 16, 1968, Lieutenant W. L. Calley led a Charlie Company platoon into My Lai and slaughtered as many as 700 unarmed villagers: "One GI is said to have thrown a grenade into a hootch where a girl of five lay that he had just raped. The young were slaughtered with the same impartiality as the old. Children barely able to walk were picked off at point blank range."[47]

When the incident was revealed a year later, several forms of psychological defiance appeared amidst the appalled reactions. Psychiatrist Robert Jay Lipton attempted to explain them: "The first is denial: 'The massacres didn't really happen or have been exaggerated.' The second is rationalization: 'All war is hell.' And the third, in a way more politically dangerous, is the mobilization of self-righteous anger: 'Stop picking on our boys. The Vietnamese had it coming to them. You [the bearer of the news] ought to be sent to Vietnam to fight.' "[48]

It should be noted that only Calley was charged with murder over My Lai (22 counts), that his sentence was eventually reduced to twenty years, and that he only served three days before being paroled. It should also be noted that Hugh C. Thompson, a warrant officer serving his second tour in Vietnam, set down his observation helicopter in My Lai, and after threatening a shoot-out with Calley's platoon, escaped with sixteen children—an act for which he won the Distinguished Flying Cross. Neither villainy nor heroism was scarce in Vietnam, just victory.

In late January 1969, Richard Nixon, the new president of the United States, inaugurated a plan called Vietnamization, designed to get America out of the war with "honor." This turned out to include secret bombing of Cambodia in 1969, invasion of Cambodia in 1970, invasion of Laos in 1971, and record "retaliatory" bombing in 1972—"endgame" escalations which only prolonged a war we lost in 1968 when we lost the belief that we could win.

On January 24, 1968, "pacification chief" Robert Komer told a Saigon press conference: "We begin '68 in a better position than we have ever been before." Six days later, during the Tet (lunar New Year) the NLF (National Liberation Front) attacked thirty-six provincial capitals and sixty-four district capitals. As international television watched, a Vietcong suicide squad, some of whom were embassy employees,[49] penetrated the American Embassy in Saigon. The same day the imperial city of Hue fell to the Communists. The four-week battle to retake it reduced the home of the Annam emperors for 250 years to rubble, but could not save the 4,800 officials and citizens who were either murdered or kidnapped and presumed murdered.[50] The mounting of so many assaults in the South proved that non-Communist control outside the major cities was an illusion. In 1946 Ho warned the French: "We will be like the elephant and the tiger. If the tiger pauses, the elephant impales him on his mighty tusks. But the tiger will not pause and the elephant will die of exhaustion and loss of blood."[51]

Lyndon Johnson initially pursued the war in Vietnam only to assure that he did not lose congressional support for the War on Poverty. The day after Congress supported the Gulf of Tonkin Resolution in 1964, it passed the Economic Opportunity Act. At the end of 1965 Johnson refused to ask for a tax hike to pay for the war for fear cuts in domestic spending would be proposed. The result was that by 1968 the United States had its largest budget deficit since World War II (and inflation for 1965–69 averaged nearly three and a half times that of 1960–64). After asking for a $12 billion military supplement, the White House was forced to eliminate $2.5 billion already authorized for social welfare in fiscal 1967.[52] As the nightmare of Vietnam forced itself upon the national consciousness, the Great Society became a forgotten dream.

War damage to the civil rights movement was as much psychological as economic. Vietnam had a way of making its presence felt in racial terms. The first people to publicly make the connection between civil rights and Vietnam were Freedom Riders and voter registrants in the South of the early sixties. As they daily risked their lives within the United States to extend to their fellow Americans rights already guaranteed to them by law, young civil rights workers formulated understandable doubts about our concerns and capabilities in Vietnam. After the disappearance of three voter registration workers in Philadelphia, Mississippi, on June 21, 1964, volunteer worker Sally Belfrage recorded this conversation between a white trainee and the Justice Department's John Doar.

"How is it that the government can protect the Vietnamese from the Vietcong and the same government will not accept the moral responsibility of protecting the people in Mississippi?"

"Maintaining law and order is a state responsibility," said Doar.

"But how is it"—the question persisted—"that the government can accept this responsibility in Vietnam?"[53]

Still, it was a shock to hear the first public statement on the war by Martin Luther King, Jr., on July 5, 1965: "It is worthless to talk about integration if there is no world to integrate in. I am certainly as concerned about seeing the defeat of Communism as anyone else; but we won't defeat Communism by guns or bombs or gases. We will do it by making democracy work."[54] On April 4, 1967, on the eve of "Burn, Baby, Burn" summer in Newark and Detroit and exactly one year before his own assassination, the 1964 Novel Peace Prize winner again warned that the replacement of right with might by a government was a powerful teaching device to its young: "I knew I could never again raise my voice against the violence of the oppressed of the ghettos without having first clearly spoken to the greatest purveyor of violence in the world today—my own government."[55]

Many antiwar leaders began in the civil rights movement and borrowed much of its terminology. During the spring of 1965, while our offensive ground forces were first landing in Vietnam, the operative resistance mode was the "teach-in," borrowed from the civil rights "sit-in." The first was at the University of Michigan on March 24, 1965, and the most ambitious occurred in Washington, D.C., on May 15, with the initial discussion connected by telephone to 122 colleges and universities around the country. The limit of the teach-in, of course, was its emphasis on reason and orderliness. Since the administration's decisions concerning the conduct of the war were already made, no amount of reasoned disagreement from a nondisruptive academia could change the course of events. They would have to, as the veteran civil rights leader Bayard Rustin suggested, "take the revolution into the streets."[56]

The first large-scale march (about 20,000 people) was coordinated by the Students for a Democratic Society (SDS) in Washington the day before Easter in 1965. However, as the numbers of demonstrations and demonstrators increased, so did the administration's desensitization toward them. At the Washington teach-in, the National Security Council's McGeorge Bundy cancelled his scheduled appearance, citing the pressure of the "real business of governing."[57] In a June 21, 1965, CBS-TV debate, Bundy countered analyst Hans Morgenthau's arguments against Vietnam by ridiculing his past predictions concerning the probable failure of the Marshall Plan and the fall of Laos to communism.[58] Secretary of State Dean Rusk referred to "academic gullibility," and Vietnam ambassador Maxwell Taylor called the war objections of Senator Wayne Morse (one of the two senators to vote against the Gulf of Tonkin Resolution) "good news to Hanoi."

Meanwhile, real opportunities to end the war passed, at least in part because we wanted no end except on our own terms. The United States refused to attend peace talks arranged by U Thant in October 1964. Under Secretary of State George Ball called the UN secretary general "naive."[59] Two years later, negotiations being conducted through the Polish government were cut off by the bombing of Hanoi, and new bombings the following February interrupted discussions between diplomatic substitutes British prime minister Harold Wilson and Soviet premier Aleksey Kosygin. Wilson told the House of Commons that "peace was in [my] grasp."[60] Perhaps. From 1965 through 1967, American officials tallied as many as two thousand attempts to initiate peace talks.[61]

Frustrated by the lack of success accompanying legal protest and illegal occupation, war resisters attempted to disrupt the war machinery itself. In August, 1965, SDS (Students for a Democratic Society) and Vietnam Day Committee members attempted for the first time to block the tracks of Marine troop trains in Oakland. In New York, on October 16, David J. Miller burned his draft card, an act which was to cost him two and a half years in jail.[62] On November 2 and November 7 respectively, Norman Morrison and Roger La Porte immolated themselves at the Pentagon and the United Nations building.[63] By April of 1967, draft card burnings had increased to 175 in a single day. In October 1967, demonstrators led by Yale chaplain William Sloane Coffin, Jr., and famed pediatrician Dr. Benjamin Spock turned 1,100 draft cards into the Justice Department without evoking a response.[64] War resisters were no longer arguing; they were clearly in opposition.

Just what they were opposing was less clear. As early as the Easter march of 1965, speakers were divided as to whether the enemy was the war or the American value system (Amerika with a k). In the November 27, 1965, Washington march, SDS president Carl Oglesby made connections that not everyone wanted to hear.

Can we understand why the Negroes of Watts rebelled? Then why do we need a devil theory to explain the rebellion of the South Vietnamese? Can we understand the oppression in Mississippi, or the anguish that our northern ghettos make epidemic? Then why can't we see that our proper human struggle is not with communism or revolutionaries, but with social desperation that drives good men to violence, both here and abroad? . . . There is one fact which describes it: with about 5 percent of the world's people we consume half of the world's goods. We take a richness that is in good part not our own, and we put it in our pockets, our garages, our split-levels, our bellies, and our futures.[65]

To examine American culture would inevitably question the effect of capitalism on our society and system of government. Many saw this as playing into the hands of the Communists. Still others thought it would detract from the war resistance. Both proved to be somewhat correct. Even as many whites felt themselves pressured to leave the civil rights movement, liberals separated from radicals in the late sixties. As early as 1964, Jack Weinberg, a veteran of the civil rights movement and the Berkeley free speech movement, warned protesters: "Don't trust anyone over thirty."[66] In 1970 the only word that could describe American society was *polarized*.

There is no doubt that a reevaluation of American society was long overdue. The war provided a perspective from which we came to challenge our traditional views of gender, race, the environment, education, economic policy, and government accountability. We learned that among the organizations receiving money from the Central Intelligence Agency were the National Student Organization, the Congress of Cultural Freedom, the National Council of Churches, the American Newspaper Guild, and the American Friends Service Committee.[67] Through the napalm manufactured by the Dow chemical company, we learned the extent to which universities were controlled by industrial research grants and recruiting. Our pursuit of an unofficial war abroad and our punishment of war resisters at home brought the judicial system into question, and any statement of our traditional ideals risked a return litany of our arms sales abroad, our support of dictators, and our apparent bondage to multinational corporations.

Vietnam: The Critics' Corner

> Theatre should be functioning at a point beyond that which the community has reached . . . a reversal of the traditional relationship in which theatre reflects the events around it; it seems to us that our times [are] moving so swiftly that we [can] not afford to let the most effective voice be the tardy one.[68]
>
> —Geraldine Lust, Open Theatre (1963)

The antiwar drama of the 1960s was in part a cultural and aesthetic phenomena, as well as a political one. In addition to the society which produced it, the theatre was forced to examine the concept of what a play is, where it should be held, and what its function should be. Any study of the attempt of the theatre of the sixties to initiate social change must also focus on the struggle of the instrument itself to break free of the proscenium arch, performance inevitability, and the limitations of language. It was the decade of Marshall McLuhan's "The medium is the message," and the justification for Andre Gide's definition of morality as a branch of aesthetics was never clearer.

The theatre of the 1960s set out to alter society by altering its modes of perception. Drawing jointly on early twentieth-century Italian futurism and mid-twentieth-century physics, sixties theatre realized that audiences did not require a naturalistically detailed picture, but only the beginning of an arc in order to infer a complete story. Thus, Peter Schumann's Bread and Puppet Theatre could mount its Uncle Fatso puppet and allow viewers to interpret its Lyndon Johnson/Uncle Sam/imperialism/patronization image for themselves. The Happening brought audience subjectivity from the modern art world and empowered it. Not only did the audience determine the meaning of the artwork, but it might also alter the form itself. The Open Theatre, the Story Theatre, and Viola Spolin's *Theatre Games* took the Suzanne Langer idea of the actor as always in the present, embodying the past, and becoming the future, and turned it into Transformation Techniques in which the process of character change became the theatrical event. Through Antonin Artaud we became aware of our inability to express ideas for which we didn't have words, and moved toward a concept of language as a thing in itself rather than as cultural symbol for something else. Jerzy Grotowski reclaimed the theatre as a ritual in which the actor/priest underwent personal change which the audience as communicants confirmed. The spectator was invited to change society by changing himself through becoming part of the process of change.

Nowhere was the necessity of audience participation more evident than in the decade's anti-Vietnam War drama. The three major categories of war protest drama—(a) antiwar activities planned for their theatricality, (b) agitprop street theatre, and (c) traditional theatre pieces in familiar playing spaces—all depended in varying degrees upon spectator involvement.

In the summer of 1969, Lee Baxandall pointed out the relationship of theatricality to politics: "Our language—the American idiom especially—seems to confirm it. We speak of a theatre of war, making a scene, properly acting in the spotlight, staging an event from behind the scenes."[69] The effectiveness of government depends upon its ability to turn its actions into spectacles which inspire the proper response from its citizenry. The discovery of the antiwar movement was that governmental machinery could be disrupted (or, at the very least, revealed) by counter-spectacles. Among the examples Baxandall cites are the 1967 march of one hundred thousand protesters in Washington, D.C., which culminated in a ritual intended to levitate the Pentagon, and the SDS-engineered pie-in-the-face greeting for the New York head of Selective Service at Columbia University in 1968. He might also have mentioned the counter-inaugural staged on the streets of Washington in opposition to Richard Nixon taking office on January 20, 1969,[70] or the yet-to-come Broadway Theatre Action, during which members of the Performance Group entered New York theatres during intermissions and took over stages for their protest.[71] There were hundreds of others.

There were probably as many street theatre agitprop plays—some by companies with considerable reputations. Robert Head's *Kill Viet Cong* invited a taxpaying passerby to get some entertainment value for the $4 million a day the United States was spending by shooting a captured Viet Cong on the spot. In a variety of embodiments, it was in the Performance Group repertoire for years. Another play that went through many forms was the Pageant Players' *The King Play*, an allegory showing how an autocratic government uses the threat of war to take away the social programs with which it has been pacifying the people. Meanwhile, Luis Valdez and El Teatro Campesino were reminding striking grape pickers with *Vietnam Campesino* that the same forces which kept the Chicano on the bottom of the social and economic pile in California could make him the point man on a Mekong Delta rifle squad.

The earliest Vietnam play listed in John Newman's bibliography is Megan Terry's *Viet Rock* (1966), a landmark in sixties drama for both content and style. Produced by the Open Theatre at Cafe La Mama (both icons of the period), this tranformational-techniques masterpiece parodies everything from war movies to rock and roll to senate investigation committees. More conventional (if more abstract) was Joseph Heller's *We Bombed in New Haven* (1968). Although Vietnam is never mentioned, the play is a striking example of sixties' mentality by a man whose novel, *Catch-22*, was one of its forming elements. In it the American war mentality is treated as a play, but those who die in "the theatre of war" are actually dead, and the process is so irreversible that an actor finds it impossible to avoid contributing his own son. As the son is taken away on a mission which the script has already revealed as doomed, the actor approaches the audience: "Now, none of this, of course, is really happening. It's a show, a play in a theatre, and I'm not really a captain. I'm an actor. . . . I'm [the actor's real name]. . . . Do you think that I [the actor's real name] would actually let my son go off to a war and be killed . . . and just stand here talking to you and do nothing?"[72] By the time the play opened, the question had been taken up by another group who were to carry their participation in the theatre of war to its ultimate conclusion.

The Trial of the Catonsville Nine

> It is hardly possible to imagine that in the atomic era war could be used as an instrument of justice.[73]
>
> —Pope John XXIII, *Pacem in Terris* (1963)

> No more war, war never again.[74]
>
> —Pope Paul VI, at the United Nations (October 4, 1965)

> The war in Vietnam is a war for civilization.[75]
>
> —Francis Cardinal Spellman, to American troops in Vietnam
> (Christmas, 1966)

We have noted in Chapter 2 the difficulty many Catholics in the 1930s had in reconciling Thomas Aquinas's concept of a "just war" with modern military technology. Still, the Roman Catholic response to war was only part of a broader, if not more important, religious question: How much should the church concern itself with earthly problems? One leading opponent of the Vietnam War, "The Catholic Worker," a radical pacifist group founded by Dorothy Day and Peter Maurin, began by feeding the poor in "Houses of Hospitality" in 1933.[76] The worker-priest movement in France set aside the priestly life-style and worked alongside manual laborers, celebrating mass during lunch breaks, and making the church a part of the everyday working life of the community. Because of its close association with the heavily Communist labor unions, this movement was suppressed by the Vatican in 1954 and ended five years later.[77]

The Ecumenical Council in Rome, Vatican II (1962–1965), sought to make religion more accessible. The modification or discarding of clerical garb, the speaking of the liturgy in the vernacular, and the turning of the altar to face the congregation symbolized a growing official Catholic concern with the world as it existed.

Yet, too many Catholics appeared to have made that accommodation already. Churches that had laid up their riches in countries wealthy and not so wealthy seemed to have no difficulty squaring their consciences with their secular Caesars' foreign or domestic policies. Dissenting individuals or Catholic groups, such as the Catholic Peace Fellowship, the Young Christian Workers, and the Interfaith Peace Mission, were as apt to be reprimanded by their own hierarchy as they were by their government.

On August 30, 1965, a federal law making draft-card burning punishable by five years in prison and a $10,000 fine went into effect. New York "Catholic Worker" David J. Miller was the first to be arrested under that law. Roger La Porte, who also was a Catholic Worker, immolated himself in front of the United Nations building. At his memorial service, Daniel Berrigan refused to call La Porte's death suicide: "He gave his life, so that others might live."[78] Berrigan subsequently was censored by his religious superiors, a punishment which did not deter a more serious challenge to war by his brother Philip.

On August 27, 1967, six days after 683 demonstrators were arrested in the March on the Pentagon, four members of the Baltimore Interfaith Peace Mission—Philip Berrigan, a Josephite priest; James Mengel, a United Church of Christ minister; Thomas Lewis, a Catholic artist; and David Eberhardt, the agnostic son of a Presbyterian minister—entered the Selective Service office of the Baltimore Customs Office and began to pour a mixture of human and animal blood on the draft files. The raiders were followed through the door by reporters and cameramen, and the FBI, arriving thirty minutes later, found all four seated on a narrow bench along the inner wall. Convicted on April 16, 1968, and scheduled to be sentenced on May 24, Philip Berrigan and Thomas Lewis set out to use the time in between constructively.[79] A press release written by Daniel Berrigan declared:

Today, May 17th [1968], we enter Local Board No. 33 at Catonsville, Maryland, to seize Selective Service records and burn them with napalm manufactured by ourselves from a recipe in the Special Forces Handbook, published by the U.S. Government. . . . We destroy these draft records not only because they exploit our young men, but because they represent misplaced power concentrated in the ruling class of America. . . . We are convinced that the religious bureaucracy in this country is racist, is an accomplice in war, and is hostile to the poor.[80]

The "Catonsville Nine" remained on the scene until the police arrived. A week later, Phil Berrigan and Thomas Lewis were sentenced to six years for their action at the Baltimore Customs Office. They were tried with the other defendants at Catonsville on October 5–9, 1968. One of their number, Daniel Berrigan, used the trial transcript to construct a docudrama.

For most of the nine defendants, all Roman Catholic clergy, former clergy, or lay workers, Vietnam only mirrored evils so deeply ingrained in American institutions that they may well be without redress. They never denied their actions, but only sought to explain their motives through their past experiences.

Philip Berrigan, the first priest in the United States to be tried and convicted of a political crime, connected the war to our internal racial inequalities. As a WWII army trainee, he saw the grinding poverty under which blacks in the South lived. This led him to join the Society of St. Joseph, an order founded after the Civil War to aid American Negroes, as a teacher and social worker in Louisiana.

For Mary Moylan, a former missionary nurse, it was the recognition that Vietnam was merely a new embodiment of a longtime foreign and domestic policy. While working in Uganda during the Congo crisis of 1959–1960, at a time when the United Nations was supposed to be acting as a peacekeeping force, she witnessed bombings from American planes flown by Cuban emigrés. She later left Uganda because of her perception that the hospital at which she worked did not exist so much to help the natives as to insure that they did not learn how to help themselves. Returning home to Washington, D.C., she became aware of the violent underside of this paternalism by watching the routine police brutality used to keep blacks "in their place."

George Mische, a Kennedy "New Frontiersman" who worked for the Alliance for Progress, was amazed at the hatred that greeted him in Latin America, until he learned that in two of the countries in which he served, Pentagon support had allowed military juntas to overthrow democratically elected governments. Most alarming was the Dominican Republic, where General Trujillo was dictator for thirty-two years without U.S. protest, not only killing all those who spoke of political rights, but mutilating them unspeakably as an example to their neighbors. Even our aid programs, such as the University of Chicago's American Institute for Free Labor Development, turned out to be CIA fronts.

When Mische returned home, he travelled throughout the United States for a year and a half, speaking to students, religious groups, and businessmen—even to a conference of eighty Catholic bishops, whom he found as unresponsive to real human needs as his government's agencies: "since they have 80 billion dollars' worth of property and ten times as much in investments, if they were really to live in the spirit of the stable in which Christ was born, then why not . . . give them to the poor?"[81]

Thomas and Marjorie Melville and John Hogan were also missionaries in a Latin American, CIA-supported dictatorship. In 1954 the elected government of Guatemala (which had taken land from the United Fruit Company and given it to the peasants) was overthrown because of the involvement of some Communists in it. The new president, Lieutenant Colonel Castillo Armas, gave the land back to United Fruit. There followed a succession of military dictatorships which U.S support (even using occupying American troops) has been unable to stabilize.

Thomas Melville, then a Maryknoll priest, began working with the peasants in Guatemala in 1957. John Hogan, a carpenter and Maryknoll brother, joined Melville in 1961, impressed by a "Father" who did not have a paternalistic attitude to the people. Marjorie Melville, then a Maryknoll nun, began as a teacher in the rich Guatemala City convent school, but later worked with student groups in the slums. Thomas Melville could not understand why there was no American aid money for farm cooperatives or village water systems when we *were* capable of supplying new police cars for the two thousand policemen trained and equipped in the United States. When the Catholic church also denied help, Melville used the title to the church building itself as collateral for a cooperative. Later, he, Marjorie, and John joined the rebels, hampering Green Beret attacks by their advertised presence. As Melville points out, the recent assassinations of our ambassador, our military attaché, and our naval attaché should make us ask why we are so unpopular in Guatemala.

For Thomas Lewis, an art teacher in the ghetto, and David Darst, a divinity student, Catonsville came about because of the lack of response to legal Vietnam protests. Darst turned down his clerical exemption and sent his draft card back to his board, but the government never brought him to trial. Lewis, who began as a civil rights demonstrator, became an antiwar protester with the Interfaith Peace Mission when his brother went to Vietnam. He recalls group vigils, prayers, marches, and the frustration of unanswered letters to congressmen and senators: "One of the vigils in Washington was at the home of Dean Rusk. Rusk said it was not his job to deal with moral matters. . . . So we turned toward the military. There was no response. They accepted no responsibility for the direction of the war. The responsibility was not theirs. They were just obeying orders." (*The Trial of the Catonsville Nine*, iii, 38–39)

German-descended George Mische also compares the Nuremberg Trials charges and American Vietnam guilt: "All of us Christians share the responsibility for having put those Jews in the ovens. If this is true, then it is also true that this is expected of me now as a Christian." (*The Trial of the Catonsville Nine*, iii, 65)

For Daniel Berrigan, Catonsville was again a question of what it meant to be a Christian. Politicized by his experience with the French worker-priests of the fifties who sought to share the life of their parishioners,

Father Berrigan saw that movement crushed by the hierarchy of the church, who believed that closeness to be a danger. Encouraged by Pope John XXIII's reforms, he turned the altar around and began saying the Mass in English. Visiting in South African in 1964, he became aware of the potential cost of living according to Christian principles. Despite opposition from Cardinal Spellman, who thought of American wars as holy wars, Father Berrigan began to speak out against Vietnam and was exiled to Latin America in 1965: "In January of 1968 an invitation came from the government in North Vietnam. Professor Howard Zinn and myself were invited to Hanoi to bring home three captive American airmen. . . . It was quite clear to me during three years of air war America had been experimenting upon the bodies of the innocent. We had improved our weapons on their flesh." (*The Trial of the Catonsville Nine*, iii, 75–77)

Between Hanoi and Catonsville, Father Berrigan visited a dying high school boy who, out of despair over the war, had immolated himself in a Syracuse, New York, cathedral. To permit the burning of children to go unchallenged is to allow the creation of a world in which the burning of children is acceptable: "So I went to Catonsville and burned some papers because the burning of children is inhuman and unbearable. . . . I did not want the children or the grandchildren of the jury or of the judge to be burned with napalm. . . . At what point will you say no to this war? We have chosen to say with the gift of our liberty, if necessary our lives: the violence stops here, the death stops here, the suppression of the truth stops here, this war stops here." (*The Trial of the Catonsville Nine*, iii, 79–82)

The Catonsville Nine are convicted, of course. The judicial system is equipped to deal only with the facts of a given incident. It is not subject to the mitigations of past experiences, religious principles, or moral right. The prosecution admits that the war might reasonably be seen as illegal and immoral. The judge draws a distinction between his views as a judge and his views as a man, but the evils—political, religious, racial, economic—to which the Nine have testified are not on trial and there seems at this moment in time no court high enough to bring proceedings. In his introduction to the play (written in 1969), Daniel Berrigan noted that many who praised their action in the spring of 1968 now see it as laughable—an attempt to use a judicial system which is itself only a tool of the forces which have committed the crimes they are fighting: "Simply, we have lost confidence in the institutions of the country, including the courts and our own churches. . . . We have lost confidence, because we do not believe any longer that these institutions are reformable. . . . We believe that this has occurred because the law is no longer serving the needs of the people; which is a good definition of morality." (*Trial of the Catonsville Nine*, v, 105)

David Darst, Mary Moylan, Marjorie Melville, and John Hogan received two-year sentences; George Mische, Thomas Melville, and Daniel Berrigan three years; Philip Berrigan and Thomas Lewis, three and a half years, to run concurrently with the six year terms set down for the blood-pouring in Baltimore. On April 9, 1970, the day they were scheduled to report to prison, George Mische, Mary Moylan, Dave Eberhardt, and the Berrigan brothers went underground. Phil Berrigan and Dave Eberhardt were captured at Stain Gregory's Church in Manhattan on April 21. Daniel Berrigan, the only priest ever to make the FBI's Most Wanted list, was arrested on Block Island (off Rhode Island) on a rainy August 11 by seventy FBI agents posing as bird-watchers. On the basis of good conduct and poor health, he was paroled on February 24, 1972. Philip Berrigan's parole (December 20, 1972) was widely interpreted as a sign of the nation's turning against the war.[82]

"In this itch for beatitude, which has nothing to do with God or our neighbor—in order to get nearer to that, we must kill all the time. In the pursuit of life, we are always dealing out death. War becomes the continual occupation and preoccupation in the minds of people who are purportedly trying to get to a better life."[83]

On September 9, 1980, Philip and Daniel Berrigan and six other peace activists entered a restricted area of the General Electric Space Division in King of Prussia, Pennsylvania. Using hammers, they dented the nose cones of two Minuteman 3 intercontinental ballistic missiles and splashed human blood and scattered ashes over tools and documents.[84] For them—and for those of whom we will now speak—the war has not ended.

Bringing the War Back Home

I think whatever experience he did have over there, it was pretty intense for him and nobody was letting him talk about it—like "Okay, you're a hero, you're home," this kind of shit—when I think he needed some time to vent somewhere and that wasn't the appropriate way. . . . I felt like pulling him aside and saying, "Let's talk about it." But I guess at that time I wasn't ready either or I didn't know how to do it."[85]

—Medical Corpsman Stephen Klinkhammer

I was watching everybody eating dinner and they were all well dressed and everything, and [my fiancée] said, "What's the matter?" And I said, "Let's get out of here. In about two minutes I'm going to get up and start busting

heads." And I said, "I don't know why." I wanted to wipe that restaurant out. It was so strong in me. My whole body was tensing up.[86]
—Philip Caputo, former Marine platoon leader

I was in a VA hospital the first time I heard anybody saying, "Those fucking guys over in Vietnam. Look what they're doing." Man, it did something to me. Like I was guilty. I was a criminal. You had sentenced me to die. These are the same people from whom I left the year before. I'm back but I don't belong. I wanted to go back to the Nam. I would have re-upped, but I was all wounded. This world was alienating, what people was talking about, what people was liking.[87]
—an anonymous wounded returning soldier

In his "Hierarchy of Needs," Abraham Maslow suggests that one can search for self-fulfillment only when biological, safety, belongingness, and esteem needs have been met. In America's greatest period of prosperity, roughly from 1947 to the "energy crisis" of 1973, more of these needs were being met for more people than ever before. The beginning of this period also coincides with the tremendous postwar population increase known as the Baby Boom. With the coming of age of the Baby-Boomers came the era of greatest Vietnam divisiveness—thus triggering Vice President Spiro Agnew's charge of "permissiveness." The sixties activists were the children of World War II's moral and material victors, who had already achieved the Depression dreams of "a chicken in every pot" and "two cars in every garage"—not to mention a God-granted nuclear umbrella to keep them dry. Our prosperity and sense of invincibility had created expectations of which previous generations had not even dreamed. "Rosie the Riveter" may have punched out at the factory and into the pages of *Better Homes and Gardens*, but her daughters would not be so easily sidetracked. The first lunch-counter sit-ins of 1960 were not peopled by starving sharecroppers who wanted the food, but well-fed college students who wanted to make a point. In his presidential campaign of 1968, Robert Kennedy was fond of quoting Tennyson's *Ulysses*: "Come, my friends. It is not too late to seek a newer world." Given their circumstances and America's traditional view of itself as the chosen people, it is not altogether surprising that so many Baby-Boomers fully expected that world to be achieved.

In a way that *their* children may never understand, this sixties generation (at least initially) expected that their quest for the grail would be government-aided. Respect for government and belief in its power to do right was probably never higher than in the twenty years following World War II. FDR had demonstrated a public commitment to the disadvantaged in the Depression which had previously been unknown in

American government. Instead of the expected return of the Depression, our standard of living grew steadily higher, accompanied by a wider dissemination of education and civil liberties. At home and away, our government was morally interventionist and could afford to be.

As with all virtues, however, the extended application of this commitment to moral action contained the seeds of vice. We believed that God had given us a military and economic mandate to perfect the world. We did not question that the application of our technology and value systems would be as advantageous to all others as it was to us. Opposition to this mandate must be overcome for the good of the opposer more than for ourselves. We could vanquish all that was evil in the world, make war on poverty and alien ideology simultaneously. Economically, this proved impossible, as the inflation statistics quoted earlier show. There were, however, other contradictions which had wider social implications.

To begin with, the ideological war was too often fought by the victims of the poverty war. According to Lawrence Basker and William Strauss's study of the draft and the Vietnam generation, *Chance and Circumstance*, 27 million men came of draft age between August 5, 1964, and March 28, 1973—America's official period of military involvement in Vietnam. But although a 1969 survey of recent high school graduates found that 75 percent saw the draft and Vietnam as "the problems young men your age worry about most," only 8 percent of the "Vietnam generation" would actually serve there. Sixty percent of those who did not see combat took active steps to avoid it. More than half of the nondraftees and nearly half of the era's noncombat soldiers believe that their own actions contributed to their escape from battle. A 1971 Lou Harris poll defined Vietnam soldiers as "suckers, having to risk their lives in the wrong war, in the wrong place, at the wrong time."[88]

It can only be concluded, therefore, that to an embarrassingly high degree, the war was fought by those who could not get out of it. The most obvious draft inequity was the 2-S deferment for students in college. In 1965–66 only 2 percent of all army draftees were college graduates. James Fallows, who went to great lengths to exempt himself from the draft, notes that the Harvard *Crimson's* antipathy to the war dated from the spring of 1968, when the deferment for graduate students was ended.[89] If an enlisted man was a college graduate, his chances of going to Vietnam were 42 percent as opposed to 64 percent for a high school graduate and 70 percent for a high school dropout. In addition, approximately half of every combat platoon in Vietnam consisted of racial minorities. Systematically denied equal combat opportunity until the Korean War, blacks comprised 24 percent of the combat dead in the

1965's Vietnam.[90] No wonder Fallows entitled his confession "What Did
You Do in the Class War, Daddy?"

Nearly 58,000 Americans died in Vietnam. Perhaps half that many
were permanently disabled, and the total of wounded numbered over
300,000.[91] If you were a sucker to be there, what were you when you
came home? The first answer is that you were likely to be a scapegoat.
Those who were against the war were likely to blame the soldier for
waging it; those who were for the war were likely to blame the soldier
for losing it.

Second, you were unlikely to be reintegrated into society. As veterans
often put it, there were "no homecoming parades," no public ceremonies
of absolution welcoming the returning warrior to the peaceful society.

Third, if you did reestablish yourself in society, having lost to the
nonveterans the time spent in service and rehabilitation, your ability to
succeed often depended upon concealing your Vietnam service. After
World War II, politicians as diverse as Joseph R. McCarthy and Lyndon
Johnson built careers on highly questionable war records. After Vietnam,
many found that in order to be successful they had to hide their
experience.

Finally, according to one Veterans Administration study, fully one-
third of the Vietnam-generation veterans did feel ashamed about the war
and nearly one-half avoided wearing their uniform on leave. When one
adds that guilt to the taboos against the veteran's discussing Vietnam, to
his ostracization and the discrimination against him for having been there,
and when one remembers that the average soldier's age was nineteen, as
opposed to twenty-six in World War II, it is not surprising to find that
between 500 and 700,000 veterans (approximately one-fourth of those
who served in Vietnam) have suffered from post-traumatic stress—the
inability to integrate the Vietnam experience into their lives.[92] For many,
their subsequent lives became extensions of Vietnam rather than the
reverse. If deaths there were meaningless, their own survivals must be
equally arbitrary. If no standards measured actions there, what moral
guides could have importance here?

As Tim O'Brien suggests in *Going After Cacciato*, what was lost in
Vietnam was a sense of certainty:

They did not have a cause. They did not know if it was a war of ideology or economics
or hegemony or spite. . . . They did not know the terms of war, its architecture, the
rules of fair play. . . . They did not know how to feel. Whether, when seeing a dead
Vietnamese, to be happy or sad or relieved; whether, in times of quiet, to be
apprehensive or content; whether to engage the enemy or elude him. They did not

know how to feel when they saw villages burning. . . . They did not know good from evil.[93]

Vietnam: The Endless Epilogue

The United States has now been officially out of Vietnam longer than we were officially in it. Unofficially, of course, many Americans of that generation will never be separated from Vietnam, but will—as Albert Camus said about the Spanish Civil War—"carry it with them like an evil wound."

It is perhaps instructive that three of the seven plays in the first anthology of Vietnam War drama, *Coming to Terms*, deal with the difficulties of returned veterans. Both Tom Cole's Medal of Honor Rag (1975) and Stephen Metcalfe's *Strange Snow* stress survivor guilt. From the standpoint of this book's emphasis on caste as well as class, the former is probably more relevant. Its two characters—a black Vietnam Congressional Medal of Honor winner and his psychiatrist, a European-born Jew—are both chance escapees from total, irrational slaughter. The soldier was the only one of his squad not in a truck blown up by the Vietcong, and the psychiatrist was the only one of his family not to die in a concentration camp. It is the psychiatrist's task to teach his patient that he need not throw away his life to compensate for not having died in Vietnam, a task in which he fails: "You got your reasons for wanting to see no more war, right?—and no more warriors. I dig that, for your sake. But a lot of folks don't want the black veteran to throw down *his* weapons so soon. Know what I mean? Like, we are supposed to be preparing ourselves for another war, right back here. Vietnam was just our basic training, see? I'm telling this to you, y'see, so you won't be too surprised when it comes."[94]

Emily Mann's *Still Life* (1980) is equally interesting for its insight into gender roles. In the play, we are shown the anger, the violence, and the guilt common to much returning-Vietnam-veteran literature. However, we are also reminded that the sixties were a time of change for women. Mark, the veteran of *Still Life*, discovered in Vietnam that he had been given a power over life and death that no legal or moral system could justify or take away. Back in the United States, he must deal with that awakened, corrupted power, in a society (his therapist-lover reminds us) whose concepts of masculinity have altered drastically in his absence. "Oh, I'm worried about men. They're not coming through. (My husband) How could I have ever gotten married? They were programmed to fuck, now they have to make love. And they can't do it. It all comes down to fucking versus loving. We don't like them in the old way anymore. And I don't think they like us, much. Now that's a war, huh?"[95]

It was a war the earliest of the homecoming plays anticipated.

Sticks and Bones

Probably no political drama was ever introduced to a larger viewing audience in a more bizarre fashion than David Rabe's *Sticks and Bones*. Rabe, an ex-Vietnam hospital corpsman, wrote a trilogy of Vietnam plays—the other two being *The Basic Training of Pavlo Hummel* and *Streamers*. *Sticks and Bones* opened at Joseph Papp's Public Theatre before moving in September 1971 to Broadway, where it won the Tony Award for the best new play of the 1971–1972 season. In August 1972, Papp contracted with CBS for a series of televised productions over a four-year period at a cost of $7 million. The first, Shakespeare's *Much Ado About Nothing*, was broadcast on February 2, 1973. On February 21, CBS announced that *Sticks and Bones* would be presented on March 9.[96]

Meanwhile, American involvement in the war was winding down. On August 12, 1972, the last U.S. combat ground troops left Vietnam. On October 26 (twelve days before President Nixon's landslide reelection) Henry Kissinger noted that "peace is at hand," and on January 23 the president announced that an agreement containing "peace with honor" had been reached. Between *Much Ado About Nothing* and the announcement about *Sticks and Bones*, the first American prisoners of war began the journey home—some after incarcerations of more than six years. In the first week of March, as CBS prepared to show a drama about a blinded, embittered veteran returning home to a family threatened by what he told them about themselves, footage of the actual returning POWs flooded the TV screen.

On March 6, CBS-TV president R. D. Wood announced that the telecast of *Sticks and Bones* was being postponed indefinitely on the grounds that its presentation "at this time might be unnecessarily abrasive to feelings of millions of Americans whose lives are emotionally dominated by returning POWs." Papp protested vigorously, calling the postponement a "cowardly cop-out and rotten affront to freedom of speech," and vowing not to honor the remainder of the contract which called for the production of eleven more plays for CBS.[97]

Perhaps both men were being disingenuous. *Much Ado About Nothing* cost $810,000 to produce, $35,000 more than CBS paid Papp. In addition, the number of viewers who watched the TV production was enough to heavily erode the theatre audience for the play, which closed at a loss of $165,000, but insufficient to provide the ratings a prime-time program needs for survival. CBS had other, more pressing, economic reasons for disassociation from the productions.

On December 18, 1972, Clay T. Whitehead, director of the newly created White House Office of Telecommunications Policy, urged that individual television stations be held responsible, at the risk of losing their licenses, for the content of all network material they broadcast, including nightly newscasts.[98] Sixty-nine of the network's 184 affiliate stations initially refused to carry the program, and only two of the twelve advertising slots were filled.[99]

On March 10, noting the delay of *Sticks and Bones* and the suggestion that funding for Public Broadcasting System news presentations would be restricted, outgoing Federal Communications Commissioner Nicholas Johnson predicted that television networks would yield to the Nixon administration's pressure to avoid controversial programming.[100] As the White House's bill on the renewal of television and radio broadcasting licenses put it three days later, stations would have to be "substantially attuned to the public needs and interests."

On March 29 the last American troops left South Vietnam. On June 26, Papp and CBS terminated their production agreement, and on July 13—two days before the expiration of their option would have allowed Papp to file legal suit—CBS rescheduled *Sticks and bones* for deep in television's dog days. On August 17, two days after American bombers flew final missions over Cambodia and President Nixon complained on television that networks had averaged twenty-two hours of Watergate coverage weekly in the last ninety days, viewers could finally make up their own minds about *Sticks and Bones*. That is, some viewers could make up their minds: 94 of CBS's 186 affiliates did not show the program and 43 others moved it out of prime time or to another day.[101] It was television drama as mind-boggling as the play itself.

As a play rather than a media event, *Sticks and Bones* is political without being ideological. Neither communism nor the policy of containing it is ever mentioned, much less attacked or defended. Mindless, commercial consumption *is* attacked, but that consumption is never identified with a particular economic philosophy. It *is* seen as a corollary of an incredibly vicious racism and dehumanization, the product of cultural conditioning which begins in the white, middle-class, hegemonic American home. The word *Vietnam* does not appear in the dialogue, although stage directions and descriptions of the war's conduct make its references perfectly clear. Religion is presented as a pop-psychology cliché, and a spiritual malaise of derailed values is literalized as internal rot. Finally, like most political drama, *Sticks and Bones* ends unhappily, suggesting not only that the rot remains but that it remains unrecognized.

Each act of the play is framed by family slides, warning us, as does *The Trial of the Catonsville Nine*, that there is a tomorrow's world to be shaped by today's values. Some of the slides we will recognize later as having been taken by Ricky, the family's second son, in the course of the play. It is to the house of Ricky's parents, Ozzie and Harriet, that his blinded brother David will return from the war.

The names immediately both inform and distance the audience. The Nelson family (Ozzie, Harriet, David, and Ricky) was the archetype of the post-World War II American middle class: white, wholesome, clean, and reverent. they life in a world unaffected by social and economic problems—an America whose slight, humorous deviances from common sense could be gently corrected within the framework of a half-hour situation comedy. Their family, beginning on radio in 1949 and appearing on television from 1952 to 1966, was a scaled-down problem-reducing mirror of our own. If its two-dimensional image was false, what did that tell us about our sense of ourselves?

The home to which David returns is worthy of the glowing TV which stands downstage with its back to the audience for much of the play. Indeed, when Ozzie can no longer hide from David's truth late in the play, he tries to hide in the television set itself, wildly changing the channels: "I flick my rotten life. Oh, there's a good one. Look at that one. Ohhh, isn't that a good one. That's the best one. That's the best one."[102]

Even in the beginning, however, there is "a sense that this room, these stairs belong in the gloss of an advertisement," not reality. (*Sticks and Bones*, I, 6) Father Donald, the basketball-playing priest, is an escapee from *Going My Way* and is not to be found in a Catholic world ranging from Cardinal Spellman to the Berrigans. There is a hunger in Harriet's piety. Ricky's carefree attitude is less a stage than an end. Ozzie is puzzled by a sense of unfulfilled promise, by a revisionism determined to deny significance to accomplishments which only he remembers, and finally, by a remembrance of David as less than ideal: "I . . . seen him do some awful things, ole Dave. He was a mean . . . foul-tempered little baby. I'm only glad I was *here* when they sent him to do his killing." (*Sticks and Bones*, I, 11)

"The Adventures of Ozzie and Harriet" followed the evening news. When the sergeant major enters the living room, refusing an offer of cake and coffee, and depositing the blind David like a parcel on the living room couch, the barrier between the two forms of television seems finally to have been breached: "When I get back they'll be layin' all over the grass; layin' there in pieces all over the grass, their backs been broken, their brains jellied, their insides turned into garbage. No-legged boys and one-legged boys. I'm due in Harlem; I got to get to the Bronx and Queens, Cincinnati, St. Louis, Reading. . . . I got deliveries to make all across this country." (*Sticks and Bones*, I, 5)

The system is breaking down. At the end of the play, the trucks will return, their urgency escalating and their cargo deteriorating. And—for a moment—it will appear as if the American television surface gloss has been shattered beyond repair. But before we reach this point, we will be exposed to what that surface covers: an ideal–co-opting materialism, dehumanization of epic proportions, and a pervasive sense of internal rot.

In his past—before Harriet, before the house they live in, before the children—Ozzie was a runner: "But it's not for the money I run. In the fields and factories, they speak my name when they sit down to their lunches. If there's a . . . prize to be run for, it's me they send for. It's to be the-one-sent-for that I run." (*Sticks and Bones*, I, 31)

Ozzie left his hometown for the hobo jungles and freight trains of the Great Depression. It was on one of those freights that he met a railroad brakeman named Hank Grenweller who threw him from the moving train into the community where he now lives. Later, Hank would become Ozzie's friend, getting him the defense plant job which exempted him from World War II, introducing him to Harriet, advising him on the purchase of their house, and talking him out of leaving town, until when he returns to the tracks where he was thrown off, "the grass in among the tiles is tall, the rails rusted. . . . No trains any longer come that way; they all go some other way." (*Sticks and Bones*, I, 45)

Ozzie is a metaphor for America, its effortless growth derailed by the Depression and its ideals channeled into a materialism as ultimately unsatisfying as Harriet's endlessly produced snacks of fudge and milk. Harriet doubts his virility, and both she and Ricky have the habit of leaving in the middle of his speeches ("You're just talking nonsense anyway"). His house is a coffin: "You made it big so you wouldn't know, but that's what it is, and not all the curtains and pictures and lamps in the world can change it." (*Sticks and Bones*, II, 65) His past has been made suspect in even his own eyes. Harriet denies that she was ever the vision he thought her, and remembers a race in which Ozzie beat Hank as an example of Hank's generosity. Ozzie is finally reduced to handing out inventories of his possessions as proof of his existence: "There's no evidence of me in the world, no sign or trace, as if everything I've ever

done were no more than smoke. My life has closed behind me like water."
(*Sticks and Bones*, II, 64)

Racism in *Sticks and Bones* is traced to the home. David recalls seeing
his mother sickened in church by the Oriental features of a Eurasian baby.
When he wished to bring home Zung, the Vietnamese girl with whom
he was in love, Harriet made it clear that she regarded the mixing of
blood as white defilement: "It is our triumph, our whiteness. We
disappear. . . . They take us back and down if our children are theirs—it
is not a mingling of blood, it is theft." (*Sticks and Bones*, II, 79)

Zung is present throughout the play, first sensed by David and
gradually recognized by Ozzie. But her danger to this metaphorical image
of America is more than miscegenation. She is evidence of the humanity
we have treated so casually because we do not recognize its existence.
After loving Zung, David no longer finds it possible to "take some old
man to a ditch of water, shove his head under, and talk of cars and money
till his feeble pawing stops and then head on home to go in and out of
doors and drive cars and sing sometimes." (*Sticks and Bones*, I, 39)
David's parents are unconcerned with his sexual relationship with Zung
so long as it has no emotional commitment: "What you mean is you
whored around. . . . I mean, it's like going to the bathroom. All glands
and secretions." (*Sticks and Bones*, I, 26)

Once Zung becomes recognizable as a human being, we will have to
accept her as human and accord her human dignity, or we will have to
commit murder without calling it by such euphemisms as "pacification"
or pretending that the victim feels no pain.

The dehumanization with which the war is associated is only a
reflection of the dehumanization already present at home—manifested in
Father Donald, who can speak of "acceptance of an alien race" as
"sickness" (*Sticks and Bones*, II, 59), and Ricky, whose description of
a girl as "a piece of tail" and "a piece of ass" is sanctioned by his father,
as long as "it wasn't any decent girl." (*Sticks and Bones*, II, 77) And if
what happened in Vietnam is acceptable, as David points out to his
mother, his red-tipped, phallus-like cane lifting her skirt, then "everything impossible [is] made possible." It is Ricky who has become the
American Dream, because he never questions the implications or consequences of his appetites. His brain is "small and scaly, a snake forever
ignorant of the fact that it crawls": "You see, Dave, where you're wrong
is your point of view, it's silly. It's just really comical because you think
people are valuable or something and given a chance like you were to
mess with 'em, to take a young girl like that and turn her into a whore,

you shouldn't when of course you should or at least might . . . on whim . . . you see?" (*Sticks and Bones*, II, 82, 89)

David has brought—through his memories and his family's growing awareness of Zung—recognition of the war into his home. Like the family, the audience is gradually enlightened to the presence of an internal rot, an odor which seems first to emanate from Vietnam, but which is slowly revealed as endemic of a congenitally diseased society. We are made aware of it by the vehemence of Ozzie's insistence of its presence in Oriental women, in the Other: "Those girls. Infection. From the blood of their parents into the very fluids of their bodies. An actual rot live in them." (*Sticks and Bones*, I, 29) David traces the sickness back to the keystone of his parents' lives, Hank Grenweller, recalling Hank's "injured" hand first from childhood, and, later, from when Hank visited him just before he went overseas: "The sickness was congenital. . . . Why did you make me think him perfect? It was starting in his face the way it started in his hand." (*Sticks and Bones*, I, 22–23)

It was Hank who gave Harriet to Ozzie—an Ozzie who cannot remember "making" David, whose blindness is never given a military explanation. Later, Ozzie will try to identify the poison as the product of Harriet's "internal female organs," but against his will David will make him search inside himself until he too can see Zung. Then the sham is past. Then the realities of war and sitcom merge. Then the trucks return.

They've stopped bringing back the blind. They're bringing back the dead now. The convoy's broken up. There's no control. . . . Tell her yes, the one with no name is ours. We'll put him in that chair. We can bring them all here. I want them all here, all the trucks and bodies. There's room. Ricky can sing. . . . They will become the floor and they will become the walls, the chairs. We'll sit in them, sleep. We will call them "home". We will give them as gifts—call them "ring" and "pot" and "cup." No, . . . we will notice them no more than all the others. (*Sticks and Bones*, II, 85–86)

Some truths are eternal, but truth-tellers are not. Earlier, when under pressure in a different context, Ozzie lashes out: "If I have to lie to live, I will." (*Sticks and Bones*, II, 68) David has underestimated the determination of the self-deceived to retain their fantasy. Ricky beats him to the floor with his guitar. Finally face to face with the reality of Zung, Ozzie strangles her, and in a metaphor for America's reassembling of its image, hides the body under the rug. All the family then cooperates in assisting David's "suicide" by razor, with Harriet prudently protecting her living room with towels and drip pans and Ricky photographing

David's deathmask for the slides we see at the beginning and end of the play.

America does not know itself, Rabe tells us, as an act of self-will. The final irony of the Vietnam adventure is that both war protesters and war veterans in the end were ostracized for the same reason: not for what they told us about the war, but for what they told us about ourselves.

Vietnam was America's tragedy because our intention in being there was to protect the children that in the end we alienated, corrupted, and destroyed. We had attained the "good life," which we wanted to bequeath to those children. In *China Gate*, Lucky Legs dies so her son can be an American. In *The Trial of the Catonsville Nine*, the defendants gave up their freedom to protest a war which kills children so that the killing of children will not become the norm. Whatever their political differences, both acts were sacrifices of self for the future. Yet, the longer the war lasted, the more corrupted the future became. Finally, the "good life" in *Sticks and Bones* became Ricky, the appetite without conscience, to which we sacrificed David, the child who held up the mirror to it. The tunnel in which we walked was paved with good intentions, and the light at the end of it was hell.

Notes

1. Quoted by William J. Lederer, *Our Own Worst Enemy* (New York: W. W. Norton, 1968), 56.

2. Nancy Zaroulis and Gerald Sullivan, *Who Spoke Up? American Protest Against the War in Vietnam 1963–1975* (Garden City, N.Y.: Doubleday, 1984), 333.

3. Lederer, *Our Own Worst Enemy*, 28–30.

4. Lederer, *Our Own Worst Enemy*, 58–59.

5. Frances FitzGerald, *Fire in the Lake* (New York: Vintage Books, 1972), 68–71.

6. When loyal Vietnamese peasants were moved from their villages into "strategic hamlets" to better protect them militarily, the South Vietnamese government and its American advisors became the enemy. George C. Herring, *America's Longest War* (New York: Alfred A. Knopf, 1986), 89.

7. FitzGerald, *Fire in the Lake*, 66.

8. Fred Halstead, *Out Now!* (New York: Monad, 1978), 4–5.

9. One of the *anti*-Communist OSS officers in Vietnam was Watergate break-in chief E. Howard Hunt. Alexander Kendrick, *The Wound Within* (Boston: Little, Brown, 1974), 35.

10. Quoted by Herring, *America's Longest War*, 9.

11. Lederer, *Our Own Worst Enemy*, 240–43.

12. Kendrick, *Wound Within*, 38.

13. American policy and military experts, who continually feared that Ho would prevail upon Communist China to intervene directly in the war with South Vietnam and its allies, should have read his replay to the angry pro-Chinese elements within the

DRV in 1946: "You fools! . . . The last time the Chinese came, they stayed one thousand years! . . . The white man is finished in Asia. But if the Chinese stay now, they will never leave. As for me, I prefer to smell French shit for five years, rather than Chinese shit for the rest of my life." "Ho Chi Minh: Asian Tito?" in *America in Vietnam*, ed. William A. Williams et al. (Garden City, N.Y.: Anchor Press/Doubleday, 1985), 95–96.

    14. Williams et al., *America in Vietnam*, 6–8.

    15. French Union losses in the first Indochina War included forty-five thousand dead, forty-eight thousand missing and presumed dead, and seventy-five thousand wounded. The economic cost (not including the American loans) was over $3 billion. Kendrick, *Wounded Within*, 91.

    16. Herring, *America's Longest War*, 22, 42.

    17. In 1967, General Lew Walt, the Marine Corps commander in Vietnam, told Congressman Riegle that military control of Vietnam would require another twelve to fifteen years. Lederer, *Our Own Worst Enemy*, 263.

    18. Herring, *America's Longest War*, 30–36.

    19. The complete Geneva Conference Declaration can be found in Walter Lefeber, ed., *America in the Cold War* (New York: John Wiley & Sons, 1969), 98–100.

    20. Kendrick, *Wounded Within*, 89.

    21. John Newman, *Vietnam War Literature* (Metuchen, N.J.: Scarecrow Press, 1988).

    22. Albert Auster and Leonard Quart, *How the War Was Remembered: Hollywood and Vietnam* (New York: Praeger, 1988), 33.

    23. Tom Stoppard, "Ambushes for the Audience: Towards a High Comedy of Ideas, *Theatre Quarterly* 4 (May-July 1974): 14.

    24. Auster and Quart, *How the War Was Remembered*, 17.

    25. Samuel Fuller, *China Gate* (Globe Enterprises, released by Twentieth-Century Fox), Republic Videotape 0648.

    26. Nicholas Garnham, *Samuel Fuller* (New York: Viking Press, 1971), 116.

    27. Phil Hardy, *Samuel Fuller* (New York: Praeger Publishers, 1970), 22.

    28. Quoted by Robert H. Wiebe, in "White Attitudes and Black Rights from *Brown* to *Bakke*," in *Have We Overcome?*" ed. Michael V. Namorato (Jackson: University of Mississippi Press, 1979), 150.

    29. Williams et al., *America in Vietnam*, 254.

    30. Kendrick, *Wound Within*, 106.

    31. Following the Buddhist self-immolations of 1963, Madame Nhu said she enjoyed the monks' "barbeques."

    32. Quoted by Michael Maclear, in *The Ten Thousand Day War* (New York: St. Martin's Press, 1981), 54–55.

    33. Chester L. Cooper, *The Lost Crusade: America in Vietnam* (New York: Dodd, Mead, 1970), 210.

    34. Herring, *America's Longest War*, 95–97.

    35. Herring, *America's Longest War*, 133.

    36. Kendrick, *Wound Within*, 175–80.

    37. Maclear, *Ten Thousand Day War*, 130.

    38. Timothy J. Lomperis, *The War Everyone Lost—and Won* (Baton Rouge: Louisiana State University Press, 1984), 62.

    39. Lomperis, *War Everyone Lost*, 59.

    40. Herring, *America's Longest War*, 146, 149.

41. Cooper, *Lost Crusade*, 489–517.

42. Maclear, *Ten Thousand Day War*, 253.

43. Maclear, *Ten Thousand Day War*, 147.

44. Kendrick, *Wound Within*, 307.

45. Gabriel Kolko, *Anatomy of a War* (New York: Pantheon Books, 1985), 144–45.

46. Lederer, *Our Own Worst Enemy*, 92–97.

47. George Walter, quoted by Maclear, *Ten Thousand Day War*, 274.

48. Robert Jay Lifton, "Americans in Vietnam: The Lessons of My Lai," in *War Crimes and the American Conscience*, ed. Edwin Knoll and Judith Nies McFadden (New York: Holt, Rinehart and Winston, 1970), 106.

49. Lederer, *Our Own Worst Enemy*, 29.

50. Herring, *America's Longest War*, 189–91.

51. Kendrick, *Wound Within*, 43.

52. Kolko, *Anatomy of a War*, 287–88.

53. Quoted by Thomas Powers, *The War at Home* (New York: Grossman Publishers, 1973), 26.

54. Quoted by Powers, *War at Home*, 139.

55. Martin Luther King, Jr., "A Time to Break Silence," in *A Testament of Hope: The Essential Writings of Martin Luther King, Jr.*, ed. James Melvin Washington (San Francisco: Harper & Row, 1986), 233.

56. Powers, *War at Home*, 55–61, 71.

57. In actuality, Bundy had flown to the Dominican Republic, where, at the beginning of May, Johnson had sent twenty-four thousand troops to contain yet another "war of liberation."

58. Morgenthau was right about Laos. It just hadn't happened yet. Powers, *War at Home*, 67–69.

59. Kendrick, *Wound Within*, 221, 191.

60. Cooper, *Lost Crusade*, 237–67.

61. Herring, *America's Longest War*, 164.

62. Powers, *War at Home*, 82–85.

63. Zaroulis and Sullivan, *Who Spoke Up?*, 3.

64. Powers, *War at Home*, 190–95.

65. Carl Oglesby, "How Can We Continue to Sack the Ports of Asia and Still Dream of Jesus?" in LaFeber, *America in the Cold War*, 18–22.

66. Quoted by Irwin Unger, in *The Movement: A History of the American New Left, 1959–1972* (New York: Dodd, Mead, 1974), 74.

67. Powers, *War at Home*, 180.

68. Geraldine Lust, quoted by Arthur Sainer, in *The Radical Theatre Notebook* (New York: Avon Books, 1975), 19.

69. Lee Baxandall, "Spectacles and Scenarios: Dramaturgy of Radical Activity," *The Drama Review* 13, no. 4 (Summer 1969): 54.

70. Sainer, *Radical Theatre Notebook*, 62–63.

71. Richard Schechner, "Guerilla Theatre, May 1970," *The Drama Review* 14, no. 3 (Fall 1970), 164–65.

72. Joseph Heller, *We Bombed in New Haven* (New York: Dell Publishing Co., 1970), II, 218.

73. Quoted by Charles A. Meconis, in *With Clumsy Grace* (New York: Seabury Press, 1979), 6.

74. Quoted by Kendrick, *Wound Within*, 216.

75. Quoted by Zaroulis and Sullivan, *Who Spoke Up?* 101.

76. Zaroulis and Sullivan, *Who Spoke Up?* 10.

77. Richard Curtis, *The Berrigan Brothers* (New York: Hawthorn Books, 1974), 28–29.

78. Quoted by Meconis, *With Clumsy Grace*, 13.

79. Curtis, *Berrigan Brothers*, 75–84.

80. Quoted by John Deedy, in *"Apologies, Good Friends"* (Chicago: Fides/Claretian, 1981), 82–83.

81. Daniel Berrigan, *The Trial of the Catonsville Nine* (Toronto: Bantam Books, 1971), iii, 64. Subsequent references to this play will be noted in the text.

82. Curtis, *Berrigan Brothers*, 110–20.

83. Quoted by Deedy, *"Apologies, Good Friends,"* 116.

84. Deedy, *"Apologies, Good Friends,"* 128.

85. Quoted by Al Santoli, in *Everything We Had* (New York: Random House, 1981), 228.

86. Quoted by A. D. Horne, in *The Wounded Generation* (Englewood Cliffs, N.J.: Prentice Hall, 1981), 112–13.

87. Quoted by Mark Baker, in *Nam* (New York: William Morrow, 1981), 288.

88. Lawrence M. Bakir and William A. Strauss, *Chance and Circumstance* (New York: Alfred A. Knopf, 1978), 3–13.

89. James Fallows, "What Did You Do in the Class War, Daddy?" in *The Wounded Generation*, ed. A. D. Horne (Englewood Cliffs, N.J.: Prentice Hall, 1981), 20.

90. Bakir and Strauss, *Chance and Circumstance*, 5–10.

91. Santoli, *Everything We Had*, xi.

92. Myra MacPherson, *Long Time Passing* (Garden City, N.Y.: Doubleday and Company, 1984), 191.

93. Tim O'Brien, "Going After Cacciato," in *The Wounded Generation*, ed. A. D. Horne (Englewood Cliffs, N.J.: Prentice-Hall, 1981), 3.

94. Tom Cole, *Medal of Honor Rag*, in *Coming to Terms: American Plays and the Vietnam War* (New York: Theatre Communications Group, 1985), 177.

95. Emily Mann, *Still Life*, in *Coming to Terms: American Plays and the Vietnam War* (New York: Theatre Communications Group, 1985), I, x, 282.

96. *"Sticks and Bones* on C.B.S. March 9," *New York Times*, February 21, 1973, p. 87.

97. "Papp's *Sticks and Bones* Put Off by C.B.S.," *New York Times*, March 7, 1973, p. 87.

98. John J. O'Connor, "How About Some Backbone?" *New York Times*, March 18, 1973, sec. 2, p. 19.

99. Albin Krebs, *"Sticks and Bones* Decision Is Called 'Cowardly,' " *New York Times*, March 9, 1973, p. 75.

100. George Gent, "Compare Attitude on Media to That of Nazi Germany," *New York Times*, March 10, 1973, p. 62.

101. Albin Krebs, "C.B.S. Stations Balk on *Sticks and Bones*," *New York Times*, August 17, 1973, p. 63.

102. David Rabe, *Sticks and Bones* (New York: Samuel French, 1972), II, 86. Subsequent references to this play will be noted in the text.

5

Civil Rights—A Caste of Millions Lights Up a Dark Theatre

Justice is pictured blind and her daughter, the Law, ought at least to be color-blind. [1]

—Albion W. Tourgee, counsel for the plaintiff in
Plessy vs. Ferguson (1896)

In October 1947, President Truman's Commission on Civil Rights produced a landmark document, *To Secure These Rights*, suggesting that the immediate equalizing of certain opportunities was required by moral and economic necessity at home and political urgency abroad. On February 2, 1948, the president made these recommendations the basis of his legislative message to Congress: (a) the establishment of a permanent Commission on Civil Rights, a Joint Congressional Committee on Civil Rights, and a Civil Rights Division in the Justice Department; (b) the strengthening of civil rights statues; (c) the providing of federal protection against lynching; (d) the protection of the right to vote; (e) the prevention of discrimination in employment by the establishing of a Fair Employment Practices Commission—a permanent successor to the one operating temporarily throughout World War II; and (f) the prohibition of discrimination in interstate transportation facilities. [2]

This program struck at the heart of "states-rights" institutionalized racism by asserting the federal government's responsibility for assuring the Negro legal, political, and economic equality of opportunity. Its last clause was a direct refutation of the 1896 *Plessy vs. Ferguson* decision which justified Jim Crow railroad cars on a "separate but equal" basis.

When it was rejected by Congress, other means of attaining equality had to be found. Some were executive, such as President Truman's Order 9981 of 1948, providing for the armed services integration. Most, however, were judicial, and in the late 1940s and 1950s the NAACP sponsored the tortuous trek to the Supreme Court for several important rulings on housing, voting and education.

Many of the civil rights judgments of the Earl Warren Court (1953–1969) followed paths laid out earlier. Four times between 1927 and 1953, the Supreme Court ruled unfavorably on Texas attempts to exclude Negroes from voting in Democratic Party primaries.[3] In the "Solid South" of pre–civil rights days, winning the Democratic primary was tantamount to election. In 1948, the Vinson Court ruled that purely private "gentlemen's agreements" which restricted housing along racial lines were not governmentally enforceable—a principle which the Warren Court used in the sixties to disallow "sit-in" convictions.[4] Even the Warren Court's most famous decision, *Brown vs. Topeka* (1954), had a number of predecessors stretching back to 1938.

On four separate occasions between 1938 and 1950, a resident Negro sought admittance to a state university graduate school, and each time the Court so ordered.[5] However, *Brown vs. Topeka*, the alphabetically first of the five cases whose adjudication banned all state-imposed racial discrimination, was far more sweeping in its implications. Seventeen states and the District of Columbia *required* segregation in 1954, and 50,000 schools and 10,500,000 students were affected.

Does segregation of children in public schools solely on the basis of race, even though the physical facilities and other "tangible" factors may be equal, deprive the children of the minority group of equal educational opportunities? We believe that it does. . . . To separate them from others of similar age and qualifications solely because of their race generates a feeling of inferiority as to their status in the community that may affect their minds and hearts in a way unlikely ever to be undone.[6]

In the late 1950s, Congress laid the groundwork for the monumental civil rights bills of the mid-sixties. In 1957, the Civil Rights Commission President Truman had called for in 1948 was finally established, with a mandate to seek out voting violations. The attorney general was empowered to seek injunctions against interference with the right to vote, and the 1960 Civil Rights Act allowed for federal representatives to register voters when local officials would not.[7] But the clearance of congressional roadblocks could not come too soon for even racial moderates who, tiring of the delay, cost, and modest accomplishments of the court system, were already testing a new method of obtaining their goals: nonviolent passive resistance.

In December 1955, Rosa Parks, a seamstress and former NAACP official, was arrested for refusing to give up her seat on a Montgomery, Alabama, bus to a white man. Within days, a bus boycott by blacks had been formed, and, reluctantly at first, Dr. Martin Luther King, Jr., a twenty-six-year-old Baptist minister, emerged as its spokesman, evolving a philosophy of Christian nonviolence even as he taught it and lived it.

The boycotters' initial demands were incredibly modest: (a) more courteous treatment of black passengers; (b) seating on a first-come, first-served basis, but with blacks continuing the current practice of filling up from the rear of the bus forward, while whites filled in from the front toward the back; and (c) hiring of black drivers on predominantly black lines.[8] To attain these goals, they did not march, sit in, or court arrest. They merely refused to ride a bus. In retaliation for their non-action, among other things, Dr. King's house was bombed and the Reverend Fred Gray's draft exemption was revoked. In February 1956, twenty-four ministers were among the nearly one hundred people arrested in Montgomery on boycott charges. Dr. King was sentenced to 386 days in jail. Nonetheless, the riders' strike continued until open seating was instituted on the buses shortly before Christmas of 1956, 381 days after the boycott began.[9]

On February 1, 1960, the same day Dr. King's Southern Christian Leadership Conference moved to Atlanta to "train our youth and adult leaders in the techniques of social change through nonviolent resistance,"[10] students from North Carolina Agricultural and Technical College "sat in" at a hitherto "whites only" Greensboro lunch counter. Almost instantaneously, that scene was repeated in dozens of cities before reshaping itself as "read-ins" in public libraries, "wade-ins" at municipal pools, "kneel-ins" at churches, and "stand-ins" at ticket windows of segregated theatres. Over 40 percent of the 1960 NAACP budget went toward defending court cases involving 1,700 student demonstrators.[11]

Within months, the demonstrators had an organization and a name— the Student Nonviolent Coordinating Committee (SNCC). SNCC members were in the vanguard of the 1961 "Freedom Riders," a direct, and frequently bloodied, challenge to the Jim Crow interstate transportation laws enshrined in *Plessy vs. Ferguson* sixty-five years earlier. In the autumn of 1961, 16 SNCC members began full-time civil rights organizing in the Deep South. By 1964, there were 150, coordinating the efforts of 650 volunteers in the voter registration "Freedom Summer" in Mississippi.[12]

In September 1957, President Eisenhower had federalized the Arkansas state militia and joined it to the 101st Airborne Division (a total of 1,000 troops) to integrate nine Negro students into Little Rock's Central High School. Personally uninterested in desegregation, Eisenhower was well aware that the rule of law must be upheld and international embarrassment avoided: "At a time when we face grave situations abroad because of the hatred that Communism bears toward a system of government based on human rights, it would be difficult to exaggerate the harm that is being done to the prestige and influence and, indeed, to the safety of our nation and the world."[13]

Opposition to university integration in the Deep South was even more fierce. Autherine Lucy was admitted to the University of Alabama on February 3, 1956, only to have riots cause her suspension four days later and her expulsion on February 29. It would not be until June 11, 1963, that Negro students—this time in defiance of Governor George C. Wallace, and escorted by federal marshals and the National Guard— would again enroll at the University of Alabama. Meanwhile, James H. Meredith, an air force veteran, began study at the University of Mississippi in September 1962—an action only made possible by 1,500 federal marshals and a Fifth Circuit Court judgment threatening Governor Ross Barnett with jailing and a fine of $10,000 a day.[14]

In 1963, the civil rights movement was achieving its deepest impression on the American sensibility. Henceforth, it would be obscured by legislation, the Black Power movement, Vietnam, and the multiple unrests which claimed our attention in the 1960s. Two events were pivotal: (a) the integration of Birmingham, and (b) the March on Washington.

In 1962, Martin Luther King, Jr., and his aides formulated a method for achieving local integration that they called Project C—for confrontation. On April 3, 1963, this plan was initiated in the citadel of southern white privilege, Birmingham, Alabama. As a television world watched in shock, naked flesh and moral rectitude clashed with the canine corps and cop clubs of Sheriff Eugene ("Bull") Connor in events timed, in a symbolic masterstroke, to coincide with the pre-Easter Christian calendar—most notably in the Palm Sunday beating of 600 demonstrators and the Good Friday arrest of Martin Luther King, Jr., and fifty of his followers.[15] On April 16, Dr. King made a prediction to white clergymen (who had called his actions "untimely" and "unwise") in his classic "Letter from a Birmingham Jail": "If [the Negro's] repressed emotions are not released in nonviolent ways, they will seek expression through violence; this is not a threat but a fact of history."[16]

On May 10, the city of Birmingham announced a four-part program to desegregate lunch counters, restrooms, fitting rooms, and drinking fountains.

In a national television address on the evening of June 11, the day the University of Alabama was integrated, President Kennedy called for a new Civil Rights Act to assure equality of accommodations, a faster school desegregation pace, and greater minority voter protection.

One hundred years of delay have passed since President Lincoln freed the slaves, yet their heirs, their grandsons, are not yet fully free. They are not yet freed from the bonds of injustice; they are not yet freed from social and economic oppression.

And this nation, for all its hopes and all its boasts, will not be fully free until all its citizens are free.[17]

For those Americans who are too young to remember the emotional climate of August 28, 1963, it may be hard to comprehend the "high" of the March on Washington, when more than 250,000 Americans—a quarter of them white—walked the mile from the Washington Monument to the Lincoln Monument. What seemed to be happening that day was the final illumination of Ralph Ellison's "Invisible Man," a self-declaration of black citizenship made before God and man in the nation's capital. "I have a dream," Dr. King said that day,

that one day this nation will rise up and live out the true meaning of its creed: "We hold these truths to be self-evident; that all men are created equal."

I have a dream that one day on the red hills of Georgia the sons of former slaves and the sons of former slave owners will be able to sit down together at the table of brotherhood. . . . This will be the day when all of God's children will be able to sing with meaning, "My country, 'tis of thee, sweet land of liberty, of thee I sing. Land where my fathers died, land of the Pilgrims' pride, from every mountainside, let freedom ring."[18]

Negro History Plays: Negative Images of White America

Emerging minority drama follows a reasonably consistent pattern: (a) the sympathy play—written for a social majority audience by one of its own, projecting an emotional identification with a social minority; (b) the protest play—written for a majority audience by a minority member for the purpose of achieving acceptance from the majority; (c) the revolutionary play—written for a minority audience by a minority author and demonstrating the minority's personal and moral superiority to the majority; and (d) the play of everyday life or postrevolutionary play— written by a minority playwright for a mixed audience and illustrating a situation in which social inequality is a fact of life without necessarily being its focus.

Insofar as such plays are political as well as social, however, the dominant minority drama genre is the history play in which the life of an event, individual, caste, class, or creed is examined from the minority viewpoint in order to accuse, excuse, educate, or inspire. Nowhere is this truer than in Afro-American theatre, whose purpose from the first published black-written play (William Wells Brown's *The Escape*, 1858) has been to bridge the gap between the history written by the winners and the history experienced by the losers. Randolph Edmond's *Denmark Vesey* and *Nat Turner* date from the 1920s, and two of the earliest Afro-American drama anthologies, Willis Richardson's *Plays and Pageants from the Life of the Negro* (1930) and (with May Miller) *Negro History in Thirteen Plays* (1935) furthered the tradition. As historian Carter Woodson wrote in 1935: "The stage in America . . . is often an agency for racial propaganda which fair-minded people are not anxious to promote. . . . Why does not the Negro dramatize his own life and bring the world unto him?"[19]

In more recent times, William Branch examined the conscience of Frederick Douglass with *In Splendid Error* (1954) and Loften Mitchell explored the range of the twentieth-century's first half with his treatments of black comedian Bert Williams (*Star of the Morning*, 1965) and the Reverend Joseph DeLaine, a civil rights pioneer (*A Land Beyond the River*, 1957). Other political and artistic leaders portrayed included Marcus Garvey (Charles Fuller's *The Rise*, 1969) and Paul Robeson, in Philip Hayes Dean's 1979 play of the same name. Malcolm X inspired at least three plays in addition to the one analyzed later in this chapter: N. B. Davidson's *El Hajj Malik* (1979), William Wellington Mackey's *Requiem for Brother X* (1966), and Jeff Stetson's 1988 *The Meeting* (about a fictional rendezvous with Martin Luther King, Jr.); as well as an opera about Malcolm and Elijah Muhammad.

Plays which attempt the whole sweep of Afro-American history are more rare. Ironically, considering its title, *Liberty Deferred*, a Living Newspaper written by John Silvera and Abram Hill for the Federal Theatre, was never performed or published. The outstanding example of such a play in the Federal Theatre era was Langston Hughes's *Don't You Want to Be Free?*, created for his own Harlem Suitcase Theatre in 1937. Subtitled *From Slavery Through the Blues to Now—and Then Some*, the play is notable today for providing a narrative context for some of Hughes's best poetry and for developing the multiple characterization, presentational acting style which later plays like *In White America* would borrow.

Beginning with the race's origins in Africa, each section of black history was given its own rhythm up to the play's finale, the 1935 Harlem riots.

Member of the Audience: Riots won't solve anything, will they, brother?

Young Man: No, riots won't solve anything.

Member of the Audience: Then what must we do?

Young Man: Organize . . . colored and white unions to lift us all up together.

Member of the Audience: You mean organize with white folks, too.

Young Man: That's what I mean! We're all in the same boat! This is America, isn't it?
   It's not all colored. Not all white. It's both. [20]

Hughes's evocation of class solidarity across caste lines was eventually to bring him before HUAC in the late 1950s, but the play's subsequent history proved the playwright to be more interested in social goals than in dogma. According to Leslie Catherine Sanders, Hughes reworked *Don't You Want to Be Free?* at least six times. In 1944 he omitted the Harlem riots entirely and concentrated on segregation in the military and the exclusion of blacks from defense industries. The 1946 version calls for continuing the fight for democracy at home after the war. Cold War conservatism results in a soft-pedaling of racial cooperation in 1952, but still equates the riots at home with the overseas battles for freedom. The 1963 Emancipation-centennial version supplants the call for labor organization with an admonition to join the NAACP and the Congress of Racial Equality.[21]

Slave Ship (1967), by LeRoi Jones (Amiri Baraka), is a restating of *Don't You Want to Be Free?* using a modernist, Artaudian tone. Rhythm is again the dominant storytelling device, but instead of Hughes's poetry and traditional spirituals and blues, Jones uses sound as a force in itself to express the terror and the pain of the Middle Passage (the Atlantic voyage of the slave ships only alluded to by Hughes) and to impact upon the nerves of the audience. Even when dialogue is used, many of the early passages are in Yoruba and unintelligible even to most black audiences. The other similarities and differences between the two plays are equally instructive. Both use a single villain who plays multiple roles, but while Hughes's villain is a white oppressor, Jones depicts a black betrayer: a house slave who sells Nat Turner for an extra pork chop, a shuffling "Steppin Fetchit" entertainer, and a nonviolent Uncle Tom preacher. The endings are also reversed. While Hughes calls for black/white unity, Jones has all his blacks conjoin in a dance which ends with the slaughter of the preacher, then turns on the unseen white voice which has been his guide:

"You haha can't touch me . . . you scared of me, niggers. I'm God. You cain't kill white Jesus God. I got long blond blow-hair. I don't even need to wear a wig. You love the way I look. You want to look like me. You love me. You want me. Please. I'm good. I'm kind. I'll give you anything you want. I'm white Jesus savior right God pay you money nigger me is good God please . . . please don't." . . . [*And then the terrible humming . . . sound, broken now, by the finally awful scream of the killed white voice.*][22]

In *The Motion of History*, the Tom character is back, now (in Baraka's evolving social analysis) as a member of the new petite bourgeoisie.

Black Politician: Black Power! [*Glassy eyed, then*] I nominate for vice-president of the United States Nelson Rockefeller, the fiend of Attica.

Ex-Black Militant: Black Power! [*Glassy eyed, then*] Black Capitalism! Let the Soul Brothers get a piece of the action.

Actor: Black Art. [*Glassy eyed, then*] Blacula! Super Fly! The Werewolf from Watts! Starsky and Hutch!

Lyndon B. Johnson: [*At one side of the stage*] We shall overcome!

Richard Nixon: [*Other side of stage*] Power to the People![23]

The Motion of History is a Marxist-Leninist analysis of the American past from 1676 Jamestown through Reconstruction and the 1960s murders of the Philadelphia, Mississippi, civil rights workers, Malcolm X, and Martin Luther King, Jr., ending in a caste-crossing Communist congress calling for the building of a party to bring about a socialist revolution. It is a long play and only intermittently actable. It is possible to sympathize with Baraka's attempt to unify white and black by giving context to the events which separate them. There is irony in his difficulty in finding a publisher for his anticapitalist plays when his "Hate Whitey" works were so commercially successful. It is unfortunate he has been forced to sacrifice dramatic effectiveness to achieve it. On that level, *In White America*—a sympathy play/protest play/history play hybrid—is its superior.

In White America

Wednesday I went with a bunch of Freedom School kids to Biloxi where we saw *In White America*. [The Free Southern Theatre] has been formed this summer to play all over the state. . . . It is pretty strong stuff—what the slave ships were like, what being a slave was like, the lynchings, Father Divine in the 30s, Little Rock, and an added scene: a speech by Rita Schwerner [wife of Michael Schwerner, a civil rights worker slain in Philadelphia, Mississippi]. . . . One of the actresses said, "You can't imagine what it was like under slavery" and a 15-year-old girl next to me said, "Oh, yes I can."[24]

In the emotional aftermath of the March on Washington, *In White America*, Martin Duberman's documentary drama, opened at the Sheridan Square Playhouse in New York City on October 31, 1963. This climate did not engender the play itself, whose final episode takes place at Little Rock's Central High School six years earlier, but it is doubtful that the play could have found a producer had not the March suggested the existence of an audience.

The first act of *In White America* begins with the slave ships and ends with Emancipation. The second act's dramatic distance—Reconstruction to Little Rock—is more psychological than chronological or legal. The order of importance of the events of Act I has long since been established. Act I also allows for the insertion of topical material like that noted earlier in the chapter. However, Act II, ending as it does in 1957, has a climax which is dramatically, but not historically, convincing. While one could claim Little Rock to be as psychologically relevant to integration as Birmingham or the March on Washington, integration itself is no longer the sole issue, and no 1963 play could expect to deal with Black Power or the economic malaise of recent years.

The classic protest play engages the audience's sympathy by associating the social victim with what the audience holds dear. The first act of *In White America* associates black slaves with a love of liberty, a strong sense of family, a true Christianity, a desire for justice and education, and the willingness to work hard, to fight, and to die for the concrete manifestation of these ideals. It then concludes, unsurprisingly, that these upholders of basic American standards deserve their freedom.

The historical passages begin with a slave ship doctor's description of a kidnapped people who, enduring starvation, filth, confinement, disease, and rape, when given the opportunity, throw themselves overboard, choosing the sharks over bondage. This account is juxtaposed against the 1790 Congress's reasons for refusing the ban the slave trade: (a) unconstitutionality, (b) harm to property values, (c) incentive to slave discontent, and (d) the teachings of the Bible. More unsettling, considering his attempt to ban slavery in the Declaration of Independence and his long relationship with Sally Hemmings, is Thomas Jefferson's conclusion that blacks are biologically inferior.

Living conditions vary from plantation to plantation, but in an unguarded moment a slave named William reveals that all slaves talk of freedom. He suggests that it would benefit both races. Working for themselves, blacks would work much harder, and white people would gain because they own all the land. Meanwhile, Nat Turner suggests the danger of *not* freeing the slaves.

Indeed, the true feelings of slaves remain hidden so long as they are in bondage. In a letter to a master who has asked him to return, one runaway reckons up the wages he and his wife should have received for a combined fifty-two years of service and asks it be sent to him as a pledge of sincerity, concluding with a cheerful "Say howdy to George Carter, and thank him for taking the pistol from you when you were shooting at me."[25] After the Civil War begins, the wife of a South Carolina senator senses danger in the very impassiveness of her slaves: "Are they stolidly stupid, or wiser than we are, silent and strong, biding their time?" (*In White America*, I, 32)

The play reminds us constantly that the need to enforce inferiority upon an "Other" is as degrading to the oppressor as to the oppressed. John Brown is heard denying that God respects racial differences, while Sojourner Truth extends the same principle to sex. But their call for recognition of individual humanity only highlights a caste system as invulnerable in the North as it is in the South. When the home of a Quaker woman in Canterbury, Connecticut, is befouled and vandalized because she opens a school for "young ladies and little misses of color," Andrew T. Judson, later a district court judge, defends the assaults: "The colored people never can rise from their menial condition in our country; they ought not to be permitted to rise here." (*In White America*, I, 28)

The demands of the Civil War suspend such sentiments, and the act ends with a white officer's account of his black troops' heroism, religiosity, and patriotism. After the reading of the Emancipation Proclamation, the soldiers break into "My Country, 'Tis of Thee," whose words might have recalled on opening night Dr. King's speech of less than ten weeks earlier: "From every mountainside, let freedom ring!" (*In White America*, I, 36)

The second act shows a legal slavery replaced with a de facto slavery. After 1865, blacks still live in a society where whites set the norms and control the law, government, and economy. In a postwar meeting with Frederick Douglass and George T. Downing, President Andrew Johnson warns that he will support the enfranchisement of blacks only if such an act represents "the will of the people," ignoring that the only way of testing that will is through a vote in which all the current voters are white and male.

In the South, Reconstruction and the Fifteenth Amendment, which grants the vote to Negro males, are met by the rise of the Ku Klux Klan. Transcripts of federal hearings provide accounts of men whipped for attending meetings and holding political opinions. There is an interview with a woman who was whipped and raped and whose child was crippled, all for the crime of owning her own house. On the floor of the U.S. Senate, "Pitchfork Ben" Tillman of South Carolina justifies more than three thousand lynchings in the thirty-five years following Reconstruction as protection of white women against rape. Meanwhile, official records cite the most frequent lynching motive as "mistaken identity." (*In White America*, II, 50)

As the twentieth century dawns, blacks cannot even agree among themselves as to what their objectives must be. The most influential Negro of the day, Booker T. Washington of Tuskegee Institute, urged that blacks concentrate their energies on manual labor and economic sufficiency: "In all things that are purely social we can be as separate as the fingers, yet one as the hand in all things essential to mutual progress." (*In White America*, II, 52) In response, W. E. B. Du Bois, one of the founders of the NAACP, argued that in order to conciliate the South, Washington was accepting the definition of blacks as inferior: "We do not expect to see the bias and prejudices of years disappear at the blast of the trumpet; but we are absolutely certain that the way for a people to gain their reasonable rights is not by throwing them away and insisting that they do not want them." (*In White America*, II, 53)

In the Depression, Father Divine, the most visible of "the New Gods of the City," was able to take the demonstrative, "sanctified," religious fundamentalism newly urbanized blacks brought with them from the South and use it to form the basis of a successful nongovernmental socialism. More philosophically influential was Marcus Garvey's post-WW I Universal Negro Improvement Association. Its "Back to Africa" principle provided the intellectual underpinnings for all subsequent black nationalism movements.

Insofar as white support for black equality was concerned, the twentieth century seemed determined to take steps backward. In 1913, Woodrow Wilson's administration reinstated segregation among federal employees for the first time since the Civil War, and oppression of blacks outside the public sector was frequently far worse.

An Elbert County, Georgia, laborer testifies concerning conditions on a peon farm where illiterate workers are signed to $3.50-per-week, ten-year contracts whose secondary provisions are not revealed to them: "It was then made plain to us that in the contracts, we had agreed to be locked up in a stockade at any time the Senator saw fit. And if we got mad and ran away, we could be run down by bloodhounds, and the Senator might administer any punishment he thought proper." (*In White America*, II, 59) At the end of ten years, when the workers try to leave, commissary bills are produced from the company store where all of them have been forced to buy their supplies. Told they are signing promises to pay later, the workers find themselves obligated to work another three years for nothing.

At the end of World War II, a sailor sums up the racial situation in a single sentence. "We know that our battle for democracy will begin when we reach San Francisco on our way home." (*In White America*, II, 62) Postwar civil rights gains are brushed by in a single sentence as the play moves to Little Rock and the major theme of Act II.

A black high school girl, attempting to enroll in Little Rock's Central High School, finds herself stopped by National Guardsmen with rifles and fixed bayonets. As she retreats to the city bus bench, members of a jeering crowd spit on her and threaten lynching: "Just then a white man sat down beside me, put his arm around me and patted my shoulder": "She just sat there, her head down. Tears were streaming down her cheeks. I don't know what made me put my arm around her, saying, 'Don't let them see you cry.' Maybe she reminded me of my 15-year-old daughter." (*In White America*, II, 64)

The scene ends with the actors facing one another rather than the audience. Will they see one another as a threatening "Other" to be killed or tolerated; or will they become family members, to be cherished and protected? "Which side are you on?" seemed such a simple question in 1963, when only a lack of will appeared to stand between us and a "Great Society." In the years that followed, however, events blurred even black and white issues, reducing perception to gray opacity.

The Rise of Black Power

On September 15, 1963—just eighteen days after Dr. King dreamed of "all of God's children" joining hands—a bomb interrupted Sunday school at the Birmingham Sixteenth Street Baptist Church. Four children died and twenty-one other people were injured. Lerone Bennett records the sight of a man screaming amid the church's rubble: "Love 'em? Love 'em? *I hate 'em!*"[26] Ten weeks after the Birmingham bombing, John F. Kennedy, who had in the first six months of 1963 moved from seeing racial problems as "low priority" to the proposal of the most comprehensive civil rights bill in America's history, was assassinated.

In retrospect, it sometimes seems that nonviolent protest was also fatally wounded that November day in Dallas. If America could not protect a president, who could blame anyone for arming in self-defense? The souring of Vietnam (already present in the assassination of Diem), the disgrace of the trial of the murderers of the Philadelphia, Mississippi, civil rights workers, the riots in Watts in 1965 and Newark and Detroit in 1967, and the concurrent murders of Malcolm X, Viola Liuzzo, George Lincoln Rockwell, Martin Luther King, Jr., and Robert Kennedy only confirmed a principle already defined.

In the same years, however, blacks made more substantial gains than in any period since the Reconstruction. In his first address to Congress following President Kennedy's death, President Johnson laid down the gauntlet: "We have talked long enough in this country about equal rights. . . . It is time now to write the next chapter, and to write it in the books of the law." The 1964 Civil Rights Act barred discrimination in public facilities (allowing the Justice Department to sue to desegregate state and municipal facilities like swimming pools, and to withhold federal funds from any state agency that delayed), forbade employer or union job discrimination, authorized the Justice Department to *initiate* school desegregation suits, and extended voting rights. When Dr. King, *Time* magazine's "Man of the Year" for 1963, was jailed in Selma, Alabama, less than two months after being named America's youngest-ever Nobel Prize winner (for Peace in 1964), Johnson said, bluntly, "Open your voting booths to all your people, and we *shall* overcome."[27] The Voting Rights Act of 1965 provided for federal registrars and observers whenever patterns of discrimination could be demonstrated, while eliminating literacy tests and the poll tax.[28]

The Open Housing Act of 1968 was the last hurrah of Lyndon Johnson's Great Society. The Nixon administration was to practice (in Daniel Moynihan's immortal phrase) "benign neglect." Nevertheless, the machinery of civil rights, now set in motion, was to produce impressive results in the next decade. At the end of 1968, 68 percent of black students still went to all-black schools. Two years later, the percentage stood at 18. Gerald Ford's solicitor general was to argue in the Supreme Court against even private schools being all-white, a logical extension of the Court's busing-for-racial-balance decision. Not even Ronald Reagan's support could gain federal subsidies for all-white private colleges in the early eighties. By 1978, there were nearly fifteen times as many black registered voters in Mississippi as in 1964. In the South as a whole, elected black officeholders increased more than twentyfold between 1964 and 1978, including twenty-one legislators in Georgia and thirteen in Alabama.[29]

And yet there was, and continues to be, a gap between equality of rights and equality of fulfillment. The basic conclusion of the National Advisory Commission on Civil Disorders (the Kerner Commission) in 1968 was that the "nation is moving toward two societies, one black, one white—separate and unequal."[30] As to which of these societies was on top, no one had any doubt. Nevertheless, discussion of the cause was practically a black national pastime. In the sixties, the two leading contenders were white evil and white economics.

Black separatism has an old, if not particularly honored, place in U.S. history. The West African country of Liberia was created, at least partially, to prevent the presence of free Negroes from inspiring their enslaved brothers to rebellion. Marcus Garvey achieved enormous popularity in the early 1920s by promising a United Africa under black rule: "There is no Law but Strength," he preached, "No Justice but Power."[31] The combination of black nationalism and religious fervor has been exploited by a number of later movements, the most visible of which in the sixties was Elijah Muhammad's "Black Muslims."

Ideologically, Muhammad taught the demonology of the white man—"Yacub's history." The first men were black. White people were the result of six hundred years of genetics and genocide practiced on the island of Patmos according to the principles of Yacub, a dissatisfied scientist who had been exiled from the holy city of Islam, Mecca. Returning to the mainland, these "blue-eyed devils" were further exiled to the caves of Europe, where Moses was to civilize them two thousand years later. They are "the serpent" the biblical Moses lifted up in the wilderness. Allah decreed that the devil white race would rule the world for six thousand years (roughly to the present) until it destroyed itself. The original people would then reclaim their heritage.[32] Elijah Muhammad called for a separate black state in America. To indicate their break with American tradition, his followers abandoned their "slave names" and adopted Islamic names. Many, such as Elijah Muhammad's most famous protégé, Malcolm X, simply substituted the letter "X" for their former last name.

It should be pointed out that black separatism was only part of a rapidly expanding black consciousness in the United States of the sixties—a consciousness which in turn reflected the reality of a rising Third World. More accurately, it was the reality of two-thirds of the world—the nonwhites who, since World War II, were rapidly passing from subject to sovereign peoples. In the wake of China and India, Ghana in 1957 became the first of a host of newly created black African nations. It does not trivialize this movement to point out how much of its impact in America was aesthetic. Swahili classes in ghetto YMCAs were certainly more important in concept than communication. Unlike the Harlem Renaissance of the twenties, when black artists produced for white critics, black beauty became a life-style emulated by whites. Even blond, "blue-eyed devils" affected dashikis, and Caucasian "naturals" were as common as "processes" among blacks in the previous decade. The Beatles struggled for "soul," as "Mo-town" recording artists leapt from obscure labels and stations far up the dial to platinum superstardom. To "tell it like it is" was to be "right on," and a decade that had begun with Franz Fanon's *Black Skins, White Masks* was threatening to go into negative. Black was more than beautiful; it had hegemony.

Still, it was easier to have soul than to keep it together with body. To do that required power—"Black Power"—and the potency of that idea may be judged by the haste with which it was condemned, not by white reactionaries, but by the Urban League and the NAACP. The term was coined by the chairman of the Student Nonviolent Coordinating Committee, Stokely Carmichael, on yet another of the famous marches of the sixties. On June 5, 1966, James Meredith, the first black student at the University of Mississippi, had undertaken a one-man pilgrimage for voting rights from Memphis, Tennessee, to Jackson, Mississippi. The following day he was ambushed and wounded. Numerous civil rights leaders volunteered to take his place, and it was on June 17 in exchanges between an SNCC faction of the marchers and blacks lining the road that the "Black Power" chant was born.[33]

On July 4, the Congress of Racial Equality (led by Floyd McKissick) adopted the concept of Black Power. Two days later, the NAACP convention—with Vice President Hubert Humphrey as its guest speaker—rejected it. In his keynote address, NAACP director Roy Wilkens called it "a reverse Mississippi, a reverse Hitler, a reverse Ku Klux Klan."[34] The Urban League's Whitney Young debated with McKissick on the August 21 edition of NBC's "Meet the Press," deploring "the country's obsession and preoccupation with the debate about a slogan which we felt deterred the country from concentrating on the problems of poverty and discrimination." Dr. King, who had on the march tried to halt the chants, was more perceptive in his analysis: "The new mood has arisen from real, not imaginary causes. The mood expresses an angry frustration which is not limited to the few who use it to justify violence."[35]

Who would control was pivotal in the Black Power debate. "I got a letter from a professor at Harvard," McKissick said on "Meet the

Press": "Explain black power. . . . Six basic ingredients are needed: One, political power; two, economic power; three, an improved self-image of the black man himself; four, the development of young, militant, leadership; five, the enforcement of federal laws, the abolishment of police brutality; and six, the development of the black consumer bloc."[36]

Carmichael raised hackles by asserting in the September 22 *New York Review of Books* that since power in America derives from racial blocs, it only made sense for blacks to take it wherever they could get it: "The reality is that this nation, from top to bottom, is racist; that racism is not primarily a problem of human relations but of an exploitation maintained—either actively or through silence—by the society as a whole. . . . It means the creation of power bases from which the black people can work to change statewide or nationwide patterns of oppression through pressure from strength—instead of weakness."[37]

Looking back at the definitions of Black Power given by Carmichael and McKissick, it is relatively easy to separate the "rap" from the reality. Beyond the evaluation of whites by Carmichael ("irrelevant . . . except as an oppressive force") and McKissick's ominous endorsement of self-defense was a demand for economic and political power roughly equivalent to social input. Such a demand signalled the end of "protest," a concept which implied that the improvement of minority status was an exercise of majority power. The exercise of Black Power, on the other hand, was an exercise in equality in that it presumed that the minority aim was control of its own destiny and not assimilation into the majority. The statement of this principle has historically been a blow to the ego of majority reformists (white liberals in America), who from time immemorial have always assumed that everyone given the opportunity would be just like them. And since black moderates were well aware that the legal gains of the preceding decade largely derived from the manipulation of the white liberal conscience, Wilkens's and Young's public distancing and King's equivocation over Black Power were understandable. Consciously or unconsciously, younger blacks were reading different cues. They were living in a country where their music, their fashions, and their rhetoric were the standard, not a deviance; in a world where *whites* were a minority, increasingly unable to enforce their will. They had chosen to emphasize the "Power in Black Power— the power to select and to deny. They understood that respect must precede acceptance; that equality cannot be granted, but must be assumed.

Black Power, Black Arts

"Black Art is the aesthetic and spiritual sister of the Black Power concept. As such, it envisions an Art that speaks directly to the needs and aspirations of Black America. A main tenet of Black Power is the necessity for Black people to define the world in their own terms. The Black artist has made the same point in the context of aesthetics."[38]

The black theatre which developed in the late sixties and early seventies sought to make its home within the black community, seeking to raise that community's consciousness and serving it as an educational center. The content of its plays was explicitly activist, if wildly uneven. Robert Macbeth of Harlem's New Lafayette Theatre bemoaned the "ten- and twenty-minute revolutionary wonders" he had to plow through to find a single playable script.[39] How serious was this revolutionary sentiment? Perhaps this depends upon how you define *serious*. Critic Geneva Smitherman has pointed out that for a people who place so much emphasis on style, rhetoric *is* performance: "While the speakers may or may not act out the implications of their words, . . . listeners do not necessarily *expect* any action to follow. As a matter of fact, skillful rappers can avoid having to prove themselves through deeds if their rap is strong enough. . . . This bad talk is nearly always taken for the real thing by an outsider from another culture."[40]

Such an explanation does not account for the simple fact that times change and people change with them. Thus, LeRoi Jones, the Greenwich Village "Beat poet" of the late fifties, could become Imamu Amiri Baraka, the black nationalist of the late sixties, and still later evolve into the avowed Marxist whose *Motion of History* (1977) could see all of America's problems as deriving from class oppression as clearly as he once saw their cause as racial oppression. And Ed Bullins, who predicted confidently in a 1968 *Newsweek* interview that "this reactionary racist government will have me killed within ten years,"[41] could go on to accept Rockefeller and Guggenheim grants, saying in 1974, "In the recent past, preoccupation in addressing mainly social and political issues may have been Black literature's major flaw."[42]

"Dr. Martin Luther King was the last prince of nonviolence. He was a symbol of nonviolence, the epitome of nonviolence. Nonviolence is a dead philosophy and it was not the black people that killed it," declared Floyd McKissick in 1968.[43] No one could have predicted the Ed Bullins of 1974 in 1968. That was the year that, as guest editor of *The Drama Review*, America's most prestigious avant-garde theatre journal, he eclipsed forever the categories of sympathetic and protest drama and established Black Revolutionary Theatre and the Theatre of Black Experience as the only viable forms of Afro-American drama. Bullins invented neither form, of course. Langston Hughes had been writing drama for forty years, and the year 1964 alone had produced three black plays which stand the test of time as both social and artistic documents: James Baldwin's *Blues for Mr. Charlie* and LeRoi Jones's *The Dutchman* and *The Slave*. But Hughes, Baldwin and Jones were distinguished authors with white-approved credentials. The contributors to *The Drama Review* for Summer 1968 were *dangerous*.

Bullins himself laid down criteria for street theatre, part of a larger plan worked out by LeRoi Jones for publicizing the revolution. In *The Bronx Is Next*, Sonia Sanchez dramatized black commandos who took over the streets from white cops, enforcing in passing their concept of what forms manhood and womanhood should take. In four short plays, Ben Caldwell took on the whole apparatus of the "Great Society"—identifying Christianity as a way of exploiting the black man, the economic opportunity organization as a way of humiliating him, birth control (induced by impotent whites) as a way of reducing his army, urban renewal as a way of diverting the revolution, and recommended open warfare as a way of countering the white devil. In *And We Own the Night* (a title taken from a Jones poem), Jimmy Garrett advocated shooting your own mother if she was counter-revolutionary. Bullins and Jones were also creating black consciousness-raising rituals at the New Lafayette Theatre in Harlem and Spirit House in Newark, respectively. What they were like, we could only guess from the plays that reached the white world.

The Gentleman Caller

On April 25, 1969, the Chelsea Theatre Center presented *The Gentleman Caller* at the Brooklyn Academy of Music as one of four one-acts under the group title *A Black Quartet*. When the curtain opens, we are in a fashionable living room located in the midst of an America parable: "Against the back wall is a gun rack with rifles and shotguns in it. Upon the wall are mounted and stuffed heads of a Blackman, an American Indian, a Viet Namese, and a Chinese."[44]

The title of the play is something of a red herring, representing as it does one of the three characters in the play who are never heard: Mr. Mann, the supposed master of the house, who is offstage most of the play, presumably shaving; a telephone caller who interrupts the action five times, trying to talk to Madame; and a sophisticated young Negro.

It is from the last of these that our dramatic reflexes have been trained to expect the answer to the play's mystery.

One of the two speaking characters is Madame herself, a society *grande dame* perhaps past her best years, but still confident in her expensive dressing gown. She is introduced offstage warbling "America"—an outburst followed by the chorus of a vigorous Negro spiritual sung by the other speaking character, Mamie Lee King, "the classic image of how a Negro maid is thought to look."

It is Mamie—"one of the truly worthwhile possessions" left by Madame's father—who opens the play energetically denying access to Madame, first to a telephone enquiry, and then to the sophisticated Negro. It is clear that Mamie disapproves of the latter—a well-dressed young black man, adorned with imported cigarettes and business cards and entering the front door—and she only reluctantly admits him on his second attempt. Madame is more cordial, seeming to recognize him, chiding him in a manner that is teasing, half-provocative. Madame insists over Mamie's protest that the Caller's tea be served first, and, after the maid rejects another phone call for Madame, works herself into a snit in order to fire Mamie.

Her anger is equally as patronizing as her employment, however, and yet another phone call later, Mamie is offered her job back with a two-dollar-per-month raise and "that new black taffeta dress [Madame] got for Aunt Hattie's funeral six years ago," (*The Gentleman Caller*, i, 242) We gather that this scene has been played many times before, but now there is a surprise ending: Mamie quits. Frustrated and enraged, Madame turns to the Caller, opening her dressing gown and inviting him in.

To her amazement, the Gentleman Caller shows no interest until she mentions her irritation at having to wait for her husband to pretend to shave. Whenever the beard is mentioned, the Caller twitches uncontrollably. When she realizes where his true desires lie, Madame dissolves into helpless laughter—a laughter punctuated by the ever-insistent demand of the ringing telephone. She snatches up the phone, only to suffer her third rejection in a row as the scene ends when no one wishes to speak with her.

In Scene 2, "Mr. Mann is stretched out in the center of the living room floor, dressed in an Uncle Sam suit, without trousers or shoes, his shorts are cut from an American flag; his socks are star-spangled." (*The Gentleman Caller*, ii, 246) Mr. Mann is dead of a slit throat. The Caller, investigating the body, is startled to find that its long white beard is false—a fact which fails to surprise Madame or Mamie. Meanwhile, the maid takes the gun down from above the mantle and shoots Madame in the head: "Boy, put down that ole piece of hair; it came from between mah granny's legs anyway. Now I've taken enough of yo silly behind stuff. Grab his feet like I said." (*The Gentleman Caller*, ii, 247)

"Times have *really* changed," Madame has mused earlier, but not even she suspects how much. The sophisticated young man is the New Negro. Genteel in manner and in taste, he is at home in fashionable white drawing rooms. He has swapped his blackness for a chance at, not the sensual delights of Madame, but rather the symbol of white power, Mr. Mann's beard. He is as surprised to find that the power is false as Madame is to find herself no longer the object of desire or the standard of beauty, or (presumably) as Mr. Mann, white America personified, is to find himself dead. The New Negro has betrayed his blackness in order to assimilate into falseness and death. The true power lies with those who have maintained their heritage, politically and aesthetically, biding their time until the opportunity comes to assume their rightful position in the world.

[*The Maid returns, wearing an exotic gown of her own design. Her bandanna has been taken off; her au naturel hair style complements her strong Black features. She picks up the phone.*]

Maid [*refined*]: Hello? Yes, you wish to speak to the madame? Yes, she is speaking. . . .

[*Slow curtain as the Maid speaks into the phone of high finance and earth-changing matters.*]

(The Gentleman Caller, ii, 247–48)

The "Gentleman Caller" has gotten through at last.

The Death of Malcolm X

"I could die at the hands of some Negro hired by the white man. Or it could be some brainwashed Negro acting on his own idea that by eliminating me he would be helping out the white man, because I talk about the white man the way I do."[45]

Malcolm X, black nationalist and internationalist, was shot while speaking at the Harlem Audubon Ballroom on February 21, 1965.

Malcolm Little was born shortly after a Ku Klux Klan raid in Omaha, Nebraska. His father, a Baptist minister and follower of Marcus Garvey, was murdered in East Lansing, Michigan, when Malcolm was six, and his mother was institutionalized when he was twelve. A hustler, dope peddler, pimp, and burglar, he was sentenced to ten years in a Massachusetts prison in February 1946, three months before his twenty-first birthday. Moved to the Norfolk, Massachusetts, prison colony in 1948, Malcolm converted to the Nation of Islam religion and to the self-education process. He was released from prison in August 1952, and was named a Muslim minister a year later. In the next decade, Malcolm became the most important and most visible of Elijah Muhammad's ministers, founding temples in Boston, Philadelphia, New York, and Los Angeles, as well as the newspaper *Muhammad Speaks*. After 1959 he was in constant demand on radio and television, and for press and magazine interviews as a Muslim spokesman for black separatism:

U.S. politics is ruled by special-interest blocs and lobbies. What group has a more urgent special interest, what group needs a bloc, a lobby, more than the black man? . . . The cornerstones of this country's operation are economic and political strength and power. The black man doesn't have the economic strength—and it will take time for him to build it. But right now the American black man has the political strength and power to change his destiny overnight.[46]

The religious dogma upon which Malcolm based his teachings was questionable—Malcolm himself was to break from it after his trip to Mecca—but the truth of what he taught about black/white relationships in America may be judged by its acceptance as common knowledge a quarter-century later and by the vehemence with which it was denounced at the time by moderates of his own race. "This twentieth-century Uncle Thomas is a *professional* Negro . . . by that I mean his profession is being a Negro for the white man . . . Black bodies with white heads."

However, Malcolm was also aware of his power to strengthen the moderates' hand. On a visit to Selma, Alabama, in January 1965, he told Coretta Scott King that his presence would help Dr. King achieve his goals: "He said he wanted to present an alternative; that it might be easier for whites to accept Martin's proposals after hearing him."[47] But that was after Malcolm had been to Mecca and had split with the Black Muslims.

The break had been coming for some time. Elijah Muhammad had become increasingly irritated by the predominance which Malcolm had assumed in the media. Asked to comment shortly after President Kennedy's assassination, Malcolm assessed the climate of violence created in white America and adjudged the murder to be a case of "the chickens coming home to roost"—a phrase which made every news broadcast and resulted in a ninety-day suspension by Mr. Muhammad. In early 1964 Malcolm founded a new mosque in Harlem and embarked on a prolonged trip to Mecca and a number of the emerging black African nations. He returned with a new view of the Islamic religion, one that expunged racial differences.

"In my past, I have made sweeping indictments of *all* white people. I never will be guilty of that again—as I know now that some white people *are* truly sincere, that some truly are capable of being brotherly toward a black man. The true Islam has shown me that a blanket indictment of all white people is as wrong as when whites make blanket indictments against blacks."[48]

Ironically, such statements did nothing to end Malcolm's difficulties at home. In Africa he had met with leaders in Egypt, Tanzania, Nigeria, Ghana, Kenya, and Uganda—going a long way to gaining their public (and internationally embarrassing) support for black rights in America. From being an articulate black spokesman in the United States, he had advanced to articulating the link between American blacks and the Third World.

The white man's racism toward the black man here in America is what has got him in such trouble all over this world with other non-white peoples. . . . And the non-white peoples of this world are sick of the condescending white man! That's why you've got all this trouble in places like Viet Nam. . . . Can you imagine what can happen, what certainly would happen if all of those African-heritage people ever *realize* the blood bond, if they ever realize they all have a common goal—if they ever unite?[49]

Strictly speaking, Amiri Baraka's *The Death of Malcolm X* is a filmscript rather than a play. With a sure sense of theatre, Baraka takes many of Malcolm's metaphors and literalizes them. The "brainwashed" blacks Malcolm predicted might someday kill him are present as surgically and culturally conditioned zombies. The "professional Uncle Toms" he scorned are personalized as a "distinguished looking Negro" leading his neat and well-mannered marchers into senseless beatings, for which *he* receives awards from equally distinguished whites. The idea of American government as the tool of special interest groups is physicalized in the breadth of the conspiracy formulated against Malcolm, and in speech in LBJ's style and accent emanating from a hand puppet. The idea of Malcolm as a representative of all the Third World is presented by cutting from his falling body to shots of people of color the world over collapsing from the same gunfire.

The Death of Malcolm X is an excellent example of American Expressionism. Malcolm, who appears only briefly, and his family and aides provide the norm against which the ingrained evil of whites is judged. In a luxurious room overlooking the Capitol building, "surrounded by human bones and skeletons," a fat Klansman in full regalia watches Malcolm control a television debate.

Malcolm: It is that simple fact that will animate the rest of the world against you! That
simple alarming fact of your unredeemable evil. You are all disqualified as human
beings. . . .

Klansman: Hahaha . . . yr right nigger . . . yr right . . . ha . . . by our evil . . .
hahaha . . . but what good will it do you?[50]

The Klan, of course, is only a part of this vast conspiracy, which
includes the executive branch of the American government, the military,
science, education, business, integrationist leaders, and, ultimately, the
whole of Western civilization.

The dominant setting for the work is the headquarters of a semisecret
paramilitary organization named Uncle Sam Central and its connected
scientific laboratories, the IABS. (Institute for Advanced Black Studies).
In the latter's operating rooms, black "mindsouls" are removed and
replaced—"white brains in black bodies," as Malcolm called them. In
special "bohemian" conditioning areas, black men are taught to value
only interracial sex. Light-skinned Negroes dance at an imitation cotil-
lion. Motion pictures screen an endless stream of black stereotypes, as
classrooms associate all culture with the highlights of Western civilization
and God with Christian institutions.

In Uncle Sam Central's administrative areas, soldiers are outfitted in
Uncle Sam suits. The officers, like Bullins's Mr. Mann, wear fake beards
to signify their rank. The higher ranked are dressed as representatives
of epochs of Western civilization: George Washington, Hernán Cortés,
Greeks, Romans, Vikings, and so forth. In the intelligence areas, radios,
dispatches, and television screens carry messages of worldwide coups,
murders, and treachery. Meanwhile, in the staging area, dazed blacks
run mindlessly through their instructions for a military operation to be
carried out in a large hotel auditorium.

In the world outside, some Negroes seem mesmerized by the antics of
a lump-faced Texas cowboy, but in the background, signs of the revolution
are appearing. White cops look up suddenly to see garbage cans hurtling
at their heads. White artists with white aesthetic systems are startled by
black revolutionaries kicking in their loft doors.

In the street, a gray-haired Negro leads a civil rights march through
a street lined with police and people in Uncle Sam suits. As the marchers
sing "We shall be white" in spiritual tones, their leader acknowledges
with nods from side to side the applause and abuse of the crowd:

[*The policemen's clubs and billies beating the demonstrators in agonizing slow
motion. . . . The grey-haired man stands, untouched, at the center of the melee. He is
beatified, a red, white, and blue halo appears illuminating around his head. . . .*]

"Go home, my children . . . we have proven our point, that love is stronger than hate!" [*People's heads are being cracked open. Women are wrestling with policemen. . . .*] "We have beaten them, I say, we are this day blessed! We will be white . . . We will be whiter than them. . . . Whiter, much whiter." [*He says the last words into a wrist radio.*] (*The Death of Malcolm X*, 10–12)

The last piece of the conspiracy is in place. That night the sky is a monstrous neon American flag, its harshness underscored by the occasional bomb or scream—"the character of a quietly hysterical American night." In the morning, shots of Malcolm and his aides preparing for his appearance at the Audubon Ballroom are interspersed with the final wrap-up of details by those who will confront him there. In a trophy room stacked with money and adorned by a shrunken head resembling Patrice Lumumba, a banker makes plans for a celebration: "The rite goes on, eh?" At a banquet, the grey-haired Negro receives an award "for meritorious service" from a white audience: a life-sized watermelon made of precious stones and gold. In an airplane above the city, the hit squad of brainwashed blacks once again runs through its afternoon instructions for Operation Sambo, stopping when the "Star-Spangled Banner" plays to lick their white officer's shoes "one at a time, in perfect order." At the Audubon Malcolm is speaking: "We speak of revolution and don't even know what it is. A revolution means land. . . . A revolution also means bloodshed. There is no revolution without bloodshed." (*The Death of Malcolm X*, 18)

In the auditorium a commotion is staged, distracting the bodyguards. Up the side hallway rush three men firing a shotgun and revolvers. In closeup we see the bullets striking Malcolm's chest, and the scene cuts to nonwhites (Africans, Asians, Latin Americans, etc.) all over the world clutching their breasts as if shot. On television, an announcer interrupts the regularly scheduled program: "Today, black extremist Malcolm X was killed by his own violence."

"[*Last image is of all the featured ofays . . . going through a weird historic ritual . . . as they put on U Sam suits, making growling unintelligible noises, but ending each phrase rhythmically with "White!" "White!" "White!" "White!" etc.*]" (*The Death of Malcolm X*, 19–20)

Postrevolutionary Black America

It is accurate to describe what has occurred since the mid-1970s as a postrevolutionary *mood*. Although the faces of those in charge are not always white, the system has not changed. Carl Stokes was elected mayor of Cleveland, Kenneth Gibson mayor of Newark, Maynard Jackson of

Atlanta, Tom Bradley of Los Angeles, and Harold Washington of Chicago (among others) without appreciably bettering the conditions of urban blacks. Gibson, who was elected with the support of such "black revolutionaries" as Amiri Baraka, lost it when he tried to meet a budget deficit by cutting school programs. By the end of the decade, a rising new conservatism was calling for the dismantling of social programs. Even the Reverend Jesse Jackson's PUSH (People United to Serve Humanity) program in the school systems of Chicago stressed self-reliance and personal effort.

By the mid-eighties, black separatism seemed increasingly a question of economic class rather than caste protest or revolutionary ideology. Of course, there never was a chance of a separate black state in America, even if ghettos continue to exist. Even the Black Muslims (under the leadership of one of Elijah Muhammad's sons) encouraged white investment in their cooperative businesses,[51] before disbanding altogether. The increasing acceptance of the Third World by America was slower to develop. Andrew Young, once an aide to Martin Luther King, Jr., was forced to resign as President Carter's United Nations ambassador when he tried to start dialogues with the Palestine Liberation Organization. Stokely Carmichael still strives to "unite the people," but does so now under the name Kwame Ture as a resident of the African republic of Guinea.

Although outstanding blacks are now more thoroughly assimilated into mainstream America than ever before, the same cannot be said of the lower classes. Even as a new, more conservative Supreme Court began to question its past decisions on education, quotas, equal opportunity, and so on, the "real power" gap—the economic gap—between blacks and whites in America loomed greater than ever. Part of this gap is doubtless due to simple physics: The last starter cannot immediately match the pace of the other runners. In America's postindustrial period, this trend is likely to become more pronounced, as the unskilled jobs are eliminated which sustained families while new generations trained.

More disturbing is the fact that the decline of segregation has actually worsened conditions for those who remain in the ghetto. The professional classes, businessmen, and civic and religious figures who previously provided the leadership and successful examples for young blacks have moved to better neighborhoods. "These figures," Elijah Anderson, a black professor of sociology at the University of Pennsylvania, reminds us, "served the black community as visible, concrete symbols of success and moral value, as living examples of the result of hard work, perseverance, decency and propriety." According to another black sociologist,

William Julius Wilson of the University of Chicago, "The result is not merely poverty, but social isolation."[52]

Many sociologists have seen a relationship between black poverty and the "feminization of poverty," that is, the number of families in which the head of the household is a woman whose earnings are below poverty level. A recent study by the Children's Defense Fund found that 90 percent of all babies of black teenage mothers are born out of wedlock.[53] This phenomenon is also related to "hard-core" poverty, defined by chronic unemployment extending to two or more generations of a single family. According to Leon Chestang, dean of Wayne State University's School of Social Work, black families can generally be divided between the "achievement-oriented" and the "survival-oriented." The achievement-oriented child—usually to be found in a two-parent, economically stable family—may view racism as a barrier to potential fulfillment, but will not internalize that barrier. The security of a strong family insures the child's self-esteem, shielding him from the emotionally debilitating effects of racism and giving him the confidence to capitalize on what opportunities do appear. The survival-oriented child also perceives injustice for blacks in a white society, but more importantly, he perceives himself as inadequate to challenge it. Since his family members are usually powerless to protect him or themselves, he is likely to accept the dead-end designation society seems determined to allot him. Lacking a role model with which he can associate a future improvement in status, he will grab what material gratification is available.[54] The child may also sense in his condition the abrogation of the social contract and conclude that the unfairness with which he has been treated relieves him of any social obligations which cannot be enforced upon him. Thus, the child takes as his mentor the street "hustler" who prospers materially by violating social codes, or takes part in "ghetto Christmas"—the looting which accompanies inner-city riots or power failures.

In *Talley's Corner*, a classic study of black "street-corner" men in a blighted section of Washington, D.C., Elliot Liebow has suggested that ghetto blacks are merely reacting to the realities of their society and the unlikelihood of ever escaping it. The larger society demands that the inner-city black man define himself by his labor and by his position as the head of a family. Unfortunately, work, when it is available to him, is frequently so menial as to offer no challenge or chance of advancement, and very little money. When he quits, he is only confirming the evaluation of the job the larger culture has already given it. Similarly, he doesn't marry for sex—which is readily available—but to fulfill his society-created definition of what it is to be a man. However, "he hedges on his commitment from the very beginning because he is afraid, not of marriage itself, but of his own ability to carry out his responsibilities as husband and father. How own father failed and . . . the men he knows who have been or are married have also failed or are in the process of doing so. He has no evidence that he will fare better than they and much evidence that he will not."[55]

His wife's male role models have also failed, and she expects this of him as well. In her eyes he sees both what he is and what society says he should be. Only on the street corner, in the company of other failed men, can he avoid this definition. Nevertheless, with so little self-gratification available, such friendships become extremely vulnerable to whatever other possibilities of self-fulfillment (sex and money) present themselves. There is never enough to go around, and the success of one man on the corner must inevitably come at the expense of another.[56]In the end, the satisfactions of work, family, and friendship are all imperiled by poverty and its concomitant lack of self-esteem.

The Postrevolutionary Aesthetic Blues

Ed Bullins called it the Theatre of Black Experience, but as the 1970s progressed and revolutionary fervor faded, it could have been named the Theatre of Bleak Prospects. In 1984 black per capita income was 57 percent of whites', exactly what it had been in 1971.[57] As the U.S. Constitution headed into its third century, from an economic standpoint at least, blacks were just what they had been at the beginning: "three-fifths of a man."

Humanity, of course, cannot be measured monetarily. It can, however, be reduced psychologically. In *Black Communication in White Society*, Roy Cogdell and Sybill Wilson discuss the concept of "black mentality," a set of attitudes blacks have developed to cope with the advantages that whites in America have numerically, economically, legally, and in culturally accepted values.

Cogdell and Wilson see "black mentality" as reflective of the psychological processes formed in neocolonial settings, and suggest that the price blacks pay for their acceptance of white value standards is self-hatred, sometimes accelerating into schizophrenia: "Possession of two separate identities—one positive (white) and the other negative (black)—and two sets of conflicting values in search of the elusive 'good life' seems to overburden many blacks."[58]

Fittingly, it has been the black artist, rather than the psychologist, who has provided us with the most-telling examples of the destructive effect of white values on the black personality. Ed Bullins's *In New England Winter* (1967) shows acceptance of white values as synonymous with suicide. In the present, Steve Benson and his half-brother, Cliff Dawson, plan a robbery. Steve hopes to return to New England and Liz, the half-insane girl he left there five years earlier. New England winter is a metaphor for white America—as Steve half-consciously realizes—for death as well: "It's snowing up there now. Snowing . . . big white flakes. Silent like death must be. . . . Death must be still and black and deep. . . . Deathly cold."[59]

Acceptance of white values is a subtle form of betrayal, for it encourages blacks to measure themselves by their triumphs over other blacks, to associate blackness with defeat. During *In New England Winter*, Steve broods over an assault on him by another gang member years earlier: "Cops and niggers. . . . In his monkey mind, he was playin' white cop . . . and I was just a nigger he could. . . . " (*In New England Winter*, i, 136) In the past, Steve has measured his competitive white superiority by seducing his half-brother's wife. Eventually, he kills to prevent Cliff from discovering his betrayal—not dreaming that his brother, who always knew, would be so irrational as to love and forgive him.

The protagonist of Charles Gordone's *No Place to Be Somebody* (1969), Johnny Williams, is a young black man whose goal in life is to break the stranglehold an Italian mobster has on the local rackets. His role model has been his foster father, a black gangster who has exchanged ten years in a federal prison for terminal consumption and a little insight: "You got the Charlie fever, Johnny. Tha's what you got. I gave it to you. Took yo' chile's min' an' filled it with the Charlie fever. Givin' you a education or teachin' you to dinner pail, didn't seem to me no way for you to grow up an' be respected like a man. . . . Couldn't copy Charlie's good points an' live like men. So we copied his bad points."[60]

The danger of internalizing white evaluations of blackness as inferior and bestial is a major theme in Leslie Lee's *The First Breeze of Summer* (1975). The play has two time frames and two protagonists. We see the past (pre–World War I North Carolina) in flashbacks experienced by an elderly black woman as she recalls the different fathers of her three children. The present is a contemporary northern city where Lucretia and her surviving children and grandchildren live. Lucretia's modern parallel is her grandson and namesake, Louis, who, as she once did, must learn to come to terms with his blackness and his sexuality.

Lou, who hopes to become a doctor, is troubled by a dilemma of his own making. He believes that the factors which hold him back are endemic to his race. By that he does not mean social barriers. Any element in his life Lou associates with blackness—for example, that his father and brother work with their hands, that his passions are aroused when he is petting with his girlfriend—he now sees as evidence of inferiority to be mercilessly suppressed.

Lou: Sometimes I'd . . . I'd like to . . . to . . . take a knife and . . . and just . . . rip this black stuff off!—just skin myself clean! I—

Nate: You'd just bleed, man, that's all . . . just bleed.[61]

One of the most effective dramatic examples of the deleterious effect of white values on black personalities is found in Charles Fuller's 1982 Pulitzer Prize winner, *A Soldier's Story*. The play is a murder mystery set in a 1944 segregated Louisiana army camp. However, we are less concerned with the identity of the murderer than the personality of the victim, and Sergeant Vernon Waters is eventually revealed to us as a suicide waiting to happen.

Encouraged by his father to shed any trace of accent, culture, or work habit that might stamp him as "colored," Walters finds that a military career is the closest he can get to real power in a white society. Walters is awarded the Croix de Guerre for World War I bravery in France, but the experience is soured when an ignorant black soldier allows himself to be humiliated for the amusement of white troops and French onlookers. Aware that he will always be judged as a black man, Walters sets out to eliminate from the army all those who cannot meet his preconceived standards of whiteness, not realizing that he is killing something in himself: "You got to be like them! And I was—but the rules are fixed. . . . It doesn't make any difference! They still hate you! . . . They still hate you!"[62]

Ironically, Walters is killed by his mirror image—a soldier who also seeks to rid the black race of what he perceives as its most undesirable element, the black carrier of white oppression.

In many plays of the postrevolutionary period, the failure to be oneself is a form of living death. Of *A Soldier's Play*, as of the drama we will study next, we can only repeat the words of one of Walters's targets for elimination: "Any man ain't sure where he belongs must be in a whole lot of pain." (*A Soldier's Play*, II, 90)

The Mighty Gents

In Memory of all the
Brothers and Sisters

who saw the light at the
end of the tunnel . . . and
chose the darkness instead.[63]

In 1970, Richard Wesley's *Black Terror*, written for the New Lafayette Theatre, sounded "the death knell of America," extolling the virtues of a black revolutionary combat team which would "rather be dead than alive in America."[64] A few years later, with the New Lafayette closed, Wesley was writing about another gang grown older and still trapped in the roles they had created for themselves.

In one of its earlier drafts, Wesley called *The Mighty Gents* "The Last Street Play." The setting is the Newark ghetto in approximately 1975. The "Mighty Gents" are a street gang which reached the zenith of its power in the early sixties. Its surviving members—Tiny, Lucky, and Eldridge—are thirty years old now, trapped in lives which are on the downslide in all aspects—not the least of which is pride and self-respect. Their leader is Frankie Sojourner, a traveller in a strange land. In a literal sense they are all newcomers to the black urban North, where only Frankie and his girlfriend, Rita, were actually born. Rita denies her Newark birth and describes how "the sun always usedta shine where I was born." In a flashback, Frankie's father attempts to end Frankie's gang fighting by sending him to his grandmother's farm in the South. More importantly, however, their current lives are a dead end—over, for all intents and purposes, unless they can find a way out.

In 1960 Rita was a Mighty Gent "deb": "I can remember seein' men who talked down to my Mama and spit on my Daddy with their eyes and voices, cringe in fear when the Mighty Gents came walkin' round and when they feared the Gents, they feared me." (*The Mighty Gents*, vii, 30)

The Mighty Gents are based, then, on a paradox. Their effectiveness as a group is based upon the fear they can inspire, but the motives of each member for belonging are the needs for love and self-love. Even Frankie's joining the Mighty Gents was an attempt to overcome self-revulsion and gain an acceptable self-concept. At fifteen, seduced emotionally and intellectually by a fascinating "older woman," he discovered his sexual initiator to be a transvestite homosexual: "I don't remember much of anything from that entire month except that I screwed every girl I could and did everything that was considered manly, extra hard. Anything to prove to myself that I wasn't a . . . well, you know. Yah, then I joined the Mighty Gents and started a lucrative career as a head-knocker. After I drew first blood against the Zombies, I didn't doubt myself ever again." (*The Mighty Gents*, i, 7)

Rita also associates the Mighty Gents with love, which she defines as never separating sex from respect: "We were special then and every day was filled with sunshine and light." (*The Mighty Gents*, v, 20) For her, the Mighty Gents are part of her battle against a future as a "grey shadow . . . like Mama and the rest of the women on the block." (*The Mighty Gents*, vii, 29–30)

The gang is a vehicle for respect. It provides a sense of belonging and ego-support in an emotionally harsh environment. Its shortcomings, however, are its functional limits: It works only so long as it is believed in; its structure allows no growth; and its code of action is essentially life-denying, not nurturing. Nowadays, the gang hangs together because it is the only way of recalling their past. The drawback is that it also reminds them of their present. Tiny's Vietnam-gained limp is their only concrete knowledge of life outside inner-city Newark. Eldridge is a born follower in a movement going nowhere, and Lucky is a sad dreamer, three times married to Martha, a former "deb" who is now dying of high blood pressure because she sees no reason to live. They cling to Frankie because he has been more successful than they in keeping the dream alive—a dream he needs even more than they do: "I'm the leader out there. Somethin' I can't be nowhere else in life." (*The Mighty Gents*, ix, 41)

But if the role of leader provides Frankie with his self-respect, it also demands of him that he follow the rules. In the flashback with his father, Frankie struggles to explain why he broke Essex Braxton's arm after a gang fight: "You got to be strong to be allowed to exist. You got to be able to command some respect and he couldn't do that. . . . I'm a Mighty Gent an' if I fail to make people respect me, I ain't got no right to live." (*The Mighty Gents*, vii, 18) Lately, however, Frankie has had the sense of "playin' by somebody else's rules an' reachin' for somebody else's prize." He is haunted by a recurring dream in which he is a wolf surrounded by his own kind, who rip the flesh from his body as he lies bleeding: "I'm scared I ain't gon' find a way out." (*The Mighty Gents*, vii, 30)

Wesley provides us with three possible outcomes to the Mighty Gents' dead-end course. They are manifested in Zeke, Essex Braxton, and Rita's knitting. Zeke is fifty-two, old before his time from having been there and having seen it all before, a derelict, capable of unctuous charm when he is cadging quarters and murderous hatred for everyone—even him-self—when he is not. Like the Gents, Zeke is still capable of deluding himself that one day he will turn the corner and reclaim his life. In a scarifying monologue performed as he panhandles the audience, Zeke tells the story of how a group of drug addicts who took him in as a teenager died from overdoses of pure Cuban heroin:

I decided that if they couldn't have dignity an' respect in life, then I'd see to it that they had it in death. Yea. Then I went to sleep, and when I woke up, rats was eatin' their bodies. . . . I swore on that day that no matter how much *I* got brutalized, I would never allow another man to think that he could control me and control what I am. I am my own man and I don't care how much you hate me, or despise me, or wish that I would go away. I am you. The real you and as long as y'all exist in this place I'm gon' be here. (*The Might Gents*, x, 44)

Braxton speaks directly to the audience as well, but although his appearance is more superficially attractive, his message is no less morally repulsive or audience implicating. Braxton was a Zombie, the gang rivals of the Mighty Gents. On his eighteenth birthday, he crept up on Frankie and Rita as they kissed on a public street, his knife permanently puncturing the Mighty Gents' hard-earned self-myth of invulnerability. From that moment the neighborhood ceased to be a place where he lived and became a place where he preyed: "They bowed down to me after that, Zombies and Mighty Gents alike. For they knew and understood, that I had acquired the gift of mercilessness . . . and I left their world forever." (*The Mighty Gents*, viii, 39–40)

Braxton sees himself as society's security guard. He has fulfilled the American Dream of upward mobility and conspicuous consumption by simply turning the ghetto's anger in upon itself. In exchange for a sumptuous living off his own kind, Braxton protects society from having to acknowledge its own underbelly—a task which he feels is sorely unappreciated.

You should be grateful to me for what I do. Because of men like me, you never have to see these cave dwellers, unless you happen to venture onto their grounds. Their lives and deaths are meaningless to most of you, as they should be, for these hopeless humans are merely surplus in today's world. Logic dictates that they should be killed off in a quick, painless, and sanitary manner; however, that would not be civilized. Hence, the need for men like me. We kill them for you. (*The Mighty Gents*, viii, 31)

Wesley's third option is more an act of faith than an escape route. This option links one of the play's repeated themes with an image that is ever present. The theme is a linking together of several phrases concerning a lost spirit which used to live in a place of magic in the land of the sun, a place where the circle could be completed. The spirit that has been lost is that of Frankie and Rita, and by extension, the rest of the gang as well. They were themselves the place of magic, perfect and immutable, until Braxton's knife penetrated their circle—a prelude to the end of the Mighty Gents as a positive functioning unit.

The land of the sun is a place Rita first associates with her childhood: "The sun always usedta shine where I was born. It wasn't paradise but it was the closest thing to it. Mama was always there to hug and Poppa was always there to tell us everything was gonna be all right." (*The Mighty Gents*, vii, 29) When the realities of the ghetto force Rita to accept that her parents cannot protect her, she associates "sunshine and light" with Frankie and the Mighty Gents.

The "magic" then is self-belief and "sunshine and light" is love and protection. When the gang melts away, only Rita is left to fight alongside Frankie. To this point, the play is a classic "coming of age" parable. To "complete the circle," all that is required is the birth of their child. For a part of this parable is the adult's acceptance of his own mortality and the placement of his hopes in a new generation. In his flashback, Frankie's father admits as much: "I wanted a son, not a damn savage. I wanted someone who would grow and take this world like I was never able to do. Someone who was gonna make me proud." (*The Mighty Gents*, iv, 17) That such hopes are not unwarranted can be seen in the gang's street-corner conversations. Tiny has a sister who is about to graduate from college, and Lucky's brothers own a successful taxi business down in Raleigh.

But Frankie has refused to abandon his sense of himself as a gang leader, and Rita has produced no baby in ten years of trying. Throughout every scene, Rita sits in a rocking chair, attempting to knit a shawl. No matter what other action is present on the stage, we are forced to consider it in light of her aims. At one points she suggests that their baby could teach her the necessary stitch to revive their magic. Later, she connects the knitting (the traditional image of approaching motherhood) with the concept of love and protection: "Knittin' is the essence of life, you know. Alla that intricate stitching. Make shawls [the old folks] said. The shawls gon' protect you against your fears and against all things harmful to you. . . . An' when the shawls are finished, then we'd be able to find our way back home." (*The Mighty Gents*, vii, 29)

In his preface Wesley has warned us about those who saw "the light at the end of the tunnel and chose the darkness instead". Humiliated by Braxton in a street-corner face-down, Frankie determines to buy a ticket out of the ghetto by robbing his old rival. "Y'all forgettin' what he did to us? What he did to the Gents? He turned us into dinosaurs, man. . . . He climbed outa here on our flesh, man!" (*The Mighty Gents*, viii, 36)

On one level it is ironic. Braxton, who saw his job as keeping "the cavemen" at one another's throats, is hit by his own kind. On another level, that Braxton's assessment of their situation is essentially correct is the tragedy of Frankie and the Gents. They exist outside of society and are aware of it, while society, if at all possible, ignores their existence entirely. "We can hit these hoods for alla they scratch an' no one would ever know who we was cause we don't exist. How they ever gon' find us? All derelicts look alike. Crooks hittin' crooks. Who gon' give a damn? Niggas hittin' niggas. Who even *cares*?" (*The Mighty Gents*, viii, 35–36)

The plan is successfully fulfilled, but so is Braxton's analysis and Frankie's prophetic dream. The gang beats Braxton and robs him of $1,200. They neglect, however, to relieve him of his gun—a neglect which Zeke, trailing the action, does not share. The cycle of wolves feeding on their own continues as Zeke confronts the Mighty Gents with Braxton's gun. Frankie is shot. As he lies on the ground, crying to his friends for help, the Mighty Gents strip him of his money, his ring, and his shoes: "Ain't no help, brotherman. You know the rules." (*The Mighty Gents*, xi, 48) And the play ends with the dying Frankie reaching toward a Rita still spotlighted knitting in her rocking chair and still repeating what could be the rallying cry of anyone whom a revolution has passed by: "I know what it is I want to do and I know what it is I have to do to get what I want, but somehow I just can't do it." (*The Mighty Gents*, iii, 11)

Notes

1. Quoted by Otto H. Olson, in *The Thin Disguise: Turning Point in Negro History* (New York: Humanities Press, 1967), 90.

2. "President Truman's Civil Rights Program (1946–1948)," in *Civil Rights and the American Negro*, ed. Albert P. Blaustein and Robert L. Zangrando (New York: Washington Square Press, 1968), 372–81.

3. "Texas White Primary Cases (1927–1953)," in Blaustein and Zangrando, *Civil Rights and the American Negro*, 395–97.

4. "Shelly vs. Kraemer: On Segregated Housing (1948)," in Blaustein and Zangrando, *Civil Rights and the American Negro*, 388–89.

5. "Brown vs. Board of Education of Topeka: The Predecessor Cases (1938–1950)," in Blaustein and Zangrando, *Civil Rights and the American Negro*," 407.

6. "Brown *vs.* Board of Education, 1954," in *The Negro in Twentieth Century America*, ed. John Hope Franklin and Isidore Starr (New York: Vintage Books, 1967), 279–80.

7. "Civil Rights Acts," in Franklin and Starr, *Negro in Twentieth Century America," 352.*

8. Vincent Harding, "So Much History, So Much Future: Martin Luther King, Jr., and the Second Coming of America," in *Have We Overcome?*, ed. Michael V. Namorato (Jackson: University Press of Mississippi, 1979), 42–43.

9. Langston Hughes and Milton Meltzer, *A Pictorial History of the Negro in America* (New York: Crown Publishers, 1968), 307.

10. Harding, "So Much History," 46.

11. Hughes and Meltzer, *Pictorial History*, 314–15.

12. Howard Zinn, *The New Abolitionists* (Boston: Beacon Press, 1964), 3.

13. "Speech by President Eisenhower Explaining Why Troops Were Being Sent to Little Rock," in Franklin and Starr, *Negro in Twentieth Century America*, 290.

14. Lerone Bennett, Jr., *Before the Mayflower: A History of the Negro in America, 1619–1964* (Baltimore: Penguin Books, 1966), 402, 410–11.

15. Bennett, *Before the Mayflower*, 347–48.

16. Martin Luther King, Jr., "Letter from a Birmingham Jail (1963)," in Blaustein and Zangrando, *Civil Rights and the American Negro*, 506.

17. "President Kennedy's Civil Rights Address (1963)," in Blaustein and Zangrando, *Civil Rights and the American Negro*, 485–86.

18. Bennett, *Before the Mayflower*, 357–58.

19. Leslie Catherine Sanders, *The Development of Black Theater in America: From Shadows to Selves* (Baton Rouge: Louisiana State University Press, 1988), 11.

20. Langston Hughes, *Don't You Want to Be Free?* in *Black Theater, U.S.A.*, ed. James V. Hatch and Ted Shine (New York: Free Press, 1974), 276.

21. Sanders, *Development of Black Theater*, 102–3.

22. Amiri Baraka, *Slave Ship*, in *"The Motion of History" and Other Plays* (New York: William Morrow, 1978), 145.

23. Amiri Baraka, *The Motion of History*, in *"The Motion of History" and Other Plays* (New York: William Morrow, 1978), IV, xv, 98.

24. Elizabeth Sutherland, ed., *Letters from Mississippi* (New York: McGraw-Hill, 1965), 99.

25. Martin Duberman, *In White America* (New York: Samuel French, 1964), I, 24. Subsequent references to this play will be included in the text.

26. Bennett, *Before the Mayflower*, 348–49.

27. William E. Leuchtenburg, "The White House and Black America: From Eisenhower to Carter," in Namorato, *Have We Overcome?*, 135–38.

28. "The Voting Rights Act of 1965," in Franklin and Starr, *Negro in Twentieth Century America*, 370–72.

29. Leuchtenburg, "White House and Black America," 139–41.

30. "Report of the National Advisory Commission on Civil Disorders," in Blaustein and Zangrando, *Civil Rights and the American Negro*, 619.

31. Bennett, *Before the Mayflower*, 295–96.

32. Alex Haley, *The Autobiography of Malcolm X* (New York: Ballantine Books, 1965), 164–67.

33. Gene Roberts, "Mississippi Reduces Police Protection for Marchers," *New York Times*, June 17, 1966, p. 33.

34. Quoted by John Hebers, in "Six Rights Leaders Clash on Tactics in Equality Drive," *New York Times*, August 22, 1966, p. 37.

35. Quoted by Hebers, "Six Rights Leaders," p. 37.

36. Quoted by Hebers, "Six Rights Leaders," p. 37.

37. Quoted by Gene Roberts, in "From Freedom High to Black Power," *New York Times Magazine*, September 25, 1966, p. 27.

38. Larry Neal, "The Black Arts Movement," *The Drama Review* 12, no. 4 (Summer 1968): 29.

39. Richard Scharine, "Ed Bullins," in *Twentieth-Century American Playwrights*, Vol. 1, ed. John Nicholas (Detroit: Gale Research Press, 1981), 33.

40. Geneva Smitherman, *Talkin' and Testifyin'* (Boston: Houghton Mifflin, 1977), 83.

41. Quoted by Mel Gussow, in "The New Playwrights," *Newsweek* 71 (May 20,1968): 115.

42. Ed Bullins, *The New Lafayette Theatre Presents* (New York: Anchor Books, 1974), 4.

43. Ed Bullins, "The King is Dead," *The Drama Review* 12, no. 4 (Summer 1968): 23.

44. Ed Bullins, *The Gentleman Caller*, in *Best Short Plays of 1970*, ed. Stanley Richards (Philadelphia: Chilton Books, 1970), i, 237. Subsequent references to this play will be included in the text.

45. Haley, *Autobiography of Malcolm X*, 381.

46. Haley, *Autobiography of Malcolm X*, 314–15.

47. Haley, *Autobiography of Malcolm X*, 243–44; 427.

48. Haley, *Autobiography of Malcolm X*, 362.

49. Haley, *Autobiography of Malcolm X*, 363.

50. Amiri Baraka, *The Death of Malcolm X*, in *New Plays from the Black Theatre*, ed. Ed Bullins (New York: Bantam Books, 1969), 9. Other references to the play will be included in the text.

51. C. G. Bunn, "Prayers and Profits," *Black Enterprise* 14 (December 1983): 28.

52. Walter Shapiro, "The Ghetto: From Bad to Worse," *Time* 130, no. 8 (August 24, 1987): 18.

53. Shapiro, "The Ghetto," 19.

54. Glen Warchol, "Value of Mentors in Lives of Black Children Extolled," *Deseret News* (Salt Lake City) January 16, 1985, sec. A, p. 12.

55. Elliot Liebow, *Talley's Corner* (Boston: Little, Brown, 1967), 210–11.

56. Liebow, *Talley's Corner*, 214–18.

57. Dick Thompson, "Unfinished Business," *Time* 134, no. 6 (August 7, 1989): 14.

58. Roy Cogdell and Sybill Wilson, *Black Communication in White Society* (Saratoga, Calif.: Century Twenty-One Publishing, 1980), 110.

59. Ed Bullins, *In New England Winter*, in *New Plays from the Black Theater*, (New York: Bantam Books, 1969), i, 137. Other references to the play will be included in the text.

60. Charles Gordone, *No Place to Be Somebody*, in *Black Theater*, ed. Lindsay Patterson (New York: New American Library, 1971), I, 661.

61. Leslie Lee, *The First Breeze of Summer* (New York: Samuel French, 1975), I, 50.

62. Charles Fuller, *A Soldier's Play* (New York: Hill and Wang, 1982), II, 97. Subsequent references to this play will be included in the text.

63. Richard Wesley, "Dedication," *The Mighty Gents* (New York: Dramatists Play Service, 1979), 4. Subsequent references to this play will be included in the text.

64. Richard Wesley, *Black Terror*, in *The New Lafayette Theatre Presents*, ed. Ed Bullins (New York: Anchor Books, 1974), 301.

6

Civil Rights Theatre Sequel I—Race

Chicanos, Native Americans, women, homosexuals, and other groups who had been systematically excluded from American cultural hegemony went through the same process of self-education and public education in the late 1960s and the 1970s as had blacks slightly earlier. This process took place on a number of different levels. Sometimes the objective was to gain sympathy and understanding from the dominant cultural group, popularly personified as the WASP (white Anglo-Saxon Protestant) heterosexual male over the age of thirty. Sometimes it was an attempt to raise the consciousness of the minority group itself by presenting an alternative view of history which explained the group's exclusion from power as the result of cultural injustice, or by viewing the plight of a minority individual whose fate is seen in context as predetermined by social assumptions rather than personal abilities. Often, the aim is to glorify qualities in the minority group which are absent in, denigrated by, or superior to those of the dominant culture.

Groups striving for recognition in the post–civil rights period had the advantage of confronting an America sensitized to the existence of social inequities. With that sensitization, however, came a backlash of disadvantages. The black focus on power rather than acceptance after the passage of the mid-sixties civil rights acts alienated many majority supporters, and the demands of racial and sexual "minorities" that their individual and cultural differences be respected were seen by some as fragmenting an already tattered social fabric. These dissenters were judged to be symbolic of national moral decay—group manifestations of a "Me Generation" which lacked commitment to anything other than the narrowest of self-interests. Conservative elements categorized attacks on the social status quo, such as Supreme Court decisions affecting prayer in the school and abortion, as evidence of a civilization permissively contributing to its own destruction. With America's self-concept in disarray and her cheap energy-dependent economy stagnant, politicians vied with one another to cut back on public support for equalizing social programs and to increase the military power with which they associated respect for America.

These roadblocks to public acceptance were also, of course, the new minorities' greatest strength. The leadership of the new movements had come from within the groups themselves, and their major concern was self-definition. A secure group identity and the political presence to make the system work for them achieved, they were more likely to be contributing members of a society than those forced to deny aspects of their cultural, emotional, and physical natures in order to receive an ever-diminishing largesse from an embattled establishment. The United States is a pluralistic rather than a homogeneous nation, its social fabric renewed rather than threatened by the necessity for flexibility and change. Furthermore, as Henry James noted in relation to immigration at the turn of the century, there are no options and definite advantages to the embracing of the alien.[1] At any rate, the education of the public could not be repossessed. Although the will of the majority might repeal laws and programs, the visibility of the minorities could not be rescinded, and their concerns must eventually be dealt with.

The Chicano Movement

Las Dos Caras del Patroncito, "The Two Faces of the Boss," is the creation of Luis Valdez and El Teatro Campesino, and was first performed on the grape strike picket line in Delano, California, in 1965. El Teatro Campesino was formed to educate and boost the morale of the largely Hispanic strikers who were being organized at Delano by Cesar Chavez and the National Farm Workers of America, later to be granted a union charter as the United Farm Workers Organizing Committee (UFWOC). *Las Dos Caras* and the Campesino's other early productions were political theatre at its most elemental—"agitprop" (agitation-propaganda) *actos* whose purpose was to "inspire the audience to social action. Illuminate specific points about social problems. Satirize the opposition. Show or hint at a solution. Express what people are feeling."[2] The subject was the strike, and the actors—themselves strikers— portrayed caricatures of people on the picket line or readily visible from it.

However, if El Teatro Campesino's relationship to the strike was clear, the context of the strike was far more complex, raising the by-now-familiar dramatic spectres of capitalism, racism, messianic Americanism.

The image of "striker as hero" conjures up Eugene V. Debs and the Pullman car workers in 1893, the National Guard slaughtering Greek miners at Ludlow, Colorado, in 1914, and assembly line workers outlasting Ford Motor Company goons in 1941. Most of all, we see in our mind's eye the Great Depression—a nation "Waiting for Lefty" and getting FDR instead. The centerpiece of this vision is the "Wagner Act" of 1935, guaranteeing to labor the right to "self-organization" and to "bargain collectively through representatives of their own choosing."

In the years following World War II, however, this vision grew steadily more distant. In 1947, the Taft-Hartley Act outlawed the closed shop, jurisdictional strike, and secondary boycott. Within ten years, nineteen states had adopted "right-to-work" laws. Between 1947 and the outbreak of the Korean War, the CIO was engaged in a constant and usually public effort to expel Communists from positions of union leadership. In 1959, the Landrum-Griffin Act was introduced to protect employees from union practices like those that had caused the AFL-CIO to expel the Teamsters Union two years earlier. In recent years, media praise has gone to union leaders sensitive to the problems of management. Some, like the United Auto Workers' Leonard Woodcock, even found themselves serving on the boards of industries in which their rank and file worked. To organize an industry from the "grassroots"—literally, in Delano—seems a dramatic anachronism.

But then the farm laborer is hopelessly behind his urban counterpart. A 1971 University of Denver study noted that the average field-worker lived only to the age of forty-six—fully twenty-five years less than nonfarm workers. With 7 percent of the work force, farm labor also suffered 22 percent of the work-related fatalities.[3] When Cesar Chavez took a job pruning grape vines near Delano in 1961, he was paid $1.25 an hour—an enviable sum when one considers that the field-workers he induced to strike four years later were only earning $1.10. When UFWOC first signed contracts with grape growers in 1970, the base pay was $1.80 an hour. Although benefits and bonuses lifted the actual earnings into the $2.92–$3.12-an-hour range, it was still a pittance in comparison with wages in unionized industry.[4] As a Florida sugar cane grower put it in 1974, "We used to own our slaves, now we rent them."[5]

Although farm workers were excluded from the Wagner Act, any thorough explanation of the position of the Hispanic farm worker depends as much on race as occupation. According to University of Southern California history professor Manuel Servin,

The Mexican, and consequently the Mexican-American, is in the vast majority . . . , whether he admits it or not, a mixture of two or three racial stocks—the once hated Hispanic European, the American Indian who was nearly exterminated, and the supposedly inferior Negro who was brutally exploited. It is this racial mixture, deriving from previously despised peoples, that accounts for the white American's exploitation and mistreatment of the early Mexican immigrant and the present-day Mexican-American.[6]

These notions were evident in our defenses of the Texas War of Independence in 1835 and the Mexican War of 1846–1848 in which the United States gained the rest of the Southwest and California. In 1842, novelist Anthony Ganilh described the pivotal battle of San Jacinto in the Texas war as a triumph of Anglo-Saxon natural supremacy: Santa Anna's foolhardy "notion that the Texans were inferior in bravery and intelligence to the peasantry of his own country, prompted him to rush into the trap prepared for him; and the fatal twenty-first of April taught him the difference between the two races."[7] On the eve of the United States' war with Mexico, Thomas Jefferson Farnham predicted the racial inevitability of North American control of the entire continent: "As the Indian and other inferior orders of the human family have ever given place to the Caucasian branch; so much, as a general law, all mixtures of that branch with these, fade before the greater intelligence of its pure blood—so certainly as the stars do before the sun."[8]

Race and occupation are united in the history of California agribusiness. Following the completion of the transcontinental railroad, California became the second-largest wheat-producing state in the country. It was also the earliest to be mechanized, resulting in the displacement of probably the worst-treated worker in American history, the native California Indian. In the early 1890s, however, the grain market collapsed, even as Luther Burbank's experiments with fruit and the refrigerator railroad car of George Westinghouse were proving successful. The water projects of the 1902 Reclamation Act were the basis of fruit and vegetable empires, which by World War II supplied 30 percent of America's farm income. But while an acre of wheat required only 13 man-hours of labor from preparation to harvest, an acre of lettuce required 125 and an acre of strawberries 500.[9] The California growers' discovery of new cash crops gave birth to their need for a new source of cheap labor.

By 1886, the Chinese, who were originally brought in to work on the transcontinental railroad, made up seven-eighths of California's farm labor force.[10] They could not, however, bring their families to the United States or apply for citizenship. The Chinese Exclusionary Act of 1882 prevented the renewal of the work force, and pressure from unemployed whites during the recession of 1893 drove many of the remaining Chinese out of the fields.[11]

The Japanese proved to be more resilient. Between 1882 and 1903, the number of Japanese field-workers in California grew from less than a hundred to thirty thousand. Through their dominance of the labor pool, they soon learned how to gain benefits and wage increases. Moreover, in spite of the Alien Land Acts of 1913 and 1919, they proved extremely successful in gaining land of their own—a possible source of the pressure to confine Japanese-Americans to internment camps during World War II and to expropriate their lands.[12]

The 1924 National Origins Act set up a quota system by which immigration limits were determined by the percentage a nationality already made up of the total population. Asians were almost entirely barred.[13] The growers first circumvented this barrier by recruiting Filipinos who had earlier emigrated to Hawaii. However, the Filipinos proved to be strong union advocates, an option with which the Mexicans were less familiar.[14]

Between 1880 and the turn of the century, Mexicans already made up 70 percent of the railroad section crews and 90 percent of the extra gangs on the principal western lines, but in the twentieth century, the Mexican-American immigrant population exploded. In the Old Mexican states of North America (Texas, Arizona, New Mexico, and California), Hispanic immigrants numbered just under 100,000 in 1900. In 1930 there were over 1,200,000. During this period, roughly a tenth of the population of Mexico immigrated to the American Southwest—most of them earning their living as farm laborers.[15]

It was as laborers that they were welcomed, if in no other way. By 1926 California lobbyist S. Friselle Parker was in Washington "to get us Mexicans and keep them out of our schools and out of our social problems." An average of 58,000 California field-workers were imported from Mexico between 1924 and 1930 and sent home during the off-season.[16] The seasonal flow was interrupted by the Depression, when even permanent residents, including some U.S. citizens and some against their will, were "repatriated" to Mexico. By 1934 the repatriates totaled 280,000[17] and would reach 500,000 by the decade's conclusion.[18]

In 1942, with defense industries depleting the Anglo agricultural work force and the Japanese-Americans incarcerated, Mexican migrants were suddenly welcome. Initiated as a wartime stopgap measure, the *bracero* importations were renewed in 1946, codified into Public Law 78 in 1951, and continued through 1964. Despite their value as strikebreakers, neither *braceros* nor their government had much control over their own working conditions. In 1948, when Mexico decided that workers should be paid $3.00 per hundred pounds for picking Texas cotton instead of the Department of Labor-approved $2.50, the U.S. government opened the borders to unemployed Mexicans, and 40,000 illegal aliens joined the 35,000 *braceros* in the fields. Cotton was soon at $1.50 per hundred-weight. Chicano support for John F. Kennedy's 1960 presidential campaign and the support of congressional Education and Labor Committee chairman Adam Clayton Powell ended the *bracero* program and paved the way for the unionizing efforts of Chavez and UFWOC after 1965. According to the Mexican-American Political Association's Bert Corona, retaliatory pressure from the growers contributed to Powell's 1967 expulsion from the House of Representatives.

The signing of contracts with the Delano table-grape growers in 1970 was followed immediately by a series of jurisdictional disputes over contracts signed by the California lettuce growers with the Teamsters Union, which dragged on until the mid-seventies. In 1975 the state passed the country's first collective bargaining act for farm workers, with the result that the average hourly wages of UFWOC workers had more than tripled by 1983.[19]

However, in the many areas of California's agribusiness industry which remain unorganized, workers wages average half those of union farm laborers, and historical circumstances are combining to keep the unions out. First, in the San Joaquin Valley, Southeast Asian refugees have taken their place in the century-long line of immigrants whose desire to find a place in their new homeland has forced down the cost of labor. Second, and most important in the long run for all agricultural workers, agribusiness is mechanizing rapidly. The 350,000 California agricultural workers employed in 1983 were already 10 percent fewer than the previous year.[20] Third, the economic troubles of Central America have also added to the flood of illegal alien field-workers in recent years.[21] Finally, poor economic prospects in Mexico continue to provide a motive that neither grower nor campesino has historically been able to resist.

When the much-maligned Simpson-Mazzoli bill was introduced into Congress in 1982, a dollar was worth 40 pesos. When it was reintroduced in 1983, a dollar was worth 140 pesos. During that year, the Border Patrol estimated that six thousand aliens a day attempted to enter the United States illegally. Mexico was generally believed to supply 50 to 60 percent of those entering, an action which their 50 percent unemployment, 100 percent inflation, and low minimum wage (one-fourth that of the United States) makes fully comprehensible. The Census Bureau estimates that there are as many as six million undocumented aliens now in the country.[22] Factoring in cost data in job displacement, education, unemployment, welfare, health, and crime, the Immigration and Naturalization Service believes that federal, state, and local governments lose $1.26 billion yearly for each million undocumented residents.[23]

The Immigration Reform and Control Act was finally passed by Congress in 1986, and its registration program went into effect two years later. That its provisions (which include amnesty for aliens who entered the United States prior to 1982 and heavy penalties for knowingly employing aliens) will effectively curb illegal immigration is unlikely. For Mexico to maintain even the same rate of employment as it currently has would require the creation of 700,000 new jobs a year.[24] If there were no differences in job availabilities, there would be no motive for illegal entry. The United States is unlikely to even consider the mass deportations which were carried out during the Depression. To begin with, no one has any idea what such an action would do to the American economy. Second, the tendency has been for whole families to slip across the border. Subsequent children born in the North are U.S. citizens, and a United States already sensitive over its Latin American image is unwilling to deport citizens or divide families again.

Las Dos Caras del Patroncito

We have to find some cross between being a movement and being a Union.
—Cesar Chavez (1965)

All of which is to say that the roots of political theatre are deep and tangled indeed. What began as the simplest of agitprop dramas referring to the most local of labor actions leads us through an elaborate warp and woof to the whole fabric of American society. In the long run, Cesar Chavez's greatest contribution to the labor movement may prove to be the recognition of the matrix that connects local working conditions to international attitudes, racial pride and civil rights to the American economy, religious conscience to political reality. Similarly, Luis Valdez's greatest artistic contribution may be his recognition that he could politically best serve his people by increasing their awareness (and that of the larger American society) of their cultural roots. Before Chavez, could one have conceived of a union leader being awarded the Martin Luther King, Jr., Nonviolent Peace Prize, as he was in 1974?[25] Before El Teatro Campesino, could one have conceived of a cultural/historical docudrama on Broadway, as *Zoot Suit* was in 1979?

Like the march from the dusty paths of the Delano fields to Broadway, *Las Dos Caras* derives from the ability of the imagination to perceive of oneself as on top. *Las Dos Caras* is a simple turnaround in which the *esquirol* (illegal migrant worker) finds himself in the role of the *patroncito* (landowning boss) and discovers that the position makes the man. The play was an exercise in counter-intimidation and grew out of improvisations held in an old pink house behind the *huelga* (strike) office in Delano. The growers were engaging in their own version of guerrilla theatre: bathing the pickets in huge clouds of dust raised by the high-speed transit of their powerful cars, cruising the area in pickups with mounted shotguns prominently displayed in their back windows, and deploying private armed guards (*la jura*, or "rent-a-fuzz") at the edge of the fields. In *Las Dos Caras*, the symbols of power revert to the worker.

The play opens with the first appearance of the farm worker. "I come here to prune grape vines. My patron bring me all the way from Mexico here to California—the land of sun and money! More sun than money. But I better get to *jalar* now because my patroncito he don't like to see me talking to strangers."[26] He is then joined by the patroncito, complete with "pig" mask, bullwhip, imaginary Lincoln Continental, and list of advantages of the worker's life in comparison to the grower's.

The first is economic. The worker gets free transportation to and from Mexico, free housing while he is here, and eats only beans and tortillas, which cost almost nothing. Of course, the transportation is in a fully packed, open truck driven straight through, stopping only for gasoline. In such a truck, a 1940 McAllen, Texas, accident took twenty-nine Mexican lives (eleven of them children under the age of sixteen) and injured another fifteen. In October 1944, Pauline Kibber counted 496 such migratory trucks passing through Lubbock, Texas.[27] The workers' cabins are rent-free and air-conditioned (largely due to the front door having fallen off)—although the air itself is seasoned by the nearby portable outhouses which line the irrigation ditches. As for the meals, the diet of the laborers to a large extent accounts for the shortness of their life span, noted earlier in this section.

Meanwhile the poor landowner must struggle to pay his taxes, insurance, and the upkeep on his apelike "rent-a-fuzz." He must maintain his $12,000 Lincoln Continental, his $350,000 LBJ-style ranch house, and his blond wife, whose mink bikini is barely large enough to hold its $5,000 price tag. And all the time he must put up with lazy, disgraceful, Communist strikers, for as California state senator Hugh Burns warned in 1967: "Even though the Delano movement is not Communist-dominated, it lends itself to Communist-type influences."[28]

In his heart, the patroncito wishes only to be one of his own field hands, contentedly shining his master's shoes and kissing his ass. Suddenly, he realizes that he has the power to make his wish come true. After all, the big growers are among California's richest men. In 1969, 12.2 percent of the farmers owned 86.4 percent of all the farmland. By 1972 there were only 40 percent as many farms as in 1945, and the average size was increasing by more than thirty acres a year.[29] The limits to a big landowner's whims are few. He exchanges clothes and identification signs with the farm worker and teaches him the fine points of obedience training the governor. See, for example, the Fresno press conference during the presidential campaign of 1968 at which Governor Ronald Reagan and presidential candidate Richard Nixon denounced the grape workers' strike from a luncheon table at which grapes were prominently displayed.[30]

The transformation is not complete, however, until the patroncito removes his mask and gives it to the *esquirol*. Slow recognition comes over the farm worker's face: "Patron, you look like me!" Thus armed with all the outward accoutrements of the boss, the *esquirol* begins to act like one. He insults and kicks his former master, laying claim to his land, car, house, and wife. When the landowner protests, the worker cuts his wages to eighty-five cents an hour.

Patroncito: I was paying you a buck twenty five!

Farmworker: I got problems, boy! Go on welfare! (*Las Dos Caros del Patroncito*, 18)

The patroncito tries to take back his material identity, but succeeds only in arousing Charlie, his paid *la jura*. Responding to the signs of power as he has been trained to do, the "rent-a-fuzz" drags out the struggling boss to a promised beating: "Somebody help me! Help! Where's those damn union organizers? Where's Cesar Chavez? Help! Huelga! HUELGAAAAAA!" (*Las Dos Caras del Patroncito*, 19)

And we are reminded—as were the picket lines at Delano—that the differences between men are circumstantial and, frequently, temporary.

The shoe may someday be on the other foot, and as Cesar Chavez told the strikers marching to Coachello in 1969: "Time accomplishes for the poor what money does for the rich."[31]

The Politics of Culture

According to a 1985 Ford Foundation report, there were twenty-nine Chicano theatre groups in the United States (including thirteen in California).[32] The Mexican-American theatre has never been far removed from its audience's political concerns. As far back as the 1860s, California's Compania Dramatica Espanola gave benefit performances for Juarez's army of liberation. Eduardo Carrillo's *El proceso y muerte de Aurelio Pompa* in the 1920s not only argued that Pompa was being unjustly accused but also raised money for his defense. Between 1930 and 1933, Gabriel Navarro's *Los emigrados*, Antonio's Helu's *Los mexicanos se van*, and Juan Bustillos Oro's *Los que vuelven* all took up the Mexican-American viewpoint on the U.S. policy of repatriation. During the Depression, *La pizca de la uva*, produced at Los Angeles's Teatro Hidalgo, supported striking Mexican farm workers, and El Paso's *El sacrificio del jornalero* was done as a benefit for the Union Internacional Obrera.[33]

The late 1960s and early 1970s produced some good-quality agitprop *actos* reminiscent of the black revolutionary plays of the same period. Guadalupe Saavedra's *Justice* (1968) is a parable of a humble but devout people who are harassed by "Honky Sam" and his dogs. Urged by the "Voice of God" to organize, the people kill one of the "dogs" (police) every time one of their own is murdered until Honky Sam is defeated. Francisco Burruel's *The Dialogue of Cuco Rocha* (1970) describes a prison warden's chess game with a Chicano activist whose spirit and political movement are as impossible to get rid of as his namesake. Jaime Verdugo's *Trampa sin salida*, "Get Out If You Can," (1972) shows how pachucos are conditioned to sell their birthright and fight one another, as well as the police.[34]

The parable continues to be a popular form in more recent Chicano dramas. Ruben Sierra (of Seattle's Group Theatre Company) has written a satirical comedy on the subject of racial purity, *La Raza Pura, or Racial, Racial*. In Alurista's *Dawn*, the forces of the Latin American Indios gods of life and redemption, Quetzalcoatl and Cihuacoatl, overcome the representatives of consumerism and death, Pepsicoatl and Cocacoatl. The inadequacy of present-day nonviolent techniques is the theme of Ysidro R. Macias's *Martir Montezuma*, a *MacBird*-like parody obstensibly set in A.D. 1524, but containing characters such as Viceroy Rigan (the Spanish viceroy in charge of Nueva Espana), Roberto Quinaidi (the distinguished young liberal senator), and his widow, Hay-tol, plus Revolucion and Justicia. In Macias's *The Ultimate Pendejada*, a Mexican-American couple, Robert (Roberto) and Mary (Maria) Gomes (Gomez), become aware of their need for roots, only to leap from the fire of empty Caucasian materialism into the frying pan of empty radical rhetoric.[35]

Every emerging minority depends upon the stage to provide them an alternative history which explains their present plight. *La victima* (1977), collectively created by El Teatro de la Esperanza of Santa Barbara, follows the lives of a Chicano mother and the son she loses during the 1930 repatriations. Adopted into an Anglo family, Sam grows up to become an official of the Immigration and Naturalization Service, so immersed in self-hatred that when a chance meeting with his now elderly mother forces him to examine his motives, he sends her back to Mexico again.[36] Carlos Morton (whose immigrant father took his last name from a Morton Salt billboard) has written several histories, working alone, with various university collectives, and with the San Francisco Mime Troupe. *Lilith*, based on the mythical story of the first wife of Adam, proposes that the past deeds of women have been inaccurately assessed. *Los dorados*, originally performed as street theatre, is a Chicano account of the discovery of California, and *Rancho Hollywood* is a California history from the Gold Rush forward, showing how Hollywood stereotypes of Chicanos, Native Americans, and blacks have been perpetuated.

The best-known play of Morton (whose reputation as a Chicano playwright is second only to Luis Valdez) is *The Many Deaths of Danny Rosales* (1983). This play, which began as a collective effort with students in San Diego, is a quasi-documentary, taking its inspiration from a newspaper article on the 1975 shooting death of Richard Morales at the hands of the Castroville, Texas, sheriff. The sheriff's wife and daughter loaded the body into the trunk of the family car and drove six hours to a relative's ranch to bury the body. The sheriff eventually pleaded guilty to aggravated assault and received a two-to-ten-year sentence.

Deputy: Did you hear? Grace Hall pleaded no contest to the charge of concealing physical evidence. She was fined $49.50 in court costs.

Rowena: $49.50! If Danny weighed 154 pounds at the time of his death, that means she got off with about thirty cents a pound. . . .

Berta: They killed my husband many times. . . . Once when he was born poor. . . . Once when he didn't get a decent education. Once with a shotgun at

the Old Alamo School Road. . . . Once with a pick and shovel near the Louisiana
border. . . . And once in a court of law. . . .

Rowena: In 1977, two years after Danny Rosales' death, we realized a great victory.
Fred and Grace Hall were indicted by a federal grand jury [and] found guilty of
violating Danny Rosales' civil rights. Fred Hall was sentenced to life in prison,
and Grace Hall was sentenced to three years in prison. But was this such a great
victory? Did you hear what happened in Mejia, Texas, a couple of years ago?
Three black men drowned while in police custody. And just last year in San
Antonio they shot Hector Santoscoy and. . . .[37]

Even as Cesar Chavez searched for a cross between a union and a
movement, Chicano political theatre has encompassed both specific
political issues and the validation of a culture. The significance of the
latter may be harder to grasp, unless one remembers the importance of
aesthetics to a revolutionary minority. Marx believed that to have
dominance in a society, the values of a cultural group had to have
hegemony, that is, the group's values had to be the norm for that society.
Although Marx was referring to a class war, the concept is even more
applicable to a caste war. One can buy into a different class, but skin
color and gender are permanent, and cultural roots are pulled up at the
cost of psychological self-denial and loss of nourishment. In Chapter 5,
we noted that the audience for revolutionary drama is the minority itself,
and that black art was the aesthetic equivalent of Black Power. It follows
then that to adopt the aesthetic system of the majority in order to speak
to it is to yield hegemony to the majority. An inevitable step in the
literature of an emerging minority is the reclamation of its cultural forms
and imagery. The attempt of the majority to adapt to or adopt those forms
and images is a hegemonic victory. When "Black is beautiful," when
Caucasians adopt Native American ecological ideals, when men take
pride in being called feminists, or when gay styles are adopted, the
minority has triumphed in a way no conscious act of tolerance or militant
force of arms can ever achieve.

When Luis Valdez and Teatro Campesino turned in the 1970s from the
agitprop *actos* that had energized the striking grape pickers of the Delano
fields to ritual spectacles incorporating Latin American Catholic symbolism and Aztec imagery, they faced intense criticism from the politically committed—most of all, ironically, from Marxist-oriented groups
which had failed to make the class/caste comparison.[38] Valdez realized
(as Lenin did not) that to speak only to the politically committed leads,
at best, to a revolt in which power changes hands, rather than to a
revolution in which the system changes. To achieve the latter, he had to
create a drama with which the lower-class campesino or descendant of

campesinos could identify, and which the upper-class Anglo would strive to emulate. Thus, the 1960s *actos* (the Mexican/American confrontation seen through Chicano eyes) became the 1970s *mitos*, or myths (the Mexican/American experience from the viewpoint of God), enlivened by the *corrida*, or traditional Mexican ballad, and expressed in the vaudeville/cabaret/circus of the *carpa*—the traditional touring tent entertainment of the pre–World War II era. If *Las Dos Caras del Patroncito* is the typical Teatro Campesino fare of the 1960s, *La Gran Carpa de los Rasquachis*—which presents the whole history of the Mexican-American in terms of a struggle between "Saint Boss's Church" and a Jose Guadalupe Posada–inspired devil—is typical of the 1970s.

Late in the 1970s, Valdez was ready for the next step: the incorporation of the *acto*, *mito*, *corrida*, *carpa*, and Living Newspaper techniques into *Zoot Suit*. At its base were two historical incidents from the Los Angeles of the early 1940s: (a) the Sleepy Lagoon murder case, in which seventeen Mexican-American young men were convicted of and imprisoned for the murder of another Chicano youth whose death may or may not have occurred during a gang-related brawl; and (b) the Zoot Suit Riots, in which locally based sailors and marines, egged on by press and police, poured into the Hispanic sections of the city for the purpose of "teaching respect" by stripping and shearing Mexican-Americans dressed in the currently fashionable "zoot suit," with its colorful draped shape, ankle-tight cuffs, reet pleats, and peg tops, complemented by lids and DA hairstyles. *Zoot Suit* rightly concludes that both incidents were signs of a Caucasian majority in search of a racial scapegoat upon which to vent wartime fears and frustrations after West Coast Japanese-Americans had been interred. The play's most striking character is El Pachuco, the alter ego of one of the Sleepy Lagoon defendants. He is at once the rebel against white authority and the rebel against white style, the street-smart Los Angeles Latino and his Inca ancestor. Clad in the garb that marks his identity, he speaks the play's hegemonic truth: "It is the secret fantasy of every *vato* to put on the zoot suit and play the part of the pachuco."[39] Stripped of the suit by vengeful sailors, he rises as a loincloth-clad Aztec god and exits the stage, his dignity intact.

Zoot Suit rewrites history from the standpoint of the minority, and does so using the minority's symbolism and language (El Pachuco speaks in *calo*, the street slang originally derived from Spanish gypsies), while exciting the admiration of the majority. *Zoot Suit* was a sensation in Los Angeles, failed on a Broadway lacking in cultural context, only to be reborn, Quetzalcoatl-like, as a film. That Mexican-American culture is translatable to filmic terms is emphasized by Valdez's *Zoot Suit* successors: *The Ballad (Corrida) of Gregorio Cortez, La Bamba*, and *Stand and Deliver*. By speaking in his own tongue, Valdez has expanded the theatre language of his audiences. By remaining so close to his own roots, he has given his plays a life which transcends the *barrio*. His Chicano theatre has become American theatre.

Native Americans

Insofar as the Western Hemisphere is concerned, the term "Indian" is social, not biological. As every American schoolchild knows, "Columbus sailed the ocean blue in fourteen hundred and ninety-two" in an attempt to find a shortcut to India (Southeast Asia). The fact that he landed in the islands off Central America and soon realized his mistake did not prevent him from labeling the natives there *los Indios*. That the term came to be applied to all Native Americans may have sealed their fate more surely than the many differences between them.

In actuality, Native Americans can be categorized by linguistics into a dozen language stocks, "each as distinct from one another as the Semitic from the Indo-European, and within each stock into languages as distinct as English from Russian."[40] Tribes tended to see themselves as not only markedly different from their neighbors, but as their superiors. From the Mikasuki (Seminoles) in Florida to the Inuit (Eskimos) in Alaska, tribal names mean roughly "We, the People," or "Human Beings."[41]

Had Native Americans initially accepted the post-Columbian definition of them all as Indians, they might have been more concerned about the annihilation of adjacent tribes and united earlier against the Europeans. Miantonomo, a Long Island Narragansett chief, proposed such a military alliance in 1642,[42] and many feel that it still might have been successful as late as the Revolutionary War.[43] By the time Native Americans did unify in the Plains Indian Wars, the whites were so numerous and technologically advanced that it was impossible to do more than delay the inevitable.

What began as a geographic mistake is too frequently today a cultural insult. To be "Indian" is not merely to have Indian ancestry in the sense that Negro blood automatically designates one as "black." Most Hispanics in Latin America have some Indian blood, but *los Indios* refers to the poor, socially isolated, politically impotent, and culturally traditional peoples, who (unlike the Hispanicized *mestizo*) have not assimilated into the dominant culture. Only those Sioux they perceive as backward are designated by Dakotans as "Indians," as are tribal Cherokee by white Oklahomans.[44]

At the time of the first white appearances in North America, the aboriginal population is estimated by anthropologist Henry Dobyns to have been between 10.5 and 12.6 million.[45] Considering the life-supporting abundance available, it is not surprising that the natives felt unthreatened by the arrival of Columbus. Within a century, however, Spanish explorers developed a saying: "If the Indians are friendly, no European has been here."[46] Today, Native Americans comprise only 0.5 percent of the US population, as opposed to 8 percent for Hispanics and 14 percent for blacks.[47] The former landlords of the continent have become the unwelcome wards of the state.

The white man wanted the red man's land, and offered him civilization for it. Neither clause was optional. Back in 1603, the Huron chief Anadabijou refused the urgings of French explorers to accept white ways, telling Samuel de Champlain to come live with the Indians and demonstrate the superiority of his life-style: "When we see all this, we shall learn more in a year than in twenty by simply hearing you discourse."[48] The stated aim of New World white governments has always been to acculturate the natives—in our case, to "make the American Indian the Indian American." Nowhere were we more successful than with the five "civilized" tribes of Georgia—the Cherokees, Choctaws, Creeks, Chikasaws, and Seminoles. The Cherokees had allied with Andy Jackson, both against antiwhite Indians and at the Battle of New Orleans. They adopted Christianity and developed a written language, a newspaper, a banking system, and that crowning mark of civilization—a slave code. Nevertheless, in 1830, President Jackson's Indian Relocation Bill authorized the tribes' transfer from their legally owned land to supposedly equivalent lands west of the Mississippi. The Cherokees protested through the law, obtaining a favorable ruling from the Supreme Court, which Jackson ignored: "John Marshall has rendered his decision, now let him enforce it." In 1838 the Georgia militia escorted the Cherokees on a march to Oklahoma called the Trail of Tears because one-quarter of the tribe died on the trip. On his purchase and resale of vacated Georgia land, Jackson made a profit of 750 percent.[49]

The saga of the Cherokees was by no means over. By 1850 they had established an exemplary school system, largely staffed by Indian teachers, administrators, and school boards, and including college-level classes in philosophy, rhetoric, Latin, Greek, and trigonometry.[50] However, under the Dawes Severalty Act of 1887, Cherokee tribal land was divided into plots too small to be profitably farmed. Much of this land was then purchased by adjacent large ranches at bargain prices. When Oklahoma became a territory in 1890, the tribal schools were closed. In

1898 Congress ordered the Cherokee, Choctaw, Chickasaw, and Creek nations dissolved.[51]

Indian tribes were treated as sovereign nations so long as they could militarily defend themselves. When the Bureau of Indian Affairs (BIA) was established in 1832, it was placed in the War Department. During the treaty-making era (1778–1871), the federal government negotiated 371 agreements with individual tribes. The military threat past, U.S. policy began to eliminate the cultural identity. In 1883, when Sitting Bull of the Hunkpapa Sioux reminded a congressional delegation of its past broken promises, Senator John Logan chastised him, stating that the government's purpose was to "civilize you and make you as white men."[52]

Anthropologist Joseph Jorgenson insists the Congressional Act of 1871 "allowed for speedier domination of Indians and expropriation of Indian resources." He groups it with the Homestead Act (1862), the Timber Culture Act (1873), the Desert Land Act (1877), and the Timber and Stone Act (1878) as rulings which "literally denied all off-reservation territory to Indians,"[53] and the Dawes Severalty Act which contributed to the loss of ninety million acres before it was ended by the Indian Reorganization Act (IRA) of 1934.[54] In 1924 American Indians were rewarded for their disproportionate service in World War I by being made full citizens. This action opened their lands to full taxation, a condition many were unaware of until their acreage was sold to pay state and local taxes.[55] Technically, the IRA restored tribal government. In actuality, reservation superintendents could veto any decisions a tribal council made, and still had full control over all individual and tribal property and financial affairs. Even the selection of a tribe's lawyer required the approval of the secretary of the interior, who usually relied on the local superintendent's recommendation.[56]

The 1950s saw a number of attempts to assimilate Indians into white society. The first was relocation, or the subsidizing of individual Indians' migration from the reservation to the city. The target of relocation was Indians aged eighteen to thirty-five. According to one Cleveland Sioux: "The old people can die on the reservation, but they want the young ones to move to the city, intermarry, forget their traditions, and disappear. It's another form of genocide."[57] The second was termination (House Concurrent Resolution 108), which would end the special standing Indian tribes had under federal law, including tax exemptions, hunting and fishing rights, medical services, and so on.[58] To the Klamath of Oregon and the Menominee of Wisconsin, that meant the loss of their timber industry. Senator Arthur Watkins of Utah called House 108 "freedom legislation," and Utah reservation Indians were refused the right to vote until 1956 on the grounds that reservation lands were untaxed.[59] The third was on-reservation state jurisdiction—enacted in Washington, Oregon, Nebraska, Minnesota, and Wisconsin through Public Bill 280 in 1954. Interference with federally guaranteed Indian fishing rights in Washington and Oregon initiated a seventeen-year court fight (1961–1978) by the Puyallups of Washington over the 1855 treaty.[60] In Nebraska, local police took advantage of the law to harass Indians on the reservation, while in Wisconsin and Minnesota the state used the law as grounds for arbitrarily removing children from their families and assigning them to foster homes. By 1970 the ratio of Indians to whites in Minnesota foster homes was twenty-four to one.[61]

In 1968, reservation Indian unemployment stood at 42 percent, and income was only a third of the national average.[62] Fifteen years later, 1968 seemed like the golden age. Jimmy Carter's last budget authorized .04 percent of all federal spending for Indians. President Reagan's first budget indicated 2.5 percent of *all* spending cuts would come out of Indian allocations, resulting in a real decrease in federal Indian spending of 35 percent. On the Navaho reservation, unemployment reached 70 percent, and on some other reservations was as high as 95 percent.[63] For the moment, it appeared as if the federal government had reverted to the philosophy of a century earlier: If it was easier to feed the Indians than to fight them, it was cheapest of all to starve them to death and be done with it.[64]

In 1905, BIA commissioner Francis E. Leupp wrote: "The Indian will never be judged aright till we learn to measure him by his own standards, as we whites would want to be measured if some more powerful race were to usurp dominion over us."[65] In short, let the Indian be an Indian.

As America approaches the twenty-first century, this will consist of following two philosophically different, but otherwise reconcilable, courses: (a) allow the Indian to pursue his life-style and avail himself of the opportunities any U.S. citizen is guaranteed under the Constitution; and (b) allow him the limited sovereignty implied in the many treaties and agreements which the U.S. government has made with his people.

One traditionally American avenue which must be allowed to remain open for the Indian is freedom of religion. From 1493, when Pope Innocent VI took it upon himself to divide the New World between Spain and Portugal without consulting its current inhabitants, the institutions of Christianity have been a mixed blessing for the Native American.[66] In 1637 Puritan John Underhill used it to justify a night's slaughter of seven hundred noncombatant Connecticut Pequots: "We have sufficient light from the Word of God for our proceedings."[67] Underhill would have agreed with Colonel John Chivington, the Methodist minister who ordered the Southern Cheyenne massacre at Sand Creek in 1864: "I have come to kill Indians and believe it is right and honorable to use any means under God's heaven to kill Indians."[68]

Years after the Plains Wars had ended, BIA officials saw the supplanting of Indian religions by Christianity as a major factor in assimilation. In 1923, Indian Affairs commissioner Charles Burke had reservation superintendents cooperate with missionaries in suppressing traditional religious activities on the Taos, New Mexico, reservations. The Pueblos, who had been fighting for their religious autonomy since 1608, protested that their religion taught them "about God and the earth, and about our duty to God, to earth, and to one another." In reply, BIA press releases suggested Pueblo opposition was financed by Communist "money from Moscow," and Burke tried unsuccessfully to induce Congress to enforce his ban on "useless and harmful performances."[69]

To advise acceptance of Indian religious freedom is not to promote any particular sect, for the religions are as diverse as the tribes which developed them. Nor is it to denigrate Christianity, which found its way into Indian religion in 1800 when Handsome Lake, a Huron prophet, grafted Quaker principles onto traditional Iroquois ways.[70] The basis of the Ghost Dance was a Second Coming of Christ, this time to the Indians.[71] Black Elk, the Ogalala Sioux medicine man, believed in both Jesus and the Sacred Pipe, and the peyote-using Native American Church, the single largest reservation domination, is by definition an Indian version of Christianity.[72]

Just as essential as freedom of religion, and probably more difficult for the average non-Indian to accept, is the right of the Native American to live in a communal, noncompetitive relationship with his fellow man and his environment. In 1810 the Shawnee warrior Tecumseh protested the ceding of lands in the treaty of Fort Wayne: "The only way to stop this evil, is for all the red men to unite in claiming a common and equal right in the land as it was at first, and should be yet, for it was never divided, but belongs to all, for the use of each."[73]

The idea of sharing all land equally was incomprehensible to the invading Europeans, the more articulate of them seeing justification in Manifest Destiny, or as General James Carleton put it, "the insatiable progress of our race."[74] As a part of his campaign to evict the Utes from their Colorado land, William Vickers wrote in the *Denver Tribune* in 1879: "The Utes are actual, practical Communists and the government should be ashamed to foster and encourage them in their idleness and wanton waste of property."[75]

A century later, however, the philosophy of the Utes no longer seems so foreign. The traditional Indian believes that the earth is his mother. He takes from it only what he needs, shares his bounty with his fellow man, and returns his body to nourish the earth when he dies. For a world anxiously watching atomic apocalypse and Malthusian madness race to become the agent for its suicide, the Indian way of life has achieved radical relevance. Vine Deloria, Jr., formerly of the National Council of American Indians, points out, "American society could save itself by listening to tribal people. The land-use philosophy of Indians is so utterly simple that it seems stupid to repeat it: man must live with other forms of life on the land and not destroy it. . . . He must give up the concept of the earth as a divisible land area that he can market."[76]

But let us suppose that the white man's becoming red is no more likely than the red man's turning white. Is not the recognition of the Native American's special relationship to the country at large worthy of maintenance? We have the continent which created their culture. Do we not, in return, owe that culture self-determination of its future? Prior to 1871, when Indian tribes could still command military respect, we dealt with them as sovereign nations. Since the Indian Reorganization Act of 1934, tribes have existed under the concept of limited sovereignty; that is, they are distinct, independent political communities, but only *within* the United States. They can make no foreign treaties, and U.S. legal action can qualify tribal sovereignty unilaterally.[77] We can expect in the immediate future, as in the recent past, that it is in such unilateral legal actions that abuses of power will take place.

In earlier decades, the U.S. government arbitrarily confiscated Indian land for a variety of uses, including railroad and highway building, exploitation of mineral rights, and for military purposes. In 1942 the War Department confiscated 500 square miles of the Oglala Sioux Pine Ridge Reservation to use as a practice bombing range. The land was never returned, and an old woman who protested receiving only two hundred dollars for the loss of a four-hundred-acre tract was called unpatriotic.[78]

Such actions are scarcely ancient history. In 1980 the government sought to locate its MX missile "race-track" system on twelve million acres of eastern Nevada owned by the Shoshone Nation. For land whose value was estimated at $2.4 trillion, the government offered to settle for $26 million.[79] In the "Four Corners" area of Utah, Colorado, Arizona, and New Mexico, a conglomerate of twenty-three electric companies runs the nation's largest strip mine while drawing hundreds of millions of gallons from the Colorado River and creating some of the nation's worst air pollution. Meanwhile, among the Navajo and Hopi, who lost sixty-five thousand acres and saw the sacred Black Mesa desecrated in the project, reservation unemployment stands at 72.4 percent, and only one Navajo home in three has electricity.[80]

The greatest support to Indian sovereignty may come from the Pan-Indian movement—a concept of multitribal nationalism which developed in the 1960s. Unified, tribes' increase in legal/political/economic power and sheer visibility can do a great deal to hinder the exploitation of any tribe individually. In 1975 twenty-two tribes united to form CERT (the Council of Energy Resource Tribes) "to promote the general welfare of energy resource owning tribes and their people through the protection, conservation, and prudent management of their oil, natural gas, uranium, coal, geothermal, and oil shale resources." The year before, ninety-seven tribal representatives met at Sitting Bull's grave on the Standing Rock Sioux reservation to urge the United States to recognize tribal sovereignty. They formed the International Indian Treaty Council, which was eventually recognized by the United Nations as an official nongovernmental organization and which was given full observer status by the Movement on Non-Alligned Nations in 1981.[81]

The most dangerous threats to Indian sovereignty will be in the name of energy needs or national defense or, most subtly of all, the welfare of the Indians themselves. A prime example is the Native American Equal Opportunity Act introduced by Washington representative John Cunningham in 1977, which called for de facto termination by abrogating all treaties, closing all Indian hospitals, schools, housing projects, and ending hunting and fishing rights.[82]

In the end, what will be to the advantage and honor of Native Americans will be to the advantage and honor of all Americans. Chief Seattle of the Suquamish put it well 130 years ago: "Your time of decay may be distant, but it will surely come, for even the white man, whose God walked and talked with him as friend with friend, cannot be exempt from the common destiny. We may be brothers, after all. We will see."[83]

Black Elk Speaks

Black Elk was born in 1863 and was either present or acquainted with participants at most of the major events of the Plains Indian Wars. His father (also an Oglala Sioux medicine man) received a lifelong limp at the Battle of the Hundred Slain (the Fetterman Massacre), an 1866 victory masterminded by Crazy Horse, Black Elk's second cousin. Black Elk himself fought at the Battle of the Little Big Horn (the Greasy Grass) River in which Custer died in 1876, and was shot by soldiers in a battle the day after the Wounded Knee Massacre on December 29, 1890. In 1930–1931, Nebraska poet John Neihardt interviewed Black Elk on the Oglala reservation. *Black Elk Speaks* had gone through twenty-eight American editions and been translated into eight foreign languages by the time Christopher Sergel dramatized it in 1976.

As a boy in 1872, Black Elk received a vision that determined the course of his life, providing the play with its theme. For, although the play's action is centered in the Plains Wars, its central idea is that of unity: first of all, unity among the Indians, the absence of which made inevitable their conquest by the white man; second, the message Indian philosophy has for the modern world—the unity of man with the earth and the entire cycle of life; and, finally, the world of the vision—the unity of the flesh and the spirit, the conscious and the subconscious.

Black Elk Speaks takes the form of a docudrama. Like *In White America*, the play consists of historical events introduced by narrators. The central action is extended warfare, but the narrators (frequently the warrior chiefs themselves) describe events with a detached irony. This is a war whose outcome is known from the beginning, and the play is less a re-creation of history than a postmortem. The famous phrases we associate with the Indian Wars are present, often delivered by characters other than those who originally spoke them. This is done partly for dramatic convenience, and partly because the consciousness that created them does not depend on a single situation. The presence throughout the play of a single narrator, Black Elk, with whom the audience can grow in identification, gives the play an advantage over *In White America*. Furthermore, as Wounded Knee, the play's culminating event, was eighty-five years in the past when the drama was being written, *Black Elk Speaks* cannot become dated, as was *In White America* almost from its opening curtain. On the other hand, by relying on its documentary sources for dialogue, *In White America* achieved a sense of period and of progression that *Black Elk Speaks*, with its unrelieved contemporary irony, lacks. Black Elk himself is outside of the action, worldly and aware—dramatically effective, but bearing little resemblance to the faith and dignity recorded by Neihardt. In 1963 *In White America* rode the rising crest of the civil rights movement. Thirteen years later, *Black Elk Speaks* was on the brink of its backlash. There are also twenty-five potential black viewers in America for every Indian. Finally, the purpose of including Black Elk in the play was probably the relevance of his vision to the ecological movement of the early seventies. The problem is that the act of conservation is not inherently visually dramatic and the audience may well not realize the relevance of the Indians' fate to their own.

The play opens with a lament for the tribes lost as the white man's presence spread across America, ending at Wounded Knee. Black Elk recounts the vision he received at the "center of the world," the highest point in the sacred Black Hills:

> I saw that the sacred hoop of my people was one of many hoops that made one circle, and being endless, it was holy with all powers becoming one power in the people without end. I was offered a wooden cup full of water, and in the water was the sky. "Take this," the Voice said. "It's the power to make live, and it's yours." I was given a mission in the form of a bright red stick that by my power I must bring to life. . . . I was to make it grow into a shielding tree that would bloom—a mighty flowering tree that would shelter the children, a tree to protect the people.[84]

To the Indian the circle is sacred, representing the endless cycle of life. Each people has a cycle of life, but all unite to make the great circle. The water is the nourishment of life, and the tree is the tree of life, whose purpose (according to Neihardt's record of the 1931 account) was "to shelter all the children of one mother and one father."[85]

The play proceeds to the arrival of Columbus, bringing baptism and a gracious acceptance that red-skinned people (unmentioned in the Bible) are indeed human beings: "Such people must be made to work, sow, and do all that is necessary. And to adopt our ways." (*Black Elk Speaks*, I, 16–17)

We next see Andrew Jackson (called by the Indians "Sharp Knife") removing the Cherokee to Oklahoma "for as long as grass grows and water flows" (*Black Elk Speaks*, I, 20), a sentiment actually expressed in the 1868 treaty ceding the Black Hills to the Sioux after the victorious war engineered by Red Cloud. The dramatic Black Elk tells Jackson what the real Black Elk said about Custer's violation of that treaty: "You can see that it is not the grass and the water that have forgotten."[86]

In the early days of the Plains Wars, the Indians are beaten by a lack of unity. We see the Santee Sioux drawn into an uprising in 1862 Minnesota by their failure to listen to their chief, Little Crow. Once the war begins, the same young braves choose to sack the town of New Ulm rather than follow Little Crow against Fort Ridgely. The Indians of the Upper Agency refuse to join in the war and return Little Crow's white hostages, unaware that the state would soon pay bounties for any Indian scalp, would sentence 303 Indians for hanging after five-minute trials, and would use the Santee uprising to banish them to a reservation in the Dakotas where one-quarter would die the first winter. On his way back from a futile attempt to convince the prairie Sioux in 1863, Little Crow himself was a victim of the bounty system.

The lack of unity is not solely intertribal. The trail of western history is littered with the careers of officers like Major Edward Wynkoop (called Tall Chief) who were too sympathetic to Indian needs. The play's most touching example of split loyalties is a sidebar story to the infamous 1864 Sand Creek, Colorado, massacre. In accepting the assurance of the army commander, Colonel John Chivington, and sending his young warriors away to hunt, Black Kettle, sworn to peace, saw 133 of his Southern Cheyenne killed—105 of them women and children. "Nits make lice," Colonel Chivington observed. Two of the wounded were George and Charlie Bent, sons of William Bent, a white rancher, and Yellow Woman, a full-blooded Cheyenne. Yellow Woman, the narrator of this section, driven to an uncontrollable hatred of all whites, confronts her husband: "We have to fight them. Fight all of them! . . . You're one of them! . . . You're a white man!" (*Black Elk Speaks*, I, 82) Less than ten months later, the historical Yellow Woman, who swore never again to deal with white men, was killed by Pawnees scouting for the Army.[87] Black Elk sums up the effect of the massacre. "Within a few minutes after dawn over Sand Creek, the soldiers achieved what no Indian statesman had been able to contrive in generations—they made us start uniting." (*Black Elk Speaks*, I, 83)

Act II begins with a reminder of Black Elk's vision and its relationship to the unity of the circle: "The Indian camp is arranged in a circle as is all nature—the circle of the prairie horizon, of the unbitten moon, of the flow of life from seed to flower back to seed again. In time of war, the holy man establishes his round tepee in the center of the camp around which the warriors wait in a circle. The holy man has visions, then comes forth, singing to the warriors of what he has seen." (*Black Elk Speaks*, II, 87)

Crazy Horse, Black Elk's second cousin, finds the genius which dominates the rest of the Plains Wars in the purification rites of his vision: "The world men live in is only a shadow of the real world which is the world of the spirit. In the real world which is the world behind this one, everything seems to float and dance and because it is made of the spirit, nothing is material." (*Black Elk Speaks*, II, 91)

After the Civil War ends, the army attempts to open the Bozeman trail to the goldfields of Montana. General Patrick Connor runs into a coalition of Hunkpapa, Oglala, and Cheyenne under Sitting Bull, Red Cloud, and

Roman Nose. The Connor expedition costs the government a million dollars per Indian killed. Crazy Horse discovers that white soldiers cannot stand to be ridiculed and, leading a decoy band of ten braves from five different tribes, steers Captain Fetterman's company into Red Cloud's trap. The Battle of the Hundred Slain (Fetterman's Massacre) will bring the Sioux the Black Hills in the Treaty of 1868. One hundred five years later, the fulfillment of its terms will be a primary negotiating point in Wounded Knee II, the American Indian movement's occupation of the place where Custer died.[88]

Before the Little Big Horn, we see a sample of Custer's handiwork at the Washita River in Oklahoma. In 1868, almost exactly four years after Sand Creek, Black Kettle and his remnant of Cheyennes are ordered to camp on the Washita. Custer is given his orders by General Phil Sheridan, historically best known for telling a Comanche chief, "The only good Indians I ever saw were dead." (*Black Elk Speaks*, II, 119) Lest we mistake what is to come, the lines and the sound effects are a replay of those that preceded Sand Creek. Of the 103 Cheyenne killed that day, only eleven were warriors. Custer, who was called Pahauska or "Long-Hair," by the Indians, is renamed Squaw-Killer.

In 1876, the Indians, now calling themselves Dakotas or allies, defeat one part of an army pincher movement under General George Crook. Crazy Horse's vision tells him to return to the Little Big Horn. After the battle, Black Elk approaches Crazy Horse.

Black Elk: I'm told it was a Santee who killed Custer.

Crazy Horse: [*Also quietly*]: Yes.

Black Elk [*Puzzled. Smiling*]: I thought probably you killed him.

Crazy Horse [*Quietly*]: Yes, I killed him too. He was killed by the Indian people. (*Black Elk Speaks*, II, 127–28)

When the dispatches reach the newsstands of the outside world, it is July 4, 1876—America's Centennial.

In September 1877, out of food and ammunition, Crazy Horse is promised a reservation if he will surrender at Fort Robinson. There, instead, he finds a cell and chains. Attempting to escape, he is bayoneted and dies at the symbolic age of thirty-three. For the Ghost Dancer, the actual Black Elk designed shirts that he had seen in a vision—shirts which were supposed to be bulletproof, one of which he was wearing when he was shot the day after Wounded Knee:

A Paiute Messiah told us God had sent Christ to earth but white people treated him badly leaving scars on his body so he had gone back to Heaven. Now he had returned to earth as an Indian, and he was to make everything as it used to be. All we had to do was dance—dance and it would bring back our dead—dance the dance of the Ghost and once more we'd be all alive and together. . . . At Pine Ridge, the agent telegraphs Washington, "Indians are dancing in the snow. We need protection." . . . a great sacred circle—the hoop of our Indian nation—and at the center is the sacred tree—and the tree is in bloom! (*Black Elk Speaks*, II, 131-33)

On December 29, 1890, four troops from the Seventh Cavalry, Custer's former unit, surrounded a band of Minneconjous under Big Foot and forced them to camp at Wounded Knee Creek. For what they were about to do, they would receive twenty-six Medals of Honor. Out of the 350 Indians encamped at Wounded Knee, 289 were killed. When the wounded reached Pine Ridge, they were temporarily hospitalized in the Episcopal Church—in straw and bedding under a banner left over from Christmas: "Peace on Earth, Good Will to Men."[89]

"And you see what else died there in the bloody mud and was buried in the blizzard. It was a people dream—a beautiful dream, as you must know. . . . Because it was your dream too! . . . It may be that some small root of the sacred tree still lives—a root that could be nourished. . . . We offer the wooden cup filled with water. It's the power to make live, and it's yours." (*Black Elk Speaks*, II, 135)

Center Stage: Center of the Universe

In the European sense of the term, there is very little Native American drama. Not much of what has been written has been published, and some of the best examples in print fall into the category of what we have called, in Chapter 5, works by "sympathetic members of the majority." Christopher Sergel is a professional playwright who has made a career out of dramatizing popular books and films for the Dramatic Publishing Company of Chicago. His adaptation of *Black Elk Speaks* was chosen as this section's chief example because it combined a factual and coherent account of the Plains Wars from an Indian viewpoint with a sense of the Native American concepts of spirituality, space, and time—concepts which, because of their incompatibility with European Christianity, hierarchial constructs, and linear time, made the war inevitable.

The other modern, white-written, "Indian" play to logically include is Arthur Kopit's *Indians* (1968). However, the focus here is on the divided feelings of the quintessential "western hero," Colonel William F. "Buffalo Bill" Cody. Although he sincerely admires the Plains Indians and would like to preserve their way of life, Buffalo Bill cannot resist the temptation to by mythologized as an example of his race's superiority.

Thus, while the western Indian is dying, the western white man's integrity dies with him. Realistic scenes of an 1890 Senate investigating committee listening to pleas by Sitting Bull's Hunkpapa Sioux that treaty obligations be met are alternated with Buffalo Bill's evolution into a phantasmagoric parody of himself for white ego justification and titillation. In the end, Cody can only exist as a "two shows a day" entertainer in a ghost town—a false emblem of a civilization he helped to destroy:

I would . . . first . . . like to . . . say a few words in defense of my country's Indian policy, which seems, in certain circles, to be meeting with considerable disapproval. . . . Indeed, in all ways, our vast country is speedily being opened for settlement. The shipment of smallpox-infested blankets sent by the Red Cross to the Mandan Indians, has, I'm pleased to say, worked wonders, and the Mandans are no more. Also, the Government policy of exterminating the buffalo, a policy with which I myself was intimately connected, has practically reached fruition. Almost no buffalo are left, and soon the Indians will be hungry enough to begin farming in earnest, a step we believe necessary if they are ever to leave their barbaric ways and enter civilization. . . . Another aspect of our benevolent attitude toward these savages is shown by the Government's policy of having its official interpreters translate everything incorrectly, thereby angering the Indians and forcing them to learn English for themselves. Which, of course, is the first step in civilizing people.[90]

When Buffalo Bill discovers that to kill the Indian way of life is to kill something in himself, he is repeating a major theme of modern Native American literature. Playwright Lynn Riggs (best known for *Green Grow the Lilacs*, which became the basis of *Oklahoma!*) faced Broadway rejection when he attempted to deal with his divided racial heritage in *The Cherokee Night* (1934). The play begins with the onstage image of a giant tepee:

In pictographs all over the tepee's front is the story of a man's life: the first deer he killed stumbles to crooked knees, a feathered arrow in its heart; three buffaloes charge his pony; he stands before a mountain with a summit of flame; a woman lifts her hand out of nowhere; a road branches out in seven ways, and on the seventh—and wildest—coils a rattlesnake; before a waterfall is a willow tree; across a deep chasm a warrior leaps, and in his hands are curious fetishes carved from granite.[91]

The story begins with a group of mixed-blood young people picnicking in 1915 at Claremore Mound—where the Cherokee massacred the Osage Indians many years earlier—follows them forward to 1931, and retraces them to the circumstances of their births in 1895. In the later years, we see them betrayed and betraying: Discovering the boy she loves to be her half-brother, a girl informs on another member of the group to the police for twenty-five dollars. In the heart of the Depression, another girl, now well-off, denies a sister whose family is starving. In the final scene, their problems are traced to a wounded thief—the unacknowledged father of two of the picnickers—who lies dying in an old Indian's cabin.

Spench: Sump'n always drove me on. The bosses! Burned down their barns, rustled their cattle, slept with their wives. Shot the bastards down! Sump'n inside—no rest. I don't know—Bad blood. Too much Indian, they tell me.

Gray Wolf: [*The revelation growing in him from what Spench has said.*] Not enough Indian. . . . I'm full blood—Cherokee. I live peaceful. I ain't troubled. I remember the way my people lived in quiet times. Think of my ancestors. It keeps me safe. You though—like my boy. He's dead. He was half-white, like you. They killed him, *had* to kill him. Not *enough* Indian. (*The Cherokee Night*, vii, 258–59)

Each year the state of Utah holds a high school one-act play contest. The entries are the usual mélange of Broadway, Off-Broadway, and classical theatre, with one exception. Every year, the students of the White Horse Lake Navajo reservation write their own play, and every year the theme is the same: the difficulty of living in two different worlds. At Mount Senario College in Wisconsin's Chippewa region, Victor Macaruso teaches a course on the image of the Indian in American literature: "Those who become bicultural gain a culture, but not without a large expenditure of psychic energy. They must be able to employ the correct set of cultural patterns at appropriate times. They must frequently have facility in two languages to organize and express two different world views. They must know which forms of behavior are acceptable in each setting and be able to respond accordingly." The alternatives to biculturalism are to reject white society entirely—scarcely feasible in a country where Indians are only two-thirds of one percent of the population—and assimilation. "Assimilated individuals frequently lose a culture and may find they are banned from entering into the culture for which they have prepared themselves. They lose their personal identity; their self-image becomes confused. They become marginal people living on the illusive fringe between cultures without a home in either culture."[92]

It is at this point that Native American theatre, without ever being polemical, becomes political. The focus of the U.S. government (when it has not been to annihilate) has been to assimilate the Indian. A key element of that assimilation process has been the banning of Native American religious dramas which promulgate Indian identity. The suppression of the Pueblos which we noted earlier and the part played by the Ghost Dance in inciting the Wounded Knee massacre are only two of the many examples of military and missionary collaboration against Indian culture. The Sun Dance which was common to all the Northern

Plains Indians was among the first ceremonies to be banned as non-Christian and a source of potential intertribal unity. As late as 1923, the commissioner of the Bureau of Indian Affairs was recommending that "Indian dances be limited to one in each month in the daylight hours of one day in midweek, and at one center in each district: the months of March and April, June, July, and August being excepted. That no one take part in the dances or be present who are under 50 years of age. That careful propaganda be undertaken to educate public opinion against the dance."[93]

Jeffrey Huntsman warns against drawing generalizations about a Native American drama of which there are as many types as there are Indian cultures. One principle that can be stated with assurance is that the aesthetic principles governing the form, content, and meaning of the artist's work are the embodiment of the community's values. What the apprentice artist learns "is not a single task or fact, but a thread of the entire fabric of society. For a Maidu the proper making of acorn bread begins with an evocation of the story of creation, and the making of a Navajo rug begins with the morning prayers, the driving of the sheep to food and water, and the gathering in of plants for dyes."[94]

Thus, the artistic process is in itself a statement and a reinforcement of the tribal identity and a factor in centering that identity in the universe: "Nowhere is this more apparent or more powerfully symbolized than in the great Navajo chantways, epic religious dramas of cosmic scope, the fundamental purpose of which is to restore and maintain the essential balance of the world, the lack of which produces sickness in mind and body. A sing, the actual curing event manifesting the chantway, restores health to the individual patient, to those gathered at the ceremony, to the nation, and ultimately to the cosmos."[95]

It is precisely the elements of traditional Native American drama that mitigate against assimilation into the larger white culture. The first of these is polychronic time—time which can be viewed not only linearly, but cyclically and eternally.[96] Euro-based culture last grasped this concept as *figura* under medieval Christianity, when all time was seen as existing simultaneously in the mind of God, with future events prefigured in the present as evidence of the Eternal Plan. The second is the point from which time is eternal, the sacred "center of the earth" at which the individual is in perfect harmony with himself, his people, all living things, and the universe. The symbol of this center is—as we have seen in *Black Elk Speaks*—the circle.

The most recent of published Native American plays, the works of Kiowa-Delaware author Hanay Geiogamah of the Native American

Theatre Ensemble, illustrate both the strength Indians derive from the circle and the destructiveness of linear time. In the five brief scenes of *Body Indian*, a young Oklahoma man on his way to a detoxification center in Norman is stripped of his land-lease money and, finally, his pawnable wooden leg, in order to provide wine for what should have been his supportive family and friends. Each scene ends with ever-closer sounds of a train, until at the final curtain, the projection of the onrushing locomotive over Bobby's body makes us realize it is the train that severed his leg—the price claimed by a civilization that runs on linear time and has no pity for those who cannot adjust to it. In *49*, a musical named after the spontaneous communal dances so popular with southwestern Indians, young people racing to and participating in the dance share stage time with an ancient Kiowa medicine man—the Night Walker—who sees it as a reincarnation of the Indian spirit, and the police who are trying to break it up.

[*To a powerful drumbeat and in gymnastic movements, they form an elaborate barricade with their bodies, allow the image to strike, then dismantle and form another in the center of the dance circle. . . . The patrol car lights slowly begin to fade one at a time as the patrols pull back. . . . From their defensive positions, the 49 group now turns toward the center of the circle, where Night Walker is standing in a shaft of colored light. He is holding a bull-roarer and a rattle.*]

Night Walker: I am the oldest man of the tribe!/ You have shown respect for me./ You will always have mine.

[*Now, at a carefully measured pace, Night Walker creates the effect of a violent storm as he speaks his final incantation. Each time he spins his bull-roarer, one of the young people is propelled to the center of the circle. . . .*]

Night Walker: We are a tribe!/ Of people with strong hearts./ Who respect fear/ As we make our way./ Who will never kill/ Another man's way of living.[97]

In the mid-1980s, the University of Oklahoma press was considering an anthology from the Native American Theatre Ensemble, but it was never printed. New plays may yet come from the Red Earth Performing Arts Company of Seattle, created by Don Mart (Flathead) and John Kaufman (Nez Perce), the Indian Performing Arts Company of Tulsa, Robert Shorty's Navajo Theatre, the Thunderbird Company of Ontario (Ojibway), Four Arrows (Mohawk), or New York's Spiderwoman Theatre Workshop, formed by Muriel Miguel (Rappahannock-Cuna).[98] Even if they are not printed, however, they will be performed. The Indians knew, long before Artaud, that the ritual event is the real drama, and that the text behind it is merely an artifact. As for assimilations, it is wise to remember that the melting pot dissolves the large as well as the small, and the words of Black Elk may in the long run mean as much to the white man as to the red: "What I know was given to me for men and it is true and it is beautiful. Soon, I shall be under the grass and it will be lost. You were sent to save it, and you must come back so that I can teach you."[99]

Notes

1. Chuck Lane, "Open the Door," *The New Republic* 192 (April 1, 1985): 20.

2. Luis Valdez and El Teatro Campesino, *Actos* (San Juan Bautista, Calif.: Cucaracha Press, 1971), 6.

3. Sam Kushner, *Long Road to Delano* (New York: International Publishers, 1975), xii.

4. Mark Day, *Forty Acres* (New York: Praeger Publishers, 1971), 168.

5. Kushner, *Long Road*, 101.

6. Manuel P. Servin, *The Mexican-Americans: An Awakening Minority* (Beverly Hills, Calif.: Glencoe Press, 1970), 1.

7. Quoted by David Leary, in "Race and Regeneration," in *The Mexican-Americans: An Awakening Minority*, ed. Manuel P. Servin (Beverly Hills, Calif.: Glencoe Press, 1970), 21–22.

8. Leary, "Race and Regeneration," 25.

9. Carey McWilliams, "The Borderlands Are Invaded," in *The Mexican-Americans: An Awakening Minority*, ed. Manuel P. Servin (Beverly Hills, Calif.: Glencoe Press, 1970), 43–45.

10. Kushner, *Long Road*, 6–9.

11. Walter Goodman, "Message of Immigration Bill Is Disputed," *New York Times*, October 12, 1984, p. 17.

12. Kushner, *Long Road*, 12–13.

13. Goodman, "Message of Immigration Bill," 17.

14. Kushner, *Long Road*, 14–17.

15. McWilliams, *Borderlands Are Invaded*, 32–36.

16. Kushner, *Long Road*, 19.

17. Emory S. Bogardus, "Repatriation and Readjustment," in *The Mexican-American: An Awakening Minority*, ed. Manuel P. Servin (Beverly Hills, Calif.: Glencoe Press, 1970), 89.

18. Goodman, "Message of Immigration Bill," 17.

19. Robert Lindsey, "Chavez and Farm Workers Adapt Tactics to the Times," *New York Times*, July 20, 1983, sec. 1, p. 20.

20. Robert Lindsey, "Shrinking Job Market Generates Violence on California Farms," *New York Times,* August 19, 1983, p. 8.

21. Larry Rohter, "Mexico's South Fights Tide of U.S. Bound Aliens," *New York Times*, April 10, 1989, p. 1.

22. Jeremiah Baruch, "Half-Open Door: The Puzzle of Immigration," *Commonweal* 110 (July 15, 1983): 389.

23. Wayne King, "Costs of Immigration Reform, Measured and Unknown," *New York Times*, October 17, 1984, p. 16.

24. George Russell and Dan Goodgame, "Trying to Stem the Illegal Tide," *Time* 126 (July 8, 1985): 28.

25. Kushner, *Long Road*, 204.

26. Luis Valdez, *Las Dos Caras del Patroncito*, in *Actos* (San Juan Bautista, Calif.: Cucaracha Press, 1971), 9. Subsequent references to this play will be included in the text.

27. McWilliams, 30.

28. Day, *Forty Acres*, 43–44.

29. Kushner, *Long Road*, 223.

30. Day, *Forty Acres*, 89.

31. Day, *Forty Acres*, 77.

32. Joanne Pottlitzer, *Hispanic Theater in the United States and Puerto Rico* (New York: Ford Foundation, 1988), 35, 44.

33. Nicolas Kanellos, *Mexican American Theater: Legacy and Reality* (Pittsburgh: Latin American Literary Review Press, 1987), 118, 121, 124.

34. Jorge A. Huerta, *Chicano Theater: Themes and Forms* (Ypsilanti, Mich.: Bilingual Press/Editorial Bilingue, 1982), 157–67.

35. The plays in the preceding paragraph are all published in Roberto J. Garza, *Contemporary Chicano Theatre* (Notre Dame: University of Notre Dame Press, 1976).

36. Huerta, *Chicano Theater*, 70–81.

37. Carlos Morton, *The Many Deaths of Danny Rosales*, in *"The Many Deaths of Danny Rosales" and Other Plays* (Houston: Arte Publico Press, 1983), 48–49.

38. Kushner, *Long Road*, 157.

39. Huerta, *Chicano Theater*, 179.

40. Murray L. Wax, "Who Is an Indian?" *The American Indians: A Rising Ethnic Force*, ed. Herbert L. Marx, Jr. (New York: H. H. Wilson, 1973), 12.

41. Alvin M. Josephy, *Now That the Buffalo's Gone* (New York: Alfred A. Knopf, 1982), 5.

42. Annette Rosenstiel, *Red and White* (New York: Universe Books, 1983), 49.

43. Robert Burnette and John Koster, *The Road to Wounded Knee* (New York: Bantam Books, 1974), 142.

44. Wax, "Who Is An Indian?" 14.

45. Steve Talbot, *Roots of Oppression* (New York: International Publishers, 1981), 16.

46. Rosenstiel, *Red and White*, 11.

47. Talbot, *Roots of Oppression*, 20.

48. Rosenstiel, *Red and White*, 42.

49. Burnette and Koster, *Road to Wounded Knee*, 106–7.

50. Burnette and Koster, *Road to Wounded Knee*, 68–69.

51. Burnette and Koster, *Road to Wounded Knee*, 112.

52. Dee Brown, *Bury My Heart at Wounded Knee* (New York: Holt, Rinehart, and Winston, 1970), 426.

53. Talbot, *Roots of Oppression*, 107.

54. Josephy, *Now That the Buffalo's Gone*, 132.

55. Burnette and Koster, *Road to Wounded Knee*, 113.

56. Josephy, *Now That the Buffalo's Gone*, 219.

57. Burnette and Koster, *Road to Wounded Knee*, 18.

58. "Recommendations for Indian Policy: Message from the President of the United States Transmitting Recommendations for Indian Policy," in *The American Indian: A Rising Ethnic Force*, ed. Herbert L. Marx, Jr. (New York: H. H. Wilson, 1973), 75.

59. Talbot, *Roots of Oppression*, 122–25.

60. Josephy, *Now That the Buffalo's Gone*, 177–89.

61. Burnette and Koster, *Road to Wounded Knee*, 133–34.

62. Talbot, *Roots of Oppression*, 6–7.

63. Josephy, *Now That the Buffalo's Gone*, 257–58.

64. Burnette and Koster, *Road to Wounded Knee*, 147–48.

65. Burnette and Koster, *Road to Wounded Knee*, 150.

66. Rosenstiel, *Red and White*, 21.

67. Josephy, *Now That the Buffalo's Gone*, 65.

68. Brown, *Bury My Heart*, 86.

69. Josephy, *Now That the Buffalo's Gone*, 107–8.

70. Rosenstiel, *Red and White*, 74.

71. Brown, *Bury My Heart*, 432.

72. Burnette and Koster, *Road to Wounded Knee*, 41.

73. Rosenstiel, *Red and White*, 114.

74. Brown, *Bury My Heart*, 31.

75. Brown, *Bury My Heart*, 376.

76. Vine Deloria, Jr., "For Survival—The Indian Way," in *The American Indian: A Rising Ethnic Force*, ed. Herbert L. Marx, Jr. (New York: H. H. Wilson, 1973), 170–71.

77. Talbot, *Roots of Oppression*, 49.

78. Burnette and Koster, *Road to Wounded Knee*, 114–15.

79. Talbot, *Roots of Oppression*, 187.

80. Talbot, *Roots of Oppression*, 155–79.

81. Josephy, *Now That the Buffalo's Gone*, 254–55, 260.

82. Talbot, *Roots of Oppression*, 48.

83. Rosenstiel, *Red and White*, 126.

84. Christopher Sergel, *Black Elk Speaks* (Chicago: Dramatic Publishing Company, 1976), I, 13–14. Subsequent references to this play will be included in the text.

85. John G. Neihardt, *Black Elk Speaks* (Lincoln: University of Nebraska Press, 1961), 43.

86. Neihardt, *Black Elk Speaks*, 18.

87. Brown, *Bury My Heart*, 108.

88. Greg Conderacci, "Wounded Knee—I," in *The American Indian: A Rising Ethnic Force*, ed. Herbert L. Marx, Jr. (New York: H. H. Wilson, 1973), 47–48.

89. Brown, *Bury My Heart*, 445.

90. Arthur Kopit, *Indians* (New York: Hill and Wang, 1969), xiii, 89–90.

91. Lynn Riggs, *The Cherokee Night*, in *"Russet Mantle" and "The Cherokee Night"* (New York: Samuel French, 1936), i, 131. Subsequent references to this play will be included in the text.

92. Victor Macaruso, "Cowboys and Indians: The Image of the Indian in American Literature," *American Indian Culture and Research Journal* 8, no. 2 (Summer 1984): 15–16.

93. Linda Walsh Jenkins and Ed Wapp, Jr., "Native American Performance," *The Drama Review* 20, no. 2 (Spring 1976): 6.

94. Jeffrey F. Huntsman, "Native American Theatre," in *Ethnic Theatre in the United States*, ed. Maxine Schwartz Seller (Westport, Conn.: Greenwood Press, 1983), 357.

95. Huntsman, "Native American Theatre," 360.

96. Nikki Hansen, "Culture and Commentary in Three Native American Plays, *Encyclia* 63 (1986): 80.

97. Hanay Geiogamah, *49*, in *New Native American Drama* (Norman: University of Oklahoma Press, 1980), xi–xii, 129–130, 132.

98. Huntsman, "Native American Theatre," 370.

99. Neihardt, *Black Elk Speaks*, x.

7

Civil Rights Theatre Sequel II—
Gender

The Introduction to this book includes the following definition of a political play: "Political theatre shows public policy, laws, or unquestioned social codes impinging unfairly and destructively upon particular segments of society." Individual though the protagonist may be, what happens to him or her is not an example of isolated fate, but rather is the result of historically alterable conditions which are inherently unfair to the group with which he or she is identified by the dominant social element. It is not for his or her individuality that the protagonist is harmed, but because he or she is a member of that group. The agents of that harm are not aberrant individuals, but are acting according to standards which, despite their unfairness, have hegemony in the society.

In the United States, with its egalitarian ideals and relatively healthy economy, caste is a more effective measurement of discrimination than class. In America, class barriers are economic walls vulnerable to cash flow (if not within this generation, then the next), but caste barriers are biological and can no more be penetrated than a man burst out of his own skin.

The most subtle of caste barriers is sex. The socially supplementary position of women is expressed in terms like "women's auxiliary" and "the better half" and titles like "Mrs." which identify women in relation to men. Women are the original hyphenated Americans. For minority women, racial classifications take precedence over gender, and even "women-identified women" (lesbians) are often ironically grouped with gay men, rather than with members of their own sex. A quarter-century into the latest of a series of women's movements as old as humanity itself, its most misplaced appellation is "sister," for most women do not recognize their own sex as a family to which they owe allegiance. This is above all a failure of self-recognition. True hegemony in any society lies with the group whose value system is accepted as the standard of the society. For most women in the United States, the standard value system is that of the patriarchy, and they do not recognize that there is any contradiction between its tenets and their rights.

That "the personal is political" is a governing precept of feminism. Cindy Nemser, former editor of *The Feminist Art Journal*, explains the resistance of many practitioners and critics to looking at women's theatre from a political standpoint: "If only an art that specifically advocated women's right was designated as feminist, then only women artists who were putting political activism into their works could be said to be making feminist art. But . . . any art that reflects a woman's immediate personal experience has the right to be called feminist art."[1] However, if we invoke the definition of political theatre above, and accept the fact that "a woman's immediate personal experience" is very often impinged upon by systems whose principles have hegemony in her society despite their inherent opposition to her needs, then most feminist theatre may be seen as political.

As stated previously, the chief barrier to women's political freedom is the patriarchal value system. Its power lies in its invisibility. Like air, it goes unrecognized and uncontemplated until we can no longer breathe in it. For discussion purposes, we are dividing the social systems which are potentially unfair to women into four groups: (a) economic/occupational, (b) familial/sexual, (c) legal, and (d) religious. In practice, of course, they are not divided, but are merely categorical manifestations of gender assumptions.

Among the traditional feminine virtues are emotional sensitivity, a nurturing nature, a communal focus, a process orientation, and patience. The perception and glorification of these qualities may also be a contributing factor to women's secondary social position. Sue-Ellen Case argues that such interpretations of women's nature is "biologism—the transformation of sociocultural determinants into the biology of gender. . . . The materialists would argue that this 'nurturing' behaviour has simply been induced by society to keep women out of the marketplace by romanticising their confinement to the domestic sphere. 'Nurturing' is an extension of that domestic, mothering role. Materialist feminists argue that to privilege this behaviour in women merely reifies their oppression."[2] The flip side of biologism associates society-perceived masculine qualities with highly valued elements of Western civilization: intellectualism and objectivity, creativity, individualism, goal-orientation, and a sense of urgency. The completeness which the feminine provides is to be sought, following Aristophanes in Plato's *Symposium*, in the Other rather than nurtured in the self. Gender is first of all, therefore, an economic issue.

The nineteenth-century anthropologist J. J. Bachofen postulated three stages of social evolution, of which patriarchy is the third. The first was sexual promiscuity and the second a state of matriarchy based on "the religious and civil primacy of womanhood."[3] Elise Boulding has proposed that society's transition from matriarchy to patriarchy coincided with its evolution from a growing/hunting economy to one based on trade. In the "agrovilles," women farmers provided 80 percent of family sustenance and were always present. Male hunters, on the other hand, were absent for long periods. During these hunting journeys, however, men began to find flint and other materials that were valued as tools or ceremonial objects. Trading networks began, with the flint gatherers receiving food and crafts in return. Because of the continuing importance of their food-producing and family-sustaining roles, women could neither specialize nor travel. Thus, when they did enter the market system, their products were marginal, more vulnerable to the factors of time and locale. This process was completed in the second milleneum B.C. when clan rights to land and property were codified into legal systems which guaranteed the administration of property by the male.[4]

The economic importance of gender roles was intensified by the industrial revolution. In an agrarian society, the division between male and female tasks was less clear. Women shared field labor with men and, because the work of the men never took place far from the home, their influence was important in the raising of children. Since labor was largely manual, the production of children (the new labor force) was important to the continuance of life. Nineteenth-century industrialization completed the categorization of labor that the trade economies had begun. Women with children found it more difficult to leave the home and go into the factory than did men. Children, who had watched their fathers on the farm until they were old enough to work with them, now spent those years as the almost total responsibility of their mothers. Children, who had been an economic necessity to the farmer, became an economic liability to the factory wage-earner.

The effect of industrialization was to change the family *line* (the reproducer of traditions and the maintainer of property) into family *unit* (the source of emotional fulfillment and refuge from the world).[5] The economic system replicated the patriarchal system in that a hierarchy developed in which the industrial society was created out of family units. In return for absolute conformity on the assembly line, the male worker was granted absolute sovereignty in his own home. Thus, his family behavior and his work behavior, which had been of a piece on the land, became fragmented in the industrial society. Sex, which had been a necessity for family physical survival, became a personal physiological pleasure, which the man had a right to demand even as his own submission was demanded at work. To complete the formula, the woman could demand that her children fulfill her, and, upon reaching adulthood, the children could expect to take their place in the industrial society.

Like all human systems, however, there proved to be a gap between the practice and the theory. Under nineteenth-century industrialization, the family at the very least was presumed to be unbroken. By the last quarter of the twentieth century, the "feminization of poverty" had become a generalization inductively reasoned from appalling statistics. Female-headed families make up less than one-fifth of all families with children under the age of eighteen in the United States, yet comprise *half* of all poor families. Possibly one out of every five unemployed women is jobless because she cannot find child care, and there may be seven million "latchkey" children caring for themselves while their parents work. This is not a problem time alone will cure. There are roughly as many working women as men, but in the 1980s their numbers increased at twice rate of men. They are earning 60 percent as much as men, and four-fifths of them have no pension plans. Therefore, when a working woman retires, she is three times as likely to be poor as her male counterpart.[6]

The obvious answer is to pay women on a comparable basis to men. The question then becomes to determine a formula for that comparison and to find the funds to carry it out. Over twenty states have recently enacted laws containing comparable-worth language. In a typical case, Wisconsin found the worth of legal secretaries (100 percent female, $14,800 annually) to be of comparable worth to public defender investigators (92 percent male, $20,600 annually).[7] The effect of correcting this injustice on the tax base of an agricultural state during a period of depressed farm economy has not been calculated, but the Washington-based Bureau of National Affairs says employer cost of proposed comparable-worth or pay-equity plans could reach $320 billion nationally and result in an annual inflation rate increase of 9.7 percent.[8]

Concealed in plain sight in all these figures is another pair of gender assumptions: that women should be limited to a select group of occupations, and that these occupations are inherently worth less to society than those which are restricted to men. The occupational result of the womanly virtues of nurturing ability, patience, and process-orientation has been a preponderance of women in the care-giving and service sectors of the economy (nursing, teaching, secretarial work), and the yielding of a whole analytical/athletic continuum of better-paying jobs to men. While it follows that one task may have more value to society at a given time than another, and that one individual may be better at that task than another, it does not follow that such divisions should consistently be along gender lines. The ironic effect has been to depress the incomes of those men in traditionally feminine occupations, but even there, inequities are frequent. I recall beginning my teaching career at an institution which had hired my wife (a proven teacher) at a 7 percent lower salary. I was head of the household, the administrator explained, and a veteran. Although the former was doubtful and the latter not of my choosing, I do suppose I could have defended my classroom in a firefight and bench-pressed more chalk than my wife.

One possible interpretation of society's economic treatment of the woman is that she is being punished for the crime of being independent from a man (although her entry into the marketplace is more often required by that independence rather than being its motive). The traditional role of woman under the patriarchy is that of economic object, not economic participant. Patriarchy is, by definition, a system of tribal government in which the leader is male, and family authority, identity, and property are passed on to the male heirs. Female descendants in this system have no sustaining family identity of their own, but rather take the name of their current male protector. Under patriarchy, women are held as property, and marriage is seen as a transfer of deed. If the property is valued, the groom must purchase it with a bride-price. If it is not, the father must add a dowry to the transaction. This concept of property is seen in English statute law which until the time of Elizabeth I defined rape as the theft of a women, an economic loss to the male head of her family.[9]

Under patriarchal law, therefore, a women who deliberately chooses independence is guilty of stealing from a man. The vestigial remains of the need to punish this crime still haunts the collective unconscious of our legal system. In her "Profile of Young Women in Wisconsin's Juvenile Justice System," state senator Barbara Lorman noted disturbing differences in the treatment of women and man: "Females were four times more likely to be locked up than male runaways. Over one-half of the young women were locked up for status offenses (related only to their youth) or public order offenses, as compared to one-fifth of the young men. . . . It takes an average of only 20 months from first offense to correctional placement for young women, while young men average 31 months." Senator Lorman points out that a female is much more likely to be imprisoned for a misdemeanor than is a male. Finally, "over three-quarters of the incarcerated females studied had suffered physical abuse resulting in injuries, about one-third had been sexually abused and about one-half had been sexually assaulted."[10]

Perhaps the saddest elements of these last statistics are the source of the abuse and rape, and the cyclical nature of their effects. According to Nancy Gilpatrick of Salt Lake City's Phoenix Institute, 90 percent of the female Utah state prison inmates whom she counsels are from incestuous homes.[11] One out of every eight children receives serious physical injury at parental hands, and 125,000 new cases of child abuse occur each year. Add to that the nearly two million cases of wife beating reported annually, and lifetimes of low self-esteem, poor self-image, and social isolation are easily explained.[12]

Often both beatings and incest are presented to the child as evidence of love. If only the child had been "good," the abuse would have been unnecessary. The incestuous relationship is "our secret." Recent studies indicate that what has been called "the last taboo" may be broken in one family in ten. In cases of father-daughter incest, the mother may well be a "silent partner" in the act—not condoning it, but failing to protest because (a) she wishes to hold the family together; (b) she is totally dependent on her husband financially; or (c) she lacks the self-esteem to challenge her husband in even so basic an area. The daughter herself is victimized by both her father's psychological coercion and her mother's lack of support. She may crave her father's affection an approval, and/or fear his anger. In *Mending Broken Children*, George and Barbara Henderson remind us that children with unmet needs cling to their parents, finding excuses even for behavior which harms them.[13]

A major tragedy of incest is the likelihood that its female victim will pass from the home to still other coercive sexual relationships. The histories of incest victims abound with self-destructive choices. Their self-concepts, typically, are weak, and they are drawn to men whose personality type and behavior pattern is similar to that of their fathers. In many cases, this is because their home situation while growing up isolated them from the rest of society. Their emotional development tends to be arrested at the point of violation and they associate affection with exploitation. The end result of sexually or otherwise physically abusing a child is seldom merely a wasted life. Incest returns generation after generation in the same family.

The concept of the female as property of the dominant male goes far to explain both incest and spouse abuse. However, there were religious justifications for the former as well. In chapter 19 of Genesis, Lot and his daughters escaped from the destruction of Sodom (leaving as a pillar of salt the wife who disobeyed God by looking back). Lot's daughters, fearing that their father's seed would vanish from the earth, seduced him with wine: "Thus were both the daughters of Lot with child by their father." (Gen. 19:36) Scripture, then, not only permitted incest, but established it as the wish (responsibility) of the daughter. Freud, although he did as much, could not have done better.

Throughout the ages, religion has been used to justify the subordinate place of women. Every patriarchal culture has as part of its mythology an incident which establishes the right of male dominance. Ancient Greece, for example, had at least three. The divine order was determined by the theomachy—a war between the gods in which the Olympians, led by Father Zeus, conquered the titans of Gaia, the Earth Mother. Zeus swallowed the mother of Athena and gave birth to the fully grown, armor-clad goddess by having his head split open—a supreme act of intellect forever supplanting the claim of mother as parent: "Farewell, dear Mother. . . . Father and mother is man and wife, man and wife is one flesh, and so, my mother." (*Hamlet*, IV, iii) Zeus also incinerated Semele by revealing his true self, and, plucking the unborn Dionysus from her ashes, inserted him in a slit in his thigh from which he was reborn.

To be twice-born is the symbol of Christianity, once from a woman and once from God the Father. Also in the Judeo-Christian culture, it is the sin of Eve (the source of evil) and her influence on Adam which condemned her to childbearing and evicted them both from the Garden of Eden. In 1 Timothy, the Apostle Paul reminds us of her sin and of the possibility of her redemption: "Let the woman learn in silence with all subjection. But I suffer not a woman to teach, nor to usurp authority over the man, but to be in silence. For Adam was first formed, then Eve. And Adam was not deceived, but the woman being deceived was in the transgression. Notwithstanding, she shall be saved in childbearing, if they continue in faith and charity and holiness with sobriety." (1 Tim. 11–15)

From Pandora's box to the chronicles of St. Augustine, the problems of mankind have been laid at women's door. Psychiatry, that religion of the twentieth century, with its "uterine biology as psychology" theories, is one in principle with the Elizabethans who accounted for woman's lower place in the Chain of Being through her moral corruptibility, which was a result of the thinness of blood emanating from a heart further left in her body than that of her brother. The female, though "bone of my bones, and flesh of my flesh," is seen by the patriarchal tradition as inferior in spirit and weaker in flesh than man, created to be his "help mate," and punished for having coveted the knowledge denied to her by God.

This historical interpretation accepted, it is clear that changes in women's social status involve challenges to dominant legal, economic, religious, scientific, and familial structures. It is also not surprising that in the recent history of the women's movement, those groups which would completely transform the legal system are merely called reformist, while those who would altar basic male/female relationships are termed radical.[14] By patriarchal definition, lesbians are the most radical because they are "woman-centered." As Adrienne Rich says, "institutionalized heterosexuality . . . demand(s) that the girl-child transfer those first feelings of dependency, eroticism, mutuality, from her first woman to a man, if she is to become what is defined as a "normal" woman.[15] Ti-Grace Atkinson, ex-president of the New York chapter of the National Organization for women (NOW), put it more succinctly: "Feminism is the theory; lesbianism is the practice."[16]

Although lesbianism is not a practical physical option for the vast majority of women, a forceful undertaking of feminist issues in the United States will require more "woman-centered" thinking from all women, and possibly from men as well. If women's values are to achieve hegemony, as painter and writer Pat Mainardi realizes, they can be no more limited to one gender than those of the patriarchy are now: "Feminist art is political propaganda art which like all political art should owe its first allegiance to the political movement whose ideology it shares. Since feminism is a political position (the social, economic, and political equality of men and women) and feminist art reflects those politics, it could even be made by men, although it is unlikely that at this point men's politics will be up to it."[17]

Fittingly, woman-centered thinking is most likely to be found in the structure of the theatre which most frequently produces feminist drama: the collective. This type of theatre takes as its operating model the consciousness-raising groups which were so much a part of the women's movement in the late 1960s. This communication strategy was notable for its flexible agenda, its emphasis on group consensus, and—in the words of Brenda Hancock—avoidance of any kind of "hierarchical power relationships associated with masculine politics."[18] The advantage of the collective theatre for women is critical, as well as creative. The vast majority of theatre reviewers are male, trained by education or experience to recognize masculine themes and a masculine structure—what Megan Terry calls "a fried egg. A beginning, a middle and an end, with a rising climax. A male orgasm."[19] Although material feminists may see some danger of insularity here, it essential that women playwrights find their own voice by listening to responses from their own gender. As time passes, women will become more confirmed in their self-worth, and the critical ranks will become increasingly integrated and/or sensitized to their message. It is probable, however, that the collective will evolve in form rather than disappear. Male writers such as Sam Shepard, David Mamet, and Lanford Wilson are in the habit of debuting their work in regional theatres in whose management they frequently take part. To that extent, it is the feminine model which has become the norm, and the lone artist who is rapidly becoming an artifact.

Getting Out

In theatre, the feminist impulse is expressed through the struggle of women for autonomy against an oppressive, sexist society. The systems with which they are in conflict permeate the most personal areas of women's economic, sociosexual, legal, and religious lives. Perhaps the best recent play which illustrates the inherent unfairness of the patriarchal systems is Marsha Norman's highly acclaimed 1978 drama, *Getting Out*. What happens to Arlene Holsclaw could not happen to every woman, but it does happen to many, and it is much more likely to happen to women than to men.

Getting Out takes place in a prison within a prison, in a present that is surrounded by—and a refection of—the past. The setting is a one-room apartment in the slum area of a large Kentucky city. It is bare and dingy, and there are bars on its single window. Its former occupant was a prostitute whose trade paid for her pimp's "green pants." Its present occupant, the prostitute's sister, Arlene Holsclaw, has just arrived from Alabama, where she has been paroled after serving eight years for a second-degree murder committed during an escape from a prison where she was serving three years for forgery and prostitution.

On a catwalk above the apartment are the locales of a prison—sometimes literal and sometimes figurative—whose chief occupant is Arlie, Arlene as a teenager: "Arlie is the violent kid Arlene was until her last stretch in prison. In a sense she is Arlene's memory of herself, called up by her fears, needs and simple word cues. . . . Arlene is suspicious and guarded, withdrawal is always a possibility. Arlie is unpredictable and incorrigible.

The change seen in Arlie during the second act represents a movement toward Arlene, but the transition should never be complete."20

The continuous action of *Getting Out* is Arlene's first day in her new home on the "outside." At the same time we see flash-backs depicting Arlie's passage from sexually abused child to juvenile delinquent to unwed mother, prostitute, and convict. In the second act, Arlie's behavior is modified—first by a guard's small favors, then by a chaplain's counseling—until after an emotional crisis which Arlene relives at the climax of the play, she becomes a model prisoner.

Inside or out, Arlene Holsclaw's life has been a succession of unfulfilled promises and withheld opportunities. In the prison announcements that set the tone for each act, the routine is broken only by the suspension of privileges: a library not open, a front lawn and picnic tables off-limits, an exercise class cancelled, a picnic postponed, a visitor mistakenly announced, and so forth. In spite of inclement weather, however, work details go on. A lost checkerboard suspends all checkers playing, and even a gift for a retiring prison volunteer is a required project.

"Completely rehabilitated," Arlene is paroled to Kentucky "in consideration of family residence and appropriate support personnel." (*Getting Out*, I, 11) She has been driven from Alabama by Bennie, her former guard, who confidently expects that Arlene will supply in his retirement years what was missing from his marriage. Here, in her sister's apartment/workplace, she will meet two people from her past— her mother and Carl, her former pimp, the unaware father of her son, and a current prison escapee—plus Ruby, an ex-con living upstairs. Here Arlene will also learn the similarity between her prison and postprison lives, as she moves closer to an understanding of her past self.

Arlene finds rapprochement with her mother impossible. Obstensibly there to help Arlene move in, her mother cleans in such a way as to eliminate Arlene from the process, then blames her for being lazy. Having never taken the time to teach her anything, including cooking or cleaning, Arlene's mother defines her as worthless, denigrating her looks and presuming she'll return to prostitution. Too uncaring to write to her in prison, much less send money, her mother accuses Arlene of turning lesbian tricks or putting out for a guard in order to survive. On the outside, she refuses to have Arlene in her home for fear she'll be a bad example to the children still living at home. She even dismisses Arlene's request to hear about Joey, the baby who was taken from her in prison: "You never really got attached to him anway. . . . Kids need rules to live by and he'll get em [in a foster home]." (*Getting Out*, I, 26) When she finds Bennie's hat under the bed, it only confirms her assumptions: "I knowed I shouldn't have come. You ain't changed a bit. . . . Same hateful brat." (*Getting Out*, I, 37)

Even a world-class loser like Carl is an improvement over Arlene's mother. A poor white imitation of a black pimp, Carl at least values her as a meal ticket. He even fantasizes for her what she wants most—a life-style which would give her something to offer to her son.

Carl: You got your choice, honey. You can do cookin an cleanin or you can do somethin that pays good. . . . Say it's dishwashin, OK? . . . An you git maybe seventy-five a week. Seventy-five for standin over a sinkful of greasy gray water fishin out blobs of bread an lettuce. . . . Eight hours a day, six days a week, to make seventy-five lousy pictures of Big Daddy George. Now, how long it'll take you to make seventy-five workin for me? . . . Two hours maybe. Now, it's the same fuckin seventy-five bills. . . . You work two hours a night for me and how much you got in a week. . . . You come with me an you git four-fifty a week. . . .

Arlene: I want to be with [Joey]. . . .

Carl: So, fly him up to see you. Take him on that boat they got goes roun the island. Take him up to the Empire State Building, let him play King Kong. (*Getting Out*, II, 68–70)

But even as a small-town pimp, Carl was a failure, renting Arlie out to men who got their kicks causing pain, and being unable to keep her out of jail. Out of his depth in New York, wanted for jail breaking, and carrying a prison-gained drug habit, his promises are as empty as his future.

As for Bennie, the crude analysis of Arlene's mother is probably accurate: "No man alive gonna drive a girl five hundred miles for nuthin." (*Getting Out*, I, 35) But such hopes do not necesarily condemn him. He has been kind to her in his fashion, and he seems in tune with her main interest. "Wish I had a kid. Life ain't, well, complete without no kids to play ball with an take fishin. Dorrie, though, she had them backaches an that neuralgia, day I married her to the day she died." (*Getting Out*, I, 43) However, Bennie, like her mother, presumes to know too much about Arlene—the way she thinks, what she wants—and thinks his assumed familiarity and past favors give him rights she has not granted. Like Carl, Bennie is uninterested in letting Arlene choose. "You don't want me to go. You're jus beginning to git interested. Your ol girlie temper's flarin up. I like that in a woman. . . . You ain't had a man in a long time. And the ones you had been no count. . . . Ain't natural goin without it too long. Young thing like you. Git all shriveled up." (*Getting Out*, I, 45)

Given her past experience, it is not surprising that Arlene is suspicious of Ruby, who seems to want nothing from her. As an ex-con who has seen some of her own attempts to go straight aborted by trusting the wrong person, Ruby is sympathetic but realistic. She even confirm Carl's assessment of what the straight life will be like if Arlene takes the dishwashing job opening up where Ruby cooks: "He tell you you was gonna wear out your hands and knees grubbin for nuthin, git old an be broke an never have a nice dress to wear? . . . He tell you nobody's gonna wanna be with you cause you done time? . . . He tell you your kid gonna be ashamed of you an nobody's gonna believe you if you tell em you changed? . . . Then he was right." (*Getting Out*, II, 72) The bars over Arlene's apartment window have delivered their message. "Completely rehabilitated," Arlene has only exchanged one prison for another.

What does it mean to "get out"? At the bitter moment when she discovers just how limited her options for the future are, Arlene tells Ruby, "Outside's where you get to do what you want." (*Getting Out*, II, 73) By this, she primarily means being free of the constrictions placed upon her by her social and economic standing in the community. Arlene has come to believe that by eliminating that part of herself that society has always objected to, the rebellious, antiauthoritarian Arlie, by becoming meek, she could "inherit the earth." The emphasis is on the tangible fulfillment of her desires. The material benefits that Carl promises—inevitably short-lived because, at worst, breaking parole will send Arlene back to prison, or because, at best, her youth and marketability are fading—are based upon her turning tricks at the customers's demand and primarily for Carl's benefit. The alternative that Bennie offers—however more socially acceptable, potentially enduring, and financially less rewarding—is no alternative in principle at all. It is still sex for pay, with Bennie this time deciding what Arlene is and what she does. If Arlene follows Ruby's lead, however, she will have sovereignty—that is, within very real financial and social limitations, control over her own life: "But when you make your two nickels, you can keep both of em. . . . You kin always call in sick . . . stay home, send out for pizza an watch your Johnny Carson on TV . . . or git a bus way out Preston Street an go bowlin." (*Getting Out*, II, 72)

If to "get out" is to assume sovereignty over one's own life, and if *Getting Out* is a political play, then the factors that mitigate against Arlene's taking charge of her life must be seen as flaws in the social system and not as purely personal problems. Therefore, we must study her first as an abused child, and then follow her progress through a sexually discriminating legal system which accurately reflects the economic, social, and educational sexual mores of the country.

In Arlie's case, as in most abusive situations, the damage was psychological as well as physical. Long before she was grown, Arlie came to understand that she was ugly, and that her ugliness was the key to her character and to society's treatment of her: "Do somethin with your hair. I always though if you'd looked better you wouldn't have got in so much trouble. . . . You always was to skinny. . . . Shoulda beat you like your daddy said. Make you eat." (*Getting Out*, I, 28)

Like many abused children, Arlie experiences psychic division as a part of her everyday life. On one level she closes rank against any outside threat to her parents, lying about the source to the money she receives from her father and beating up the classmate who accuses her mother of using the family cab for prostitution. On another, she feels intense but unreleasable anger. Arlie attempted to poison her father by substituting toothpaste for mayonnaise in his sandwich and received yet another mother-condoned beating. The rest of Arlie's world pays dearly for that thwarted impulse.

Unable to achieve a fulfilling relationship with her parents, Arlie willingly becomes pregnant. She names the baby Joey, after the teddy bear with which she consoled herself as a child. Psychoanalyst D. W. Wennicott notes that children playing with dolls often create what they perceive as a perfect environment.[21] Abused girls frequently have children as early as possible in order to get the uncritical love they feel has been denied them. Unfortunately, that need and the lack of a family role model leave them woefully unprepared for the realities of child rearing, and the sad result is often a new generation of battered children. Arlie sees herself and her baby in a pact against inadequate authoritarian adults:

What you gonna be when you grow up, pretty boy baby? You gonna be a doctor? You gonna give people medicine and take out they . . . No, don't be no doctor . . . be . . . a preacher. . . . Sayin Our Father who is in Heaven . . . Heaven, that's where people go when they dies, when doctors can't save em or somebody kills em fore they even git a chance to . . . No, don't be no preacher neither. . . . Go to school an learn good . . . se you kin . . . make everybody else feel so stupid all the time. Best thing you to be is stay a baby cause nobody beats up on babies or puts them. . . . That ain't true, baby. People is mean to babies, so you stay right here with me so nobody kin get you an make you cry an they lay one finger on you . . . an I'll beat the screamin shit right out of em. (*Getting Out*, I, 44)

When the baby is taken away from her, Arlie loses control. She escapes from prison, in the process killing a man—a cabdriver like her father and mother—who tried to assault her.

Arlie's tie to Carl, who is her pimp as well as her lover, is a common, rather than an unusual, situation. Bennie is drawn to Arlene at least partially because her reputation as "damaged goods" excites him, and because it gives him as her "moral superior" the right to determine how those goods will be distributed. Bennie has been Arlie's keeper and, to retain this role, he will presume knowledge of feelings she has not revealed, use elements of her past to keep her place, and invade her body even as he has invaded her privacy. Significantly, Bennie does not even recognize his actions as rape until Arlene points it out to him. And why should he? He has simply traded small kindnesses for complete power over her—the same power exercised by her father and Carl before him, the same power every school and prison Arlie was ever in has demanded over her (as evidenced by the requirement of Alabama State Women's Prison that she transmigrate into Arlene the meek before she can "get out") In taking advantage of Arlene's low self-esteem to make her do something she doesn't want to do, Bennie reflects the rule of the system, not its exception.

It is her final rejection of self that causes the prison to decide Arlie is rehabilitated. The shell she has developed to hostility and they neglect is vulnerable to kindness and attention. In prison she comes to rely on the chaplain who renames her Arlene, teaching her that Arlie was her evil side that God would help her destroy. The destruction of Arlie was God's will, so that Arlene might join the meek that inherit the earth. Then, without telling Arlene before he left, the chaplain was transferred away:

They said it was three whole nights at first, me screamin to God to come gt Arlie an kill her. They give me this medicine an thought I's better. . . . Then that night it happened, the officer was in the dorm doin count . . . an they didn't hear nuthin but they come back out where I was an I'm standin there tellin em to come see, real quiet I'm tellin em, but there's all this blood all over my shirt an I got this fork I'm holdin real tight in my hand. . . . An there's all these holes all over me where I been stabbin myself an I'm sayin Arlie is dead for what she done to me, Arlie is dead an it's God's will. I didn't scream it, was jus sayin it over an over . . . Arlie is dead, Arlie is dead. . . . They couldn't git that fork outta my hand til . . . I woke up in the infirmary an they said I almost died. (*Getting Out*, II, 74–75)

What is still alive is Arlene, knitter of sweaters, the best housekeeper in the dorm, honor-cottage assignee, and early parole material. The final exploitation has occurred. Arlie is now Arlene, the patriarchal society's perfect woman: domesticated, in legal bondage, permanently economically subservient, and unable (or unwilling) to defend herself.

Given the commonality of Arlie's experience, it may be extraneous to mention that it is she who serves time for prostitution, not Carl or her clients—even those whose specialty is beating her up; or that Arlie was imprisoned for killing the cabdriver with his own gun in self-defense; or that her state of mind at the time of the killing was scarcely stable. The depth of the state's concern for Arlene is probably best represented by its program for her rehabilitation and release. In prison she is trained as a beautician.

Mother: Said you was gonna work.

Arlene: They got a law here. Ex-con can't get a license.

Mother: Shoulda stayed in Alabama, then. Worked there.

Arlene: They got a law there, too. (*Getting Out*, I, 29)

She is then paroled to Kentucky "in consideration of family residence and appropriate support personnel" (*Getting Out*, I, 11), presumably to her mother and siblings: "I ain't hateful, how come I got so many hateful kids? Poor dumb-as-hell Pat, stealin them wigs, Candy screwin since day one, Pete cuttin up ol Mac down at the grocery, June sellin dope like it was Girl Scout cookies and. . . . Thank God I can't remember it all." (*Getting Out*, I, 31) As Carl succinctly puts it: "Who you know ain't a 'convict'?" (*Getting Out*, II, 67)

In addition to its other values, *Getting Out* is an economic primer for American women. Even if society had not acted in character and had allowed Arlene to practice her prison-learned trade, it would have placed limits on what she could have earned. If she had achieved her heart's desire, the custody of Joey, they would have joined the 325,000 American families of the early 1980s affected by reductions in benefits for Aid to Families with Dependent Children.[22] If she had achieved the social ideal of a husband, only to find herself and perhaps other children in the abusive situation with which she was so familiar, her options would have been few. On the eve of the July 1985 Nairobi conference marking the end of the United Nations' Decade for Women, the Justice Department suspended a $625,000 to the National Coalition Against Domestic Violence, which supports five-sixths of the nearly nine hundred American shelters for battered women and children, on the basis of a charge that the coalition was a "pro-lesbian, pro-abortion, anti-Reagan radical feminist group." Since, as columnist Ellen Goodman pointed out, the grant itself was earmarked for a public-awareness campaign, a national referral plan, and a program to train police workers, the charge was clearly specious: "Indeed, the subtext of the attack was much more important: the familiar charge that shelters are the subversive creation of anti-family types who are really out to break up homes."[23] It would appear that even self-protection is a sign to some Americans of a threatening feminine independence.

Given, then, the magnitude of this problem (and we have not even considered the plight of women who are members of racial or sexual minorities), how is it to be approached politically?

We know at least that, although the size of the overall effort is incalculable, its beginning and ending must be personal. Again, *Getting Out*'s Arlene points us in the right direction. It is the inseparable triumvirate of female bonding, social awareness, and self-acceptance that makes change possible. This should come as no surprise, for each minority group we have studied has suffered from a lack of unity, a lack of an alternative history which affirms its rights in society, and a lack of self-pride. Many social factors have separated women from one another. Even as it was the chaplain's counsel that quelled the rebelliousness in Arlie, religion has been through the ages to justify women's subordinate place, dogmatizing their baseness and their need to be redeemed by "God the Father." In addition, legal systems have recognized them only in relation to men, and economic systems have forced them to compete against one other for a man's protection or his employment residue.

Arlene comes to trust Ruby's political analysis and accept her friendship because Ruby is able to validate Arlene's experience by showing its similarity to her own. The acceptance by another of her views is to Arlene the beginning of the end of her alienation, her awakening to a history of which she is a part, and the subsequent strengthening of her self-concept. When Arlene describes her suicide attempt, the "murder" of Arlie, it is Ruby who convinces her that "you can still love people that's gone." (*Getting Out*, II, 75) The play ends with Arlene and Arlie sharing a pleasant memory—an acceptance by Arlene of her past and of the qualities in Arlie without which the battle for the future will be lost.

The struggle that is the claiming process of women will outlast this play, but it cannot outlast the concepts of self-worth, sexual history, and unity. For if the history of the women's movement in nineteenth- and twentieth-century America has taught us anything, it is that when these concepts are forgotten, the energy of the movement is diverted. In the past 150 years, with help of organized women, slavery has been abolished and the former male slaves enfranchised, several wars have been won and one ended. For themselves, women have the vote and certain legal (often unenforced) protections. What convinced women that their own causes were less worthy than those they helped to bring to fruition? Even the so-called sexual revolutions of the twenties and the seventies soon degenerated to techniques within traditional sexual relationships rather than generating a new understanding of the nature of sexual relationships themselves.[24] It is sad to read of Colorado representative Pat Schroeder's refusal to attend the Nairobi UN Decade for Women conference: "After the Decade for Women, there is really nothing to celebrate."[25]

Meanwhile, the bars on Arlene's window remain. Men have placed them there—Bennie insists—"to keep folks from breakin in." Perhaps—in some men's eyes—this is true. When will the bars be removed? Perhaps when men realize that keeping a caste in its place is as socially limiting to the confiner as to the confined. Perhaps when women recognize that they're there.

Biological Determinism versus Personal Control

The major political theme feminist dramatists have had to deal with in the United States of the twentieth century is whether the destinies of women will be controlled by conventional assumptions about gender or by their individual needs. On the one hand, it is easy (and accurate) to blame women's political problems on patriarchal ideas about who women are and what they are capable of, and to state the necessity for a united feminist front to combat those problems. On the other, it is well to remember that many women and factions of women are as dogmatic about the feminine nature as are the patriarchs and their Phyllis Schlafly fellow travellers.

The age-old question, "What do women want?" should rightly have as many answers as there are women, but the generic answer must be "control over themselves." Abortion, for example, is not a feminist issue. Shorn of special circumstances, no rational human being wants to see a potential human life terminated. The issue is whether a women will have the decision about carrying a child to term made for her by law (China—to illustrate the flip side of the same principle—has practiced state-ordered abortions in recent years) or if she will make this physically/economically/religiously/culturally/familially very difficult determination for herself. As in any important personal decision, the individual factors involved for a women of the white, Anglosaxon, Protestant hegemonic class are multitudinous. For a lesbian, a woman of color, or a woman of the ethnic/religious minority, the consideration may be similar, dissimilar, or multiplied, but they will continue to be individual. As noted above, the great failure of the suffrage movement was not in getting the vote, which women won and have cast with more consistency than men, but in their failure to control the agenda—to insist on the consideration of women's issues, the most important of which is the right to make decisions about their own lives.

The key political action of *Getting Out* occurs when Arlene drops the telephone numbers of both Carl and Bennie into the wastebasket—a defiance of the gender assumption that a woman must exist as the satellite of a man. Acts of resistance against biological determinism are the focus of all the feminist dramas described below. Limited (perhaps unwisely) to those plays which are individually rather than collectively authored, these dramas illustrate gender assumptions taking the form of intrafamily and sexual pressures, economic/legal restrictions, and religious mores, and the special constraints faced by lesbians and women of color. Because of the frequency with which such plays touch several of the issues involved, their discussion has been arranged in chronological order.

It is also helpful to divide our considerations into two time periods: those written before the dawn of the latest women's movement of the 1960s, and those that were inspired by it. Susan Glaspell's *Trifles* (1916), the most anthologized one-act play ever written by an American woman, has as its basis an incident from the reporting background of the Provincetown Players cofounder and future Pulitzer Prize winner. The wives of two rural county officials searching for a motive for a farmer's murder read the telltale signs of the brutalizing of his wife in her kitchen and hide them: "I might have known she needed help! I know how things can be—for women. I tell you, it's queer, Mrs. Peters. We live close together and we live far apart. We all go through the same things—it's all just a different kind of the same thing."[26]

One of those things is probed by Mary Burrill's *They That Sit in Darkness* (1919), a script by a black playwright whose theme is colorless. A visiting nurse agonizes over her inability to legally help a sharecropping woman prematurely aged by giving birth to ten children: "My heart goes out to you poor people that sit in darkness, having, year after year, children that you are physically too weak to bring into the world—children that you are unable not only to educate but even to clothe and feed."[27] Molly Newman and Barbara Damashek will explore the same situation more than six decades later in one of the patches from *Quilters*, a musical about the pioneer women of the Great Plains. When doctors can offer no relief to a woman who has already borne twelve children, neighbors who have suffered the same fate quietly help her end her pregnancy.

The title of Sophie Treadwell's 1928 expressionist classic, *Machinal*, describes a system which consumes dreamers without fulfilling dreams. Based on the famous Ruth Synder murder case, "its villain is not Helen's materialistic husband [with his] smugness, selfishness, and banal jokes. . . . Nor is it the cavalier lover (played in the original production by Clark Gable) who considers her just another conquest while she sees him as a romantic escape. Rather, the villain is a rigid society that has no room for human feelings . . . especially those of women"[28]

Because the economy superseded all other concerns, the thirties were not a fruitful time for focusing on women's concerns. The leading woman dramatist coming into the 1930s, Rachel Crothers, penned her most pointed challenge to the patriarchy in *A Man's World* back in 1909, and despite the centrality of her women protagonists, Lillian Hellman's themes are not feminist-oriented. The freedom of the war years was to till more fertile earth. Elsa Shelley's *Pick Up Girl* (1944) depicted the trial of a fifteen-year-old prostitute, whose trade had supplied her with an abortion and a social disease. When one reviewer attacked the play as "innocent" and "sentimental," *New York Evening Post* reporter Willella Wyatt unearthed the following information: "90 percent of the youth who were being supervised in juvenile shelters in New York City were under 18 years of age and 50 percent were girls under sixteen. *Pick Up Girl*, Wyatt concluded, was 'a timely but horrifying warning . . . for anyone with a social conscience.' "[29]

The first black woman playwright with a social conscience was probably Angelina Grimke (*Rachel*, 1916), but Beah Richards combined that tradition with that of the older, one-woman show in *A Black Woman Speaks* (1950). Her target audience was the white woman who failed to see a similarity to her own slavery:

And they sold you here even as they sold me. . . . If they counted my teeth, they did appraise your thigh. Sold you to the highest bidder the same as I. And you did not fight for your right to choose whom you would wed. But for whatever bartered price that was the legal tender, you were sold to a stranger's bed in a stranger land. Remember? And you did not fight. Mind you, I speak not mockingly, but I fought for freedom. I'm fighting now for our unity. We are women all. And what wrongs you murders me . . . eventually marks your grave. So we share a mutual death at the hand of tyranny.[30]

The black feminist fight continued throughout the next decade. Lorraine Hansberry's seemingly apolitical *A Raisin in the Sun* (1959) is still the best protest play ever written because of its ability to turn an audience's perception of "them" into a mutual "we." The end of *The Drinking Gourd* (1960) is harsher. In a war for equality, there will be casualties. During the 1860s, a slave woman decides to lead her children to the Underground Railroad rather than save the dying patriarch who had been her kindly "master" all her adult life. Having commissioned a televised version for the centennial year of the Civil War, NBC-TV found America unready and cancelled its production. Alice Childress lived longer but felt the same resistance. The heroine of her 1955 Obie Award winner, *Trouble in Mind*, finds her career stymied when she refuses to play a stereotyped mammy who does nothing while her son is being lynched. *Wedding Band*, which waited nine years for its first New York production (1972), challenged the miscegenation laws which made it illegal for an interracial couple to cohabit, much less marry, and the divorce law which denied freedom to a wife beaten, humiliated, and deserted by her husband. Childress's *Wine in the Wilderness* (1969) upheld the validity of a lower-class black woman's personal experience with the daily battle for "black pride" in America's ghettos against the trendy pseudo-Africanism of a "yuppy" artist.

If the views of women onstage were limited, lesbians were virtually invisible. "A lesbian was like a vampire; she looked in the mirror and there was no reflection."[31] Marjean Perry's *A Trap Is a Small Place*, one of the first treatments of lesbianism for other than sensational purposes, appeared as early as 1953. Nevertheless, getting *A Late Snow*—Jane Chambers's play about a college professor's attempt to achieve emotional fulfillment and still retain her job—produced Off-Broadway proved a monumental task in 1974.

Quincey: One person, a sophomore, tried to form a Gay Lib group. . . . They kicked her out of the dorm. . . . The rest of the kids we rallied and picketed and the trustees had a hearing. They let her stay in school—if she lived off campus. She couldn't live in the dorm. . . .

Ellie: It was four years ago. The administration has changed. There are some radical groups on campus now.

Quincey: The faculty's still in the closet. (*A Late Snow*, I, 44)

By the end of the 1970s, sexual love between women was a central feature of black playwrights Alexis DeVeaux (*A Season to Unravel*) and P. J. Gibson (*Long Time Since Yesterday*), and the awakening of a woman to her homosexuality is the theme of *Giving Up the Ghost* (1984) by Hispanic poet Cherrie Moraga. As the years pass, DeVeaux's ideal comes to seem more possible: "New worlds/a new path/new context for living and working together. Equally. Whole. . . . Not as homosexuals and heterosexuals but as sexual beings. Free from the domination of race, sex and class. This is my naked stance: These are my feminist priorities."[32]

Giving Up the Ghost was produced at Minneapolis's Foot of the Mountain Theatre, one of the most durable of women's collectives. By the 1970s, collectives were contributing to the theatrical literature as well as to the theatrical and *regional* experience of the women's movement. To parody the popular Gretchen Cryer musical of the decade, feminism was "Getting My Act Together and Taking It on the Road." Martha Boesing was resident playwright of the Foot of the Mountain and, through the bride's multiple personalities in *River Journal*, depicted the fragmenting power of patriarchal marriage. Although the San Francisco Mime Troupe was not primarily feminist, in *The Independent Female* (1970) Joan Holden contributed an analysis of women's position in the workplace which was *commedia del l'arte* in style, but accurate in content. Megan Terry founded the Omaha Magic Theatre and in the 1970s wrote such plays for it as *Babes in the Bighouse*, which made its sexual points partly through cross-gender casting, and *American King's English for Queens* (1978), which examined the sexist nature of critical language.

In 1980 two women playwrights were presenting the dilemma of the black middle-class family choosing between bourgeois respectability and a honest assessment of their race's treatment in the United States: Diane Houston's *The Fisherman* at the Black Alley Theatre in Washington, D.C., and Kathleen Collins's *In the Midnight Hour* for the Women's Project, which was inaugurated by Julia Miles of New York's American Place Theatre. Among the other Women's Project plays are *Killings on the Last Line*, Lavonne Mueller's remarkable study of the lives of nine working women in a Chicago nuclear reactor parts factory during 1979, the United Nations' Year of the Child, and Joan Shenkar's *Signs of Life*. Shenkar highlights the different positions of men and women in society by parodying such familiar literary figures as Virginia Woolf's "Shakespeare's sister" (through Henry James and his sister Alice), *Washington Square's* Dr. Sloper, and the protagonist of *The Elephant Man* (through P. T. Barnum's "Elephant Women").

The consciousness-raising of the collectives also stressed a new perception of religion, largely in attempts to revive the spirit of the matriarchy and the holistic power of women healing one another. In Aishah Rahman's *Unfinished Women Cry in No Man's Land* (1977), five women in a home for unwed mothers share a split stage with a dying Charlie Parker—offering an explanation for both abandoned women of color and seduced black art: "Following the music's heartbeat I took a journey I could no longer avoid and along the way I helped a woman toss her newborn baby overboard a slaveship. I joined hands with my mother as she took *her* mother's hand and I took my place in the circle of black women singing old blues."[33] In the end, the whole women's movement may be best explained by the words of Ntozake Shange, whose *spell #7*

(1979) utilized the minstrel show to illustrate the co-opting of the black artist, and her *for colored girls who have considered suicide/when the rainbow is enuf*, which brought a new sensibility of poetry to the theatre: "i found god in myself/& i loved her fiercely."[34]

Gay Liberation

> My criticism of the gay rights movement is that it isn't asking for civil rights, it is asking for a recognition and acceptance of an alternative life-style which I do not believe society can condone, nor can I.[35]
> —Ronald Reagan (November 1980)

Although it is possible to disagree with our fortieth president over society's capacity for "recognition and acceptance," Mr. Reagan is correct in defining the gay movement's focus as being as much cultural as legal. However, far from being unusual in seeking validation of a distinctive life-style, gay liberation is only mirroring the struggle being engaged in the other groups in this chapter and, by extension, the young, the elderly, and all other culturally nondominant minorities in America.

In a very real sense America's racial problems arrived with its first settlers, while its masculine/feminine conflicts are as old as Eve (or at least the Judeo-Christian concept of her). On the other hand, the gay life-style—itself inseparable from the question of gender roles—could only manifest itself according to a gay culture found in a gay community—both relatively recent social phenomena.

As we noted earlier, the classification of society according to gender roles was a product of the industrial revolution. Behavior was evaluated in terms of its support of the industrial model (normal) or its detraction from the model (deviant). Following the organizing principle of the time, deviant behavior was categorized. Drunken laborers who broke the rhythm of the assembly line, anarchists who refused to maintain their "place," and women who were discontent in the home were all deviants. The worst deviants were those who threatened the family unit (and, by extension, the industrial society) by finding sexual fulfillment outside the function of gender roles. In 1869, Karoly Marie Benkert, a Hungarian doctor, named this category of deviates "homosexuals."[36]

Benkert's definition provided no new insights into the same-sex erotic act itself, of which every known society provides examples.[37] What it did do was to shift the emphasis from the act to the actors, identifying in the process a cultural minority for whom same-sex love was the "norm." For, while deviance is a crime under the law, a sin under religion, and a sickness under medicine, the "natural" practices of a cultural minority are (or should be) none of these things. What to the majority culture is a social issue is to the minority a way of life.

In *The Love That Dared Not Speak Its Name*, H. Montgomery Hyde suggests that Old Testament homophobia (fear of same-sex eroticism) was a stratagem required for racial survival: "No doubt the basis for its condemnation was similar to that of withdrawal in coitus, or Onanism . . . namely that it was the duty of the Jews to increase and multiply and any interference with the normal sexual function to this end was to be reprobated."[38] D. S. Bailey, Anglican clergyman and historian, believes that condemnations of homosexuality may also have been a means of separating Jewish culture from that of their Middle Eastern neighbors. The only Old Testament passages specifically referring to homosexual acts, Leviticus 18:22 and 20:23, condemn male homosexuality and prescribe the death penalty respectively, but fail to indicate to what period and legal code they belong. The most frequently cited biblical reference is the Genesis story of Sodom's residents demanding to "know" the angelic visitors to Lot. However, K. Boyd's reading of the Hebrew text indicates that the sin of Sodom was inhospitality, not homosexuality. Nevertheless, there can be no doubt that defenders of homophobia in Judeo-Christian cultures have always used the Bible as a weapon in their campaign.[39]

The thirteenth century Christian theologian Thomas Aquinas rated "unnatural vice" (bestiality, sodomy, other homosexual venereal acts, and masturbation) as worse than "intemperate lust" (adultery, seduction, or rape) because by precluding the possibility of children, it was a crime against God rather than persons.[40] The position of the Catholic church on homosexuality remains largely unchanged since the time of Aquinas.[41]

Thus, although the industrial revolution changed the function of the family, and although Christianity became entrenched in the Western world, both family and church continued to block any relaxation of the moral sanctions against homosexuality. If Benkert's definition was accurate, a same-sex preference is the norm to a sizable population. Therefore, sanctions cannot be enforced without a certain amount of repression. Maturing industrialized societies offered two outlets for such repression: art and imperialism.

It is no accident that the concept of "art for art's sake" was born in late-nineteenth-century Western Europe—a society which had already established the socially stabilizing value of pleasure. While art has always been both enjoyable and a personal expression of the artist, in earlier times its utilitarian function (praising the gods, recording social history, conveying moral lessons, etc.) had been stressed. Under industrialism, art, like sex, began to be explored for its beauty alone. In the twentieth century, the subject of art would not be an object or story. It would be the way in which the object was described or the story told. The emphasis in both art and sex would be on perceived personal experience—process instead of product. The gay sensibility, which has always divorced sex from procreation, has also been the mark of a proportionately large number of artists.

It is probably impossible to know how many explorers, traders, and colonial administrators sought more than their fortunes in what they perceived to be primitive and sexually less repressed areas of the world. The literature of Western imperial countries abounds with stories of darker, less civilized, less driven lands whose unquestioning embrace of pleasure proves seductive to the Caucasian overachiever. Works as diverse as Somerset Maugham's "Rain" and Margaret Mead's *Coming of Age in Samoa* (to list a pair of bisexual writers) come to mind. The strong homosexual tradition in American literature has three components: (a) male bonding, (b) in an uncivilized environment, (c) between a white man and an "noble savage."[42] Examples of such friendships include Natty Bumppo and Uncus, Ishmael and Queequeg, the Lone Ranger and Tonto, and Captain Kirk and Mr. Spock. These relationships are acceptable because they are "natural" and because they have as their purpose the civilizing of the frontier. The white male hero is functioning in a setting outside of the laws of society. His tools (long rifle, sixgun, laser, etc.) and his use of them may be barbarous, but his aim is to create an environment in which they will not be necessary. His ally this task is an alien (less human) male who in fact will be out of place in the civilization the hero is engaged in creating, but who contributes out of love for the hero. Ironically, the alien's purity derives (in the Romantic tradition) from his lack of experience with the civilization of which his friend is trying to create a more sanctified version.

The tradition stipulates the alien's death in the service of the white ideal—a sacrifice all the more genuine because the others of his own kind resist it. It also demands that neither friend form a permanent relationship that will supersede their tie to one another. For example, a mutual attraction grows between Uncus and Cora Munroe even as he and Natty attempt to protect Cora and her sister from the sexual intentions of the evil Indian, Magua. Both Uncus and Cora die in the attempt to rescue her, leaving Natty to avenge them.

It is also true that the hero will be no more comfortable in his "brave new world" than his alien friend. Thus, the Lone Ranger is already fading into the distance before we can ask, "Who was that masked man?" and Admiral Kirk gladly leaves his desk job to once again "boldly go where no man has ever gone." In short, American literature shows the male-bonding relationship as counter to the essence of the developing civilization, but condones and glorifies it as both purer than the old civilization and necessary if a New Jerusalem is to be created.

"Coming out of the closet" instead of going into the wilderness often means forfeiting such traditional supports as family and church, risking jobs and professional advancement, and exposing oneself to a legal system whose sanctions may not be as stringent as when Thomas Jefferson urged castration of same-sex lovers as a humane substitution for the death penalty, but which can be all the more devastating for the capriciousness of its application.[43] Even friends who are supportive of the individual homosexual may urge the seeking of medical treatment, which in the last century has included castration, hysterectomy, vasectomy, removal of the ovaries and clitoris, lobotomy, the administration of hormones, LSD, hypnosis, shock treatment, behavior modification, pornography, and psychiatry for the purpose of "curing" the patient rather than achieving self-acceptance.[44]

Benkert's 1869 definition of same-sex lovers as a minority group with specific characteristics endemic to it was a one-hundred-year time bomb insofar as gay liberation was concerned. It would take that long for the historical circumstances to appear that would allow so submerged a minority to recognize its own existence and to affirm its right to live openly as homosexual.

The first known homosexual emancipation organization in the United States was the Society for Human Rights, located in Chicago and chartered by the state of Illinois on December 10, 1924. Its objective of combating "public prejudices . . . by the dissemination of facts according to modern science among intellectuals of mature age"[45] did not prevent its officers from being arrested and their diaries and publications seized without warrant the following year. The Society for Human Rights, with its emphasis on educating the more perceptive among the majority toward acceptance of homosexuals, is an early example of what Toby Marotta has termed the homophile movement. It was not until the 1950s that such educationally oriented organizations would again form, most notably the Mattachine Society (Los Angeles, 1951, and New York, 1955) and the Daughters of Bilitis (San Francisco, 1950; New York, 1958).[46]

But the 1950s were not the easiest time to educate Americans on a subject commonly termed a threat to America's "family structure, moral fiber, and way of life." In his McCarthy-era parable of New England witchcraft, *The Crucible*, Arthur Miller saw this fear as the natural reaction of a people who believed their survival had been a sign of God's favor, but now were no longer certain: "The witch-hunt was a perverse manifestation of the panic which set in among all classes when the balance began to turn toward greater individual freedom. When one rises above the individual villainy displayed, one can only pity them all, just as we shall be pitied someday. It is still impossible for man to organize his social life without repressions, and the balance has yet to be struck between order and freedom."[47]

The concepts of "individual freedom" and "social life without repressions" were just what the homophile movement was about, and it did not take long for some people to draw the conclusion that one underminer of America (communism) must necessarily be in league with another (sexual freedom).

On July 17, 1950, Senator Kenneth Wherry of Nebraska, cochairman of a committee ferreting out sexual deviates in government, told a *New York Post* reporter: "You can't hardly separate homosexuals from subversives. Mind you, I don't say every homosexual is a subversive, and I don't say every subversive is a homosexual. But a man of low morality is a menace in the government, whatever he is, and they are all tied up together."[48]

In 1951 the State Department fired 2 employees for homosexuality, and 117 others faced with similar charges resigned. By January 1955, when the Civil Service Commission reported the results of the first sixteen months of its security program, "655 cases involving sex perversion" had resulted in individuals being "dismissed or deemed suspect for reasons unrelated to disloyalty or subversion".[49]

Such wholesale firings might be more difficult today, but government agencies still try to avoid *hiring* gays. To cite the best-known case, Air Force Sergeant Leonard Matlovich spent six years in court fighting the less-than-honorable discharge that followed his coming out in 1975, finally accepting a cash settlement in lieu of reinstatement.[50] Former governor Ruben Askew (a 1984 presidential candidate) stated during his 1979 confirmation hearings as President Carter's Special Trade Representative that "I will not have a known homosexual on my staff."[51] In 1985, the New York City Council voted for the seventh consecutive time not to include homosexuals under the antidiscrimination section of the city's hiring laws.[52]

In America, the appearance of greater sexual freedom has always been greeted as a prelude to revolution. Those unable to comprehend the homophobia of the fifties may better remember the hysteria of the sixties when boys with long hair and girls in jeans and without foundation garments stirred the wrath of their elders. In his account of the 1970 National Guard shooting of thirteen students at Kent State University in Ohio, James Michener found that many townspeople justified the killings on the basis of the students' sexual life-styles:

A businessman will be saying, "The thing I can't stand is the way they dress," but he will add, "And it's disgusting the way the girls sleep around." Or a Kent housewife will explain, "I could tolerate them if they had any manners," but she will conclude in a lower voice, "And the way they sleep together in those dormitories!" . . . It could not have been coincidence that so many women referred with a sense of hatred to the young girls who were appearing in town without bras; this became a fixation with many, and was apparently an intuitive reaction to a symbol.[53]

"And what's the point of a revolution without general copulation?" [54] Certainly gay liberation was born out of the revolutionary sentiments of the sixties. Considering their heightened awareness of social injustice, it is not surprising that many gay activists had previously been participants and leaders in the civil rights movement and the anti-Vietnam War struggle. Perhaps more important, the decade established the primacy of the "counterculture" mentality—the right to (and the importance of) doing "your own thing."[55]

Benkert's time bomb exploded on Christopher Street in New York's Greenwich Village on the evening of June 27, 1969. The Public Morals Section of the New York Police Department was making a routine raid on a gay bar known as the Stonewall Inn. Employees were arrested, and patrons who were unable to produced identification were detained for questioning:

Three of the more blatant queens—in full drag—were loaded inside, along with the bartender and doorman, to chorus of catcalls and boos from the crowd. A cry went up to push the paddywagon over, but it drove away before anything could happen. With its exit, the action waned momentarily. The next person to come out was a dyke, and she put up a struggle—from car to door to car again. It was at that moment that the scene became explosive. . . . But the blaze of flame which soon appeared in the window of the Stonewall was still a shock.[56]

What came to be known as the Stonewall Riots continued for the next several nights. Gays were uniting and fighting back for the first time. Before the year was out, the Gay Liberation Front had succeeded the Mattachine Society as the most important of the gay political groups, and in 1970 it in turn was superseded by the Gay Activists Alliance. The third wave, the lesbian feminist movement, also emerged in 1970, under the title of Radicalesbians.[57] Although male and female gays were to unite still again as the National Gay Task Force, this bewildering formation and disintegration of groups in the seventies underscores two divisive factors in the movement which have yet to be resolved: (a) the needs of lesbians and gay men cannot always be met by the same political actions; and (b) the inability of gays to determine whether the attainment of legal rights or the right to a gay life-style should have priority.

The word *homosexual* comes not from the Latin *homo* (man), but rather from the Greek *homos* (same). Since what distinguishes lesbians and gay men from the majority culture is that they are same-sex lovers, it is not surprising that differences arise between the two groups. Although many gay men sincerely like women, many others just as sincerely do not and are perfectly willing to perpetuate patriarchal, hierarchical relationships within homosexual organizations. When Harry Britt, a gay male, was elected a San Francisco supervisor in 1979, Sally Gearhart pointed out that the achievement of gay male aims would not necessarily benefit women:

We'll see to it that gay people are not discriminated against in housing or employment while at the same times the ERA may fail to be ratified, thus perpetuating the lower economic and social status of women (fifteen or twenty percent of them lesbians); we may succeed in getting "homosexual acts" decriminalized in this country while every sixty seconds somewhere there will still be a woman being raped, [and] . . . at the same time less and less protection will be given to battered women and children who are victims of precisely the same kind of violence that anonymous sex perpetuates.[58]

The insensitivity that some lesbians perceived gay males displaying to their problems was doubly distressing to those who had experienced similar discrimination within the women's movement. Because of their refusal to accept patriarchal judgments, the women's liberation pioneers of the sixties had often been taunted as lesbians. Some, like Ti-Grace Atkinson, who resigned as president of the National Organization for Women's New York chapter in October 1968, saw the connection between women's need for economic and political independence from men and the emotional and physical independence lesbians had achieved already. Others, like Betty Friedan, the author of *The Feminine Mystique*, opposed any recognition of the lesbian issue at all, calling it a "lavender herring." The 1971 New York NOW elections were the scene of bitter lesbian-baiting, but the national convention passed a strongly worded prolesbian resolution (which New York did not ratify until several years later): "Asking women to disguise their identities so they will not 'embarrass' the group is an intolerable form of oppression, like asking black women to join us in white face. "59

Gay civil rights gains were numerous after 1969. In 1974 the American Psychological Association decided homosexuality was not a mental disorder. In 1978 the Briggs Initiative which would have banned un-closeted gays or their friends from California school jobs was defeated. Seventy-five declared gays were 1980 Democratic National Convention delegates. Federal courts ended the law banning gay immigration in 1982, and by 1983 twenty-seven had passed bills allowing sex between con-senting adults of the same sex.60

Nevertheless, as President Reagan pointed out at the beginning of this essay, the issue was life-style as well as civil rights. Nor could the freedom achieved be limited to gays. If—as Benkert's definition implies—homo-sexuals and heterosexuals differ only in the focus of their yearnings, then the achievement of sexual liberty for the former can never be assured while the latter remain repressed:

Erotophobia is such a tenacious strain of Western culture that it affects every aspect of our lives. It informs our attitudes towards women, children, race, class, and towards sexuality in general. It has perpetuated strict sexual and gender roles which in turn support and reinforce the erotophobia which fostered them. Homosexuality, with its blatant disregard for sexual assignments, flies in the face of this system. Homosexual-ity represents an antithesis of Western cultural teaching about sex and gender and is by definition the rejection of erotophobic values.61

From the Closet to the Footlights

If somebody insults you—sock 'em in the jaw. If you don't like the sex laws, attack them. . . . You wanna get a petition? I'll sign one. . . . But, David, please get over the notion that your particular sexuality is something that only the deepest, saddest, the most nobly tortured can know about. It ain't—it's just one kind of sex—that's all. And, in my opinion—the universe turns regardless.62
—Lorraine Hansberry's *The Sign in Sidney Brustein's Window* (1964)

It is tempting to think of any play involving a social group outside the hegemonic norm as political. However, even as the presence of a homosexual character does not make a play "gay," a play with a gay theme need not be political. Lillian Hellman's concern in *The Children's Hour* (1934) is no more homosexual than the concern of Ibsen in *Ghosts* is syphilis, and the self-destructive guilt felt by the lesbian character presently mitigates against its production. The same could be said of Mart Crowley's *The Boys in the Band* (1968), which in its day was an enormously significant shatterer of taboos. On the other hand, while the characters and plot of Gore Vidal's *The Best Man* (1960) seem mired in another century, the 1989 smears of Congressmen Tom Foley and Barney Frank make the decision of Vidal's candidate not to reveal a homosexual episode in his opponent's past pertinent indeed. Politics, like drama, is a time-and-space art.

American gay dramas with some political content go back as far as Mae West's *The Drag* (1927), which (surprisingly) has in spots all the clinical dullness of a Eugene Brieux-dramatized lecture. However, positive gay messages are rare until after Stonewall. The production showing the most immediate results was of Jonathan Katz's *Coming Out* in 1975, which one night inspired its patrons to stage a successful sit-in at a neighborhood bar that discriminated against gay patrons.[63] *Coming Out* is a documentary in the tradition of *In White America*—also by a gay playwright, Martin Duberman—and along the way we meet Walt Whitman, Horatio Alger, Willa Cather, Gertrude Stein, and Allen Ginsberg. Chronologically, its scenes stretch from the "unclean practices" for which five New England boys were hanged in 1629 to the 1973 case of a black New Jersey high school teacher whose homosexuality is the excuse used to destroy his cultural and political influence among the Afro-American young. Another scene which reinforces solidarity across caste lines is the "lavender menace" incident at the 1970 New York NOW convention:

What is a lesbian? A lesbian is the rage of all women condensed to the point of explosion. Lesbian is the word that holds women in line. When a woman hears this word tossed her way she knows she is stepping out of line. Lesbian is a label invented by the Man to throw at any woman who dares to be his equal, who dares to challenge his prerogatives, who dares to assert the primacy of her own needs. For in this sexist society for a woman to be independent means she can't be a *woman*—she must be a *dyke*.[64]

History, of course, has a built-in alienation effect, allowing straight audiences to decry the oppression of gays without feeling personally guilty. Martin Sherman's *Bent* (1979) was a major Broadway hit, with its protagonist growing in acceptance of his homosexuality even as his status under the value system of Nazi persecution declined. Eric Bentley's *Lord Alfred's Lover* (1979), about Oscar Wilde's coming to terms with his homosexuality, has received only regional productions. Perhaps it is safer to hate Nazis than the Victorian middle class, or perhaps concentration camps are inherently more dramatic than drawing rooms.

Plays which deal with contemporary incidents of gay oppression in America remain rare. In *The Ovens of Anita Orangejuice* (1978), Ronald Tavel tried without much success to apply Ridiculous Theatre techniques to Anita Bryant's attempt to make her Florida antigay crusade national. More effective was Doric Wilson's *West Street Gang* (1977), a production by his own The Other Side of Silence theatre. Staged at a gay bar, the play depicted a response to a recent series of New York "gay-bashings." Best of all was *Execution of Justice* (1984), Emily Mann's documentary treatment of the 1978 murders of San Francisco mayor George Moscone and gay city supervisor Harvey Milk. In what was widely perceived as an antigay backlash, the assassin (city supervisor Dan White) was only convicted of voluntary manslaughter:

> The city was divided all during that period. It divided on emerging constituencies like the gay constituency. That's the one that was used to cause the most divisive emotions more than any other, so the divisiveness in the city was there. I mean, that was the whole point of this political fight between Dan White and Moscone and Milk: The fight was over who controlled the city. The Right couldn't afford to lose Dan. He was their saving vote on the Board of Supervisors. He blocked the Milk/Moscone agenda. Obviously, Harvey Milk didn't want Dan White on the Board. So, it was political, the murders.[65]

Of interest are the political implications of the recent trend toward gay romantic comedy. Richard Hall's *Love Match* (1977) deals with the economic aspects of homophobia in its story of a movie with a gay theme that *almost* doesn't get made. Hall's *Prisoner of Love* (1978) also suggests the necessity for gay liberation reformers to lighten up and enjoy a little of the world they are striving to hard to improve for oppressed minorities.

Almost too palatable are Harvey Fierstein's enormously successful *Torch Song Trilogy* (1979) and *La Cage aux Folles*(1983), probably the most popular "protest" plays to hit Broadway since Lorraine Hansberry's *A Raisin in the Sun*: "*Torch Song* thus tells critics and public what they hope to hear: gay people are just like straight people; all they want is a loving spouse, nice inlaws and a kid who gets good grades. It is this message, perhaps, that led Jack Kroll of *Newsweek* to write that the play has, 'so help me, something for the whole family.' "[66] In contrast, Doric Wilson's *A Perfect Relationship* (1979) suggests that it is possible to demonstrate emotional commitment with something other than sexual fidelity—a concept with which Broadway audiences remain uncomfortable.

Perhaps no better example of our ambivalence toward sexual freedom can be found than in the phenomenon of Aquired Immune Deficiency

Syndrome, "the Gay Plague." First, it was ignored, or (by some) secretly welcomed as nature's revenge on an "unnatural act." Then, by its presence in the entertainment and fashion industries of Hollywood and New York, it forced us to recognize the source of the sexual images that fuel our imaginations and our economy. Finally, as it spread from the homosexual ghetto into the larger society, we realized what Paul Goodman tried to tell us years ago about the nature of a minority: "The minority is always a repressed part of the majority," and we cannot long ignore its problems before we discover that they are ours.[67]

A Plague on Both Your Houses

AIDS is an acronym for Aquired Immune Deficiency Syndrome, and nobody ever died of it. AIDS victims die of diseases called toxoplasmosis, cytomegalovirus (CMV), pneumocystis carinii pneumonia, Kaposi's sarcoma (KS), cryptosporidiosis, and other "opportunistic infections." They get the opportunity because certain cells in the lymph system whose job it is to neutralize these infections or make them relatively harmless have been crippled. The first case appeared in 1979, although the pattern would not be identified until 1981 and the name would not be coined until a year later. By early 1985 the number of victims was doubling roughly every nine months, and the Department of Health and Human Services was predicting that AIDS would be the nation's sixth leading killer by 1991.[68] Over 70 percent of AIDS victims are homosexual men and about 25 percent are intravenous drug users.[69] News reports periodically support hopes of prevention and even cure, but even when medicine has done its best, the social and political questions unearthed during the AIDS crisis will remain behind to plague the American psyche.

When AIDS hysteria reached a media peak in the summer of 1983, *Time* magazine recorded a relatively rare psychological phenomenon in American medicine—the patient as leper:

A WABC-TV crew refused to enter the Gay Men's Health Crisis office to cover a story on AIDS. . . . Three nurses at a hospital in San Jose, California, quit rather than deal with AIDS cases; some staff members at San Francisco General Hospital refused to carry trays to such patients. . . . Several conservatives, including columnist Pat Buchanan, have raised the question of whether homosexuals should be barred from all food-handling jobs, and diners in several cities boycotted restaurants rumored to have gay chefs. . . . A Worcester, Massachusetts, woman wondered if she should banish her gay son from her home, just on the chance he might have AIDS. . . . In San Francisco, one man with AIDS was induced to leave a jury by those chosen to serve with him. Two other AIDS victims scheduled to appear on a local TV show were instead relegated to the makeup room, where they had to field questions by telephone. The purpose of the show: to ease anxiety over AIDS.[70]

Human Events, a right-wing weekly, suggested quarantining AIDS victims lest through donations "[they] deliberately contaminate the blood supply, thus spreading the condition into the general population, as a way to make certain that there is increased pressure on the federal government to find a cure."[71]

The perceptive reader will no doubt have noted that, in a number of examples above, no mention is made of the shunned subject having AIDS. It was sufficient merely to be a recognized homosexual male engaged in ordinary social intercourse. In this equation, Gay = Disease = Threat of contamination. Such unlikely journalistic bedfellows as *The New Statesman*, *The New Republic*, *Time*, and *Rolling Stone* have commented thoughtfully on the similarities between the psychological reactions to AIDS and to the Black Plague which killed a third of the population of Europe in the Middle Ages:

AIDS . . . has become the basis for an authoritarian metaphor about the dangers of dissent. The AIDS metaphor, like the metaphor of cancer, is . . . "implicitly genoci-dal": it prescribes "radical" treatment. For the Nazis, Jewry was the cancer of Europe. . . . The AIDS metaphor has developed in stages, the first of which effects an identification of gayness with the disease. This identification is culturally feasible because we already have a contagion theory of *desire*: gay men "recruit" young straight men, and young straight men can be recruited, because homosexuality is itself conceived of as a virus that can be transmitted. . . . If AIDS is in some sense continuous with homosexuality, then it follows that the condition is a punishment for pleasure.[72]

Both *The New Statesman*'s Andrew Britton and *Time*'s Lance Morrow see the fear of AIDS as a manifestation of the concern over the potential nuclear termination of existence we lived with daily.[73] God has sent us the plague to warn us to repent our sins, but beware of the fire next time. Like the Martians in *The War of the Worlds*, the aliens in our midst are being destroyed by a bacteria to which the chosen people are immune. Our physical sickness derives from our failure to control our bestial desires, of which homosexuality is only a current visible example; "We are recoiling from the liberation of the few decades (and are more likely now to call it permissiveness); but, as we are still reluctant to express this change of heart in moral terms, we invoke nature as the arbiter. Thus, herpes, as benign an infection as one can image, became the medical sensation of 1982, nature's way of telling us that sexual liberation had gone too far. AIDS—which doesn't itch, it kills—is an even better metaphor."[74]

As Is

Some of the most effective discussion of these questions is presently taking place on the stage. When Paul Selig's *Terminal Bar* was first performed at the end of 1983, the audience was confused as to the nature of the plague it describes. "By the time of the New York premiere three years later, there could be no doubt in anyone's mind."[75] In May of 1985, *Time* magazine counted seven theatrical productions which focused on AIDS, including *Warren* by Atlanta's Seven Stages. San Francisco's Arcaids company (consisting entirely of AIDS victims) segues from a robed Gregorian chant into a chorus line kick: "In the mornin', in the evenin', ain't we got AIDS!"[76] Jeff Hagedorn's *One* has a less upbeat but equally arresting opening: "I have acquired a disease that means I am going to die."[77]

Larry Kramer's *The Normal Heart*, performed at New York's Public Theater, may be the most overtly political of the plays. *Rolling Stone*'s David Black says the play "is to AIDS what Arthur Miller's *The Crucible* was to the McCarthy era."[78] In a diatribe against government inaction, press misinformation, and gay irresponsibility, Kramer offers celibacy as the only legitimate response to so life-threatening a situation.[79] William Hoffman's *As Is*, with its concentration on a relatively monogamous couple and its montage style which links their problems to those of the larger gay community, may in the long run be more politically effective.

Like many other political plays, the message of *As Is* is encapsulated in its title. Saul, the alienated lover of Rich, the AIDS victim, accepts him "as is"; diseased, with a very high potential for a physically repulsive death; and broke, with both his finances and his capacity for earning destroyed by the disease and its social aura. This acceptance precedes the discovery by Rich's brother that, sexual preference and debilitating illness aside, he too still loves Rich. Most important, "as is" signifies Rich's acceptance of himself (and his sexuality) as separate from his disease—the victim of a virus, not a damned soul singled out for divine retribution.

As Is begins with a monologue by a hospice worker. An ex-nun, eased out of the convent for her fanaticism, she has, over the years, become what she describes as less "idealistic." By this, she means she expects less in the way of deathbed conversions, less in term of confirmation of her own values. We will meet her again at the end of the play.

Saul and Rich are breaking up their household. It is a scene made instantly comprehensible by the audience's recognition of the residue of a thousand similarly destroyed relationships: hurt feelings and communal property. Saul is both betrayed and concerned, still in love with Rich and (despite himself) bitchily jealous of his usurper. His role is that of the wife in this "marriage," while his successor, Chet, plays the mistress. As Rich explains it later to Saul: "I loved you but I wanted someone to write poems to."[80] Rich is irritable, impatient to leave behind what he cannot separate from Saul.

But there are other causes for their irritability. Saul's terror of AIDS affects his every moment. His waking thoughts are invaded by account after account of acquaintances, friends, and even former lovers now dead or in every preceding state of the disease. Less noticeably, Rich, an avid cook, is eating out a lot and has recently lost weight.

When Rich is diagnosed, we see a montage of the full cycle of reactions to AIDS from Rich's lover, brother, business partner, and friends, and its almost instant evolution from disbelief and sympathy to paranoia and rejection. In a matter of moments, Hoffman captures AIDS's most terrifying side effect—the manner in which the victim is isolated at a time when he needs human support the most. The decline of Rich's catering business and the withdrawal of his brother's annual Christmas invitation are the norm, rather than the anomaly.

In the early stages of his illness, Rich struggles with what has become the gay dilemma in the AIDS crisis: the attempt to balance individual sexual needs with a responsibility to others. Drawn to gay bars and clubs, Rich begins by attempting to warn his prospective pickups of his medical condition, and ends by simply discouraging the interest of those who are attracted to him, Internally, he is bitter that the world that supplies him with his identity has been denied to him. The homosexual lives his or her life honestly only at a great social price. To have paid the price and be denied the product is doubly frustrating.

While he watches a developing assignation between two "clones" (the term used by gay men to indicate an unknown—and, presumably, duplicable—sexual partner), a beer is accidentally spilled on Rich. For that moment, his response is that of the homophobe, aroused to fury by the easy gay access to sex which he cannot have: "I'll kill ya, faggot! . . . What's a matter, can't you fight like a man?" (As Is, 23)[81]

Just the possibility of AIDS is potentially sexually inhibiting for all gay men. For a social group whose identity is derived from their sexuality, the loss of promiscuous sex, or, as Rich wryly puts it, "nondirective, noncommitted, nonauthoritarian sex" (As Is, 27) is devastating:

"The belief that was handed to me was that sex was liberating and more sex was more liberating,"says Michael Callen, 28, one of New York City's 847 AIDS victims [as of mid-1983]. "[Being gay] was tied to the right to have sex." As a result, says Richard Failla, a professed homosexual who is a prominent New York City judge, "the psychological impact of AIDS on the gay community is tremendous. . . . Some people are saying, 'Maybe we *are* wrong—maybe this is a punishment.'"[82]

Even before AIDS, Saul and Rich have personified in their lives the homosexual dilemma: the conflict between a sexually promiscuous drive and the psychological need for sustained, secure relationships. In one of the play's most moving scenes, their description of the ordinariness of their lives together achieves a poetic intensity, heightened by a montage sequence in which the cast describes the shadow cast over their individual lives in four short years by a disease that seemed initially so exotic and far away. Now, as Rich discovers, even such mundane social underpinnings as health insurance melt away in the disese's corrosive power. In San Francisco, one man, his immune system destroyed, was dying of cryptosporidiosis, a disease usually found in calves. Social Security officials told him that since the disease was found was only in animals, "therefore he couldn't have it, therefore be couldn't be disabled, therefore he couldn't have [Social Security compensation]."[83]

In the meantime Rich must also go through the requisite psychological stages, an important one of which is denial that he has the disease. He refuses to participate in his AIDS support group which includes one-half of a monogamous gay couple, a wisecracking designer of robots, and, most poignant, the pregnant wife of a police officer and secret drug addict: "At least when I come here I don't have to lie 'Bernie's doing better, I'm fine.' I can even crack up if I want to. Don't worry, I won't do it two weeks in a row. I mean, who's there to talk to in Brewster. These things don't happen in Brewster. Police officers don't shoot up heroin, cops don't come down with the 'gay plague'—that's what they call it in Brewster." (*As Is*, 43)

Coleen Johnson, assistant director of psychological services for AIDS/Los Angeles, recounts the story of a family in which a man with AIDS had given the disease to his pregnant wife. The only healthy family member was a five-year-old girl, who asked her mother, "Are you going to die?"

"Yes," the mother said.

"Is Daddy going to die?"

"Yes."

"Is the new baby going to die?"

"Yes."

"Can I come with you?" the girl asked.[84]

As Rich and Saul's bedroom becomes a hospice room, we eavesdrop on two volunteer workers for an AIDS hotline who must allay the concerns of others without ever being able to solve their own. Legitimate cases fight for time with hysteria calls and hate calls—not to mention people who are merely lonely—while their listeners cope with problems ranging from lost lovers to ungrateful patients.

One such ingrate is Rich, who responds to such varied AIDS-related phenomena as Chet's death and an orderly's demand for extra pay to clean his room,[85] by being as difficult a patient as possible. In a quieter mood, Rich recalls the heartbreak of growing up homosexual in a society that regarded him as sick, sinful, or just invisible—so desperate to discover people like himself that he searched for them in the indexes of books under 'H'.[86] But now—before the disease struck—his life seemed to be coming together: "I wrote a lot of poetry and the catering was booming and the *New Yorker* published a story of mine and I ran in the Marathon. I was on a roll. . . . The next morning I woke up with the flu and stayed in bed for a couple of days and felt much better. But my throat stayed a little sore and my glands were a little swollen." (*As Is*, 58–59)

More than anything, Rich feels betrayed. Raised in a strong Catholic family, he had come to feel, because of his fulfilled life, that God did not hate him for what he was. The onset of the disease does not so much destroy his religious faith as it does his hard-earned self-acceptance. Sending Saul out to Christopher Street to buy "downers" for a suicide attempt, Rich faces his brother—determined to be the rejector before he can be rejected: "Say, have heard about the miracle of AIDS? . . . It can turn a fruit into a vegetable. . . . [*Making the sign of the cross over his brother, chanting*] I hereby exonerate you of the sin of being ashamed of your queer brother and being a coward in the face of—" (*As Is*, 62–63)

To Rich's surprise, his brother dissolves into tears and embraces him, as guilty and unhappy over the alienation between them as Rich has been. He makes plans to return the next day, bringing with him Rich's favorite niece—the only one in the family to combine his love of poetry and sports.

Saul also returns, having purchased and then thrown away drugs—not only for Rich's suicide, but for his own. He tells of standing in the rain in front of the neon light in the window of a Greenwich Village sex shop: "Don't you see, I just don't have the right to take your life or mine. Maybe I'm being selfish, but I want you here. I need you. . . . I'll take you as is." (*As Is*, 71–72)

As the play comes to an end, it leaves many questions without answers. Some of them, such as the fate of its characters, are personal. Some of them, such as the continued lack of funding for AIDS research, are political. It is hard to understand, sometimes, that the two are often perceived as separate. In an earlier era, Ralph Waldo Emerson urged Americans to have the courage to be themselves: "To believe your own thought, to believe that what is true for you in your private heart is true for all men—that is genius."[87]

Like many another minority, homosexuals—AIDS victims or not—are part of a system that often fails to see their needs as part of the general welfare, perceiving their individuality rather as evidence of their unwillingness to conform to accepted standards. Hegemonic changes come slowly and are accompanied by much backsliding, but they can only begin when those within the minority demand to be accepted according to their own definition.

It is fitting that we should last see Rich and Saul in the act of love as the curtain is closed around Rich's bed. It is also fitting that the last word should go to hospice worker we met at the beginning. We too have lost some of our "idealism," our need for "dramatic deathbed conversions," and have gained a joy in letting others be what they are: "The other night, Jean-Jacques—he's this real 'queen'—there's no other word for it—he told me what he missed most in the hospital is his corset and high heels. I mean he weighs all of 90 pounds and he's half dead. . . . Last night I painted his nails for him. Flaming red. He loved it." (*As Is*, 77)

Notes

1. Quoted by Dinah Leavitt, in *Feminist Theatre Groups* (Jefferson, N.C.: McFarland, 1980), 11.

2. Sue-Ellen Case, *Feminism and Theatre* (New York: Methuen, 1988), 55.

3. Michele Wender Zak and Patricia A. Moots, *Women and the Politics of Culture* (New York: Longman, 1983), 9.

4. Elise Boulding, "Familial Constraints on Woman's Work Roles," in *Women and the Politics of Culture*, ed. Michele Wender Zak and Patricia A. Moots (New York: Longman, 1983), 199–201.

5. Jeffrey Weeks, "Capitalism and the Organization of Sex," in *Homosexuality: Power and Politics*, ed. Gay Left Collective (London: Allison and Busby, 1980), 15.

6. Ruth Messinger, "Feminization of Poverty Is Detailed in Report," *Nation's Cities Weekly* 7 (November 12, 1984): 7.

7. Robert J. Samuelson, "The Myths of Comparable Worth," *Newsweek*, April 22, 1985, p. 57.

8. Linda R. Woodhouse, "Report on Comparable Worth Issue," *Nation's Cities Weekly* 7 (October 1, 1984): 5.

9. Nazife Bashar, "Rape in England Between 1500 and 1700," in *The Sexual Dynamics of History*, ed. London Feminist History Group (London: Pluto Press, 1983), 30.

10. Barbara Lorman, "Capitol Comments," *Whitewater* (Wisconsin) *Register*, November 25, 1982, n.p.

11. Author's interview with Nancy Gilpatrick, Phoenix Institute (Salt Lake City, Utah), August 1983.

12. Frances Summerell Hinchey, "Parenting and Behavioral Patterns in Mothers from Violent Homes" (Ph.D. dissertation, Department of Educational Psychology, University of Utah, 1982), 6–9.

13. George and Barbara Beard Henderson, *Mending Broken Children* (Springfield, Ill.: Charles C. Thomas, 1984), 36.

14. Jo Freeman, "The Origins of the Movement," in *Women and the Politics of Culture*, ed. Michele Wender Zak and Patricia A. Moots (New York: Longman, 1983), 401.

15. Adrienne Rich, *Of Woman Born: Mother hood as Experience and Institution* (New York: W. W. Norton, 1986), 218.

16. Case, *Feminism and Theater*, 76.

17. Quoted by Leavitt, *Feminist Theatre Groups*, 10.

18. Quoted by Elizabeth J. Natalie, *Feminist Theatre: A Study in Persuasion* (Metuchen, N.J.: Scarecrow Press, 1985), 11.

19. Kathleen Betsko and Rachel Koenig, "Megan Terry," in *Interviews with Contemporary Women Playwrights* (New York: William Morrow, 1987), 399.

20. Marsha Norman, *Getting Out* (New York: Avon Books, 1980), Preface, 5. Subsequent references to this play will be listed in the text.

21. Nancy Friday, *My Mother/My Self* (New York: Dell Publishing Co., 1977), 27.

22. Messinger, "Feminization of Poverty," 7.

23. Ellen Goodman, "Domestic Violence Transcends Politics," *Janesville* (Wisconsin) *Gazette*, July 16, 1985, p. 6A.

24. Sheila Jeffreys, "Sex Reform and Anti-Feminism in the 1920's," *The Sexual Dynamics of History*, ed. London Feminist History Group (London: Pluto Press, 1983), 177–78.

25. Quoted by Jill Smolowe, "A Global Feminist Critique," *Time*, July 22, 1985, 44.

26. Susan Glaspell, *Trifles*, in *Plays by American Women: 1900–1930*, ed. Judith E. Barlow (New York: Applause Theatre Book Publishers, 1985), 84.

27. Mary Burrill, *They That Sit in Darkness*, in *Black Theater U.S.A.*, ed. James V. Hatch and Ted Shine (New York: Free Press, 1974), 182.

28. Barlow, *Plays by American Women*, xxviii–xxix.

29. Judith Olauson, *The American Woman Playwright: A View of Criticism and Characterization* (Troy, N.Y.: Whitson Publishing Co., 1981), 59.

30. Beah Richards, *A Black Woman Speaks*, in *Nine Plays by Black Women*, ed. Margaret B. Wilkerson (New York: New American Library, 1986), 34–35.

31. Jane Chambers, *A Late Snow* (New York: JH Press, 1989), I, 46. Other references to the play will be noted in the text.

32. Quoted by Wilkerson, *Nine Plays by Black Women*, 136.

33. Aishah Rahman, *Unfinished Women Cry in No Man's Land While a Bird Dies in a Gilded Cage*, in *Nine Plays by Black Women*, ed. Margaret Wilkerson (New York: New American Library, 1986), vi, 221.

34. Ntozake Shange, *for colored girls who have considered suicide/when the rainbow is enuf* (New York: Macmillan, 1977), 51.

35. Denis Altman, *The Homosexualization of America, the Americanization of the Homosexual* (New York: St. Martin's Press, 1982), 9.

36. Michael Bronski, *Culture Clash: The Making of a Gay Sensibility* (Boston: South End Press, 1984), 21.

37. For homosexual and bisexual contributions to civilization, see Jim Kepner's *Becoming a People: A 4,000-Year Gay and Lesbian Chronology* (Hollywood: National Gay Archives, 1983). For an example of the special roles allotted homosexuals in certain cultures, see the accounts of the Native American *berdache* in Jonathan Katz's *Gay American History* (New York: Thomas Y. Crowell, 1976), 281–334.

38. Quoted by Ruth Simpson, *From the Closet to the Courts* (New York: Viking Press, 1976), 59.

39. Readers interested in the interpretations of biblical references to homosexuality are referred to Derrick Sherwin Bailey's *Homosexuality and the Western Christian Tradition* (Hamden, Conn.: Archon Books, 1975) and John Boswell's *Christianity, Social Tolerance, and Homosexuality* (Chicago: University of Chicago Press, 1980).

40. K. Boyd, "Homosexuality and the Church," in *Understanding Homosexuality*, ed. J. A. Loraine (New York: American Elsevier Publishing Co., 1974), 171.

41. Ruth Simpson believes the Catholic Church "must fight changes in attitude toward the church-state laws on homosexuality (or: abortion, divorce, prostitution, gambling) or it will lose its moral credibility. But the vigilance of the Church against sexual law reform [has] another basis—the carefully guarded tax-exempt status of the Church." Simpson, *From the Closet to the Courts*, 60–61.

42. Bronski, *Culture Clash*, 15.

43. For the history of legal penalties for homosexuality in the United States, see Katz, *Gay American History*, 11–128, and "Lesbians and the Law," in *Our Right to Love*, ed. Ginna Vida (New York: National Gay Task Force, 1978), 196–219. For the jobs from which homosexuals are excluded by state laws, see Simpson, "Lesbians and the Courts of Justice," in *From the Closet to the Courts*, 178–80. For a defense of society's right to punish homosexual acts, see N. H. Fairbairn, "Homosexuality and the Law," in *Understanding Homosexuality*, ed. J. A. Loraine (New York: American Elsevier Publishing Co., 1974), 160–64.

44. Katz, *Gay American History*, 129–207.

45. Katz, *Gay American History*, 385.

46. Toby Marotta, *The Politics of Homosexuality* (Boston: Houghton Mifflin, 1981), 9–16.

47. Arthur Miller, *The Crucible* (New York: Penguin Books, 1981), 7.

48. Katz, *Gay American History*, 95.

49. Katz, *Gay American History*, 101–5.

50. In 1987 Leonard Matlovich died of AIDS.

51. Altman, Homosexualization of America, 26.

52. Ron Miller and Glenn Lovell, "AIDS Blacklist Started," (Salt Lake City) *Deseret News*, August 10, 1985, p. 7D.

53. James Michner, *Kent State: What Happened and Why* (New York: Random House, 1971), 404, 406.

54. Peter Weiss, *The Persecution and Assassination of Jean Paul Marat as performed by the Inmates of the Asylum of Charenton under the Direction of the Marquis de Sade* (New York: Atheneum, 1975), xxx, 93.

55. A factor in the decision of women and gays to form their own groups was that the combating of patriarchy and homophobia had no priority in the "revolutionary" policy of the black and New Left organizations of the sixties.

56. Marotta, *Politics of Homosexuality*, 71–72.

57. Marotta, *Politics of Homosexuality*, x.

58. Altman, *Homoesexualization of America*, 131–32.

59. Barbara Sinclair Deckard, *The Women's Movement* (New York: Harper & Row, 1983), 340–43.

60. Kepner, *Becoming a People*, 74–79. The 1986 Supreme Court upholding of the Georgia antisodomy law in 1986 suggests such gains are tenuous.

61. Bronski, *Culture Clash*, 197.

62. Lorraine Hansberry, *The Sign in Sidney Brustein's Window*, in *"A Raisin in the Sun" and "The Sign in Sidney Brustein's Window"* (New York: Signet Books, 1966), I, ii, 247–48.

63. Richard Hall, "Gay Theater: Notes from a Diary," in *Three Plays for a Gay Theater* (San Francisco: Grey Fox Press, 1983), 167.

64. Jonathan Katz, *Coming Out! A Documentary Play About Gay Life and Liberation in the U.S.A.* (New York: Arno Press, 1975), II, 53.

65. Emily Mann, *Execution of Justice*, in *The Best Plays of 1985–1986*, ed. Otis L. Guernsey, Jr., and Jeffrey Sweet (New York: Dodd, Mead, 1987), II, 242.

66. Hall, "Gay Theater," 174.

67. Paul Goodman, "Notes from a Journal," in *Nature Heals: Psychological Essays*, ed. Taylor Stoehr (New York: Free Life Editions, 1977), 246.

68. "AIDS a Leading Killer by '91," *Denver Post*, June 13, 1986, p. 1A.

69. David Black, "The Plague Years," Part 1, *Rolling Stone*, March 23, 1985, 50.

70. John Lee et al., "The Real Epidemic: Fear and Despair," *Time* 122 (July 4, 1983): 56.

71. Charles Krauthammer, "The Politics of a Plague," *The New Republic*, August 1, 1983, 20.

72. Andrew Britton, "AIDS–Apocalyptic Metaphor," *The New Statesman* 109 (March 15, 1985): 24.

73. Lance Morrow, "The Start of a Plague Mentality," *Time* 126 (September 23, 1985): 92.

74. Krauthammer, "Politics of a Plague," 21.

75. Paul Selig, Introduction, *Terminal Bar*, in *Gay Plays*, Vol. 3, ed. Michael Wilcox (London: Methuen, 1988), 39.

76. "AIDS and Theatre in the Blood," *Callboard* 13, no. 5 (May 1988): 10.

77. William A. Henry III, "A Common Bond of Suffering," *Time* 125 (May 13, 1985): 85.

78. David Black, "The Plague Years," Part 2, *Rolling Stone*, April 25, 1985, 41.

79. Henry, "Common Bond of Suffering," 85.

80. William H. Hoffmann, *As Is* (New York: Random House, 1985), 58. Other references to the play are noted in the text.

81. David Black describes two spontaneous manifestations of homophobia which shed light on Rich's reaction. In the first, a committed radical friend became angry after comparing the vast number of sexual encounters experienced by the average AIDS victim with his own relatively few conquests. In the second, Black found himself yelling "faggot" at a man who had harassed him in the midst of a Gay Health Conference anti-AIDS display. Black, "The Plague Years," Part 1, 49–51.

82. Tom Morganthau et al., "Gay America in Transition," *Newsweek* 102 (August 8, 1983): 30.

83. Black, "The Plague Years," Part 2, 43.

84. Black, "The Plague Years," Part 2, 58.

85. Such demands are far from unusual. See, for example, Lee, "The Real Epidemic," 56.

86. Actual examples of homosexuals who searched for others of their kind in book indexes include New York judge Richard Failla (Vincent Coppola et al., "Coming Out of the Closet," *Newsweek* 102 [August 8, 1983]: 34) and New York Daughters of Bilitis founder Barbara Gittings (Katz, *Gay American History*, 421).

87. Ralph Waldo Emerson, "An Original Relation to the Universe," *Emerson: A Modern Anthology*, ed. by Alfred Kazin and Daniel Aaron (Boston: Houghton Mifflin, 1958), 99.

8

Looking Ahead: Political Themes in the American Drama of the 1990s

History is cyclical. Back in 1924, Arthur Schlesinger, Sr., analyzed the periods of public and private focus which have alternated throughout America's existence, and determined that conservative (nationalistic/capitalistic/individualistic) eras have always followed liberal (international/labor-emphasizing/communal) eras, and vice versa. Schlesinger made further studies of the cycle theory in 1939 and 1949, predicting that the current conservative (private) focus which he saw as having begun in 1947 would continue until 1962, to be followed by a liberal (public) focus until 1978, and a new conservatism thereafter. His son, Arthur Schlesinger, Jr., picked up the thread in the mid-1980s. "If the . . . rhythm holds, then the 1980s will witness the burnout of the most conservative ascendancy, and the age of Reagan, like its earlier versions in the 1950s, 1920s, and 1890s, will fade into historical memory."[1]

Given that the one predictable factor about an audience is its desire to see its own interests represented onstage, characters who question public policy should experience a resurgence in the 1990s. However, their concerns may be somewhat different than in the past. As we have seen, politics on the stage is 95 percent invisible because the principles manifested have hegemony with the audience, that is, they reflect the audience's values. Recognizable political theatre occurs when the American norm (political/economic/social system) is depicted as unjust or destructive. This has usually been a reaction to our use of the "Devil theory" for purposes of empowerment. Institutionalized injustice in the

United States (as elsewhere) is usually presented as a way of combatting a demonic threat to a divinely conceived order. Thus, the persecution of our own citizens during the Cold War was "necessary" to counter a Communist subversion which, if unchecked, would betray America into the hands of an ideology whose godlessness and abhorrence of individualism was a direct challenge to the Divinity that shapes our ends. Thus, the racial and sexual apartheid which was the rule of law in the United States throughout much of its history had its roots in an economic system and its justification in the Book of Genesis. Historically, inequities of both class and caste have been disguised as articles of faith.

The face of the Devil may be harder to recognize in the decade to come. As these words are being written in late 1989, Alexander Dubcek has just returned to an overjoyed Prague, having been "rehabilitated" for the crime of premature *glasnost*. Hungary has declared itself a "bourgeois democracy," Poland is striving to find a role for the Communist Party in its government, and both East and West are contemplating (with some uneasiness) the prospect of a reunified Germany. Furthermore, the architect of this democratic/capitalist outbreak is America's designated Antichrist, the general secretary of the U.S.S.R.'s Communist Party. The duration of this Cold War *chinook* is as unpredictable as its onset. (A year ago we might have seen China as the most likely candidate for such a breakthrough.) Still, the announced goal of Russian foreign policy—to deny the United States an enemy—has been taken seriously enough for the secretary of defense to consider budget cuts of $180 billion over the next six years.

It is also possible that such caste demons as the mark of Cain, the sin of Eve, and the curse of Sodom may be in remission. In the 1989 elections, Virginia elected as the nation's first black governor a political insider whose bread-and-butter issue was a prochoice abortion stance. (Ironically, what appeared in early summer to be fatal Supreme Court weakening of *Roe vs. Wade* proved in autumn to be a rallying point for a prochoice backlash.) In mayoral races, a black candidate's victory in New York derived from the hope that he would heal racial divisiveness, not exploit it. In largely white Seattle, a white aspirant who ran an antibusing campaign lost to a black. In Cleveland, both candidates were black.[2]

Gender and religion also proved to be powerful crossover issues as the eighties came to an end. Even as a prochoice stance regained mainstream viability for the first time in a decade, the 101st Congress for the first time seriously considered child care legislation. Although a proposal to grant benefits to registered partners of gay city employees in San

Francisco was narrowly defeated, one Lutheran church in that city voted overwhelmingly to install a lesbian couple as assistant pastors. The United Church of Christ ordained its first avowedly homosexual clergyman in 1972. National Methodist and Presbyterian groups are reconsidering their stands on homosexuality. It was recently estimated that at least one in every ten Catholic priests is gay.[3] Women priests are no longer a rarity among the Episcopals. The Latter-Day Saints, which granted the priesthood to black men as recently as 1978, are now experiencing pressure within their own ranks to grant it to women.

Unfortunately, those who might deduce from the above facts that the resurging social sensitivity of the nineties will lack for subject matter are mistaken. Social inequities categorizable by class and caste will continue to exist, but they may be more difficult to disguise under the definitions of national security and divine plan as we have known them in the past. The key will be an economics which will be unmeasurable in money or gross national product, because neither of these terms takes into account the finite nature of the resources—including space, water, and air—with which we must work. The following are a set of worst-case scenarios which political theatre might have to combat or hopefully, might be able to prevent.

The gap between the rich and the poor (already roughly where it was at the beginning of the Depression) could widen as the defense industry joins already-declining domestic heavy industries. New employment opportunities will be largely in the service sector, whose traditionally lower pay scale deriving from its history as unorganized labor staffed by the young and the lower-caste (women, racial minorities, etc.) will make it impossible for even full-time workers to stay above the poverty line. The second-generation homeless will join the second-generation unemployed as a permanent underclass.

As America's defense requirements decline, industry will pressure government (and government will pressure other countries) to increase international arms shipments in the name of foreign aid. In order to influence other governments to adopt policies favorable to the U.S. economy, more of the American worldwide military presence will be engaged in covert action (or in the training of pro-U.S. "liberation forces"). To avoid congressional oversight committee interference with such actions, intelligence agencies will finance their agendas through the importation of drugs, at the same time as the military takes a more and more active part in drug warfare. The end result will be a Grenada-style border war in a Latin American country over a drug operation in which factions of our government will find themselves on both sides.

Elected officials who require more and more campaign funding to stay in office will become more indebted (to be repaid legislatively) to corporations and entities who can finance those campaigns. Thus, state and federal governments will find more innovative ways of lowering taxes for the rich, justifying these cuts on the grounds that the reinvestment of the savings will energize the economy for everyone. However, as the business of American business becomes less and less the making of products and more and more the paying of dividends, the money saved will be used to manipulate the stock market into registering values which do not reflect real worth, eventually producing a crash all the more sustained because of government attempts to delay it. At the same time, as the tax base shrinks, school systems and the infrastructure will decline, leading to privatization for those who can afford it—a whole new basis upon which to build a class war.

Technology (which will be depicted as the savior of the American life-style) will aid the economy at the risk of the environment. As the single-family farm vanishes, corporation farming will chemically increase production by depleting soil reserves on the best land, while collecting huge government subsides from inferior land withheld from production in the name of conservation. Meanwhile, multinational corporations will continue to strip the world of its natural resources for U.S. consumption, an act which will further cripple our economy by increasing international indebtedness and the percentage of our national income required to pay debt interest. In order to meet debts owed to U.S. banks, Third World countries will exploit their cheap labor in order to compete with our industry, and strip their forest land, thus hastening the greenhouse effect. Business will experience a temporary stimulus by the sale of pesticides and fertilizers to these countries, increasing their short-term production at the cost of long-term soil damage. To meet such immediate competitions, we will find it necessary to nationalize those mineral and water resources still under the control of Native Americans, who by an act of incorporation we will make full American citizens with all of the rights and none of the special privileges such an honor implies.

As fossil fuels decline in volume and air pollution levels increase, nuclear reactor proposals will surface again. The resulting waste will threaten wilderness areas already endangered by developers who want its resources and those who would exploit its tourist potential. To avoid the regional political costs of such a threat, we will trade our economic and military support of developing nations for the right to establish waste dumps, thus making radioactive pollution an international problem while contributing to the genocide of those nation's intransigent indigenous peoples.

However, the most insidious technological danger of the nineties will not be the nuclear holocaust which has been our forty-year nightmare, but rather the seeming life-affirmation of birth technology. Under the guise of promising children for the infertile and eliminating the heartbreak of physical handicaps, a "brave new world" mentality could create a new division between the technologically enhanced children of the rich, who bear all of the socially favored caste marks, and the children whose physiological diversity will be a sign of their parents' caste and class. The two terms will become—except for historical reference—one, as declining world resources increase their impact on the nation's economic range. Alternatively, birthing choices could become a government function, as it already is in China, but the economic and political pressure wielded by the manufacturers and recipients of this technology (assisted by some religious factions and appeals to American "individualism") make this unlikely.

The possibility of all of these scenarios coming to pass is, of course, nil. Nevertheless, plans which could result in some of them are already in effect, and a few plays which anticipate them have already been written. The pleasure of playing Cassandra, one of the earliest characters in Western drama, is guaranteed: vindication if one is right or relief if one is wrong. Rightly or wrongly, no look forward would be complete without the suggestion of subjects which may inspire future playwrights.

The courtroom trial play will continue to be a political theatre staple because of its ability to focus in on issues of guilt and innocence, as will the congressional hearing. However, such hearings will not be pure docudramas, as they must often examine the motives of the congressmen themselves. In a situation like that of the "Keating Five" savings and loan case, elected representatives must study their own ambivalence when a positive attempt to preserve constituent jobs is also a favor to a heavy political contributor.

The political musical will make a comeback all over the country, in the form of narrative monologues based upon interviews with the homeless, using as their model the musical version of Studs Terkel's *Working*. A TV situation comedy set in a homeless shelter, with an unemployed writer as a central character, will attempt to become the "M*A*S*H" of the nineties. Broadway will see an epic musical on the scale of *Les Misérables* closely replicating the Oliver Stone film *Wall Street*, the morality play of an economic Everyman.

History plays will re-create past American foreign policy/military adventures as a means of providing insight into our current problems. Plays depicting the CIA-engineered overthrows of the governments of Iran in 1953 and Guatamala in 1954 will join studies of more recent events, such as Keith Raddin's *Rum and Coke*, about the 1961 Bay of Pigs invasion, Rafael Lima's *El Salvador*, Larry Gelbart's *Mastergate*, and Aaron Sorkin's *A Few Good Men*.[4] Such dramas need not be purely realistic. The belief that we are the victim of our hubris will culminate in the presentation of a Frankenstein myth which will bear a close resemblance to the career of Manuel Noriega.

Frankenstein will vie with Faust as the negative extreme of America's never-temperate affair with technology reasserts itself. As the fear of nuclear holocaust investigated in such eighties plays as JoAnne Akalaitis's *Dead End Kids*,[5] Arthur Kopit's *The End of the World*,[6] Lee Blessing's *A Walk in the Woods*,[7] and Connie Congdon's *No Mercy*[8] subsides, new issues will arise. Among them will be nuclear waste, as in Bruce Dale's *White Mountains*,[9] and in vitro fertilization, as in Australian playwright Sandra Shotlander's *Angels of Power*. Our belief in the quick fix will be pilloried in a play in which an ex-soldier guilty over his abandonment of Saigon in 1975 attempts a Peace Corps "green revolution" in an emerging nation and succeeds only in destroying the methods which kept the natives alive for thousands of years.

Nor will history plays be limited to foreign policy. To David Feldshuh's recent treatment of the "Tuskegee Experiment" (a 1942–1972 study in which black syphilis sufferers were denied penicillin in order to chart the development of the disease) will be added other dramatizations of blatant historical discrimination against minorities, for example, a play about the court martial of the black soldiers involved in the "Brownsville Massacre" in 1906 Texas. Luis Valdez will return to his dramatic beginnings with a biographical treatment of Cesar Chavez, which will not only stress the' Chicano economic struggle but will reveal the farm workers' movement as an attempt to assert the legitimacy of cultural diversity. A television miniseries will also present a revisionist view of American history by showing us the Battle of the Alamo from three points of view—those of the United States, Texas, *and* Mexico. The battle itself will be the climax of the final evening, with the larger part of the airtime devoted to the political machinations which brought it about. It will end with a trailer showing the fate of the Mexican War architects and the ideals they represented.

JoAnne Akalaitis's *Green Card*[10] will be the first of many attempts to deal with the difficulties faced by immigrants, as the 1986 Reform and

Control Act proves to be an inadequate answer to the foreign influx. As further limitations in school funding provide an economic justification for immigration limitations (as well as for a constitutional amendment designating English as the official U.S. language), a countering docudrama using actual transcripts of government deliberation and case histories will make most of America aware of Depression-era Hispanic repatriation for the first time.

Ecology will combine with caste as docudramas again examine the treaty circumstances during which the Native Americans were deprived of their land. This time, however, the focus will not be on the injustices suffered by the Indian, but rather on the danger to the land in the passage from a human culture which saw it as a being as alive as itself to one which sees it only as a thing to be exploited. The importance of Afro-American culture to American survival will also be examined. Black rhythm and physical expressiveness, frequently denigrated in the past as a contributor to racial stereotypes, will be celebrated as essential to a healthy personality. Following the premise set forward in sociologists Alfred Pasteur and Ivory Toldson's *Roots of Soul*,[11] adoption of the Afro-American ability to unite cognitive, affective, and psychomotor activities may prove to be the salvation of Western civilization.

A *Heidi Chronicles*-style play on the breakdown of a "superwoman" will dramatize the mistake of the feminist movement in calling for "equality" with men, when what was needed was the right to be judged honestly as a woman, by values that were applicable only to women and that were given the credibility of those used to judge men. "Generations" plays will appear in which older women, reliving the moment in which they were diverted into making choices for the good of mankind, or the movement, or another person, will support the right of younger women to choose their true destinies.

As the third millennium after Christ approaches, it may well be that the salvation of the United States lies not in the rethinking of American principles but in fully applying their freedoms for the first time. It is possible that what appeared for much of the century to be class and caste challenges to American hegemony was only the evolutionary upheaval of its renewal. It may be that our ideal is Proteus rather than Zeus, and that the demands of racial, cultural, and sexual diversity are the birth cries of a new nation, not the death rattle of an old one. If our society can demonstrate its vitality as a living organism by growing and changing in harmony with the environment which provides its sustenance, perhaps we will find that both heal themselves—manifestations of a Gaia principle in which ecology, politics, and art are but elements in the service of survival.

Notes

1. Arthur M. Schlesinger, Jr., *The Cycles of American History* (Boston: Houghton Mifflin, 1986), 45.

2. Laurence L. Barrett and Don Winbush, "Breakthrough in Virginia," *Time* 134, no. 21 (November 20, 1989): 55–57.

3. Richard M. Ostling, "The Battle over Gay Clergy," *Time* 134, no. 20 (November 13, 1989): 89–90.

4. Keith Reddin, *Rum and Coke* (New York: Broadway Play Publishing, 1986). Plays named but not documented are not yet in publication.

5. JoAnne Akalaitis, *Dead End Kids*, in *Theater* 12, no. 3 (Summer/Fall 1981).

6. Arthur Kopit, *The End of the World* (New York: Hill and Wang, 1984).

7. Lee Blessing, *A Walk in the Woods* (New York: Dramatists Play Service, 1988).

8. Connie Congdon, *No Mercy*, in *Seven Different Plays* (New York: Broadway Play Publishing, 1987).

9. Bruce Dale, *White Mountains*, in *Women with Guns: Six New American Plays* (New York: Broadway Play Publishing, 1985).

10. JoAnne Akalaitis, *Green Card*, in *Theater* 18, no. 2 (Spring 1987).

11. Alfred B. Pasteur and Ivory L. Toldson, *Roots of Soul* (Garden City, N.Y.: Anchor Press, 1982), 45–46.

Appendix A: Milestones in American Political Drama since the 1930s

I. **The Great Depression**

    A. The Decline of the Rugged Individualist

        1931: <u>1931--</u> (Claire and Paul Sifton)

        1933: <u>Both Your Houses</u> (Maxwell Anderson)

        1935: <u>Dead End</u> (Sidney Kingsley)

               <u>The Petrified Forest</u> (Robert E. Sherwood)

    B. The Rise of the Collective Hero

        1931: <u>Can You Hear Their Voices?</u> (Hallie Flanagan and Margaret Ellen Clifford)

        1934: <u>Stevedore</u> (Paul Peters and George Sklar)

        1935: <u>Waiting For Lefty</u> (Clifford Odets)

    C. The Government Takes Responsibility

        1936: <u>Triple-A Plowed Under</u> (Staff of the Living Newspaper)

        1937: <u>Power</u> (Arthur Arent)

               <u>One-Third of a Nation</u> (Arthur Arent)

        1938: <u>Spirochete</u> (Arnold Sundgaard)

II. **World War II**

    A. The Antiwar Drama

1932: Men Must Fight (Reginald Lawrence and S. K. Laurens)

1933: Peace on Earth (George Sklar and Albert Maltz)

1935: If This Be Treason (John Haynes Holmes and Reginald Lawrence)

1936: Johnny Johnson (Paul Green and Kurt Weill)

      Bury The Dead (Irwin Shaw)

      Idiot's Delight (Robert E. Sherwood)

1937: The Ghost of Yankee Doodle (Sidney Howard)

B. The Interventionists

1934: Judgement Day (Elmer Rice)

1935: Til the Day I Die (Clifford Odets)

1937: It Can't Happen Here (Sinclair Lewis and John Moffit)

1939: Key Largo (Maxwell Anderson)

1940: Flight to the West (Elmer Rice)

1941: Watch on the Rhine (Lillian Hellman)

C. America and Post-war Racism

1945: Deep Are the Roots (Arnaud d'Usseau and James Gow)

1946: Home of the Brave (Arthur Laurents)

      Jeb (Robert Ardrey)

III. The Cold War

A. Anti-Communist Plays

1947: The Traitor (Herman Wouk)

1950: Darkness at Noon (Sidney Kingsley)

1951: Barefoot in Athens (Maxwell Anderson)

1955: Time Limit (Henry Denker and Ralph Berkey)

B. Hidden Protests

1952: <u>Slaughter of the Innocents</u> (William Saroyan)

1953: <u>Tea and Sympathy</u> (Robert Anderson)

1954: <u>Sing Me No Lullaby</u> (Robert Ardrey)

1955: <u>Inherit the Wind</u> (Jerome Lawrence and Robert E. Lee)

C. Cold War Autopsy

   1964: <u>In the Matter of J. Robert Oppenheimar</u> (Heinar Kipphardt)

   1970: <u>Inquest</u> (Donald Freed)

   1972: <u>Are You Now or Have You Ever Been</u> (Eric Bentley)

IV. **Vietnam**

A. Early Prowar Films

   1957: <u>China Gate</u> (Samuel Fuller)

   1958: <u>The Quiet American</u> (Joseph Mankiewicz)

   1963: <u>The Ugly American</u> (George Englund)

   1967: <u>The Green Berets</u> (John Wayne)

B. The Critics' Corner

   1966: <u>Viet Rock</u> (Megan Terry)

   1968: <u>We Bombed in New Haven</u> (Joseph Heller)

   1969: <u>The Trial of the Catonsville Nine</u> (Daniel Berrigan)

   1970: <u>Vietnam Campesino</u> (Luis Valdez)

C. The Endless Epilogue

   1971: <u>Sticks and Bones</u> (David Rabe)

   1975: <u>Medal of Honor Rag</u> (Tom Cole)

   1980: <u>Still Life</u> (Emily Mann)

   1982: <u>Strange Snow</u> (Stephen Metcalfe)

V. **Civil Rights**

A. Black History Plays

1930: Nat Turner (Randolph Edmonds)

1938: Don't You Want to Be Free? (Langston Hughes)

1954: In Splendid Error (William Branch)

1963: In White America (Martin Duberman)

       A Land Beyond the River (Loften Mitchell)

1968: El Hajj Malik (N. B. Davidson)

       The Rise (Charles Fuller)

1969: Slave Ship (Amiri Baraka)

1977: The Motion of History (Amiri Baraka)

1978: Paul Robeson (Philip Hayes Dean)

B. Black Revolutionary Plays

1964: Blues For Mr. Charlie (James Baldwin)

       Dutchman (LeRoi Jones)

       The Slave (LeRoi Jones)

1969: The Gentleman Caller (Ed Bullins)

       The Death of Malcolm X (LeRoi Jones)

1970: Black Terror (Richard Wesley)

C. The Postrevolutionary Black Blues

1969: No Place to Be Somebody (Charles Gordone)

1975: The First Breeze of Summer (Leslie Lee)

1976: The Mighty Gents (Richard Wesley)

1982: A Soldier's Play (Charles Fuller)

VI. The Children of Civil Rights I--Race

A. The Chicanos

1965: Las dos caros del patroncito (Luis Valdez)

1979: Zoot Suit (Luis Valdez)

1980: Many Deaths of Danny Rosales (Carlos Morton)

B. The Native Americans

1936: The Cherokee Night (Lynn Riggs)

1968: Indians (Arthur Kopit)

1972: Body Indian (Hanay Geiogamah)

1975: Night Walker (Hanay Geiogamah)

1976: Black Elk Speaks (Christopher Sergel)

VII. **The Children of Civil Rights II--Gender**

   A. Women

1944: Pick Up Girl (Elsa Shelley)

1950: A Black Woman Speaks (Beah Richards)

1953: A Trap Is a Small Place (Marjean Perry)

1955: Trouble in Mind (Alice Childress)

1960: The Drinking Gourd (Lorraine Hansberry)

1966: Wedding Band (Alice Childress)

1969: Wine in the Wilderness (Alice Childress)

1970: The Independent Female (Joan Holden)

1974: American King's English for Queens (Megan Terry)

      A Late Snow (Jane Chambers)

1976: for colored girls who have considered suicide/

      when the rainbow is enuf (Ntozake Shange)

1977: River Journal (Martha Boessing)

      Unfinished Women Cry in No Man's Land, While a

      Bird Dies in a Gilded Cage (Aishah Rahman)

1978: Babes in the Bighouse (Megan Terry)

      Getting My Act Together and Taking It on the

      Road (Gretchen Cryer)

      Getting Out (Marsha Norman)

1979: spell #7 (Ntozake Shange)

1980: The Fisherman (Diane Houston)

      In the Midnight Hour (Kathleen Collins)

      Killings on the Last Line (Lavonne Mueller)

Signs of Life (Joan Shenkar)

1984:   Giving Up the Ghost (Cherrie Moraga)

B. Gays

1960:   The Best Man (Gore Vidal)

1968:   The Boys in the Band (Mart Crowley)

1975:   Coming Out! (Jonathan Katz)

1977:   Love Match (Richard Hall)

1978:   Prisoner of Love (Richard Hall)

Torch Song Trilogy (Harvey Fierstein)

1979:   Bent (Martin Sherman)

1980:   Lord Alfred's Lover (Eric Bentley)

1983:   Terminal Bar (Paul Selig)

1985:   As Is (William M. Hoffman)

Execution of Justice (Emily Mann)

The Normal Heart (Larry Kramer)

Appendix B: Annotated Bibliography of Representative Films and Videotapes

For complete documentation of the following selections and
he discovery of alternative works which might be more suitable or
eadily available, consult the source below, which can be found in
ost college, university, and public libraries.

ilm & Video Finder (1987), Volumes 1-3
ational Information Center for Educational Media
 Division of Access Innovations, Inc.
.O. Box 40130
lbuquerque, New Mexico 87196

. **The Great Depression**

   Boom and Bust (1981. 20 min. 16mm film, 3/4" or 1/2" video).
1e modern consumer society created when the mass production of
1e industrial revolution reaches the common man for the first time
s destroyed by the Depression.

   Clifford Odets (1964. 30 min. 16mm film). The author of
1iting for Lefty discusses the effect of news-media bandwagon
sychology on the creativity of the modern artist.

FDR and the New Deal (1972. 30 min. 3/4" or 1/2" video).

Herbert Hoover and Political Capitalism (1981. 30 min. 3/4" or 1/2" video). Hoover's equation of economic theory with national character is shown as his downfall.

Promise Fulfilled and the Promise Broken (1972. 26 min. 16mm film, 3/4" or 1/2" video). The unlimited prosperity promised at the end of the "War to End All Wars" is destroyed by the Depression and returns only with World War II.

Recognition of Russia: A Climate of Mutual Distrust (1978. 26 min. 16 mm film, 3/4" or 1/2" video). Relationships between the U.S. and Bolshevism (1917-1933) explain Cold War attitudes.

Rise of Labor (1969. 30 min. 3/4" or 1/2" video). Traces the growth of labor unions from Eugene V. Debs to the present.

II. World War II

Demand for a Double "V" (1969. 30 min. 16mm film). Wartime pressures encourage black leaders to try for an integration of the armed forces as a first step in a double victory over fascism abroad and racism at home.

FDR and Hitler: The Dynamics of Power (1978. 26 min. 16mm film, 3/4" or 1/2" video). Two opposing leaders build their power in the 1930s by their ability to use mass communications.

Radio, Racism, and Foreign Policy (1978. 26 min. 16mm film, 3/4" or 1/2" video). War-inspired isolationism is reflected also in racism and ethnic discrimination.

Roosevelt vs. Isolation (1965. 25 min. 16mm film, 3/4" or 1/2" video). FDR outmaneuvers pacifists and isolationists to get lend-lease and military aid to Britain and France.

Spanish Civil War (1978. 26 min. 16mm film, 3/4" or 1/2" video). Preliminary rounds of World War II are fought in Spain, with Franco's fascists being aided by Germany and Italy, while the Republican government is supported by Russia and an International Brigade (including American volunteers), although all sides pretend neutrality.

Versailles: The Lost Peace (1978. 26 min. 16mm film, 3/4" or 1/2" video). Despite President Wilson's idealistic plans, the punitive World War I treaty sows the seeds for World War II.

War Years: Fabulous 1939, Then Global Conflict (1976. 35 min. 16mm film, 3/4" or 1/2" video). Hollywood portrays German and Japanese evil while glorifying our heroes.

III. **The Cold War**

An American Ism--Joe McCarthy (1979. 84 min. 16mm film, 3/4" or 1/2" video). Archival footage and interviews with those who knew him provide a biography of Joseph McCarthy.

Arthur Miller (1982. 25 min. 3/4" or 1/2" video). Parallels dramatized scenes from The Crucible with Miller's recorded testimony before the House Un-American Activities Committee, revealing Miller's concern for personal and group freedom.

Cold War (1967. 30 min. 3/4" or 1/2" video). Early Cold War years and the attempts to ferret out Communists in America.

Communist Blueprint for Conquest. n.d. 103 min. 3/4" or 1/2" video). "The Communist Weapon of Allure/Communist Target--Youth," narrated by Robert Kennedy, illustrates how Communists work through the young to gain power.

Day After Trinity (1980. 88 min. 16mm film, 3/4" or 1/2"

video). J. Robert Oppenheimer's childhood, his rise to prominence as head of the Los Alamos A-bomb project, and his fall from grace during the McCarthy era.

Post-War Era: The Film Noir and the Hollywood Ten (1976. 20 min. 16mm film, 3/4" or 1/2" video). Films reflect the cynicism of the postwar era and the effects of the Cold War and McCarthyism on entertainment, including the arrest of the Hollywood Ten by the House Un-American Activities Committee.

Truth About Communism (n.d. 30 min. 3/4" or 1/2" video). The communist threat from its birth to Nikita Khrushchev. Introduced by Alexander Kerensky and narrated by Ronald Reagan.

IV. **Vietnam**

Accusation (1968. 20 min. 16mm film). News footage and stills of American atrocities presented at the Bertrand Russell International War Crimes Tribunal in Stockholm.

America's Disrupted Lives (n.d. 29 min. 3/4" or 1/2" video). America's treatment of Vietnam veterans, refugees, and antiwar dissenters.

Holy Outlaw (1970. 60 min. 16mm film). Daniel Berrigan's last interview before his arrest charts his political radicalization.

Kennedy and Confrontation (1981. 16 min. 16mm film, 3/4" or 1/2" video). Kennedy's reaction to Southeast Asian events in light of the Bay of Pigs, the Berlin Crisis, and the Cuban Missile Crisis.

Some to Demonstrate, Some to Destroy (1970. 23 min. 16mm film). Police preparation and actions in dealing with demonstrators during Moratorium weekend (Nov. 15, 1969).

Vietnam: A Television History (1983. 13 episodes, 60 min. each. 16mm film, 3/4" or 1/2" video). Events in Vietnam form the 1945 revolution against the French to America's April 1975 evacuation from Saigon.

Vietnam Perspective (1985. 32 min. 16mm film, 3/4" or 1/2" video). Chronology of foreign involvement in Southeast Asia.

War Within (n.d. 60 min. 3/4" or 1/2" video). Six highly decorated veterans relive nightmares of Vietnam at the Veterans Treatment Center in Menlo Park, California.

Whole World Is Watching (1972. 28 min. 16mm film). The motives of those who wanted to shut down the government during Washington's 1971 "May Day Spring Offensive".

Why Vietnam (1965. 32 min. 16mm film or 3/4" video). Lyndon Johnson, Dean Rusk, and Robert McNamara explain U.S. support in Southeast Asia.

V. Civil Rights

Afro-Americans and Radical Politics (1969. 30 min. 16mm film). Black radical politicians from Frederick Douglass to members of the American Communist Party.

America: Black and White (1982. 73 min. 3/4" or 1/2" video). Welfare, unemployment, and increased prison populations among blacks, and renewed racism among middle-class whites.

Black Family Summit (1984. 29 min. 3/4" or 1/2" video). The May 1984 conference of the NAACP and the National Urban League on strategies to aid the black family.

Black Paths of Leadership (n.d. 28 min. 16mm film, 3/4" or

1/2" video). Different paths taken by three black men--Booker T. Washington, W.E.B. DuBois, and Marcus Garvey--in fighting for black rights.

Freedom Ride (1961. 18 min. 16mm film). An integrated bus rides into the Deep South following the Supreme Court's ending of segregation in interstate transportation.

In Motion: Amiri Baraka (n.d. n.t. 3/4" or 1/2" video). The activities of the author of The Death of Malcolm X during the two weeks prior to and including his trial and conviction for resisting arrest during the 1967 Newark riots.

Interview with Bobby Seale (n.d. 15 min. 16mm film). In jail in December 1969, the Black Panther leader discusses the Black Nation, women's liberation, and the rise of U.S. fascism.

Malcolm X Speaks (1970. 44 min. 16mm film). The life and thought of Malcolm through his speeches and interviews, and the comments of those who knew him best.

Martin Luther King, Jr. (1981. 24 min. 16mm film, 3/4" or 1/2" video). Nonviolent protest and its impact on the Public Accommodations Act, the Voting Act, and the Open Housing bill.

Urbanization: The Expansion of the Ghetto (1969. 30 min. 16mm film). Effects of urbanization on black education after World War II, including the growth of the northern black population, school segregation, and the rise of the black university.

VI. The Children of Civil Rights (Chicanos and Native Americans)

All Is But a Beginning (1972. 30 min. 3/4" or 1/2" video). John G. Neihardt, author of Black Elk Speaks, talks about a recurring dream he had as a child, and how he found the spirit of

Branch, William. *In Splendid Error*, in *Black Theater*, ed. Lindsay Patterson. New York: New American Library, 1971.

Brown, William Wells. *The Escape*, in *Black Theater, U.S.A.*, ed. James V. Hatch and Ted Shine. New York: Free Press, 1974.

Bullins, Ed. *The Gentleman Caller*, in *Best Short Plays of 1970*, ed. Stanley Richards. Philadelphia: Chilton Books, 1970.

_____. *In New England Winter*, in *New Plays from the Black Theatre*, ed. Ed Bullins. New York: Bantam Books, 1969.

Burrill, Mary. *They That Sit in Darkness*, in *Black Theater*, U.S.A., ed. James V. Hatch and Ted Shine. New York: Free Press, 1974.

Chambers, Jane. *A Late Snow*. New York: JH Press, 1989.

Childress, Alice. *Trouble in Mind*, in *Black Theater*, ed. Lindsay Patterson. New York: New American Library, 1971.

_____. *Wedding Band*. New York: Samuel French, 1973.

_____. *Wine in the Wilderness*. New York: Dramatists Play Service, 1969.

Cole, Tom. *Medal of Honor Rag*, in *Coming to Terms: American Plays and the Vietnam War*. New York: Theatre Communications Group, 1985

Collins, Kathleen. *In the Midnight Hour*, in *The Women's Project: Seven New Plays by Women*, ed. Julia Miles. New York: Performing Arts Journal Publications, 1980.

Congdon, Connie. *No Mercy*, in *Seven Different Plays*. New York: Broadway Play Publishing, 1987.

Crothers, Rachel. *A Man's World*, in *Plays by American Women: 1900–1930*, ed. Judith E. Barlow. New York: Applause Theatre Book Publishers, 1985.

Cryer, Gretchen. *Getting My Act Together and Taking It on the Road*. Garden City, N.Y.: Doubleday, 1980.

Dale, Bruce. *White Mountains*, in *Women with Guns: Six New American Plays*. New York: Broadway Play Publishing, 1985.

Davidson, N. B. *El Hajj Malik*, in *New Plays from the Black Theatre*, ed. Ed Bullins. New York: Bantam Books, 1969.

Dean, Philip Hayes. *Paul Robeson*. Garden City, N.Y.: Doubleday, 1978.

Denker, Henry, and Ralph Berkey. *Time Limit*. New York: Samuel French, 1956.

Duberman, Martin. *In White America*. New York: Samuel French, 1964.

d'Usseau, Arnaud, and James Gow. *Deep Are the Roots*. New York: Random House, 1945.

Edmonds, Randolph. *Nat Turner*, in *Black Heroes: Seven Plays*, ed. Errol Hill. New York: Applause Theatre Book Publishers, 1989.

Fierstein, Harvey. *Torch Song Trilogy*. New York: Gay Presses of New York, 1979.

Flanagan, Hallie, and Margaret Ellen Clifford. *Can You Hear Their Voices*? Poughkeepsie, N.Y.: Experimental Theatre of Vassar College, 1931.

Freed, Donald. *Inquest*. New York: Hill and Wang, 1970.

Fuller, Charles. *The Rise*, in *New Plays from the Black Theatre*, ed. Ed Bullins. New York: Bantam Books, 1969.

_____. *A Soldier's Story*. New York: Hill and Wang, 1982.

Garrett, Jimmy. *And We Own the Night*. The Drama Review 12, no. 4 (Summer 1968).

Geiogamah, Hanay. *Body Indian*, in *New Native American Drama*. Norman: University of Oklahoma Press, 1980.

_____. *Night Walker*, in *New Native American Drama*. Norman: University of Oklahoma Press. 1980.

that dream expressed again in the words of Black Elk.

Chicano (1971. 23 min. 16mm film, 3/4" or 1/2" video). Shows the bias, discrimination, and oppression facing Mexican-Americans, as well as the goals and organizations of the Chicano movement.

Decision at Delano (1968. 26 min. 16mm film). In the 1966 election, Cesar Chavez leads the attempt to unionize California grape pickers.

El Teatro Campesino (1971. 61 min. 16mm film). Origins, progress, and purpose of El Teatro Campesino, from its beginnings as a support group of the Delano grape pickers.

End of the Trail: The American Plains Indian (1967. 53 min. 16mm film, 3/4" or 1/2" video). Treaties, the reservation system, and the buffalo genocide are used to take Indian land.

Last Menominee (1966. 30 min. 16mm film). When the Menomineee Indians lose reservation status, they lose hunting and fishing rights, medical facilities, and educational and employment opportunities.

Migrants 1980 (1980. 52 min. 16mm film, 3/4" or 1/2" video). NBC documents use of child labor, substandard housing, and illegal aliens among Hispanic migrant workers.

AIDS: Facts and Fears, Crisis and Controversy (n.d. n.t. 3/4" or 1/2" video). Defining AIDS, its means of contraction, misconceptions about it, and the problems faced by its victims.

American Parade: We the Women (1974. 30 min. 16mm film, 3/4" or 1/2" video). Comparing the women's rights movement of the nineteenth century with women's liberation in the 1970's.

<u>Before Stonewall: The Making of a Gay and Lesbian Community</u> (1984.   16mm film, 3/4" or 1/2" video).   Social, political, and cultural development of the gay community since the 1920s.

<u>Coming Out is Like Peeling an Onion</u> (1982.   50 min.   3/4" or 1/2" video). Seven gay men recount their experiences with friends, family, and teachers on revealing their homosexuality.

<u>Feminist Theatre</u> (n.d.   28 min.   3/4" video).   Two actresses discuss what it means to be a feminist in the theatre and the future of feminist theatre groups.

<u>Lesbian Mothers and Child Custody</u> (n.d.   58 min.   3/4" video). Lesbian mothers struggle for the custody of their children when their sexual orientation becomes the only issue in court.

<u>Mary Daly Presents Gyn/Ecology</u> (n.d.   80 min.   3/4" video). Global dimensions of atrocities against women explain the creation of a radical feminist.

<u>Pink Triangles: A Study of Prejudice Against Lesbians and Gay Men</u> (1982.   34 min.   16mm film).   The nature of discrimination against lesbians and gay men and social attitudes toward homosexuality are challenged.

<u>Sergeant Matlovich vs. the U.S. Air Force</u> (1979.   98 min. 16mm film, 3/4" or 1/2" video).   The story of Sergeant Leonard Matlovich who was drummed out of the Air Force in 1975 because of his homosexuality.   In 1988 he died of AIDS.

Bibliography

The Plays

Akalaitis, JoAnne. *Dead End Kids*. *Theater* 12, no. 3 (Summer/Fall 1981).
_____. *Green Card*. *Theater* 18, no. 2 (Spring 1987).
Alurista. *Dawn*, in *Contemporary Chicano Theatre*, ed. Roberto J. Garza. S
      Bend, Ind.: University of Notre Dame Press, 1976.
Anderson, Maxwell. *Barefoot in Athens*. New York: William Sloane, 1951.
_____. *Both Your Houses*. New York: Random House, 1933.
_____. *Key Largo*. Washington, D.C.: Anderson House, 1939.
_____. *Knickerbocker Holiday*. New York: Anderson House, 1938.
Anderson, Maxwell, and Harold Hickerson. *Gods of the Lightning*. New
      Longmans, Green, 1928.
Anderson, Robert. *Tea and Sympathy*. New York: Random House, 1953.
Ardrey, Robert. *Jeb*, in *Plays of Three Decades*. New York: Atheneum, 1968.
_____. *Sing Me No Lullaby*. New York: Dramatists Play Service, 1955.
_____. *Thunder Rock*. New York: Dramatists Play Service, 1950.
Arent, Arthur. *One-Third of a Nation*, in *Federal Theatre Plays*, ed. Pierre de
      New York: Random House, 1938.
_____. *Power*, in *Federal Theatre Plays*, ed. Pierre de Rohan. New York:
      House, 1938.
Behrman, S. N. *Rain from Heaven*. New York: Samuel French, 1936.
Bentley, Eric. *Are You Now or Have You Ever Been*. New York: Harper a
      1972.
_____. *Lord Alfred's Lover*. Toronto: Personal Library, 1981.
Berrigan, Daniel. *The Trial of the Catonsville Nine*. Toronto: Bantam Books
Blessing, Lee. *A Walk in the Woods*. New York: Dramatists Play Service, 1
Boessing, Martha. *River Journal*, in *Journeys Along the Matrix*. Minneapoli
      Press, 1978.
Boothe, Clare. *Kiss the Boys Goodbye*. New York: Random House, 1939.

Glaspell, Susan. *Trifles*, in *Plays by American Women: 1900–1930*, ed. Judith E. Barlow. New York: Applause Theatre Book Publishers, 1985.

Gordone, Charles. *No Place to Be Somebody* in *Black Theatre*, ed. Lindsay Patterson. New York: New American Library, 1971.

Green, Paul. *Johnny Johnson*. New York: Samuel French, 1971.

Grimke, Angelina. *Rachel*, in *Black Theater, U.S.A.*, ed. James V. Hatch and Ted Shine. New York: Free Press, 1974.

Hall, Richard. *Love Match* in *Three Plays for a Gay Theater*. San Francisco: Grey Fox Press, 1983.

_____. *Prisoner of Love*, in *Three Plays for a Gay Theater*. San Francisco: Grey Fox Press, 1983.

Hansberry, Lorraine. *The Drinking Gourd*, in *Les Blancs: The Collected Lost Plays of Lorraine Hansberry*, ed. Robert Nemiroff. New York: Random House, 1972.

_____. *A Raisin in the Sun*. New York: Random House, 1959.

Head, Robert. [HED]. *Kill Viet Cong. Tulane Drama Review* 10, no. 4 (Summer 1966).

Heller, Joseph. *We Bombed in New Haven*. New York: Dell Publishing Co., 1970.

Hellman, Lillian. *The Children's Hour*. New York: Dramatists Play Service, 1961.

_____. *The Searching Wind*. New York: Viking Press, 1944.

_____. *Watch on the Rhine*, in *Modern American Plays*, ed. Frederic G. Cassiday. Freeport, N.Y.: Books for Libraries Press, 1970.

Hoffman, William M. *As Is*. New York: Random House, 1985.

Holden, Joan. *The Independent Female*, in *A Century of Plays by American Women*, ed. Rachel France. New York: Richard Rosen Press, 1979.

Holmes, John Haynes, and Reginald Lawrence. *If This Be Treason*. New York: Macmillan, 1935.

Houston, Diane. *The Fishermen*, in *Center Stage*, ed. Eileen Joyce Ostrow. Oakland: Sea Urchin Press, 1981.

Howard, Sidney. *The Ghost of Yankee Doodle*. New York: Charles Scribner's Sons, 1938.

Hughes, Langston. *Don't You Want to Be Free?* in *Black Theater, U.S.A.*, ed. James V. Hatch and Ted Shine. New York: Free Press, 1974.

Jones, LeRoi [Amiri Baraka]. *The Death of Malcolm X*, in *New Plays from the Black Theatre*, ed. Ed Bullins. New York: Bantam Books, 1969.

_____. *Dutchman*, in *"Dutchman" and "The Slave."* New York: William Morrow, 1964.

_____. *The Motion of History*, in *"The Motion of History" and Other Plays*. New York: William Morrow, 1978.

_____. *The Slave*, in *"Dutchman" and "The Slave."* New York: William Morrow, 1964.

Katz, Jonathan. *Coming Out! A Documentary About Gay Life and Liberation in the U.S.A.* New York: Arno Press, 1975.

Kaufman, George S., and Moss Hart. *I'd Rather Be Right*. New York: Random House, 1937.

_____. *You Can't Take It With You*. New York: Random House, 1937.

Kingsley, Sidney. *Darkness at Noon*. New York: Samuel French, 1951.

_____. *Dead End*. New York: Random House, 1935.

Kipphardt, Heinar. *In the Matter of J. Robert Oppenheimer*. New York: Hill and Wang, 1968.

Kopit, Arthur. *The End of the World*. New York: Hill and Wang, 1984.

_____. *Indians*. New York: Hill and Wang, 1969.

Kramer, Larry. *The Normal Heart*. New York: New American Library, 1985.

Laurents, Arthur. *Home of the Brave*, in *Famous American Plays of the 1940s*, ed. Henry Hewes. New York: Dell Publishing Co., 1960.

Lawrence, Jerome, and Robert E. Lee. *Inherit the Wind*. New York: Random House, 1955.

Lawrence, Reginald, and S. K. Laurens. *Men Must Fight*. New York: Samuel French, 1933.

Lee, Leslie. *The First Breeze of Summer*. New York: Samuel French, 1975.

Lewis, Sinclair, and John Moffit. *It Can't Happen Here*. New York: Dramatists Play Service, 1938.

Macias, Ysidro R. *Martir Montezuma*, in *Contemporary Chicano Theatre*. South Bend, Ind.: University of Notre Dame Press, 1976.

_____. *The Ultimate Pendejada*, in *Contemporary Chicano Theatre*, ed. Roberto J. Garza. South Bend, Ind.: University of Notre Dame Press, 1976.

Mackey, William Wellington. *Requiem for Brother X*, in *Black Drama Anthology*, ed. Woodie King and Ron Milner. New York: New American Library, 1971.

Mann, Emily. *Execution of Justice*, in *New Plays USA*, Vol. 3, ed. James Leverett and Elizabeth Osborn. New York: Theatre Communications Group, 1986.

_____. *Still Life*, in *Coming to Terms: American Plays and the Vietnam War*. New York: Theatre Communications Group, 1985.

Metcalfe, Stephen. *Strange Snow*, in *Coming to Terms: American Plays and the Vietnam War*. New York: Theatre Communications Group, 1985

Mitchell, Loften. *A Land Beyond the River*, in *The Black Teacher and the Dramatic Arts*, ed. William Reardon and Thomas Pauley. Westport, Conn.: Negro Universities Press, 1970.

_____. *Star of the Morning*, in *Black Theater, U.S.A.*, ed. James V. Hatch and Ted Shine. New York: Free Press, 1974.

Moraga, Cherrie. *Giving Up the Ghost*. Los Angeles: West End Press, 1986.

Morton, Carlos. *Los Dorados*, in *"The Many Deaths of Danny Rosales" and Other Plays*. Houston: Arte Publico Press, 1983.

_____. *The Many Deaths of Danny Rosales*, in *"The Many Deaths of Danny Rosales" and Other Plays*. Houston: Arte Publico Press, 1983.

_____. *Rancho Hollywood*, in *"The Many Deaths of Danny Rosales" and Other Plays*. Houston: Arte Publico Press, 1983.

Mueller, Lavonne. *Killings on the Last Line*, in *The Women's Project: Seven New Plays by Women*, ed. Julia Miles. New York: Performing Arts Journal Publications, 1980.

Norman, Marsha. *Getting Out*. New York: Avon Books, 1980.

Odets, Clifford. *Till the Day I Die*, in *Six Plays of Clifford Odets*. New York: Modern Library, 1939.

_____. *Waiting for Lefty*, in *Twenty One-Act Plays*, ed. Stanley Richards. Garden City, N.Y.: Doubleday, 1978.

Perry, Marjean. *A Trap Is a Small Place*, in *A Century of Plays by American Women*, ed. Rachel France. New York: Richard Rosen Press, 1979.

Peters, Paul, and George Sklar. *Stevedore*. New York: Covicis, Friede, 1934.

Rabe, David. *Sticks and Bones*. New York: Samuel French, 1971.

Rahman, Aishah. *Unfinished Women Cry in No Man's Land, While a Bird Dies in a Gilded Cage*, in *Nine Plays by Black Women*, ed. Margaret Wilkerson. New York: New American Library, 1986.

Reddin, Keith. *Rum And Coke*. New York: Broadway Play Publishing, 1986.

Rice, Elmer. *American Landscape*. New York: Coward-McCann, 1939.

_____. *Flight to the West*. New York: Coward-McCann, 1941.

_____. *Judgement Day*. New York: Coward-McCann, 1939.

Richards, Beah. *A Black Woman Speaks*, in *Nine Plays by Black Women*, ed. Margaret Wilkerson. New York: New American Library, 1986.

Riggs, Lynn. *Cherokee Night*, in *"Russet Mantle" and "The Cherokee Night."* New York: Samuel French, 1936.

Sanchez, Sonia, *The Bronx Is Next*, in *The Drama Review* 12, no 4 (Summer 1968).

Saroyan, William. *The Slaughter of the Innocents*, in *Theatre Arts*, 36, no. 2 (November 1952).

Selig, Paul. *Terminal Bar*, in *Gay Plays*, Vol. 3, ed. Michael Wilcox. London: Methuen Drama, 1988.

Sergel, Christopher. *Black Elk Speaks*. Chicago: Dramatic Publishing Company, 1976.

Shange, Ntozake. *for colored girls who have considered suicide/when the rainbow is enuf.* New York: Macmillan, 1977.

_____. *spell #7*, in *Nine Plays by Black Women*, ed. Margaret Wilkerson. New York: New American Library, 1986.

Shaw, Irwin. *Bury the Dead*, in *New Theatre and Film, 1934 to 1937*, ed. Herbert Kline. San Diego: Harcourt, Brace, and Jovanovitch, 1985.

_____. *The Gentle People*. New York: Dramatists Play Service, 1939.

Shelley, Elsa. *Pick Up Girl*. New York: Dramatists Play Service, 1946.

Shenkar, Joan. *Signs of Life*, in *The Women's Project: Seven New Plays by Women*, ed. Julia Miles. New York: Performing Arts Journal Publications, 1980.

Sherman, Martin. *Bent*. New York: Avon Books, 1979.

Sherwood, Robert. *Abe Lincoln in Illinois*. New York: Charles Scribner's Sons, 1939.

_____. *Idiot's Delight*. New York: Charles Scribner's Sons, 1936.

_____. *There Shall Be No Night*. New York: Charles Scribner's Sons, 1941.

Sierra, Ruben. *La Raza Pura, or Racial, Racial*, in *Contemporary Chicano Theatre*, ed. Roberta J. Garza. South Bend, Ind.: University of Notre Dame Press, 1976.

Sifton, Claire, and Paul Sifton. *1931—*. New York: Farrar & Rinehart, 1931.

Sklar, George, and Albert Maltz. *Peace on Earth*. New York: Samuel French, 1936.

Sundgaard, Arnold. *Spirochete*, in *Federal Theatre Plays*, ed. Pierre de Rohan. New York: Random House, 1938.

Terry, Megan. *American King's English for Queens*, in *High Energy Musicals from the Omaha Magic Theater*. New York: Broadway Play Publishing, 1983.

_____. *Babes in Bighouse*, in *High Energy Musicals from the Omaha Magic Theater*. New York: Broadway Publishing, 1983.

_____. *Viet Rock*, in *Tulane Drama Review* 11, no. 1 (Fall 1966).

Thurber, James, and Elliot Nugent. *The Male Animal*. New York: Random House, 1940.

Treadwell, Sophie. *Machinal*, in *Plays by American Women: 1900–1930*, ed. Judith E. Barlow. New York: Applause Theatre Book Publishers, 1985.

Triple-A Plowed Under, ed. Staff of the Living Newspaper, in *Federal Theatre Plays*, ed. Pierre de Rohan. New York: Random House, 1938.

Valdez, Luis. *Las dos caros del patroncito*, in *Actos*. San Juan Bautista, Calif.: Cucaracha Press, 1971.

_____. *Vietnam Campesino*, in *Actos*. San Juan Bautista, Calif.: Cucaracha Press, 1971.

Vidal, Gore. *The Best Man*. Boston: Little, Brown, 1960.

Wesley, Richard. *Black Terror*, in *The New Lafayette Theatre Presents*, ed. Ed Bullins. New York: Anchor Books, 1974.

_____. *The Mighty Gents*. New York: Dramatists Play Service, 1979.

Wexley, John. *They Shall Not Die*. New York: Alfred A. Knopf, 1934.

Wilson, Doric. *A Perfect Relationship*. New York: Seahorse Press, 1983.

Wouk, Herman. *The Traitor*. New York: Samuel French, 1949.

Historical Context

Altman, Denis. *The Homosexualization of America, the Americanization of the Homosexual*. New York: St. Martin's Press, 1982.

Bailey, Derrick Sherwin. *Homosexuality and the Western Christian Tradition*. Hamden, Conn: Archon Books, 1975.

Baker, Mark. *Nam*. New York: William Morrow, 1981.

Bakir, Lawrence M., and William A. Strauss. *Chance and Circumstance*. New York: Alfred A. Knopf, 1978.

Baldwin, James. *The Fire Next Time*. New York: Dell Publishing Co., 1964.

Bennett, Lerone, Jr. *Before the Mayflower: A History of the Negro, 1619–1964*. Baltimore: Penguin Books, 1966.

Bentley, Eric. *Thirty Years of Treason*. New York: Viking Press, 1971.

Blaustein, Albert P., and Robert L. Zangrando, eds. *Civil Rights and the American Negro*. New York: Washington Square Press, 1968.

Borchard, Edwin, and William Lage. *Neutrality for the United States*. New Haven: Yale University Press, 1937.

Boswell, John. *Christianity, Social Tolerance, and Homosexuality*. Chicago: University of Chicago Press, 1980.

Bronski, Michael. *Culture Clash: The Making of a Gay Sensibility*. Boston: South End Press, 1984.

Brown, Dee. *Bury My Heart at Wounded Knee*. New York: Holt, Rinehart, and Winston, 1970.

Burnette, Robert, and John Koster. *The Road to Wounded Knee*. New York: Bantam Books, 1974.

Butler, John S. *Inequality in the Military: The Black Experience*. Saratoga, Calif.: Century Twenty-One Publishing, 1980.

Chatfield, Charles. *For Peace and Justice: Pacifism in America 1914–1941*. Knoxville: University of Tennessee Press, 1971.

Cogdell, Roy, and Sybill Wilson. *Black Communication in White Society*. Saratoga, Calif.: Century Twenty-One Publishing, 1980.

Cole, Wayne S. *Roosevelt and the Isolationists*. Lincoln: University of Nebraska Press, 1983.

Cooper, Chester L. *The Lost Crusade: American in Vietnam.* New York: Dodd, Mead, 1970.

Curtis, Richard. *The Berrigan Brothers.* New York: Hawthorn Books, 1974.

Dalfiume, Richard M. *Desegregation of the Armed Forces.* Columbia: University of Missouri Press, 1969.

Davis, Elmer. *By Elmer Davis.* Ed. Robert Lloyd Davis. Indianapolis: Bobbs, Merrill, 1964.

Day, Mark. *Forty Acres.* New York: Praeger Publishers, 1971.

Deckard, Barbara Sinclair. *The Women's Movement.* New York: Harper & Row, 1983.

Deedy, John. *"Apologies, Good Friends."* Chicago: Fides/Claretian, 1981.

Devine, Robert A. *The Illusion of Neutrality.* Chicago: University of Chicago Press, 1962.

_____. *The Reluctant Belligerent.* Chicago: University of Chicago Press, 1965.

Drummond, Donald. *The Passing of American Neutrality, 1937–1941.* Westport, Conn.: Greenwood Press, 1968.

DuBois, W.E.B. *The Souls of Black Folk.* New York: New American Library, 1969.

Dulles, Foster Rhea, and Melvyn Dubofsky. *Labor in America.* Arlington Heights, Ill.: Harlan Davidson, 1984.

Dzienwanowski, M. K. *A History of Soviet Russia.* Englewood Cliffs, N.J.: Prentice-Hall, 1979.

Ellis, Edward. *A Nation in Torment: The Great American Depression 1929–1939.* New York: Coward-McCann, 1970.

Engelbrecht, H. C., and F. C. Hanighen. *Merchants of Death: A Study of the International Armament Industry.* New York: Dodd, Mead, 1934.

Faulk, John Henry. *Fear on Trial.* New York: Grosset & Dunlap, 1976.

Fausold, Martin. *The Presidency of Herbert C. Hoover.* Lawrence: University Press of Kansas, 1985.

Fenwick, Charles G. *American Neutrality: Trial and Failure.* New York: New York University Press, 1940.

Feuerlicht, Roberta Strauss. *Joseph McCarthy and McCarthyism.* New York: McGraw-Hill, 1972.

FitzGerald, Frances. *Fire in the Lake.* New York: Vintage Books, 1972.

Foner, Jack D. *Blacks and the Military in American History.* New York: Praeger Publishers, 1974.

Franklin, John Hope, and Isidore Starr, eds. *The Negro in Twentieth Century America.* New York: Vintage Books, 1967.

Friday, Nancy. *My Mother/My Self.* New York: Dell Publishing Co., 1977.

Gay Left Collective. *Homosexuality: Power and Politics.* London: Allison and Busby, 1980.

Goodchild, Peter. *J. Robert Oppenheimer: Shatterer of Worlds.* Boston: Houghton Mifflin, 1981.

Haley, Alex. *The Autobiography of Malcolm X.* New York: Ballantine Books, 1965.

Halle, Louis J. *The Cold War as History.* New York: Harper & Row, 1967.

Halstead, Fred. *Out Now!* New York: Monad, 1978.

Hammond, Paul Y. *Cold War and Détente.* New York: Harcourt Brace Jovanovich, 1975.

Hansen, Chadwick. *Witchcraft at Salem.* New York: George Braziller, 1969.

Hellman, Lillian. *Scoundrel Time.* Boston: Little, Brown, 1976.

Henderson, George, and Barbara Beard Henderson. *Mending Broken Children.* Springfield, Ill.: Charles C. Thomas, 1984.

Herring, George C. *America's Longest War.* New York: Alfred A Knopf, 1986.

Herz, Marvin F. *How the Cold War Is Taught.* Washington, D.C: Georgetown University Press, 1978.

Higgins, Hugh. *The Cold War.* New York: Barnes and Noble, 1974.

Horne, A. D., ed. *The Wounded Generation.* Englewood Cliffs, N.J.: Prentice-Hall, 1981.

Hughes, Langston, and Milton Meltzer. *A Pictorial History of the Negro in America.* New York: Crown Publishers, 1968.

Josephy, Alvin M. *Now That the Buffalo's Gone.* New York: Alfred A. Knopf, 1982.

Katz, Jonathan. *Gay American History.* New York: Thomas Y. Crowell, 1976.

Kehr, Harvey. *The Heyday of American Communism.* New York: Basic Books, 1984.

Kepner, Jim. *Becoming a People: A 4,000-Year Gay and Lesbian Chronology.* Hollywood, Calif: National Gay Archives, 1983.

Kendrick, Alexander. *The Wound Within.* Boston: Little, Brown, 1974.

King, Martin Luther, Jr. *A Testament of Hope: The Essential Writings of Martin Luther King, Jr.,* ed. James Melvin Washington. San Francisco: Harper & Row, 1986.

Knoll, Edwin, and Judith Nies McFadden, eds. *War Crimes and the American Conscience.* New York: Holt, Rinehart and Winston, 1970.

Koestler, Arthur. *Darkness at Noon.* London: Hutchinson of London, 1973.

Koko, Gabriel. *Anatomy of a War.* New York: Pantheon Books, 1985.

Kushner, Sam. *Long Road to Delano.* New York: International Publishers, 1975.

Latham, Earl, ed. *The Meaning of McCarthyism.* Boston: D. C. Heath, 1965.

Lederer, William J. *Our Own Worst Enemy.* New York: W. W. Norton, 1968.

LeFeber, Walter, ed. *America in the Cold War.* New York: John Wiley & Sons, 1969.

Levering, Ralph B. *The Cold War, 1945–1972.* Arlington Heights, Ill.: Harlan Davidson, 1982.

Levine, Issac Don, ed. *Plain Talk.* New Rochelle, N.Y.: Arlington House, 1976.

Liebow, Elliot. *Talley's Corner.* Boston: Little, Brown, 1967.

Little, Douglas. *Malevolent Neutrality: The United States, Great Britain, and the Origins of the Spanish Civil War.* Ithaca, N.Y.: Cornell University Press, 1985.

Lomperis, Timothy J. *The War Everyone Lost—and Won.* Baton Rouge: Louisiana State University Press, 1984.

London Feminist History Group. *The Sexual Dynamics of History.* London: Pluto Press, 1983.

Loraine, J. A., ed. *Understanding Homosexuality.* New York: American Elsevier Publishing Co., 1974.

McElvaine, Robert. *The Great Depression: America 1929–1941.* New York: Times Books, 1984.

MacLear, Michael. *The Ten Thousand Day War.* New York: St. Martin's Press, 1981.

MacPherson, Myra. *Long Time Passing.* Garden City, N.Y.: Doubleday, 1984.

Mandelbaum, David G. *Soldier Groups and Negro Soldiers.* Berkeley: University of California Press, 1952.

Marx, Herbert L., Jr., ed. *The American Indians: A Rising Ethnic Force.* New York: H. H. Wilson, 1973.

May, Ernest R. *"Lessons" of History*. New York: Oxford University Press, 1973.

Meconis, Charles A. *With Clumsy Grace*. New York: Seabury Press, 1979.

Michner, James. *Kent State: What Happened and Why*. New York: Random House, 1971.

Millis, Walter. *Road to War: America 1914–1917*. Boston: Houghton Mifflin, 1935.

Morotta, Toby. *The Politics of Homosexuality*. Boston: Houghton Mifflin, 1981.

Namorato, Michael V., ed. *Have We Overcome?* Jackson: University Press of Mississippi, 1979.

Nash, Gerald. *The Great Depression and World War II: Organizing America 1933–45*. New York: St. Martin's Press, 1979.

Neihardt, John G. *Black Elk Speaks*. Lincoln: University of Nebraska Press, 1961.

Olson, Otto H. *The Thin Disguise: Turning Point in Negro History*. New York: Humanities Press, 1967.

Orwell, George. *A Collection of Essays by George Orwell*. San Diego: Harcourt Brace Jovanovich, 1946.

Parenti, Michael. *The Anti-Communist Impulse*. New York: Random House, 1969.

Pasteur, Alfred B., and Ivory L. Toldson. *Roots of Soul*. Garden City, N.Y.: Anchor Press, 1982.

Powell, Adam Clayton, Jr. *Marching Blacks*. New York: Dial Press, 1945.

Powers, Thomas. *The War at Home*. New York: Grossman Publishers, 1973.

Rees, Goronwy. *The Great Slump: Capitalism in Crisis 1929–1933*. New York: Harper & Row, 1970.

Rose, Arnold. *The Negro in America*. New York: Harper & Brothers, 1948.

Rosenstiel, Annette. *Red and White*. New York: Universe Books, 1983.

Santoli, Al. *Everything We Had*. New York: Random House, 1981.

Sargent, Porter. *Getting US into War*. Boston: Porter Sargent, 1941.

Schlesinger, Arthur M., Jr. *The Cycles of American History*. Boston: Houghton Mifflin, 1986.

Seabury, Paul. *The Rise and Decline of the Cold War*. New York: Basic Books, 1967.

Seldes, George. *Iron, Blood, and Profits*. New York: Harper & Brothers, 1934.

Servin, Manuel P., ed. *The Mexican-Americans: An Awakening Minority*. Beverly Hills, Calif.: Glencoe Press, 1970.

Simon, Rita James, ed. *As We Saw the Thirties*. Urbana: University of Illinois Press, 1967.

Simpson, Ruth. *From the Closet to the Courts*. New York: Viking Press, 1976.

Smith, Gaddis. *Dean Acheson*. New York: Cooper Square Publishers, 1972.

Smith, Gene. *The Shattered Dream: Herbert Hoover and the Great Depression*. New York: William Morrow, 1970.

Smitherman, Geneva. *Talkin' and Testifyin'*. Boston: Houghton Mifflin, 1977.

Stoehr, Taylor, ed. *Nature Heals: Psychological Essays*. New York: Free Life Editions, 1977.

Sutherland, Elizabeth, ed. *Letters from Mississippi*. New York: McGraw-Hill, 1965.

Talbot, Steve. *Roots of Oppression*. New York: International Publishers, 1981.

Ulam, Adam B. *A History of Soviet Russia*. New York: Praeger Publishers, 1976.

Unger, Irwin. *The Movement: A History of the American New Left, 1959–1972*. New York: Dodd, Mead, 1974.

Upham, Charles W. *Salem Witchcraft*, Vol. 2. New York: Frederick Unger Publishing Co., 1959.

Vida, Ginna, ed. *Our Right to Love*. New York: National Gay Task Force, 1978.

Waskow, Arthur. *From Race Riots to Sit-in, 1919 and the 1960's*. Garden City, N.Y.: Doubleday, 1966.

Williams, William A., ed. *America in Vietnam*. Garden City, N.Y.: Anchor Press/Doubleday, 1985.

Wittner, Lawrence S. *Rebels Against War: The American Peace Movement, 1941–1960*. New York: Columbia University Press, 1969.

Zak, Michele Wender, and Patricia A Moots. *Women and the Politics of Culture*. New York: Longman, 1983.

Zaroulis, Nancy, and Gerald Sullivan. *Who Spoke Up? American Protest Against the War in Vietnam 1963–1975*. Garden City, N.Y.: Doubleday, 1984.

Zinn, Howard. *The New Abolitionists*. Boston: Beacon Press 1964.

Theatre History and Theory

Auster, Albert, and Leonard Quart. *How the War Was Remembered: Hollywood and Vietnam*. New York: Praeger Press, 1988.

Betsko, Kathleen, and Rachel Koenig. *Interviews with Contemporary Women Playwrights*. New York: William Morrow, 1987.

Boal, Augusto. *Theater of the Oppressed*. New York: Urizen Books, 1979.

Brown, Janet. *Feminist Drama: Definition and Critical Analysis*. Metuchen, N.J.: Scarecrow Press, 1979.

Case, Sue-Ellen. *Feminism and Theatre*. New York: Methuen, 1988.

Clark, Barrett H., ed. *European Theories of the Drama*. New York: Crown Publishers, 1947.

Clurman, Harold. *The Fervent Years*. New York: Hill and Wang, 1945.

Demetz, Peter, ed. *Brecht: A Collection of Critical Essays* Englewood Cliffs, N.J.: Prentice-Hall, 1962.

Flanagan, Hallie. *Arena*. New York: Duell, Sloan and Pierce, 1940.

Foster, Hal. *Recoding*. Port Townsend, Wash.: Bay Press, 1985.

Garnham, Nicholas. *Samuel Fuller*. New York: Viking Press, 1971.

Goldstein, Malcolm. *The Political Stage: American Drama and Theater of the Great Depression*. New York: Oxford University Press, 1974.

Hardy, Phil. *Samuel Fuller*. New York: Praeger Publishers, 1970.

House, Jane, ed. *Political Theatre Today*. New York: Institute on Western Europe, Columbia University, and Center for Advanced Study in Theatre Arts, City University of New York, 1988.

Huerta, Jorge A. *Chicano Theatre: Themes and Forms*. Ypsilanti, Mich.: Bilingual Press/Editorial Bilinque, 1982.

Itzin, Catherine. *Stages in the Revolution*. London: Eyre Methuen, 1980.

Jiji, Vera, ed. *Showcasing American Drama: "One Third of a Nation."* New York: Research Foundation of CUNY, 1984.

Kanellos, Nicolas. *Mexican American Theater: Legacy and Reality*. Pittsburgh: Latin American Literary Review, 1987.

Kirby, Michael. *A Formalist Theatre*. Philadelphia: University of Pennsylvania Press, 1987.

Leavitt, Dinah. *Feminist Theatre Groups*. Jefferson, N.C.: McFarland, 1980.

Nammes, Casper H. *Politics in the American Drama*. Philadelphia: University of Pennsylvania Press, 1950.

Natalie, Elizabeth J. *Feminist Theatre: A Study in Persuasion*. Methuchen, N.J.: Scarecrow Press, 1985.

Newman, John. *Vietnam War Literature*. Metuchen, N.J.: Scarecrow Press, 1988.

Nicholas, John., ed. *Twentieth-Century American Playwrights*, Vol. 1. Detroit: Gale Research Press, 1981.

O'Connor, John, and Lorraine Brown. *Free, Adult, Uncensored*. Washington, D.C.: New Republic Books, 1978.

Olauson, Judith. *The American Woman Playwright: A View of Criticism and Characterization*. Troy, N.Y.: Whitson Publishing Co., 1981.

Pottlitzer, Joanne. *Hispanic Theater in the United States and Puerto Rico*. New York: Ford Foundation, 1988.

Rabkin, Gerald. *Drama and Commitment: Politics in the American Theatre of the Thirties*. Bloomington: Indiana University Press, 1964.

Reynolds, R. C. *Stage Left: The Development of the American Social Drama in the Thirties*. Troy, N.Y.: Whitston Publishing Co., 1986.

Index

ABOUT THE AUTHOR

RICHARD G. SCHARINE is Professor of Theatre at the University of Utah, where he specializes in political and Black-American theatre. He has contributed to the books *Twentieth Century American Playwrights, Vol. 1* and *Themes in Drama 11*, and is the author of *The Plays of Edward Bond*.